POPULATION PATTERNS IN THE PAST

STUDIES IN SOCIAL DISCONTINUITY

Under the Consulting Editorship of:

CHARLES TILLY
University of Michigan

EDWARD SHORTER
University of Toronto

POPULATION PATTERNS IN THE PAST

Edited by

RONALD DEMOS LEE

Department of Economics and Population Studies Center
University of Michigan

In collaboration with

RICHARD A. EASTERLIN
Department of Economics and
Population Studies Center
University of Pennsylvania

PETER H. LINDERT
Department of Economics
University of Wisconsin

ETIENNE VAN DE WALLE
Population Studies Center
University of Pennsylvania

ACADEMIC PRESS   New York   San Francisco   London

A Subsidiary of Harcourt Brace Jovanovich, Publishers

This (material) was prepared with the support of National
Science Foundation grant No. SOC70-02316 A04. Any opinions,
findings, conclusions or recommendations expressed herein are
those of the authors and do not necessarily reflect the view of the
National Science Foundation.

ACADEMIC PRESS, INC.
111 Fifth Avenue, New York, New York 10003

United Kingdom Edition published by
ACADEMIC PRESS, INC. (LONDON) LTD.
24/28 Oval Road, London NW1

Library of Congress Cataloging in Publication Data

Main entry under title:

Population patterns in the past.

(Studies in social discontinuity series)
Papers presented at a conference held at the University
of Pennsylvania in October 1974, and sponsored by the
Mathematical Social Science Board.
Includes bibliographies and index.
1. Population—History—Congresses. I. Lee, Ronald,
Date II. Mathematical Social Science Board.
III. Title.
HB849.P684 301.32'9 76-27446
ISBN 0-12-441850-3

Contents

List of Contributors

Numbers in parentheses indicate the pages on which the authors' contributions begin.

BARBARA A. ANDERSON (277), Department of Sociology, Brown University, Providence, Rhode Island

LUTZ K. BERKNER (53), Department of History, University of California at Los Angeles, Los Angeles, California

H. LE BRAS (297), National Institute of Demographic Studies, Paris, France

M. DEMONET (297), School of Advanced Studies in the Social Sciences, Paris, France

J. DUPÂQUIER (297), Laboratory of Historical Demography, Paris, France

E. A. HAMMEL (113), Department of Anthropology, University of California, Berkeley, Berkeley, California

SUSAN B. HANLEY (165), Institute for Comparative and Foreign Area Studies, University of Washington, Seattle, Washington

DAVID HERLIHY (135), Department of History, Harvard University, Cambridge, Massachusetts

ALBERT I. HERMALIN (71), Population Studies Center, University of Michigan Ann Arbor, Michigan

RONALD DEMOS LEE (337), Department of Economics and Population Studies Center, University of Michigan, Ann Arbor, Michigan

PETER H. LINDERT (229), Department of Economics, University of Wisconsin, Madison, Wisconsin

MASSIMO LIVI-BACCI (311), Department of Statistics, University of Florence, Florence, Italy

R. M. McINNIS (201), Department of Economics, Queen's University, Kingston, Ontario, Canada

DANIEL SCOTT SMITH (19), Department of History, University of Illinois at Chicago Circle, Chicago, Illinois

ETIENNE VAN DE WALLE (71), Population Studies Center, University of Pennsylvania, Philadelphia, Pennsylvania

KENNETH W. WACHTER (113), Department of Statistics and Center for Population Studies, Harvard University, Cambridge, Massachusetts

POPULATION PATTERNS IN THE PAST

Introduction

Interest in the study of historical populations did not become widespread until the late 1950s, when Gautier and Henry's now classic study of the French parish of Crulai was published (Gautier & Henry, 1958). This study established both a scientific methodology for the exploitation of parish registers—*family reconstitution*—and a range of questions that might be addressed by the methodology. The study yielded a richly detailed description of the demographic behavior of individual families in Crulai—more detailed, indeed, than could be derived for modern populations from modern sources. In addition to this descriptive output, the study yielded an important behavioral conclusion: Fertility within marriage was at natural levels for the people of Crulai. It was not regulated by individual couples aiming for particular family sizes. Dozens of reconstitution studies from many countries have followed; like the original, these studies are primarily concerned with description and measurement. Such a limited focus reflects the newness of the research area, the nature of the materials (mostly parish registers) so far exploited, and the fact that this particular school of historical demography is really a branch of analytic demography, which has always been mainly descriptive.

A different approach has been taken by some social and economic historians who have considered population change in a broader context, following the important works of Goubert (1960) and Chambers (1965). These historians have developed behavioral models following prevailing currents in sociology and economics. The models, however, have typically been verbal, and have not been formulated in ways permitting clear tests. In general, attempts to test the models against historical data have either been confined to glances at broad historical patterns, or, if more detailed, have been statistically and demographically unsophisticated.

These two lines of analysis in historical demography need to be

1

linked with a more rigorous approach to the formulation, estimation, and testing of behavioral models. A growing number of scholars are doing this kind of research, although much of the research is still unpublished. To merge the tasks of descriptive measurement and model testing more quickly, using the available quantitative tools, a conference on the topic of Behavioral Models in Historical Demography was organized, and held in October of 1974.[1] The conference was designed to facilitate interaction of model-oriented researchers in historical demography, both with one another and with other historical demographers. There were about 30 participants; their backgrounds included demography, history, sociology, anthropology, economics, and statistics. For all the diversity of the participants' backgrounds, the outcome was surprisingly close to the intent of the organizers. Some new models and hypotheses were developed and tested, and old hypotheses were scrutinized with the help of new statistical techniques.

THEORIES AND HYPOTHESES

It is all very well to invoke models as a source of rigor, precision, and dramatic new insights, but models are at best as good as the theories they attempt to embody, and good theories are rare. To set the background for this book, it is useful to focus on several theories that have been used or might be used in historical research on fertility. These include the theories of homeostasis, natural fertility, marriage–inheritance, the new home economics, and relative income. The newcomer to the field of historical population studies may want a more general introduction to the literature. Consequently, a brief and highly selective bibliography, which includes several excellent surveys, is provided at the end of this chapter.

The Homeostasis Hypothesis

The homeostasis or "autoregulation" hypothesis asserts that many preindustrial societies incorporated institutional or biological mechanisms that not only kept population *growth rates* close to zero over the long run, but also controlled living standards by regulating population size in relation to resources. Malthusian population theory comes under this heading, as do models discussed by Sauvy (1969), Wrigley (1969),

The conference took place at the Population Studies Center of the University of Pennsylvania. It was sponsored by the Mathematical Social Sciences Board (MSSB) and funded by the National Science Foundation (NSF). The organizers gratefully acknowledge this support.

Lee (forthcoming), and others. A special case of the homeostatic model results from combining the natural fertility hypothesis with the marriage–inheritance hypothesis. This particular homeostatic model, which is of special interest in the context of preindustrial Europe, will be developed in more detail after the two constituent hypotheses are discussed.

The Natural Fertility Hypothesis

The natural fertility hypothesis asserts that in preindustrial Europe fertility behavior *within marriage* was not subject to voluntary control in any parity-dependent way. This hypothesis excludes any sort of "target fertility" behavior, although voluntary practices (e.g., prolonged lactation) affecting fertility at all parities are consistent with natural fertility. Many reconstitution studies, starting with Gautier and Henry (1958), have strongly confirmed this hypothesis. The early studies show that age-specific marital fertility is independent of age at marriage, as is age of mother at last birth. Some subsequent reconstitution studies (e.g., Charbonneau, 1970) have found a relationship between age-specific marital fertility and age at marriage, even when fertility behavior conformed in other respects to the natural fertility hypothesis.

Reconstitution data also provide another kind of evidence bearing on the natural fertility hypothesis: the reactions of couples to the loss, by death, of infants or young children. Evidence from a number of reconstitution studies indicates that couples made no attempt to replace such losses by altering their subsequent fertility (Knodel, 1975; Smith, 1972). The inference is that married couples did not attempt to control completed parity.

The theory received a severe blow from Wrigley's (1966) reconstitution of Colyton, which found substantial secular changes in marital fertility, and positive evidence of parity-specific control. The covariation of marital fertility with the harvest cycle or business cycle has also been established (Lee, forthcoming). However, such behavior could have had biological rather than voluntary origins; even if voluntary, it could have been independent of parity and thus consistent with natural fertility. In any case, this theory, generally accepted in the 1960s, is now highly controversial.

The Marriage–Inheritance Hypothesis

It is widely agreed that in much of preindustrial Europe having the means to a sufficient livelihood was prerequisite to marriage and that frequently such means was obtained through actual or anticipated inheritance. Hence in some instances marriage had to be delayed until the death of the father, and if this delaying were sufficiently common, then variations in mortality would entail variations in nuptiality and hence fertility, both cross-sectionally and over time.

Of course marriages were also based on wage labor or other income, which weakens the implications of the inheritance model; in their chapter Hermalin and van de Walle counter this point with the suggestion that even if inheritance of *land* was not always necessary, the inheritance of other forms of property may have been so. In any case, the qualitative prediction of the model—that higher mortality should cause younger and/or more frequent marriage—still holds. Berkner and Mendels (forthcoming) give an excellent review of this literature.

More detailed predictions of the theory depend on the kind of inheritance scheme in effect. Under an impartible inheritance system, the property passes to one favored child, who can marry; the other children emigrate or find local positions as servants or laborers, in which case they would marry late or not at all. Under this system, the number of households should vary little from one generation to the next, and population size should remain in neutral equilibrium. There should also be a relatively high proportion of stem families, since the favored child and his or her spouse might co-reside with a surviving parent, or sometimes with both parents.

Under a partible inheritance system, all children share equally in the patrimony. Thus all have some likelihood of marriage. A partible inheritance system often led to subdivision of the holding. Population could then grow from generation to generation, emigration would be less, stem families would occur much less frequently, and the proportions married would be high. Ohlin (1961) has provided a useful analysis of how such a system responds to variations in mortality.

I have so far assumed that the number of landholdings or houses is fixed. More realistically, the number depends on resources. Changes in trade, technology, or social organization produce changes in the number of holdings, thus altering the situation. And, of course, in frontier areas with available land the potential number of holdings is far greater than the actual. We would then expect high fertility resulting either from early and universal marriage (within limits imposed by often imbalanced sex ratios) or higher marital fertility (as parents anticipate bright prospects for their children, or find them particularly useful).

The Natural Fertility and Marriage–Inheritance Models Combined

Much of the literature in the field of historical demography, including some of the chapters in this volume, accepts both the natural fertility and the marriage–inheritance hypotheses. Combined, these describe a simple homeostatic system, which is often used to describe the institutional regulation of population in preindustrial Europe. For this reason I will pause to develop more explicitly the properties of this system.

Suppose that the number of hearths or stylized landholdings in a region is fixed by custom or economic opportunity at some level, say H. Couples cannot marry unless they acquire one of these landholdings intact, typically by the death of a parent. Suppose further that every hearth (or a constant proportion of hearths) has a reproductive-aged couple bearing children at the natural rate, f. Then the annual number of births, B, is simply $B = fH$, so that under these circumstances the number of births per year is constant.

What of the population size? In the long run, population size, P, will be given by life expectancy at birth, e_0, times the number of births: $P = Be_0$, or $P = e_0fH$. In other words, population size will vary in proportion to life expectancy, even though the number of hearths and the number of births are constant. This social mechanism, although it does temper the effect of mortality change on population size, provides at best only partial control.

What is the effect on living standards of changes in e_0? If the output, Q, is fixed in the region, then output per head, $q = Q/P$, will be inversely proportional to life expectancy. More realistically, if additional hands can augment output, then although q will vary inversely with e_0, the variation will be less than proportional.

Suppose, for example, that $Q = A^{1-\beta}P^\beta$ so that a 1% increase in population induces a β% increase in Q. (A is a parameter to be discussed later.) Plausible values for β would be between .5 and .8. An increase of 1% in life expectancy, and hence population, will cause a decline in per capita output, q, of $(1 - \beta)$%. If, for example, life expectancy increased from 25 to 35 years, or 40%, then per capita output might fall by 10 or 20%.

However, as is emphasized by Herlihy (in this volume) and others, the number of hearths does not remain constant. It varies in response to changes in economic opportunities as reflected by the constant A in $Q = A^{1-\beta}P^\beta$. Changes in economic opportunities in this sense will reflect changes in technology, trade, climate, arable land, and so on. If the number of hearths varies in proportion to economic opportunities over the long run, then we may write $H = hA$, where h is the constant of proportionality. Changes in opportunities will then induce offsetting changes in population, leaving the standard of living unchanged.

To summarize, a change in economic opportunity would induce a proportionate change in population and total output, leaving per capita output unaffected. A change in life expectancy would induce a proportional change in population, or less than proportional change in total output, and a decline in per capita output. Evidently even this rigid link of marriage to impartible inheritance could provide only limited societal control over population size and living standards. To the extent that marriages were not so strictly tied to inheritance, variations in population size and living standards would have been still greater.

The New Home Economics Hypothesis

The new home economics theory of fertility develops a general conceptual framework of rational choice for household decision-making. It assumes that couples choose or demand the number of children that will maximize their expected utility, where utility is derived from numbers of surviving children, "quality" of children, and consumption of other goods. The maximizing decision also depends on the couple's potential income, on child mortality, on relative prices, on the wife's potential wage, and on her productivity at home. It is recognized that couples may get more or fewer children than they want, for the usual reasons. Applications of this theory to historical populations are few, but two in particular should be mentioned. O'Hara (1975) used the model effectively to analyze the impact of declining mortality on the number and quality of children demanded, with reference to the demographic transition. Nerlove (1974) has argued that a self-sustaining tendency for quality inputs to increase from generation to generation explains not only the secular fertility decline of the past century, but also the mortality decline and industrialization.

The new home economics model may well be applicable to the period of demographic transition. Indeed, many of the insights it formalizes have been in the transition literature for years. However, it is not clear whether the model can be used to explain fertility behavior in the pretransition period. In the first place, the early microlevel demographic data sets come mainly from reconstitution studies. Although in some cases linkage with socioeconomic data is possible, even elaborate modern data sets are generally deemed inadequate to support tests of the theory.

But there is a deeper difficulty: The new home economics theory explains why couples strive for certain desired family sizes; as we have seen, however, advocates of the natural fertility hypothesis have mustered considerable evidence indicating that, in preindustrial Europe, there was no attempt by married couples to control completed parity. If the natural fertility hypothesis is right, then only age at marriage is left for the economic theory to explain. Of course, there still might be important opportunities for the application of the new home economics model in preindustrial areas outside Europe.

The Relative Income Hypothesis

According to the relative income hypothesis, the important variable for fertility or nuptiality decisions is not income itself but, *how income is perceived relative to some standard*. The standard, in turn, varies over time and across individuals, social classes, and societies. This notion played an important role in the population theory of Malthus and later classical writers, who used it to explain changes in fertility over time (the "moving standard") and across cultures (the Chinese were held to marry early and be impoverished because they had a low "standard of misery"). However, the relative income argument suffered from arbitrary application and circular reasoning until Easterlin gave testable empirical specifications of how the standard was formed and applied these successfully in both modern and historical contexts (Easterlin, forthcoming).

The theory may be viewed as a complementary modification of the income or wealth concepts in other theories. Thus the relative income concept may be incorporated in the new home economics model. Likewise, it could be combined with the marriage–inheritance model, since what constitutes a sufficient material basis for marriage is determined not absolutely, but in relation to some individual or social standard.

DISCUSSION OF THE CHAPTERS

Preindustrial Institutions and Population Control

In a novel use of village reconstitution studies, Dan Smith has investigated the evidence for aggregate level homeostasis in populations whose individual members exhibit seemingly uncontrolled family histories. He has done this by treating the average reconstitution results of parishes preselected for natural fertility as cross-sectional observations of populations with different mortality, nuptiality, and marital fertility. In this way, he has been able to study the covariations of demographic parameters across seventeenth and eighteenth century parish populations, mostly French, and in particular, to study the demographic correlates of natural fertility. He has found that although mortality, nuptiality, and marital fertility varied considerably across parishes, these variations tended to be offsetting, leaving growth rates close to zero. This evidence indirectly supports the homeostasis hypothesis; unfortunately, however, Smith has been unable to consider either the extent to which population size (as opposed to growth rate) was controlled or variations over time in the vital rates.

The average demographic profile Smith has calculated is of considerable interest, as is the detailed study of interrelations. Concern with the inheritance mechanism is actually peripheral. In support of the inheritance mechanism, Smith has found that higher mortality was associated with earlier marriage; it was also associated with higher natural fertility. However, he has also obtained the unexpected result that, cross-sectionally, earlier marriage was associated with completely offsetting reductions in natural fertility. This finding raises some questions about the mortality–inheritance–nuptiality–fertility mechanism. However, it is not clear whether these findings are applicable in the context of temporal change. Although similar cross-sectional associations for nuptiality and marital fertility are known to have existed in the later nineteenth century, these have usually been attributed to the beginnings of fertility control.

In any case, the inheritance system is only one of many possible explanations for a nuptiality–mortality link; more direct evidence is clearly necessary. The chapter by Lutz Berkner provides some. It examines the demographic consequences of partible versus impartible inheritance by comparing two villages in lower Saxony, similar except for inheritance customs. Berkner has found that differences in household structure conform to expectations under the inheritance model. For example, there was a much higher proportion of stem families and more servants under impartible inheritance than under partible inheritance. He has also found that population growth was twice as rapid over the course of a century in the village with partible inheritance. Thus his findings strongly support the marriage–inheritance model.

Although there are advantages to conducting a local comparative study such as Berkner's, there are also advantages to using a sample size large enough to permit multivariate statistical inference. The chapter by Hermalin and van de Walle attacks the partible–impartible issue by using regression analysis across French departments categorized by inheritance system for various time periods from 1806 to 1881. Some results support the standard model; others do not. Thus Hermalin and van de Walle did find a larger household size and higher rate of net emigration for impartible areas as hypothesized. Marriage age was lower, and marriage proportions higher when mortality was high, as expected. They also found a lower mean age at marriage in impartible areas, about which the model is agnostic. However, the strongest prediction of the model—that proportions ever marrying should be higher in partible areas—was not confirmed by the empirical analysis, dealing the model a fairly heavy blow. In view of this, it is not surprising that Hermalin and van de Walle have found no dramatic changes attributable to enactment of the Napoleonic Code, which imposed universal partible inheritance.

The relation between inheritance system and household complexity, confirmed empirically by Berkner and by Hermalin and van de Walle, has been examined in greater detail by Hammel and Wachter, who have used a very different approach. Employing a stochastic microsimulation program, developed in connection with an ongoing research project, these researchers have pinpointed the effects of two different forms of impartible inheritance: primogeniture and ultimogeniture. They have found wide differences in household structure—for example, stem families occurred about twice as frequently under primogeniture as under ultimogeniture. This controlled historical "experiment" demonstrates the difficulties of generalizing about the demographic effects of impartible inheritance, and of drawing inferences from observed distributions of household types. It also confirms once again the well-established result that even with the most favorable systems of inheritance, under preindustrial regimes only a minority of households would contain stem families.

The same marriage–inheritance mechanism claimed to link mortality, nuptiality, and fertility cross-sectionally should also produce compensating changes over time. The analysis and explanation of such temporal covariations is a focal point of David Herlihy's study of economic–demographic interrelations in medieval Tuscany. Access to a hearth or household (with its associated livelihood) was a prerequisite for marriage; high mortality vacated holdings and thus stimulated marriage and fertility. The number of hearths in this way limited the effect that mortality variations might have on population size when economic conditions were otherwise unchanged. At the same time, the number of hearths was not fixed; it varied with the opportunities afforded by the economy. These features of the inheritance model—resistance in the face of mortality swings, flexibility in response to economic change—have been presented and empirically supported most clearly in Herlihy's chapter.

Herlihy has also stressed fundamental urban–rural differences. For example, in Florence, wealth was associated with later marriage; in the countryside, it was associated with earlier marriage. Another intriguing finding is that females married very young by the western European standards of later centuries. In 1427, the female singulate mean age at marriage was only 18 years. In the same year, men married at between 26 and 30 years depending on the area. This fits the later European pattern, but the implied age difference of spouses definitely does not.

Hanley's study of Tokugawa Japan portrays a demographic situation that in some respects resembled the preindustrial European patterns described earlier, but which in many important respects was strikingly different. As in Europe, female marriage was late and significant proportions of women ever married. Also as in much of Europe, living standards were well above subsistence, perhaps due to social control of population size. But in contrast to Europe, there is strong evidence of fertility control *within* marriage: Marital fertility was very low, and women typically terminated childbearing in their early or mid-thirties. The sex ratio of lastborn children was quite high, suggesting that sex-selective infanticide was practiced. There is also evidence that abortion was used. Perhaps most striking, however, is the widespread practice of adoption. Combining figures for four villages, there were almost exactly half as many adoptions as marriages. The adoptions were used to compensate for child deaths, to divest families of "excess" children, and to ensure the existence of a male heir. In short, adoption was an effective institutional remedy for the uncertainties of contraception, child attributes, mortality, and fortune.

I earlier suggested that the new home economics model of fertility might not be applicable to preindustrial Europe, since the fertility behavior of couples showed no reflection of family size preferences. Hanley's study of preindustrial Japan, by contrast, portrays a reproductive system of dazzling rationality, for which the economic theory of fertility might be highly appropriate. Many of this theory's difficulties, such as absence of a market for children, irreversibility of childbearing decisions, uncertainty about attributes, and contraceptive failure, are removed by the widespread practice of abortion, infanticide, and adoption. The villagers apparently surpassed the hypothetical "perfect contraceptive population," which, after all, could neither control sex and other attributes nor so easily compensate for unexpected child deaths or economic misfortune.

To sum up this first group of chapters, most suggested that economic opportunities, including those created by high mortality, influenced nuptiality and fertility through institutions tying family formation to the availability of wealth. It may also be that preindustrial societies had crude forms of fertility control that were analogous to the mechanisms linking such standard-of-living variables as land availability and prior family income to fertility in more modern settings. Perhaps in the end we will confirm the view that both preindustrial and modern societies control fertility in response to the perceived ease of maintaining established living standards, first by controlling marriage and later by controlling fertility within marriage. At times the conference contributions suggested as much, yet they also sounded notes of caution to be heeded by future research. As stated earlier, Smith's paper raised questions about whether fertility was really affected by differences in nuptiality—and inheritance institutions by the mechanisms usually hypothesized. And in many settings the response of nuptiality and fertility to changing mortality and economic opportunity was apparently quite slow. We are getting closer to an answer to the question of how and to what degree preindustrial societies developed "preventive checks," yet ample research opportunities remain on this unresolved issue.

Socioeconomic Determinants of Modern Demographic Behavior

McInnis's chapter studies the fertility of a sample of individual farm families in Upper Canada in 1861. He is able to confirm that the well-established aggregate relationship between density of settlement and fertility does indeed reflect the behavior of individual couples. Fertility was positively related to farm size, to the proportion of the farmer's land developed, and to land availability in the area. Although his measures are rough, it appears that these variables affected fertility not by way of age at marriage but rather through marital fertility. Unfortunately, the data do not enable McInnis to distinguish among a number of competing models considered.

Peter Lindert's chapter on post–Civil War fertility swings in the United States stands apart from all the others, both because of the period covered (up to the present) and because of the model employed (a blending of Easterlin's relative income hypothesis with the new home economics fertility model). Lindert's model has been estimated and tested on interstate data for censuses from 1900 to 1970. He has succeeded in interpreting secular trends, long fluctuations, and cross-sectional differences within a common theoretical framework, and his version of the relative income hypothesis performs particularly strongly. As a peripheral aside, Lindert has confirmed once more the positive effect of land availability on fertility in the late nineteenth century United States.

Barbara Anderson's analysis of internal migration in Russia in the

1890s is the last chapter in the collection to deal with the socioeconomic causes and effects of demographic behavior. She has used aggregate cross-section data to test numerous hypotheses about the determinants of migration decisions and has included variables characterizing populations at the origin. She has concluded that the degree of cultural modernization at the origin exercised a strong positive effect on propensities to migrate to culturally modern destinations such as Saint Petersburg and Moscow, and that this effect transcended individual characteristics. The parallel results did *not* hold for industrial modernity. She also found that the natural growth rate of population at the origin was not associated with migration rates, and concluded that population pressure was not a significant cause of out-migration.

New Methods for Analyzing Aggregate Demographic Data

The remaining three chapters discuss new methods for the analysis of aggregate demographic data, methods developed specifically for use in the historical context.

The imprecision of many socioeconomic studies reflects the heavy use made of aggregate data such as time-series of baptisms, burials, and marriages, often in relation to other socioeconomic series. Since data on the size and structure of the base population are lacking, it is difficult to distinguish behavioral phenomena from manifestations of demographic structure. Attempts to calculate more meaningful measures rely on such statistics as the ratio of baptisms to marriages. The properties of these statistics have not been well established and are often seriously misleading. The shortcomings of such measures are demonstrated by Smith's chapter (Tables 2 and 3), which shows, for example, a low correlation of only .25 between the baptism–marriage ratio and reconstitution estimates of total marital fertility.

The methods described in the last three chapters help to put such research on a more rigorous demographic and statistical footing, and thereby enhance the possibilities for the study of substantive socioeconomic interactions with demographic variables. In addition, such methods facilitate communication between the aggregate and the microlevel (reconstitution) domains of analysis. It becomes possible to make consistency checks, to draw additional inferences, to supplement incomplete data in one domain with that from the other, and so on.

Demonet, Dupaquier, and Le Bras discuss a new set of model stable populations they have developed specifically for use with historical data, thus filling a long-felt need in historical demography. Existing sets of stable populations incorporate alternate assumptions about fertility and mortality; this new set also incorporates assumptions about nuptiality and marital fertility, and it employs a more flexible set of "double entry" life tables. This greater detail makes it possible to fit stable populations to reconstitution estimates, which will in turn make possible consistency checks of actual aggregate data with the implied stable population models. In addition to the usual descriptive output of age structure, rates of growth, and so on, these tables give such measures as birth–marriage ratios. They therefore provide the simulation data needed for a study of the properties of such easy-to-estimate measures.

A vast amount of historical demographic data is available in the form of long series of births, deaths, and marriages. In some cases the events forming the series can be linked and analyzed using nominative (e.g., reconstitution) methods; however, this is very time consuming, and usually only a fraction of the events can be successfully linked, raising the possibility of selectivity bias (see, e.g., Hollingsworth, 1969, pp. 181–196). In other cases, only the bare numbers of events are available. The chapters by Livi Bacci and Lee develop new methods for extracting useful information from these long series. Both chapters discuss the estimation of vital rates; Lee's study also discusses the use of these series to study determinants of variation in the rates.

The chapters differ in their approaches to estimation. Lee's method (developed more fully in Lee, 1974) relies heavily on the formal model of population renewal and it attempts to reconstruct recursively the population size, age structure, gross reproduction rate, and life expectancy at 5-year intervals. This method will give accurate results only when distortions due to underregistration and net migration are offsetting; because it is recursive, there is a danger of cumulative errors seriously and progressively biasing the results.

Livi Bacci's methods, on the other hand, are nonrecursive, so that although they give less detail (e.g., no age structure) they are more "robust" and less sensitive to persisting deficiencies in the data. In addition, he has extended his methods to nuptiality and marital fertility, which are not treated in Lee's paper (however, see Lee, forthcoming). Among the variables measured by Livi Bacci's methods are the modal age at marriage, the proportion marrying, life expectancy, and marital fertility. The methods are tested with considerable success on a number of historical data sets.

Most of Lee's chapter is devoted to showing the many important hypotheses that can be tested using aggregate series without ever having to estimate the rates. Hypotheses modeled and tested in his paper include the source of the 30-year cycle in baptism series; the existence of Malthusian oscillations; the mortality–nuptiality link of births to deaths; and the influence of climate and grain prices on vital rates. Spectral analysis is used to perform illustrative tests on parish data.

CONCLUSION

I will offer a few very subjective thoughts on promising directions for future model-oriented research in population history. High on the list must be studies of the effects of population change, a subject ignored by virtually all the chapters in this book. This topic is of particular importance because of its relevance for the situation of the currently developing countries.

Hanley's exciting paper on Tokugawa Japan illustrates the feasibility and high promise of historical studies of non-European populations, and the dangers of concentrating exclusively on European materials. Her findings also suggest that Japan is a more fruitful area than Europe for the application of the new economic theories of fertility.

A number of scholars are now working on data sets that will permit linkage of socioeconomic data with reconstituted families. We can hope for publication of new studies along these lines soon, and perhaps a clearer view of the socioeconomic correlates of individual behavior. To what extent models will help in these investigations is not yet clear.

Several chapters in this book present new methods for the exploitation of aggregate data. We can look for a closer integration of reconstitution results with aggregate evidence, as well as increased use of aggregate series themselves for demographic inference. Because a considerable quantity of social and economic data exists in the form of time-series, these advances in the use of demographic time-series may facilitate the development and testing of hypotheses with socioeconomic content.

Thanks to the Princeton Project's series of monographs on the demographic transition In Europe, many sets of time-series of cross sections have recently become available. These data lend themselves to the use of models and econometric techniques that have been successfully used on data from currently developing countries (see, e.g., Schultz, 1973).

Here, Hermalin and van de Walle's work on France illustrates the promise of what should be a very fruitful research area in coming years.

REFERENCES

Berkner, Lutz, & Mendels, Franklin (forthcoming). "Inheritance Systems, Family Structure and Demographic Patterns in Western Europe (1700–1900)," in Charles Tilly, ed., *Historical Studies of Changing Fertility*. Princeton, N.J.: Princeton University Press.

Chambers, J. D. (1965). "Three Essays on the Population and Economy of the Midlands," in D. V. Glass & D. E. C. Eversley, eds., *Population in History*. London: Edward Arnold.

Charbonneau, Hubert (1970). *Tourouvre-au-Perche Aux XVIIe et XVIIIe Siècles*. Paris: Presses Universitaires de France.

Easterlin, Richard (forthcoming). "The Economics and Sociology of Fertility: A Synthesis," in Charles Tilly, ed., *Historical Studies of Changing Fertility*. Princeton, N.J.: Princeton University Press.

Gautier, Etienne, & Henry, Louis (1958). *La Population de Crulai*. Paris: Presses Universitaires de France.

Goubert, Pierre (1960). *Beauvais et le Beauvaisis de 1600 à 1730*. Paris: S.E. V. P.E.N.

Hollingsworth, T. H. (1969). *Historical Demography*. Ithaca, N.Y.: Cornell University Press.

Knodel, John (1975). "Influence of Child Mortality on Fertility in European Populations in the Past: Results from Individual Data," in Committee for International Coordination of National Research in Demography, *Seminar on Infant Mortality in Relation to the Level of Fertility*. Paris: CICRED.

Lee, Ronald (1974). "Estimating Series of Vital Rates and Age Structures from Baptisms and Burials: A New Technique, with Applications to Preindustrial England," *Population Studies*, Vol. 28, No. 3 (November), pp. 495–512.

Lee, Ronald (forthcoming). "Models of Preindustrial Population Dynamics, with Applications to England," in Charles Tilly, ed., *Historical Studies of Changing Fertility*. Princeton, N.J.: Princeton University Press.

Nerlove, Marc (1974). "Household and Economy: Toward a New Theory of Population and Economic Growth," *Journal of Political Economy*, Vol. 82, No. 2, Supplement (March/April), pp. S200–218.

O'Hara, Donald J. (1975). "Microeconomic Aspects of the Demographic Transition," *Journal of Political Economy*, Vol. 83, No. 6 (December), pp. 1203–1216.

Ohlin, Goran (1961). "Mortality, Marriage, and Growth in Pre-industrial Populations," *Population Studies*, Vol. 14, No. 3 (March), pp. 190–197.

Sauvy, Alfred (1969). *General Theory of Population*. New York: Basic Books.

Schultz, T. Paul (1973). "Explanation of Birth Rate Changes over Space and Time," *Journal of Political Economy*, Vol. 81, No. 2, Pt. 2 (March–April), pp. 238–274.

Smith, Daniel (1972). "The Demographic History of Colonial New England," *Journal of Economic History*, Vol. 32, pp. 165–183.

Wrigley, E. A. (1966). "Family Limitation in Pre-Industrial England," *Economic History Review*, Vol. 19, No. 1, pp. 82–109.

Wrigley, E. A. (1969). *Population and History*. New York: McGraw-Hill.

INTRODUCTORY BIBLIOGRAPHY FOR
HISTORICAL POPULATION STUDIES

Periodicals

Annales de Demographie Historique
Local Population Studies

Surveys

Guillaume, Pierre, & Poussou, Jean-Pierre (1970). *Demographie Historique*. Paris: Armand Colin.

Hollingsworth, T. H. (1969). *Historical Demography*. Ithaca, N.Y.: Cornell University Press.

Reinhard, Marcel; Armengaud, Andre, & Dupaquier, Jacques (1968). *Histoire Generale de la Population Mondiale*. Paris: Montchrestien.

van de Walle, Etienne, & Kantrow, Louise (1974). "Historical Demography: A Bibliographical Essay," *Population Index*, Vol. 40, No. 4 (October), pp. 611–622.

Wrigley, E. A. (1969). *Population and History*. New York: McGraw-Hill.

Collections

Glass, D. V., & Eversley, D. E., eds. (1965). *Population in History*. London: Edward Arnold.

Glass, David V., & Revelle, Roger (1972). *Population and Social Change*. London: Edward Arnold.

Imhof, Arthur E. (1975). *Historische Demographie als Sozialgeschicte*. Darmstadt und Marburg: Selbstverlag der Hessischen Historischen Kommission Darmstadt und der Historischen Kommission für Hessen.

Laslett, Peter, & Wall, Richard, eds. (1972). *Household and Family in Past Time*. London: Cambridge University Press.

Tilly, Charles, ed. (forthcoming). *Historical Studies of Changing Fertility*. Princeton, N.J.: Princeton University Press.

Monographs and Research Articles

Coale, Ansley (1973). "The Demographic Transition Reconsidered," *Proceedings of the International Population Conference, Liege*, Vol. 1, pp. 53–72. [This paper reviews findings of the Princeton Project monographs on the fertility decline in Europe.]

Gautier, Etienne, & Henry, Louis (1959). *Crulai, Demographie d'une Paroisse Normande au XVIIe et au XVIIIe Siècles*. Cahier No. 33. Paris: Institut National d'Etudes Démographiques, Travaux et Documents.

Goubert, Pierre (1960). *Beauvais et le Beauvaisis de 1600 à 1730*. Paris: S. E. V. P. E. N.

Hajnal, J. (1965). "European Marriage Patterns in Perspective," in D. V. Glass & D. E. C. Eversley, eds., *Population in History*. London: Edward Arnold.

Wrigley, E. A. (1966). "Family Limitation in Pre-Industrial England," *Economic History Review*, Vol. 19, No. 1, pp. 82–109.

Manuals

Drake, Michael (1974). *Historical Demography: Problems and Projects.* Bletchley, England: Open University Press.

Henry, Louis (1967). *Manuel de Demographie Historique.* L'Ecole Pratique des Hautes Etudes, la IVe Section, Centre de Recherches d'Histoire et de Philologie, Serie 5, No. 3. Geneva/Paris: Librairie Droz.

Wrigley, E. A., ed. (1966). *An Introduction to English Historical Demography from the Sixteenth to the Nineteenth Century.* Cambridge Group for the History of Population and Social Structure, Publication No. 1. London: Weidenfeld and Nicholson.

A Homeostatic Demographic Regime: Patterns in West European Family Reconstitution Studies

DANIEL SCOTT SMITH

University of Illinois at Chicago Circle

In the period from the late 1950s to the mid-1970s, historical demographers reconstituted the families of early modern western European villagers and social groups. The linking of vital records into genealogies has yielded estimates on the complete range of demographic variables in the old regime of high fertility and mortality; these studies have provided the first estimates of the level and age-pattern of marital fertility in seventeenth and eighteenth century populations. The findings are surprising and puzzling. Scholars have found, instead of a constant biological maximum, marked variation in marital fertility over time and space (Demeny, 1968; Goubert, 1970; Wrigley, 1966). Beyond the noting of regional patterns, interpretation has not kept pace with the flood of reconstitution studies. This remarkable demographic diversity, particularly in the level of marital fertility, demands analysis and an attempt at systematic explanation.

The concept of the *demographic transition*—the contrast between the lower vital rates in currently advanced societies and the higher rates of premodern populations—provides both a useful analogy and a starting point for the interpretation of premodern demographic patterns. Although variability also characterizes the historical experience of declining vital rates, the concept of the demographic transition remains heuristically essential (Coale, 1969). Just as in the more general case of modernization theory, neither historical anomalies nor theoretical critiques have eliminated the need for a bold disjunction of before and after (Bendix, 1967).

As a theory the demographic transition refers to two sets of relationships. The broader socioeconomic argument connects lower vital rates to higher levels of modernity. At the core of transition theory in the narrow demographic sense is neither the contrast between higher and lower fertility and mortality nor the argument that a decline in the latter induces a decrease in the former. These statements rest on an underlying functionalist assumption—that societies strive to maintain equilibrium. Conversely, any disequilibrium tends to generate a correcting or homeostatic response. According to this reasoning, therefore, the rate of population growth in all populations will be more constant than the components of population change—mortality, marriage patterns, marital fertility, and migration. (For an early statement see Marshall, 1929/1965). A population fully using its economic resources, having a relatively fixed technological capacity, should tend toward a zero rate of population growth. In the longest run, of course, the growth rate of all populations must approach zero; if not, societies would either disappear or attain absurd densities.

Homeostatic patterns and arguments are widespread in the literature of historical demography. Davis, for example, has pointed to the multiple responses—overseas migration, delayed marriage, and the limitation of marital fertility—of the Japanese population to the stimuli of declining mortality and economic modernization (1963). Urban and overseas migration served, Friedlander (1969) has argued, as alternatives to birth control for the rural population of nineteenth century England. Several demographers have argued that marriage age and fertility within marriage can function as alternative sources of population increase (Demeny, 1968, p. 514; Henry, 1961; Lesthaeghe, 1971, Table 4, p. 419; van de Walle, 1968, p. 494).[1] Since marriage required an independent economic base in preindustrial western Europe, Ohlin (1960) has theorized that mortality and age at marriage would be inversely related. Since higher adult mortality would lead to an earlier age at male inheritance, the age at marriage for both sexes would presumably decline. In its classic Malthusian version, the homeostatic hypothesis has mortality serving as the ultimate or positive check on population growth. Although Lee (1973) has rejected the optimistic implication (the maintenance in the long run of a constant real wage of

[1] Nowhere do birth rates approach the levels arithmetically inherent in the combination of the Asian pattern of early marriage with the high levels of predecline west European marital fertility. See Kumar (1971, p. 274).

labor) of the classical theory, he found a positive correlation between English mortality and fertility over the half-millennium before 1750.

Western European family reconstitution studies supply data ideally suited to the purely demographic version of the homeostatic hypothesis. Population pressed on the relatively fixed economic potential of these villages; significant productivity change was absent. These tiny places also represent distinct and meaningful units of social life. Since the studies estimated the values of demographic variables over periods ranging from several decades to over a century, the assumption of a constant economic situation within individual villages approaches realism. If the homeostatic argument is correct, the demographic variables should tend to check each other.

Although these village populations generally approached the ceiling of economic production and productivity, one need not assume economic uniformity to test the demographic version of the homeostatic hypothesis. Marked economic shifts might impinge on the components of population change in the same direction. Wrigley (1966) has argued that sharply worsening economic conditions in the seventeenth century led to higher mortality, later marriage for women, and limitation of fertility within marriage in the English parish of Colyton. Such variation produced by economic circumstances tends to be obscured in the very long periods covered by family reconstitution studies. It is unfortunate, however, that these studies do not provide usable data on economic structure or conditions. This limitation in the data prevents the exploration of relationships between economic variables and the set of demographic parameters; further, these economic–demographic interrelationships may conceal correlations among the demographic variables themselves.

Although I will consider various demographic interrelationships, my focus will be on the explanation of the marked variation in the level of uncontrolled or "natural" marital fertility.[2] Natural fertility is a defining concept of pre–demographic transition populations. Following the Malthusian tradition, demographers have typically focused on the balancing of mortality and age at marriage. Marital fertility has been assumed to be fixed or determined by variations in biological fecundity. The perspective here is that all the demographic components form a system.

To be included in this study a population had to exhibit natural fertility. If there was a relationship between age at marriage or duration

---

[2] *Natural fertility* involves the absence of conscious control; such control exists if "the behavior of the couple is bound to the number of children already born and is modified when this number reaches the maximum which the couple does not want to exceed [Henry, 1961, p. 81]."

of marriage and fertility rates or the age at last birth in a reconstitution study, the data were excluded from analysis. Studies not reporting both age at marriage and age-specific marital fertility rates also were omitted. Several subperiods were combined in some instances, and each population provides only one observation. Estimates for the other variables were taken, inasmuch as was possible, from the time period for which marital fertility estimates were available. The majority of the 38 populations meeting these criteria are from eighteenth century France; 27 of the total were French-speaking. Only 2 fall entirely before 1700, 11 include both seventeenth and eighteenth century data, 20 are completely within the eighteenth century, and only 3 extend into the nineteenth century.

DESCRIPTIVE SUMMARY

As very important exercises in descriptive demography these family reconstitution studies have established the general contours of the natural fertility demographic regime of western Europe. Table 1 reports means, number of samples, and standard deviations; the major variables for the individual samples appear in the appendix.

Nuptiality

In the average village, women were nearly 26 when they wed for the first time; their husbands were slightly more than 2 years older. About a tenth of all women dying after menopause had never married. Widowers who remarried did so in less than 16 months on the average, whereas widows who remarried waited over 3 years.

Marital Fertility

A woman who married at age 20 exactly, and survived to age 45 with her husband would bear nine children. Although this total marital fertility rate was high, it is only 84.5% of the standard maximum fertility schedule of the Hutterites. In larger families the average interval between each of the second to fifth births was just over 2 years. Birth intervals increased with measured parity (and implicitly with the age of the mother). The second child was born 21.8 months after the first, the fifth arrived 26.8 months after the fourth, and the last followed 35.2 months after the next-to-last. Women in the average village completed their childbearing experience just after the fortieth birthday. Some women, of course, stopped earlier or were childless. Sterility characterized 5.0, 8.8, 17.1, and 38.9% of all married women at ages 25, 30, 35, and 40 respectively.

TABLE 1

Average Values of Demographic Variables in Family Reconstitution Studies

Description of variables		Mean	Cases	s
1. Nuptiality				
1. Female age at first marriage		25.7	38	1.74
2. Male age at first marriage		28.0	38	1.96
3. Age difference of spouses		2.27	38	1.23
4. Maximum spinsterhood percentage		13.3	19	7.0
5. Minimum spinsterhood percentage		8.6	15	6.6
6. Interval from widowhood to	Males	15.5	10	6.3
7. remarriage (months)	Females	39.2	9	15.8
Mortality				
8. Infant mortality, $_1q_0$, per 1000		212	35	51.2
9. Childhood mortality, $_4q_1$, per 1000		177	24	59.3
Fertility				
10. Age-specific marital fertility,	20-24	475.2	38	54.3
per 1000 woman-years	25-29	450.0	38	50.7
	30-34	398.2	38	59.5
	35-39	315.7	38	55.3
	40-44	158.0	38	39.7
11. Total marital fertility, 5 x 20-44		8.99	38	1.12
12. Percentage sterile (age)	25	5.0	12	3.7
	30	8.8	12	4.6
	35	17.1	12	6.0
	40	38.9	10	14.7
13. Illegitimacy per 1000 births		21.1	32	17.0
14. Premarital pregnancy ratio (percentage within 7 complete months of marriage)		12.0	36	6.7
15. Female age at last birth		40.1	23	.94
Fertility-birth intervals (months)				
16. First in larger families		21.8	26	2.3
17. Second in larger families		24.0	26	2.5
18. Third in larger families		25.7	23	3.3
19. Fourth in larger families		26.8	20	2.8
20. Next-to-last in larger families		29.5	23	2.6
21. Last in larger families		35.2	24	3.2
22. "Normal" birth interval		27.9	15	3.3
23. Interval after infant death		20.9	15	2.1
Fertility-seasonality of conception				
24. Ratio of the mean of the three highest contiguous months less the mean of the three lowest to a monthly mean of 100		37.7	23	10.7

Nonmarital Conceptions

By nineteenth century standards both illegitimacy and bridal pregnancy were infrequent (Shorter, 1971). Only 12% of legitimate first births came before the completion of 7 months of marriage, and a mere 2% of all births in the average village were illegitimate.

Mortality

The studies consistently reported estimates only for infant mortality ($_1q_0$) and for mortality in early childhood ($_4q_1$). Some 79% of babies celebrated their first birthday, but only 82% of this fortunate fraction reached age 5. The level of early childhood mortality was high relative to the infant mortality rate; this pattern corresponds closely to the North rather than the West variant in the widely used Coale–Demeny regional model life tables.[3]

Generation and Stable Measures

Combining variables in the family reconstitution studies permits an estimate of the more conventional demographic rates. Women marrying at the average age and surviving to age 45 with their husbands would bear 5.78 children on the average.[4] Using the estimates of illegitimacy and permanent celibacy, including the slight contribution of the earliest (15–19) and latest (45–49) age groups to total fertility, and making a guess about the impact of widowhood on fertility, we may suppose that this index of completed family size was about 15% higher than the total fertility rate. A total fertility rate of 5 implies a gross reproduction rate of 2.45.

The infant mortality rate of 212.2 fits level 6.6 in the Princeton life tables (Coale & Demeny, 1966). Female and male life expectancies at birth are thus 34.0 and 31.1 years in the North tables. Assuming a West mortality pattern after age 5 raises life expectancies at birth to only 34.1 and 31.6 years respectively. With 31 as the mean age of maternity, the net reproduction rate is 1.26, the birth and death rates for both sexes are 37.8 and 29.1, and the growth rate is therefore 8.7 per 1000.

VALIDITY OF RECONSTITUTION RESULTS

Although the technique of family reconstitution has revolutionized the study of early modern demographic history, doubt persists about

[3] In the 24 studies reporting both $_1q_0$ and $_4q_1$, the average values were 212.4 and 177.2 per 1000. In the model North tables an infant mortality rate of 212.4 is associated with a $_4q_1$ of 179.5; in the West tables the same infant mortality rate corresponds to a $_4q_1$ of 131.9 (Coale & Demeny, 1966). According to van de Walle (1974, p. 74), French mortality before the second half of the nineteenth century fits the North rather than the West pattern.

[4] The index of completed family size was calculated by adding three components reflecting the pattern of marital fertility by age: (1) The difference between the mean age at last birth and the mean age at marriage was multiplied by average fertility between 25 and 40. (2) The difference between the overall mean age at marriage and the mean marriage age in each sample was multiplied by average fertility between 20 and 30. (3) The difference between the overall and sample mean ages at last birth was multiplied by the average fertility between 35 and 45.

the representativeness of the results. A rather small number of families—from less than 50 to several hundred—is included in each study. Much more important, only a minority of all marriages can be reconstituted. This loss of data primarily derives from migration. Since movement in and out of these villages undoubtedly does not select randomly, family reconstitution studies do not capture a true cross-section of the population.

Variation in the quality of the underlying data hampers accurate comparison; by necessity this analysis assumes all published figures are equally accurate. Furthermore, the demographic estimates within each study do not pertain to the same population. The age at first marriage, for example, is known for more couples than can be included in the calculation of marital fertility. Estimates of the illegitimacy ratio and the proportion remaining permanently single come from the complete vital register. Justification of the reanalysis of these studies must rest in large part on their importance in the literature of historical demography and on the absence of alternative data for the period before modern census-taking and national vital registration.

Comparing certain reconstitution results with aggregative measures of the same or substantively related phenomena gives some quantitative indication of the representativeness of the reconstituted minority within each village. Dividing the birth rate of 37.8 per 1000—estimated indirectly from the reconstitution data by the ratio of births to deaths in the register (1.297)—implies a death rate of 29.1 and a growth rate of 8.6 per 1000, estimates identical to those obtained from the reconstitution studies. Given the approximations used in deriving the stable measures, the agreement must be regarded as partially fortuitous. Congruence of the reconstitution and aggregative measures does not guarantee the absolute accuracy of either. In both approaches mortality is probably underregistered compared to fertility. The higher correlations of $_4q_1$ than $_1q_0$ with the aggregative measures of mortality suggest that differential underregistration of infant mortality is an important source of error (see Table 2). Several of the authors also point to the underenumeration of deaths. Finally, the overall growth rate of 8.6 per 1000 appears to be rather high for eighteenth century populations. Henry (1965) estimates, for example, that the French growth rate between 1700 and 1770 was between 2.0 and 2.6 per 1000.

In general, however, the two techniques produce consistent results. The correlations in Table 2 demonstrate that variations in mortality and growth calculated from the complete register correspond to variations in analogous variables in the reconstitution studies. The commonly used birth-to-marriage ratio is not highly correlated with the level of total marital fertility. Nor is an earlier age at marriage associated with a

TABLE 2
Correlations of Family Reconstitution Parameters with Aggregative Ratios of Vital Events

Family reconstitution parameter	Aggregative ratios				
	Births to deaths	Deaths to all events	Marriages to all events	Births to all events	Births to marriage
15	.60*	-.73**	.75*	.52*	-.56*
$_1q_0$	-.40	.57**	-.54**	-.46*	.15
$_4q_1$	-.62*	.72**	-.79***	-.50	.57
Total marital fertility from 20 to 45	.03	.07	-.21	-.01	.25
Female age at first marriage	.25	-.16	.10	.12	.16
Mean value	1.297	.403	.105	.492	4.825
Number of cases	23	22	22	22	24

*p < .05.
**p < .01.
***p < .001.

TABLE 3
Correlations between Family Reconstitution and Aggregative Nuptiality and Nonmarital Fertility Variables

Reconstitution results	Aggregative results		
	Illegitimacy ratio	Proportion maximum	Never-marrying minimum
Male age at first marriage	.50**	.23	.41
Female age at first marriage	.51**	.47*	.52
Premarital pregnancy ratio	.29	-.42	-.48
Maximum number of samples	32	19	15

*p < .05.
**p < .01.

higher proportion of marriages in all vital events. Since the same information is being organized by two different methods, one might expect somewhat closer agreement between variations in reconstitution and aggregative analysis.

Substantively related demographic phenomena measured by the two methods are also correlated in the right direction. A significant relationship exists between the female age at first marriage in the reconstitution studies and the percentage of women dying over age 45 reported as single or of unknown marital status (Table 3). As would be expected from other results, the illegitimacy ratio is significantly higher in later-marrying samples, and is positively correlated with the premarital pregnancy ratio in the reconstitution studies. In sum, extreme doubt about the representativeness of family reconstitution studies is not warranted. Underregistration of vital events distorts estimates produced by both reconstitution and aggregative analysis. Ecological comparisons, however, are affected only by differentials in underregistration.

EXPLAINING VARIATION: TWO PRELIMINARY APPROACHES

Regional Differences

The averages for the studies in Table 1 conceal very marked variation. There was a range of 10 years in the mean age of first marriage; total marital fertility varied from 6.3 to 11.0 children; and infant mortality encompassed a span from 125 to 344 per 1000. Regional variation is a frequently cited source of this demographic heterogeneity. With the limited number of samples, only four groupings were feasible: (1) the southern and central parts of France, (2) the Paris region and the north of France, (3) northwestern France, and (4) a German-language region including three parishes in northeastern France. Physical contiguity and similarity in the level of marital fertility were used to group the samples from a more detailed geographic classification.

Although Table 4 reveals some differences of interest, a serious discussion of regional variation requires a larger number of samples. Some comparison can be made with other discussions of regional differences. As among departments in 1831, marriage was later in the villages in northwestern France (van de Walle, 1974, Map 7.7, p. 183). Marital fertility, on the other hand, was lowest in the south of France (Henry, 1973; van de Walle, 1974, Map 7.3, p. 175). Surprisingly, there was no tendency for the difference between $_1q_0$ and $_4q_1$ to follow the model West pattern in any region.

No differences among the regions for 13 major variables, with the exception of the illegitimacy ratio, were statistically significant in a one-way analysis of variance. The regional classification used here was too gross to detect demographic variations arising from populations sharing the same area and experiencing similar conditions of life and cultural traditions. Early modern western Europe, as nearly all historians have emphasized, was stamped with local peculiarities. Regional

TABLE 4
Regional Variation in Family Reconstitution Studies

Variable	South and central France (N=7)	Paris and northern France (N=6)	Northwestern France (N=14)	German language region (N=8)
1. Female age at first marriage	24.9	25.3	26.0	26.0
2. Male age at first marriage	27.3	26.8	28.0	28.8
3. Age difference of spouses	2.4	1.5	2.1	2.8
4. Age-specific marital fertility rates				
20-24	430	528	485	446
25-29	416	508	459	425
30-34	358	460	404	381
35-39	279	365	319	305
40-44	142	163	162	156
5. Total marital fertility (children)	8.13	10.12	9.15	8.56
6. Age at last birth	39.3(4)[a]	40.4(4)	40.4(7)	39.9(5)
7. Mean of first four birth intervals in larger families	25.5(5)	22.4(6)	24.1(9)	26.0(4)
8. Next-to-last birth interval	30.3(5)	28.3(5)	29.7(9)	29.6(3)
9. Last birth interval	35.5(5)	35.6(6)	34.5(9)	36.5(3)
10. Infant mortality, $1q_0$, per 1000	241	231	196(12)	199
11. $4q_1$, per 1000	225(4)	193(5)	141(11)	130(3)
12. $1q_0$ for same samples as 11	250(4)	226(5)	200(11)	172(3)
13. Illegitimacy ratio, per 1000	11.0(5)	7.8	26.5(13)	28.6
14. Premarital pregnancy ratio, per 1000	107(6)	101	120	142
15. Seasonality index	50.2(5)	32.1(5)	36.6(12)	41.8(1)
16. Percentage of total marital fertility in 20-24 age group	26.5%	26.1%	26.6%	26.4%

[a]Unless otherwise indicated by parentheses, data are reported in all cases.

differences in nineteenth century French departmental-level data conceal this more detailed local variation. For this analysis each sample falls, in effect, into a separate "region." Both theoretical considerations and the absence of information on the economic, social, and cultural characteristics of the villages argue against attempting to account for demographic variation on a case-by-case basis.

Conscious Control—The Shape of Marital Fertility

The variation in marital fertility could be caused by its conscious control in Henry's sense (Henry, 1961). Since the small number of years-at-risk in many of the studies prevents firm conclusions, a vary-

TABLE 5
Correlations of the Shape of Marital Fertility (Proportion of Total Marital Fertility from 20 to 44 in the 20-24 Age Group) with Measures of Marital Fertility and Other Demographic Variables

Variable	Correlation	Cases
Marital fertility rates		
20-24	.20	38
25-29	-.42**	38
30-34	-.58***	38
35-39	-.48***	38
40-44	-.52***	38
Total marital fertility, 20-44	-.44**	38
Total marital fertility, 25-44	-.60***	38
Birth intervals in larger families		
First	.22	26
Second	.50**	26
Third	.55**	23
Fourth	.46*	20
Next-to-last	.51*	23
Last	.63***	24
Normal interval	.22	15
l_5	-.04	24
$_1q_0$	-.09	35
Female age at first marriage	-.07	38
Age difference of spouses	.26	38
Index of seasonality	-.02	23
Size of place (number of vital events per year)	-.04	22

*$p < .05$.
**$p < .01$.
***$p < .001$.

TABLE 6
Correlations among Age-Specific Marital Fertility Rates and Birth Intervals in Larger Families (5+ or 6+ Children)

Age group	Age group					
	20-24	*25-29*	*30-34*	*35-39*	*40-44*	*20-44*
20-24	1.00	.69***	.61***	.59***	.37*	.79***
25-29		1.00	.85***	.73***	.48**	.90***
30-34			1.00	.86***	.50**	.92***
35-39				1.00	.63***	.91***
40-44					1.00	.68***
Cases	*30*	*38*	*38*	*38*	*38*	*38*

Birth interval	Order of birth interval					
	First	*Second*	*Third*	*Fourth*	*Next-to -last*	*Last*
First	1.00	.77***	.76***	.60**	.60**	.13
Second		1.00	.93***	.80***	.83***	.48*
Third			1.00	.88***	.83***	.50*
Fourth				1.00	.78***	.31
Next-to-last					1.00	.55**
Cases	*26*	*26*	*23*	*20*	*23*	*24*

*p < .05.
**p < .01.
***p < .001.

ing fraction of couples within some of the villages may have made fertility decisions on the basis of parity. Despite my attempt to exclude such patterns of conscious control from this analysis, the age-pattern of marital fertility in the 38 studies diverges from a maximum schedule. Compared to early eighteenth century French Canadian rates the divergence is progressive—93, 91, 82, 77, and 73% for the five age groups from 20–24 to 40–44.[5]

Coale's distinction between the shape and level of marital fertility serves to eliminate the possibility that conscious control was the sole source of variation (1971). Since individually controlled marital fertility concentrates births in the earlier years of childbearing, the proportion of total marital fertility in the initial 20–24 age group provides an index

[5] French Canadian total marital fertility between the ages of 20 and 45 (10.63) is identical to that of the standard Hutterite schedule (10.65). See Henry (1961, Table 1, p. 84).

of the shape of the marital fertility curve. This "shape" variable accounts for 19.4% of the variance in total marital fertility (Table 5). Although the shape index is correlated with marital fertility rates and birth intervals, it has little relationship to the other important demographic variables listed at the bottom of Table 5. Variation in the shape of marital fertility is a distinct dimension of the structure of overall fertility. What also needs to be explained are the high intercorrelations of the age-specific marital fertility rates and birth intervals (Table 6).

NUPTIALITY, MARITAL FERTILITY, AND COMPLETED FAMILY SIZE

Even in populations that practice contraception, women who marry early have more children than those who marry later. An operational definition of natural fertility is the absence of a relationship between female marriage age and age-specific fertility rates within marriage. Despite this relationship existing at the level of individual couples, an earlier female age at first marriage correlates with a lower total marital fertility rate at the village level. With this same contrast holding for pre-fertility decline in Austria-Hungary, early nineteenth century France, and western Europe in comparison to non-European populations, this paradox should no longer be surprising. In the 38 samples female age at first marriage explains 18.7% of the variance in total marital fertility (Table 7).

This positive correlation does not exhaust the influence of nuptiality on marital fertility. To the familiar paradox a puzzle is added. A larger difference between spouses in age at first marriage lowers marital fertility; this effect explains slightly more (22.3%) of the variance in total marital fertility than female age at first marriage. Compared to the overall average total marital fertility of 8.99 children, a hypothetical village with the average male age at first marriage but with a female marriage age 1 year older than the mean would have a total marital fertility rate of 9.58 children. Increasing age at marriage by 1 year for men and women raises total marital fertility to 9.25.[6]

---

[6] An inherent measurement error slightly exaggerates the effect of an increase in the age at marriage of females on marital fertility rates. The true relationship is distorted by the spreading out of the shorter interval from marriage to first birth over several age groups in later-marrying villages. (A rough calculation based on one early- and one late-marrying sample results in an estimate that this distortion adds .042 children per year of later female age age at first marriage to the total marital fertility rate. The observed effect is more than six times as large—.26 children per year of later marriage.)

TABLE 7
Variance in Total Marital Fertility from 20 to 44 Explained by Nuptiality, the Shape of the Fertility Curve and Size of Place

Variables	R^2 (%)	Significance	Cases
1. Female age at first marriage	18.7	.01	38
2. Age difference between spouses	22.3	.01	38
3. Shape of marital fertility	19.8	.01	38
4. Size of place (number of births per year)	16.8	.05	27
5. 1 and 2 combined	35.3	.001	38
6. 1 and 3 combined	32.1	.001	38
7. 2 and 3 combined	33.4	.001	38
8. 1, 2, and 3 combined	42.9	.001	38
9. 1, 2, and 4 combined	49.8	.001	27
10. 1, 3, and 4 combined	52.8	.001	27
11. 1, 2, 3, and 4 combined	54.4	.001	27

The relationship between nuptiality and marital fertility obliterates the obvious association of earlier marriage with a larger index of completed family size. Only a slight and statistically insignificant correlation ($-.18$) exists between completed family size and female age at first marriage. In the hypothetical village with the average male age at first marriage and a female marriage age a year later than average, completed family size is 5.83 children compared to 5.74 in the average sample. Part of this increase results from a .48-year increase in age at last birth per year of later marriage age. Earlier marriage for individual women does lead to larger complete families, but this logical result does not hold for the group.

Natural fertility for individual couples is compatible with its control on the aggregate level. Underlying Henry's definition (1961) is an implicit separation of age at marriage, spacing of children, and the age at termination of childbearing. Henry's definition fits, with qualifications,[7] the fertility behavior of modern couples equipped with effective

---

[7] Probably no population fits Henry's definition empirically. According to Henry, controlled fertility is a function of parity. In both noncontracepting and contracepting populations, women at a higher parity at a given age in the childbearing span will have more children after that age than women at a lower parity. Differential fecundity presumably explains the first case; differences in fecundity, in the effectiveness of contraceptive use, and in desired family size account for the latter case. The modernity of Henry's definition is clear from its formulation in terms of children born rather than

contraception. These couples know, more or less, how many children they want at marriage, bear them rapidly, and then use contraception and abortion to prevent additional births. In historical populations the three parts of completed family size may be more of a coherent sequence, especially on the group level. Even on the individual level the idea that marriage age and fertility within marriage are integrated should not be casually dismissed. In Ireland after 1911, for example, the decline in fertility was most marked for women who married late in life (Kennedy, 1973, p. 179). Age at marriage was an important regulator of fertility in premodern Europe, but these findings suggest that it was not the only variable mechanism in population growth.

The relatively low rates of geographical exogamy evident in the marriage data of the family reconstitution studies indicate that the village was an isolated-enough environment to maintain idiosyncratic demographic norms; most of the population movement was contained within a short radius. It is not unreasonable to suppose that customs of extended nursing would develop in villages in need of lower marital fertility. A correlation between the greater incidence and duration of nursing and earlier marriage age is apparent among villages in early twentieth century Germany (Knodel & van de Walle, 1967).[8] Community sanctions severely constrained the choices individuals could make in many intimate situations in early modern Europe. Indeed, the predominance of group control over individual choice defines the meaning of the sociological concept of *Gemeinschaft*.[9]

A simultaneous increase in the age at marriage for both males and females does result in a decline in completed family size from 5.74 to 5.58 children. Male marriage age appears to be an important independent variable in determining the level of marital fertility. In the 38 studies, an additional year of age between spouses reduces fertility between ages 30 and 44 from 6.2% to 5.4% (controlling for female age at marriage). In an earlier study I found that a decrease of 2.5% per additional year of age difference between spouses characterized fertility patterns over the same age span for women in seventeenth and

---

children currently living; differentials in infant mortality are not considered. (For an emphasis on the control of spacing in the natural fertility regime see Dupaquier & Lachiver, 1969.)

[8] The correlation between the percentage not nursing in 1903–1908 and I_m (an index of nuptiality) in 1880 in 15 provinces of Bavaria, Hessen, and Baden was −.70; for I_m in 1900 and the percentage not nursing in 1903–1908 the correlation was −.79. (Results based on unpublished data presented by John Knodel at the University of Pennsylvania conference.)

[9] For a description and analysis of the communal control of sexual and marital customs see Shorter (1975, pp. 44–53, 103–108, 121–147, and 218–227).

eighteenth century Hingham, Massachusetts (Smith, 1972, pp. 180–181). More recently Anderson (1975) has found evidence in contemporary Soviet Central Asia and early twentieth century Ireland pointing to the independent effect of husband's age on the marital fertility of the wife.

Why this relationship exists is unclear. Male biological fecundity apparently does not deline before age 45, but there are no adequate medical studies (MacLeod & Gold, 1953). Applying some scattered data to a model of birth spacing demonstrates that lower coital frequency in marriages with older husbands also cannot explain the magnitude of the effect in the west European or Hingham studies. Assuming a 17-month dead time for pregnancy and postpartum sterility, the relationship between coital frequency and the probability of conception in a modern population, and an estimated decline of .07 in male weekly coital frequency with each additional year of age, increasing the age difference between spouses by one year would lengthen the average birth interval by only .7%.[10] Since women are not at risk of pregnancy during most of the birth interval, frequency of coitus has only a minor impact on fertility.

Biological, social, and spurious causes may all be involved in the apparent effect of spouse's age difference on the marital fertility rates. It is unfortunate that none of the studies reports a tabulation of fertility by the husband's age relative to that of the wife. It is quite possible that no simple relationship exists on the individual level within these villages. Since an earlier female age at marriage is associated with a larger age gap between spouses, the age-difference effect should produce an apparent positive correlation between marriage age and marital fertility. Such a pattern would also point to consciously controlled fertility, a phenomenon absent here.

Another peculiarity of the early modern demographic system further complicates the situation. The wives of higher status or landholding men tended to marry earlier, have older husbands, and bear children at higher rates than the wives of lower status or landless men.[11] If the

---

[10] This model was based on several sources: Keyfitz (1971, p. 113); Barrett (1971, Table 2, p. 310) for data on coital frequency and on the probability of conception for women over 30; and Kinsey, Pomeroy, and Martin (1948, Table 46, p. 252) for the relationship of male age to coital frequency. The linear trend of marital coitus with wife's age in the Kinsey study is parallel to those in the methodologically superior 1965 and 1970 national fertility surveys (Westoff, 1974, Table 2, p. 137).

[11] Studies showing this class pattern for the three variables are Giacchetti and Tyvaert (1969, pp. 54–55, 61), Charbonneau (1970, pp. 75, 108, 111, 159), and Thestrup (1972, pp. 21, 24). Showing higher marital fertility for the higher status group but no difference in

ecological pattern (later female marriage age and a small age gap between spouses being associated with higher marital fertility rates) was typically reversed on a class basis within villages, then neither nuptiality parameter would show much correlation with the marital fertility of couples. The high degree of socioeconomic group endogamy suggests the possible relevance of class norms in explaining demographic behavior. (For an example of high class endogamy, see Charbonneau, 1970, pp. 84–88.) What appears to be natural fertility is not just uncontrolled fertility; rather it may well be the product of the interaction of several compensating sets of social controls.

FERTILITY, NUPTIALITY, AND MORTALITY

Just as variations in female age at first marriage and marital fertility rates tend to counterbalance, the level of mortality is also positively correlated with the index of completed family size. Although individual couples may not have attempted to replace dead children,[12] the fertility behavior of the group was oriented, or so it appears, toward the production of survivors, not babies. Fifty-five percent of a given decrease in the proportion surviving to age 5 is compensated for by a larger completed family size. Although $_1q_0$ or $_4q_1$ does not significantly assist in the prediction of total marital fertility l_5 explains 23.6% of the variance in complete family size in the 15 villages reporting all the necessary variables. The correlations in Table 8 are higher for early childhood mortality than for infant mortality, suggesting either that the shortening of the birth interval following an infant death is less important than the social replacement of dead children or that differential underregistration is higher for $_1q_0$ than for $_4q_1$.

Higher mortality is also associated with a lower age at first marriage, especially for males, and a smaller sex differential in the age at first marriage. An absolute 10% decrease in the proportion surviving to age 5 implies a decline of 1.2 years in male marriage age and a narrowing of the age difference between spouses of more than .7 years. Assuming the typical correlation between the levels of childhood and adult mortal-

---

marriage age is Terrisse (1961, p. 290). Higher fertility and later marriage for higher-status women appear in Deniel and Henry (1965, p. 583). Exhibiting no difference in marital fertility by class are Ganiage (1963, p. 85), Lachiver (1969, p. 165), and Knodel (1970, pp. 370–371).

[12] The European studies do not test this possibility directly. Indirect tests tend not to support the "replacement hypothesis." See Knodel (1974).

TABLE 8
Correlations among Nuptiality, Fertility, and Mortality Variables

Variable	1	2	3	4	5	6	7	8	9
1. $_1q_0$	1.00	.75***	-.93***	-.28	-.14	-.27	.44	.15	.30
2. $_4q_1$		1.00	-.94***	-.56**	-.28	-.50*	.49*	.21	.13
3. 15			1.00	.49**	.21	.49	-.48*	-.19	-.21
4. Male marriage age				1.00	.79***	.48**	-.38*	.09	.36
5. Female marriage age					1.00	-.16	-.18	.43**	.32
6. Age difference of spouses						1.00	-.25	-.47**	.11
7. Complete family size index							1.00	.70***	-.30
8. Total marital fertility, 20-45								1.00	-.15
9. Difference between normal interval and interval after infant death									1.00

*p < .05.
**p < .01.
***p < .001.

ity, this relationship supports Ohlin's hypothesis (1960) linking male age at marriage to mortality through the age of inheritance.[13]

Ohlin's argument implicitly assumes an equal response in marriage age for both sexes. In an intriguing analysis of female age at marriage in seventeenth century England, Elliott (1976) criticizes this untested assumption and shows that the early death of fathers forced daughters to migrate as servants to London, thus delaying their marriage. Higher mortality concomitant with worsening economic conditions might produce demographic effects further checking population increase.

The larger impact of mortality on male age at first marriage is also consistent with the relationship between mortality level and the sex ratio among young adults in the corresponding stationary populations. As mortality declines the ratio of males aged 20–35 to females aged 20–29 increases linearly in the model West life tables; higher mortality rates provide males of marriageable ages with relatively more females. An increase in infant mortality from 160 to 280 per 1000 reduces the young adult sex ratio from 142.7 to 138.6. This sex ratio variable is correlated .30 with male age at first marriage and .29 with the age difference between spouses. In the regression analysis the age difference variable may be viewed as a proxy for the level of mortality. The zero-order correlation of $-.25$ between spouse's age difference and completed family size withers to .02 when l_5 is introduced as a control variable. In predicting total marital fertility, on the other hand, introducing the age-difference variable eliminates the contribution of infant and childhood mortality to the explanation of the variance. The varying number of villages reporting a given set of demographic parameters is a cause of these ambiguous results; more important are the inherent limitations of ecological analysis for sorting out effects potentially important at the individual level or over time within a given population.

Mortality is also related to fertility through the cessation of lactation and amenorrhea following an infant death. After an infant death the average birth interval was 20.9 months compared to 27.9 months if the previous child survived to his first birthday. Some control over the spacing of births may be inferred from the variation in these two intervals. The birth interval after an infant death was slightly more regular (coefficient of variation of 10.0%) than if the previous child lived (coefficient of variation, 11.7%). The correlation of the difference

[13] Support for Ohlin's argument was found on the individual level in the relatively land-abundant environment of seventeenth and eighteenth century Hingham, Massachusetts. Men whose fathers died before age 60 married 1.6 to 2.0 years earlier than men whose fathers lived past that age. See also Smith (1973, Table 1, p. 423). An identical relationship has been found for Concord, Massachusetts. See Gross (1976, p. 211).

between these intervals—a measure related to the duration of nursing—with the normal interval was .79 (significant at the .001 level), but only an insignificant − .30 with the infant mortality interval. After an infant death women in the several villages gave birth again without much variation. The differences in overall fertility are much more closely related to the length of the normal birth interval; the latter interval reflects controlled delay as well as the dead time of pregnancy and postpartum sterility. (For a summary of contemporary views, see van de Walle & van de Walle, 1972.)

VILLAGE SIZE, SEASONALITY OF CONCEPTION, AND THE HOMEOSTATIC HYPOTHESIS

Although the portrayal of demographic parameters as counterbalancing forces is logical and has empirical usefulness in explaining variation in these family reconstitution studies, the causal mechanisms necessarily remain uncertain. It is possible that the coherent patterns arise from some other factor not included in the analysis. Wealthier (or poorer) villages, for example, may have had lower fertility and mortality for reasons quite distinct from the group regulation of the interaction of the demographic variables. The only available index of the extent of socioeconomic complexity of the samples—the size of place measured by the number of births or the number of vital events per year—is obviously not a sensitive indicator. Since the area of a parish is doubtlessly correlated with these measures, even a simple density index would be superior. Nevertheless, these measures do relate to socioeconomic complexity; the only five parishes designated as urban are among the six highest in the number of vital events per year.

As Table 9 indicates, larger village size is associated with increased completed family size, fertility within marriage, and mortality. Excluding the urban samples diminishes but does not eliminate the correlations. Because of the small and varying number of samples involved in each regression, the effect of village size, when included with the other variables, is somewhat ambiguous. In the prediction of total marital fertility, the spouse's age-difference variable is not surprisingly the most vulnerable to the addition of the village size indices. Female marriage age, on the other hand, becomes more significant in conjunction with the size variables.

The demographic plausibility of these results gives them credence. Yet the importance of the village size variable must cast some doubt on the homeostatic hypothesis, at least in its purely demographic version. Perhaps demographic homeostasis should not be viewed as hypothesis but as a pervasive empirical pattern whose causes need explication.

TABLE 9
Correlations of Village Size Index with Demographic Variables

Variable	1	2	3	4	5	6	7	8	9
1. Births per year	1.00	-.14	-.42*	.36	-.57*	-.76**	.41	-.44	.54*
1a. Same, nonurban	1.00	.07	-.22	.47*	--	--	.31	-.43	--
2. Female marriage age		1.00	-.16	-.14	.22	.20	.43**	-.08	-.18
3. Spouse's age difference			1.00	-.27	.49*	.23	-.47**	.32	-.25
4. $_1q_0$				1.00	-.93***	-.62*	.15	-.07	.44*
5. l_5					1.00	.24	-.18	.19	-.49*
6. Normal birth interval						1.00	-.49*	-.51*	-.63**
7. Total marital fertility							1.00	-.58**	.70***
8. Seasonality index								1.00	-.63**
9. Complete family size index									1.00

*$p < .05$.
**$p < .01$.
***$p < .001$.

Scholars trained in history are naturally suspicious of sentences with societies as their subjects. Although groups have norms, only individuals act, and the aggregate is the sum of the behavior of individuals. Sociologists, on the other hand, have been too content with the illustration of general functionalist notions and have ignored the problem of detailed explanation.

Isolating the causal factors and intermediate variables behind the homeostatic patterns cannot be carried very far here. The systematic analysis of variation over time rather than among places should be the focus of future research in the natural fertility area (see, e.g., Levine, forthcoming). Ecological analysis is an inexpensive way of suggesting what the important variables may be. A final pattern in these studies is of interest on these grounds. Variation in the seasonality of conception (births lagged 9 months) appears to be a crucial intermediate piece in this puzzle. Lower marital fertility and longer birth intervals are associated with larger fluctuations in the monthly number of conceptions. (The seasonality index was defined as the ratio of the difference between the average of the three highest and three lowest contiguous months to a standardized monthly mean of 100 conceptions. This index was adopted to minimize the effect of sample size and to code data presented only in graphs in the studies. In the 18 samples with tabular display of monthly births, this index was correlated .986 with the standard deviation.) The correlation of the size measures with the seasonality index raises the possibility of a spurious relationship. The negative correlation between seasonality and total marital fertility persists, however, after the introduction of a sample size variable. Nor did the relationship disappear when the five smallest (under 2000 births) villages were excluded from the analysis. The seasonality index is not a proxy for sample size.[14]

Why were babies conceived most frequently in the spring and least often in the autumn? (See Table 10.) Hypotheses abound—seasonal migration of labor during the harvest, or more vaguely a fertility pattern linked to the passage of the agricultural cycle, voluntary abstinence during certain periods (unlikely but reflected in the secondary low during Lent in March), or a less well nourished population in smaller places without markets and a regular food supply.[15] Here it is only possible to point out several suggestive relationships.

[14] The relationship between urbanization and lower seasonality in conception has been pointed out by Kenneth A. Lockridge in his unpublished paper "On Monthly Variation in the Level of Conception as a Tool in Historical Analysis" (1969). I am indebted to Professor Lockridge for his permitting me to read this wide-ranging paper.

[15] Henri Leridon (1973) conveniently summarizes the literature on seasonality in fertility patterns.

TABLE 10
Seasonality of Conception and Death

Month of death and conception	Death (N=13)	Conception (N=18)	Conceptions coefficient of variation	Correlations of monthly conceptions with:		
				Seasonality index (N=18)	Total marital fertility (N=18)	Birth intervals in large families (N=14)
January	117	91	12.2%	-.50*	.29	-.55
February	112	98	12.2	-.52*	-.05	-.08
March	114	91	13.4	-.54*	.07	-.30
April	118	111	8.2	.04	-.03	-.48
May	97	119	12.6	.75***	-.17	.41
June	82	128	13.3	.87***	-.61**	.90***
July	74	107	7.9	.27	-.13	.63*
August	89	92	11.8	.08	.25	.12
September	107	82	10.4	-.28	.23	-.11
October	98	84	6.8	-.39	.46	-.43
November	95	94	10.7	-.02	.21	-.14
December	104	96	8.7	-.64*	.06	-.67**

*p < .05.
**p < .01.
***p < .001.

Seasonality of conception is a source of marked variation in fertility. In the 18 samples with a tabular presentation of monthly birth data, the average birth rate in the 3 highest contiguous months was 37% higher than in the 3 lowest contiguous months. Although seasonal fluctuation in births has now greatly diminished, historical demographers should not ignore this poorly understood aspect of the premodern demographic world.

The focus of speculation on the causes of seasonality in conception centers on why the trough occurs in the early fall. Some connection with the harvest is usually cited. Since the timing of the peak in part determines the trough in a high fertility population (pregnant women are protected against pregnancy), this approach has a logical flaw. Since the peak in conceptions also coincides with the usual annual high in food prices, nutrition probably is not a major factor. The demographic "crisis" and the regular annual cycle of birth are distinct phenomena.

Because the 3 lowest death months (June to August) slightly lag the peak in conceptions (April to July), one may infer that the peak summer months of conception were also months of relatively low pregnancy wastage. The intersection of the cycle of fertility and mortality is also apparent in the 9-month gap separating the months of highest mortality (January to April) from the peak months of conception. The negative correlations between the seasonality index and the monthly conceptions (column 5, Table 9) are not so marked in the trough as during the December to March interval. It is possible that birth rates in the villages were more nearly equal during the April–June peak, whereas the variation in fertility arose during the rest of the year, not just in the trough. The substantive causes of seasonal fluctuation in conception remain obscure. It is sufficient here to point out its considerable magnitude and, more important, to observe its relationship to variations in the overall level of marital fertility.

SUMMARY

The variation and diversity that appear to characterize the demographic experience of communities in the early modern Europe are misleading. Striking differences in mortality, age at marriage, and marital fertility did not generate equally extreme differences in the rate of natural population increase. Early marriage was associated simultaneously with lower marital fertility rates and with higher mortality in childhood. This homeostatic pattern in demographic components among communities was related to differences in the size of communities and presumably rested on variation in socioeconomic characteristics. Within villages, however, individual demographic patterns did not mirror the relationships apparent on the ecological level.

Inasmuch as the relatively higher fertility of larger communities and the upper strata came, via the mechanism of wet-nursing, at the expense of the more rural areas and the lower strata, local and class variation also conceal an overall tendency toward demographic equilibrium. The apparent connection between the seasonal patterns of death and conception reinforces the importance of analyzing demographic parameters as an integrated set. The whole of the population engine of early modern Europe makes considerably more sense than any of its parts examined in isolation.

Empirical sense—the homeostatic patterns—must, however, represent a beginning and not an end of this line of inquiry. As a macro theory of long-run consequences, functionalism should be able to organize ecological variation in the many decades of demographic experience reported in family reconstitution studies. The limitations of the reconstitution studies have forced a rigid distinction between the purely demographic and the socioeconomic–demographic versions of the homeostatic argument. More properly, the former argument investigated in this chapter is really a special case of the latter. How the homeostatic patterns come into existence and are maintained needs to be investigated. An explanation in terms of norms, for example, will be more persuasive if demographic changes within particular villages during the natural fertility era also fit the homeostatic model. The individual-level data provided by family reconstitution studies can be more fully exploited to test for homeostatic mechanisms, e.g., the connection between father's age at death and son's age at marriage, or the possibility that the death of children will cause couples to increase their fertility. Historical demographers, in sum, need to go beyond data gathering and description. They must now begin to explore the range of possible relationships between the seemingly uncontrolled demographic behavior of individuals and the obvious structuring apparent in aggregate patterns.[16]

APPENDIX

The appendix consists of two tables on basic data beginning on the following page, and a list of the sources from which the data were taken.

---

[16] For an illuminating theoretical perspective on the possible sources of homeostatic demographic patterns see Wrigley (forthcoming).

APPENDIX TABLE I
Basic Data for Samples

Name and location	Source	Period of marital fertility rates	Mean age at first marriage		Marital fertility rates				
			Males	Females	20-24	25-29	30-34	35-39	40-44
I. South France									
Bilheres-d'Ossau	8	1740-1779	29.4	27.1	414	400	353	319	013
Lévignac-sur-Save	13	1750-1799	29.7	25.6	396	424	308	253	096
Sérignan	27	1653-1786	25.8	23.5	423	392	363	284	143
Thézels-Saint-Sernin	32	1700-1792	26.9	24.7	385	335	290	242	067
II. Central France									
Argentenay, Lézinnes and Vireaux	7	18th cent.	27.1	25.6	500	491	436	304	138
Bléré	24	1707-1765	26.0	23.0	489	440	377	309	142
Saint-Agnan	19	1730-1793	26.0	24.7	403	429	378	242	246
III. Paris region									
Argenteuil	11	1740-1770	26.4	25.3	554	521	478	360	147
Coulommiers	28	1670-1695	24	23	522	482	439	305	128
Meulan	25	1660-1739	26.5	25.1	519	507	503	379	157
Rumont	29	1720-1790	26.8	25.3	496	504	444	370	186
IV. North France									
Le Mesnil-Théribus, Marcheroux et Beaumont-les-Nonains	9	1740-1780	25.8	24.6	527	515	448	368	144
Sainghin-en-Melantois	5	1690-1769	31.4	28.6	555	520	447	407	216
V. West France									
Crulai	10	1674-1742	27.2	24.6	419	429	355	292	142
Ingouville	30	1730-1770	28	26	428	436	409	292	091
Isigny	23	-1780	28.1	25.0	439	468	382	256	108
Lonrai	2	1670-1792	28.7	26.0	573	428	320	240	117
Saint-Méen-le-Grand	1	1720-1792	27.9	26.3	582	548	476	385	202
Saint-Patrice	23	1640-1780	28.4	26.5	526	459	443	405	202

44

Saint-Pierre-Égliss	26	1705-1790	29.6	28.8	517	400	474	410	237
Saint-Vigor-le-Grand	23	-1780	30.7	25.4	419	466	340	278	176
Sotteville-les-Rouen	12	1760-1790	27.4	26.2	491	440	429	297	125
Tamerville	33	1640-1792	30.2	26.0	487	470	403	278	167
Tourouvre-au-Perche	4	1665-1765	27.0	24.6	424	419	378	314	162
Treviéres	23	-1780	28.2	26.7	517	419	397	340	182
Troarn	3	1660-1760	26.3	26.5	480	444	388	304	144
Villedieu-les-Poëles	20	1711-1790	25	25.2	498	506	466	371	214
VI. Northeast France (German-speaking)									
Boulay	18	-1780	28.2	25.5	480	452	391	341	183
Seven villages around Boulay	15	-1780	28.8[a]	26.5[a]	418	419	414	342	174
Hirschland	21	18th cent.	25	22	376	335	327	253	115
VII. German									
Anhausen	22	1692-1899	28.1	26.8	477	512	492	359	158
Boitin	17	1740-1809	29.4[a]	26.2[a]	410	349	219	162	118
Kreuth	17	1740-1809	34.1[a]	31.7[a]	472	488	456	396	201
Remmesweiler	16	-1780	28.2[a]	23.6[a]	462	387	371	292	152
Volkhardinghausen	17	-1810	28.5[a]	25.9[a]	482	457	376	295	145
VIII. Other									
Elversele (Flemish)	6	1608-1796	28.9	27.5	485	459	400	358	190
Geneva bourgeoisie	14	-1650	28.3	23.8	461	426	380	281	132
Glostrup (Danish)	31	1677-1790	31.0	27.4	558	426	380	314	191

[a]Median only reported; mean estimated from relationship of the mean and median in studies reporting both.

APPENDIX TABLE II
Basic Data

Name of sample	Infant mortality per 1000	Illegitimacy ratio per 1000	Premarital pregnancy ratio (%)	Age at last birth[a]	Seasonality index[b]	Average of first four[c]	Birth intervals		
							Last	After infant death	Normal[d]
I. South France									
Bilheres-d'Ossau	182	--	12.9	40.0	0.82	27.0	38.5	21.7	32.3
Lévignac-sur-Save	210	--	--	--	--	--	--	--	--
Sérignan	344	020	19.9	--	0.45	--	--	--	--
Thézels-Saint-Sernin	191	010	4.4	39.4	0.58	29.2	38.3	26.1	31.9
II. Central France									
Argentenay, Lézinnes, and Vireaux	229	005	7.2	38.5	0.30	23.1	33.5	21.6	23.8
Bléré	281	008	5.5	39.5	0.36	21.9	35.4	18.6	22.8
Saint-Agnan	250	012	9.1	--	--	26.5	32.0	--	--
III. Paris region									
Argenteuil	256	013	10.5	39.9	0.19	20.8	33.3	--	--
Coulommiers	269	002	4	--	0.31	22	37	--	--
Meulan	244	006	8	40.7	0.30	21.4	35.9	22.4	26.3
Rumont	164	009	9.0	39.2	0.50	23.4	34.2	21.5	27.3
IV. North France									
Le Mesnil-Théribus, Marcheroux et Beaumont-les-Nonains	212	007	14.0	40.6	0.31	23.1	35.2	21.4	27.2
Sainghin-en-Melantois	239	009	15.2	41.7	--	23.7	38.0	--	--
V. West France									
Crulai	205	007	2.8	40.0	0.63	25.9	33.0	20.6	29.6
Ingouville	286	052	14.7	--	--	--	--	--	--
Isigny	166	037	12.1	--	0.35	--	--	--	--
Lonrai	196	003	7.1	40.1	0.46	27.6	42.5	--	--

Saint-Méen-le-Grand	236	013	8.9	41.1	0.28	23.0	33.0	--	--
Saint Patrice	--	027	9.9	41.2	0.19	24.5	34.2	16.5	29.4
Saint-Pierre-Église	--	--	9.0	--	0.34	--	--	--	--
Saint-Vigor-le-Grand	125	047	22.0	--	0.41	--	--	--	--
Sotteville-les-Rouen	244	015	30.1	--	--	20.6	30.0	19.3	24.1
Tamerville	155	026	13.0	39.9	0.35	25.9	35.9	--	--
Tourouvre-au-Perche	257	008	5.0	39.8	0.41	24.2	33.5	20.7	30.0
Trévières	134	048	17.3	--	0.15	--	--	--	--
Troarn	192	024	13.9	41	0.28	25.4	32.7	20.8	30.6
Villedieu-les-Poëles	154	041	2.6	--	0.32	19.8	32.6	--	--
VI. Northeast France (German speaking)									
Boulay	196	008	11.0	40.6	--	25.6	--	--	--
Seven villages around Boulay	180	008	8.0	40.6	--	--	--	--	--
Hirschland	187	012	6.4	38.1	0.42	33.6	--	--	--
VII. German									
Anhausen	329	036	15.3	39.9	--	--	--	19.9	22.9
Boitin	181	035	28.5	--	--	27.8	43.7	--	--
Kreuth	193	065	2.7	--	--	22.1	33.8	--	--
Remmesweiler	140	013	21.3	39.5	--	--	--	--	--
Volkhardinghausen	186	052	20.8	--	--	28.4	32.0	--	--
VIII. Other									
Elversele (Flemish)	172	--	17.1	41.6	--	--	--	--	--
Geneve bourgeoisie	--	--	6.9	38.5	--	23.9	--	22.1	29.5
Glostrup (Danish)	255	--	--	--	--	26.1	34.8	20.3	30.7

[a] For complete families only.

[b] Restricted to larger families; typically six or more children, in some cases five or more, in one case eight or more.

[c] With the average month standardized to have 100 births, the seasonality index is the average of the three highest contiguous months less the average of the three lowest contiguous months. In the 18 samples with monthly data, the seasonality index is correlated +.986 with the standard deviation of monthly births.

[d] Normal interval refers to previous child surviving to his first birthday.

47

Sources

(1) Yves Blayo (1969). "Trois paroisses d'Ille-et-Vilaine," *Annales de démographie historique*, Vol. 16, pp. 191–213.

(2) Pierre-Marie Bourdin (1968). "La Plaine d'Alençon et ses bordures forestières: Essai d'histoire démographie et médicale (XVIIe-XVIIIe siècles)," *Cahier des Annales de Normandie*, No. 6, pp. 205–515.

(3) Michel Bouvet (1968). "Troarn: Étude de démographie historique (XVIIe-XVIIIe siècles), *Cahier des Annales de Normandie*, No. 6, pp. 17–202.

(4) Hubert Charbonneau (1970). *Tourouvre-au-Perche aux XVIIe et XVIIIe siècles: Étude de démographie historique*. Paris: Presses Universitaires de France.

(5) Raymond Deniel and Louis Henry (1965). "La population d'un village du Nord de la France, Sainghin-en-Mélantois, de 1665 à 1851," *Population*, Vol. 20, pp. 563–602.

(6) P. Deprez (1965). "The Demographic Development of Flanders in the Eighteenth Century," in D. V. Glass and D. E. C. Eversley, eds., *Population in History*. London: Edward Arnold. Pp. 608–630.

(7) Dominique Dinet (1969). "Quatre Paroisses du Tonnerrois," *Annales de demographie historique*, pp. 62–85.

(8) Michel Fresel-Lozey (1969). *Histoire Démographique d'un Village en Béarn: Bilheres-D'Ossau, XVIIIe-XIXe Siècles*. Bordeaux: Biscaye Frères.

(9) Jean Ganiage (1963). *Trois villages de l'Ille-de-France aux XVIIIe siècle: Étude démographique*. Paris: Presses Universitaires de France.

(10) Etienne Gautier and Louis Henry (1958). *La Population de Crulai, paroisse Normande*. Paris: Presses Universitaires de France.

(11) J. C. Giacchetti and M. Tyvaert (1969). "Argenteuil (1740-1790)," *Annales de démographie historique*. Vol. 6, pp. 40–61.

(12) Pierre Girard (1959). "Aperçus de la démographie de Sotteville-lès-Rouen vers la fin du XVIIIe siècle," *Population*, Vol. 14, pp. 485–508.

(13) Louis Henry, "The Population of France in the Eighteenth Century," in Glass and Eversley, eds, *Population in History*, pp. 434–456.

(14) Louis Henry (1956). *Anciennes Familles Genevoises: Étude Démographique, XVIe-XXe Siècle*. Paris: Presses Universitaires de France.

(15) Jacques Houdaille (1971). "La population de sept villages des environs de Boulay (Moselle) aux XVIIIe et XIXe siècles," *Population*, Vol. 26, pp. 1061–1072.

(16) Jacques Houdaille (1970). "La population de Remmesweiler en Sarre aux XVIIe et XIXe siècles," *Population*, Vol. 25, pp. 1183–1191.

(17) Jacques Houdaille (1970). "Quelques résultats sur la démographie de trois villages d'Allemagne de 1750 à 1879," *Population*, Vol. 25, pp. 649–654.

(18) Jacques Houdaille. "La population de Boulay (Moselle) avant 1850," *Population*, Vol. 22, pp. 1055–1084.

(19) Jacques Houdaille (1961). "Un village du Morvan: Saint-Agnan," *Population*, Vol. 16, pp. 301–312.

(20) Marie-Hélène Jouan (1969). "Les originalités démographiques d'un bourg artisanal normand au XVIIIe siècle: Villedieu-les-Poëles (1711-1790)," *Annales de démographie historique*, Vol. 6, pp. 87–124.

(21) Jean-Pierre Kintz (1969). "Deux études Alsaciennes," *Annales de démographie historique*, Vol. 6, pp. 261–292.

(22) John Knodel (1970). "Two and a Half Centuries of Demographic History in a Bavarian Village," *Population Studies*, Vol. 24, pp. 353–376.

(23) Mohamed El Kordi (1970). *Bayeux aux XVIIe et XVIIIe Siècles*. Paris: Mouton.

(24) Marcel Lachiver (1969). "Une étude et quelques esquisses," *Annales de démographie historique*, Vol. 6, pp. 215–240.

(25) Marcel Lachiver (1969). *La Population de Meulan du XVIIᵉ au XIXᵉ Siècle (vers 1600-1850): Étude de démographie historique*. Paris: Presses Universitaires de France.

(26) Jacques Lelong (1969). "Saint-Pierre-Église," *Annales de démographie historique,* \ pp. 125–135.

(27) Alain Molinier (1968). "Une paroisse du bas Languedoc: Sérignan, 1650-1792," *Mèmoires de la Société Archéologique de Montpellier*, Vol. XII, pp. viii, 216.

(28) J. C. Polton (1969). "Coulommiers et Chailly-en-Brie, *Annales de démographie historique*, Vol. 6, pp. 14–32.

(29) Patrice Robert (1969). "Rumont (1720-1790)," *Annales de demographie historique*, Vol. 6, pp. 32–40.

(30) Michel Terrisse (1961). "Un faubourg du Havre: Ingouville," *Population*, Vol. 16, pp. 285–300.

(31) Poul Thestrup (1972). "Methodological Problems of a Family Reconstitution Study in a Danish rural Parish before 1800," *Scandinavian Economic History Review*, Vol. XX, pp. 1–26.

(32) Pierre Valmary (1965). *Familles Paysannes au XVIIIᵉ Siècle en Bas-Quercy: Étude démographique*. Paris: Presses Universitaires de France.

(33) Philippe Wiel (1969). "Une grosse paroisse du Cotentin aux XVIIᵉ et XVIIIᵉ siècles: Tamerville," *Annales de démographie historique*, Vol. 6, pp. 136–189.

REFERENCES

Anderson, Barbara A. (1975). "Male Age and Fertility: Results from Ireland prior to 1911," *Population Index*, Vol. 41, pp. 561–567.

Barrett, J. C. (1971). "Fecundability and Coital Frequency," *Population Studies*, Vol. 25, pp. 309–313.

Bendix, Reinhard (1967). "Tradition and Modernity Reconsidered," *Comparative Studies in Society and History*, Vol. 9, pp. 292–346.

Charbonneau, Hubert (1970). *Tourouvre-au-Perche Aux XVIIᵉ et XVIIIᵉ Siècles*. Paris: Presses Universitaires de France.

Coale, Ansley J. (1969). "The Decline of Fertility in Europe from the French Revolution to World War II," in S. J. Behrman, Leslie Corsa, & Ronald Freedman, eds., *Fertility and Family Planning: A World View*. Ann Arbor: University of Michigan Press.

Coale, Ansley J. (1971). "Age Patterns of Marriage," *Population Studies*, Vol. 25, pp. 193–214.

Coale, Ansley J., & Demeny, Paul (1966). *Regional Model Life Tables and Stable Populations*. Princeton, N.J.: Princeton University Press.

Davis, Kingsley (1963). "The Theory of Change and Response in Modern Demographic History," *Population Index*, Vol. 29, pp. 345–366.

Demeny, Paul (1968). "Early Fertility Decline in Austria-Hungary: A Lesson in Demographic Transition," *Daedalus*, Vol. 97 (Spring), pp. 502–522.

Deniel, Raymond, & Henry, Louis (1965). "La population d'un village du Nord de la France, Sainghin-en-Mélantois, de 1655 à 1851," *Population*, Vol. 20, pp. 563–602.

Dupaquier, J. J., & Lachiver, M. (1969). "Sur les debuts de la contraception en France ou les deux malthusianismes," *Annales: Économies, Sociétés, Civilisations*, Vol. 24, pp. 1391–1406.

Elliott, Vivien Brodsky (1976). "An Analysis of Age at First Marriage in Seventeenth Century London, Essex, and Hertfordshire," *Newberry Papers in Family and Community History*, No. 4.

Friedlander, Dov (1969). "Demographic Responses and Population Change," *Demography*, Vol. 6, pp. 359–381.

Ganiage, Jean (1963). *Trois villages de l'Ille-de-France*. Paris: Presses Universitaires de France.

Giacchetti, J. C., & Tyvaert, M. (1969). "Argenteuil," *Annales de Demographie Historique*, Vol. 6, pp. 40–61.

Goubert, Pierre (1970). "Historical Demography and the Reinterpretation of Early Modern French History: A Review Article," *Journal of Interdisciplinary History*, Vol. 1, pp. 37–48.

Gross, Robert A. (1976). *The Minutemen and Their World*. New York: Hill and Wang.

Henry, Louis (1961). "Some Data on Natural Fertility," *Eugenics Quarterly*, Vol. 8, pp. 81–91.

Henry, Louis (1965). "The Population of France in the Eighteenth Century," in D. V. Glass & D. E. C. Eversley, eds. *Population in History*. London: Edward Arnold.

Henry, Louis (1973). "Fecondite des mariages dans le quart nord-ouest de la France de 1670 a 1829," *Population*, Vol. 28, pp. 873–922.

Kennedy, Robert E., Jr. (1973). *The Irish: Emigration, Marriage, and Fertility*. Berkeley: University of California Press.

Keyfitz, Nathan (1971). "How Birth Control Affects Births," *Social Biology*, Vol. 18, pp. 109–121.

Kinsey, Alfred C.; Pomeroy, Wardell B.; & Martin, Clyde E. (1948). *Sexual Behavior in the Human Male*. Philadelphia: W. B. Saunders.

Knodel, John (1970). "Two and a Half Centuries of Demographic History in a Bavarian Village," *Population Studies*, Vol. 24, pp. 353–376.

Knodel, John (1974). "The Influence of Child Mortality on Fertility in European Populations in the Past: Results from Individual Data." Unpublished manuscript.

Knodel, John, & van de Walle, Etienne (1967). "Breast Feeding, Fertility and Infant Mortality: An Analysis of Some Early German Data," *Population Studies*, Vol. 21, pp. 109–131.

Kumar, Joginder (1971). "A Comparison between Current Indian Fertility and Late Nineteenth Century Swedish and Finnish Fertility," *Population Studies*, Vol. 25, pp. 269–282.

Lachiver, Marcel (1969). *La Population de Meulan*. Paris: S.E.V.P.E.N.

Lee, Ronald (1973). "Population in Preindustrial England: An Econometric Analysis," *Quarterly Journal of Economics*, Vol. 77, pp. 581–607.

Leridon, Henri (1973). *Natalité, Saisons et Conjoncture Economique*. Paris: Presses Universitaires de France.

Lesthaeghe, R. (1971). "Nuptiality and Population Growth," *Population Studies*, Vol. 25, pp. 415–432.

Levine, David (in press). "The Demographic Implications of Rural Industrialisation: A Family Reconstitution Study of Shepshed, Leicestershire, 1600–1851," *Social History*, Vol. 1.

Lockridge, Kenneth A. (1969). "On Monthly Variation in the Level of Conception as a Tool in Historical Analysis." Unpublished manuscript.

MacLeod, John, & Gold, Ruth Z. (1953). "The Male Factor in Fertility and Infertility, VII, Semen Quality in Relation to Age and Sexual Activity," *Fertility and Sterility*, Vol. 4, pp. 194–203.

Marshall, T. H. (1929/1965). "The Population Problem during the Industrial Revolution: A Note on the Present State of the Controversy," in D. V. Glass & D. E. C. Eversley, eds., *Population in History*. London: Edward Arnold. Reprinted from *Economic History*, Vol. 1.

Ohlin, Goran (1960). "Mortality, Marriage and Growth in Pre-Industrial Populations,"
   Population Studies, Vol. 14, pp. 190–197.

Shorter, Edward (1971). "Illegitimacy, Sexual Revolution, and Social Change in Modern
   Europe," *Journal of Interdisciplinary History*, Vol. 2, pp. 237–272.

Shorter, Edward (1975). *The Making of the Modern Family*. New York: Basic Books.

Smith, Daniel Scott (1972). "The Demographic History of Colonial New England," *Journal
   of Economic History*, Vol. 32, pp. 165–183.

Smith, Daniel Scott (1973). "Parental Power and Marriage Patterns: An Analysis of
   Historical Trends in Hingham, Massachusetts," *Journal of Marriage and the Family*,
   Vol. 35, pp. 419–428.

Terrisse, Michel (1961). "Un faubourg du Havre: Ingouville," *Population*, Vol. 16, pp.
   285–300.

Thestrup, Poul (1972). "Methodological Problems of a Family Reconstitution Study in a
   Danish Rural Parish before 1800," *Scandinavian Economic History Review*, Vol. 20,
   pp. 1–26.

van de Walle, Etienne (1968). "Marriage and Marital Fertility," *Daedalus*, Vol. 97 (Spring),
   pp. 486–501.

van de Walle, Etienne (1974). *The Female Population of France*. Princeton, N.J.: Princeton
   University Press.

van de Walle, Etienne, & van de Walle, Francine (1972). "Allaitmement, sterilité et
   contraception: les opinions jusq'au XIXe siècle," *Population*, Vol. 27, pp. 685–701.

Westoff, Charles F. (1974). "Coital Frequency and Contraception," *Family Planning
   Perspectives*, Vol. 6, pp. 136–141.

Wrigley, E. A. (1966). "Family Limitation in Pre-Industrial England," *Economic History
   Review*, 2nd ser., Vol. 16, pp. 82–109.

Wrigley, E. A. (forthcoming). "Fertility Strategy for the Individual and the Group," in
   Charles Tilly, ed., *Historical Studies of Changing Fertility*. Princeton, N.J.: Princeton
   University Press.

Peasant Household Organization and Demographic Change in Lower Saxony (1689–1766)*

LUTZ K. BERKNER

University of California, Los Angeles

The relationship between peasant household organization and demographic change in western Europe has often been closely linked to differences in inheritance systems. Patterns of inheritance are enormously complex and varied, but they can be grouped into two basic types according to the ultimate disposition of the land: impartible systems, in which peasants do not divide their land, and partible systems, in which they may divide it. These provide two contrasting models of social change, household and family organization, and population growth.

In regions of impartible inheritance, where the land is not divided, peasant families are able to maintain their status over long periods of time by keeping their holdings intact. Because the land is inherited by only one heir, impartible inheritance also tends to be associated with a *stem-family structure*, which results in households composed of the parental couple and one married child during one phase of the developmental cycle of the family. The demographic consequences oper-

* The research for this chapter was supported by the Ford and Rockefeller Foundations Program in Support of Social Science and Legal Research on Population Policy. I want to thank the Past and Present Society for permission to reprint some material which originally appeared in Berkner (1976).

ate primarily through control over marriage and migration: Since only one child may marry and stay at home, the other children who cannot marry into local households must either remain celibate or emigrate from the community, unless they can establish themselves as cottagers or landless laborers. If no new lands are cleared and the community restricts settlement so that cottagers or landless persons cannot enter the community, the rate of new household formation will be very low and the population will grow slowly.

The model for regions of partible inheritance is quite different. The social status of families tends to change in every generation; only those who are "fortunate" enough to have few surviving children are able to maintain their position. In the long run the land will be fragmented into increasingly smaller holdings. Families will become poorer and will often be forced to turn to part-time artisanal activities, seasonal migration, or day labor in order to support themselves. Each child is given a portion of the land at marriage, and the parents often keep one part for themselves. This means it is less likely that a parental couple will live in the same household with one of the married children, and the predominant pattern will be one of independent nuclear family households. Because partibility leads to the creation of new holdings, all the children are provided with at least a minimal economic base with which to marry and stay in the community. The result is a relatively high rate of new household formation, high marriage rates, and low out-migration—all of which lead to rapid population growth.[1]

In theory, these two inheritance systems should result in radically different patterns of population growth. In reality, there are many complicating and mitigating factors. First of all, inheritance can only explain the behavior of those who have something to inherit—that is, peasants who own property or hold it under some form of secure

---

[1] The following discussion is based on Berkner and Mendels (forthcoming). This work provides a critical analysis of the general argument presented here. The best presentation of the two models is by H. J. Habakkuk (1955). George Homans (1941) used a similar version of the two models, stressing the relationship between impartible inheritance, stem families, emigration, celibacy, and late marriage. His arguments were supported by H. E. Hallam (1958), who showed that there were more young marriages and less emigration in a village with widespread partibility than in one where partibility was limited. The Irish case described in Arensberg and Kimball (1968) is a classic description of the stem family and its effect on demography. William Petersen (1960) also adopts the impartible model as a cause of slow population growth before the demographic transition. J. Hajnal (1965) cautiously suggests that the stem family may explain the peculiar western European marriage pattern of late marriage and high celibacy. Here I have excluded marriage age and marital fertility from the models, both because the relationships are not conceptually clear and because I have no data on either one.

hereditary tenure. In areas where much of the land is held on short-term leases, or where the majority of the population is landless, these models can explain very little. If the peasants' land is owned by nobles or bourgeois, the inheritance customs of the peasants are not going to make much difference. If there are no restrictions on settlement, so that day laborers and artisans can build cottages in a community, the fact that the landholding peasants do not divide their property will not prevent the formation of new households of landless classes, who may eventually outnumber the peasants and alter the demographic and social patterns of the region.

A second problem is that inheritance practices are not necessarily fixed. In fact, it is often difficult even to find out what they are, for there may be discrepancies between inheritance laws, inheritance customs, and actual practice. Laws may conflict with customs. Probably the most famous example of a law encouraging partible inheritance is the Napoleonic Code of France—but in regions with strong customs of impartibility, holdings were in fact rarely divided (Brandt, 1901). On the other hand, the professed customs may not be followed in practice. When it is customary to divide the land, but further fragmentation will destroy the economic viability of the farm, various monetary arrangements may be made so that the holdings are in actuality managed by only one of the children.[2]

Finally, demographic or economic changes may act to alter the household organization, the population growth patterns, or the inheritance practices themselves. If mortality is high, so that there are fewer than two surviving children per household, there ought to be no difference in either model in the migration or marriage rates of the children. However, if mortality is low, and more than two children survive per household, peasant families in partible regions will be put under pressure to make arrangements limiting the erosion of their economic base through fragmentation.

Although demographic pressure or economic changes may alter inheritance practices, impartible systems are generally more resistant to change, primarily because they are often linked to land tenure laws enforced by the state or the manor to prevent fragmentation. Partible systems, however, are inherently unstable. Partibility is only conditional—peasants *may* divide, but they are not forced to do so. Whether division actually takes place depends on a variety of circumstances. In preindustrial Europe, on the average, some 20% of all

---

[2] This is shown in the excellent comparative study of inheritance by Cole and Wolf (1974, chap. 8).

families had no surviving heirs, and another 20% had only one (Wrigley, forthcoming). In either case, the land did not have to be divided. If there were more than two surviving children, it was still possible to transfer the holding to only one of them, and pay off the others in cash. And even if a division did take place, there is no reason that the retired parents or widow could not have stayed in the household of one of the children. All these things tend to reduce the difference in the demographic and social consequences of the two models.

These complications have led some demographers to reject the entire argument. Kingsley Davis, for example, has written:

> [I]f there is no sustained natural increase in a settled agrarian area, any system of inheritance will work. If the opposite is the case, then no inheritance system will work, unless, of course, there is some real solution available. Despite the vogue of inheritance systems in population theory, it is doubtful that they play any determinant role in demographic change [1963, p. 351].

In the long run this view is probably correct, because peasants will adjust their family strategies to changing economic and demographic circumstances. But in the short run, peasants in partible and impartible regions do not have the same options. The inheritance system leads to a different choice of family strategies, and these in turn may have quite different social and demographic consequences.

Keeping all these difficulties in mind, I would like to demonstrate the differences in these two models by comparing the household organization and population growth of two regions having different inheritance systems in the northwest German province of Lower Saxony between 1689 and 1766. The first region is the territory of Calenberg, which lies near the city of Hanover (see Map 1), where holdings were impartible and the peasants practiced single-heir inheritance. The second is the territory of Göttingen, which lies to the south around the city of the same name. Here peasant holdings could be divided, and inheritance followed the German common law of equal division among the children.

Politically, both regions were part of the Electorate of Hanover, one of the larger German states. There were no major differences in the legal, economic, or social conditions of the peasantry in the two regions at the end of the seventeenth century.[3] The peasants were free of personal

---

[3] All the following descriptions of social structure, land tenure, and inheritance in Lower Saxony are based on the classic study of the peasantry in the region by Wittich (1896, chaps. 1 and 2).

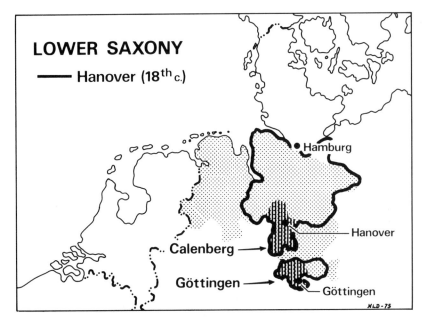

Map 1.

serfdom and hereditary estate subjection of the type found in Prussia, but they did fall under a manorial system. Except for a few noble estate farms and large domainal farms owned by the state, most of the land consisted of peasant holdings. The social structure was overwhelmingly peasant and agrarian. There were relatively few full-time artisans, although part-time linen weaving was widespread.

The peasants were divided into status groups that roughly correspond to social classes: *Häuslinge* (lodgers), *Brinksitzer* (cottagers with little or no land), *Kleinköter* or *Köter* (smallholders), *Grossköter* (middle peasants), and various degrees of *Meier* (peasants farming from a quarter-holding to a full holding). These groups are roughly equivalent to social classes, although the actual holding size could vary considerably within each category. If we look at the distribution of households by status (Table 1), there are many more *Meier* with large holdings in the impartible region of Calenberg (27%) than in the partible region of Göttingen (12%) and a much smaller proportion of *Köter* (smallholders) in Calenberg (27%) than in Göttingen (46%). But if we examine the distribution of the size of the holdings, there is less difference between

TABLE 1
Social Structure in 1689

		Calenberg (impartible)		Göttingen (partible)	
Status groups					
Lodgers	*(Häuslinge)*	6%	(53)	13%	(132)
Cottagers	*(Brinksitzer)*	22%	(188)	14%	(145)
Small holders	*(Kleinköter)*	11%	(89)	23%	(238)
	(Köter)	16%	(132)	23%	(232)
Middle peasant	*(Grossköter)*	12%	(101)	7%	(73)
Large holder	*(Halbmeier)*	7%	(57)	11%	(115)
	(Vollmeier)	20%	(170)	1%	(10)
Not indicated		6%	(49)	8%	(81)
Size of holdings					
No land		24%	(197)	30%	(304)
1-10 Morgen[a]		35%	(296)	35%	(361)
10-20		12%	(97)	16%	(163)
20-30		8%	(70)	9%	(93)
30-40		4%	(30)	4%	(42)
40 or more		10%	(85)	6%	(65)
Not indicated		7%	(64)	--	
Total households			839		1028

[a] 1 Morgen = .6 acre.

the two regions, except that there is a slightly larger proportion of very large holdings in Calenberg.

The difference in the inheritance systems in the two regions is closely linked to the land tenure situation and to the development of a land law known as *Meierrecht*. The *Meierrecht* defined holdings held under certain forms of tenure as legally impartible units. In Calenberg this applied to almost all the peasant land; in Göttingen it applied to less than one-third of the land (Borries, 1864, pp. 258–259).

Along with the strict impartibility imposed by the *Meierrecht*, a number of institutional arrangements evolved in Calenberg. These ensured that the impartible holding would remain intact, free of debt, and economically viable to pay taxes and dues.[4] The first was the *Anerbenrecht*, the law of single inheritance. Only one child could become the

---

[4] Besides the basic material in Wittich (1896), there is a description of inheritance arrangements in Grossmann (1900, Part 1).

legal heir to the impartible farmland; the other children had claims only to the personal property and what was designated as *allodial* property—the buildings, equipment, animals, produce, and any parcels of freehold land. Those who were not heirs were compensated for their claims in the form of marriage portions paid by the heir when his brothers and sisters left home. They could not claim these portions as long as they remained in the household, but the heir was not required to support them after they reached the age of 14.

In Calenberg the legal transfer of ownership to the heir was often made before the death of the parents upon their retirement. The retirement conditions (called *Leibzucht*) were usually written into the heir's marriage contract, and stipulated the specific amounts of food, produce, and income that were to be given the parents, who ordinarily retired to a room in the farmhouse. A widow with young children who remarried continued to manage the farm until the heir reached the age of majority, when she and her second husband could claim full retirement rights. The transfer of the impartible farmland to a single heir, the weak claims of the other children, and the strong retirement rights of the parents were the underlying principles for the stem-family household organization among the landed peasantry in Calenberg.

In the territory of Göttingen, where division of the land was not restricted by the conditions of tenure, inheritance was governed by the common law, which provided equal portions for all the sons and daughters. The marriage contract of the parents usually stipulated that the surviving spouse would divide the property with the children, but the children often received their portions when they married. Without a systematic reconstruction of individual family histories, the evidence that the peasants in Göttingen actually were dividing their holdings is all indirect. First, the land tenure allowed division and the common law sanctioned it. Second, in the eighteenth century local authorities were constantly complaining that there was too much fragmentation of holdings in the region because of the custom of partibility.[5] Third, according to a nineteenth century survey, partible inheritance was still the custom; Göttingen was one of the few regions in the province of Lower Saxony where division of holdings took place (Grossmann, 1900). Fourth, the 1831–1832 land survey showed a much higher proportion of small holdings in this region than in any other part of the province (Borries, 1864, p. 259).

---

[5] See "Anlagen," pp. 44–45 in Wittich (1896). Niedersächsiches Staatsarchiv Hannover (hereafter NSSA), Hann. 74 Münden E 954, described division in 1713.

Now let us examine the evidence for the household organization of the peasants in the two regions in 1689 and in 1766, and the demographic change that took place between these two dates. The sources for the comparison are household lists prepared for the purpose of tax assessment. The 1689 lists are so detailed that they are virtually equivalent to a nominative census (Burchard & Mundhenke, 1940–1972). They vary somewhat from village to village but usually include the names, ages, and status of all the members of the immediate family and their relationship to the head of the household, and also list any relatives, lodgers, and servants living with him.

The 1766 lists are not as detailed.[6] They give only the names of the household heads and record their status in only a few villages. The household membership is indicated as the number of persons falling into each of 20 categories: *male head, female head, children, relatives, male servants, female servants, lodgers, lodgers' children,* and *lodgers' servants.* The categories *children, relatives,* and *lodgers' children* are further divided into the categories *male, female, over 14,* and *under 14.* So there are no exact ages at all, and no ages for the household heads. It is not clear how many lodger family units there were. We also do not know the relationship of the relatives to the head of household.

In 1689 there was a marked difference in the family structure in the households of the two regions (Table 2). Extended families were found in 30% of the households in the impartible villages of Calenberg, and in only 7% of the households in the partible villages of Göttingen. Moreover, only the impartible region had a stem-family structure.

As mentioned earlier, the stem family was organized according to the rule that only one child will marry and stay on the farm with his parents, taking over the holding and supporting his parents in their old age. The other children would eventually leave, but as long as they stayed they had to remain celibate. These rules are implicit in a system of single inheritance and undivided holdings, and they are the basis for the institutional arrangements described for Calenberg.

Unfortunately there is no simple, neat method of determining stem-family *structure* from sources that describe only household *composition.* The stem-family structure does not consist of just one particular household form; it follows a series of phases over the family life cycle consisting of combinations of the head couple, the retired parents, and unmarried brothers and sisters (Berkner, 1972). A full sequence of phases would include the following relatives in addition to the head couple: (1)

---

[6] These are in NSSA, Dep 7 C 730-2.

TABLE 2
Family Structure in 1689

	Calenberg (impartible)		Göttingen (partible)	
Nuclear family				
Head couple without relatives	65%	(549)	87%	(900)
Stem family forms				
Retired parents (couple)	7%	(58)	1%	(12)
Widowed parent and child(ren)	3%	(28)	<1%	(2)
Widowed parent alone	8%	(64)	3%	(36)
Unmarried siblings of head	6%	(49)	<1%	(4)
Married child of head	2%	(17)	<1%	(5)
Other extended family forms	4%	(35)	1%	(15)
Nonfamily forms				
Unrelated persons or families	5%	(39)	6%	(64)

the retired parents living with or without unmarried children (the brothers and sisters of the head), (2) a widowed parent and unmarried children, (3) a widowed parent only, and (4) the unmarried brothers or sisters only. Not every family went through all these phases or followed the same sequence. Some couples had no heirs at all; some heirs did not marry until both parents had died; some heirs had no surviving brothers and sisters. This means that the proportion of stem families in the population is not equivalent to the proportion of households composed of co-resident couples. It is only an indirect measure, and the figure will always be low at any given time. In the case of Calenberg, only 12% of the households had a full stem-family composition including either a retired parental couple, a widowed parent and child, or a married child who had not yet inherited the farm. But in Göttingen these forms amounted to only a little more than 1%. The only relatives found with any frequency (3%) in Göttingen were widowed parents. In Calenberg widowed parents were found in 8% of the households, and when we calculate the mean age of the head of the household for each stem-family form in Calenberg, the widowed parents fall into their logical place in the sequence of phases (see Table 3).

TABLE 3
The Stem Family Cycle in Calenberg (1689)

Stem family phase	Mean age of the male head of household	n
Retired parental couple	32	58
Widowed parent and child(ren)	33	28
Widowed parent alone	37	64
Unmarried siblings of head	40	49
Nuclear (no relatives)	46	549
Married child of head	58	17

In 1689 the model relating family structure and inheritance fits quite well. (For a more detailed analysis of 1689 lists, see Berkner, 1976.) The second question is whether the demographic prediction that population growth should be considerably less in the impartible region because of the restrictions on the rate of household formation also holds. In the 80-some years after 1689, the population of both regions grew, but it increased 60% in the partible villages and only 30% in the impartible ones. An even greater difference is found in the addition of new households: There were 40% more households in the partible region in 1766, but only 15% more in the impartible (Table 4).

In the impartible region of Calenberg some new households were formed, but they accounted for less than half the population growth (since family size also increased). The primary mechanism of growth

TABLE 4
Population Change 1689–1766

	Calenberg			Göttingen		
	1689	1766	Increase	1689	1766	Increase
Household heads	1560	1829	269 (17%)	1865	2592	727 (40%)
Children	1877	2294	417 (23%)	1974	3011	1037 (53%)
Nuclear family	3437	4123	686 (20%)	3839	5603	1764 (46%)
Relatives	517	737	220 (43%)	125	659	534 (430%)
Servants	330	453	123 (38%)	280	333	53 (19%)
Lodgers	281	668	387 (139%)	95	437	342 (360%)
Total R, S, L	1128	1858	730 (65%)	500	1429	929 (186%)
Total population	4565	5981	1416 (31%)	4339	7032	2693 (62%)
Total households	839	961	122 (15%)	1028	1430	402 (39%)

was the internal expansion of existing households, which added more relatives, servants, and especially lodgers (Table 5). These three groups account for 50% of the additional population in the area. The increase in lodgers (from 6% of the population to 11%) explains almost the entire change in the social distribution of population. Taking in lodgers is one way that communities can accommodate more families without creating new holdings. In terms of households, the largest change was among relatives: The number of households with relatives rose from 30 to 44%. Overall, the locus of population growth was within the existing household and family structures.

TABLE 5
Social Composition of the Population in 1689 and 1766

	Calenberg (impartible)				Göttingen (partible)			
	1689		1766		1689		1766	
Number of persons								
Household heads	1560	(34%)	1829	(31%)	1865	(43%)	2592	(37%)
Children	1877	(41%)	2294	(38%)	1974	(46%)	3011	(43%)
Nuclear family	3437	(75%)	4123	(69%)	3839	(88%)	5603	(80%)
Relatives	517	(11%)	737	(12%)	125	(3%)	659	(9%)
Servants	330	(7%)	453	(8%)	280	(7%)	333	(5%)
Lodgers	281	(6%)	668	(11%)	95	(2%)	457	(7%)
Total population	4565	(100%)	5981	(100%)	4339	(100%)	7052	(100%)
Number of households								
With relatives	249	(30%)	410	(44%)	74	(7%)	441	(33%)
With servants	206	(25%)	288	(30%)	201	(20%)	232	(17%)
With lodgers	146	(17%)	210	(23%)	44	(4%)	145	(11%)

In the partible area of Göttingen, households also adjusted to population pressure by adding relatives and lodgers, but not servants. The proportion of households with relatives jumped from 7 to 33%, the proportion of households with lodgers rose from 4 to 11%, and the *number* of relatives and lodgers increased fivefold. Despite these dramatic changes in the composition of households and the shift in the social distribution of the population, relatives, servants and lodgers explain only one-third of the population growth in Göttingen. *Two-thirds* of the increased population is accounted for by members of nuclear families in new households.

Thus the difference in the population growth of the two regions is consistent with the models. In the region of partible inheritance, the population grew twice as fast and the number of households increased three times as much as in the impartible. Moreover, the stem-family structure was maintained in the impartible region. In the partible region the family structure changed under population pressure, and a new kind of household organization appeared. It looks as if a stem-family pattern also developed in the partible region, but since the 1766 lists do not indicate the exact relationships (only whether the relatives were male or female, over or under 14), comparisons are difficult to make. However, in Calenberg (impartible) 20% of the households included only one adult relative (presumably a widowed parent), whereas 23% included some more complex combination of two or more adult or young relatives. In Göttingen also 20% of the households have one adult relative, but only 12% have a more complex form (Table 6).

The appearance of one adult relative in the household does not necessarily indicate any particular inheritance practice since it is always possible for a widowed parent to continue to live with one of the children under any system. But the appearance of the more complex forms of extended families in the partible region in 1766 raises the fundamental problem of determining causality. The inheritance system is itself subject to change under different demographic conditions, and household structure may reflect demographic patterns as much as determining them. On the one hand it appears that the inheritance practices changed to a single heir/retirement system under the pressure of the authorities who were opposed to division, aided by the reluctance of the peasants to continue fragmentation.[7] On the other hand—and this would explain the increased number of relatives in Calenberg—with declining mortality more parents would have lived to retirement age than in the seventeenth century.[8] The important point is that in Calenberg impartible inheritance acted to slow population growth and the existing household structure was able to absorb much of the increase that did occur, whereas in Göttingen the effect of partibility was to create population pressures that in turn led to more complex forms of household organization.

Although the family structure and perhaps even the inheritance prac-

[7] Official attempts to restrict partibility in the region are described in "Anlagen," pp. 44–51 in Wittich (1896) and in NSSA, Hann. 74 Münden E 954.

[8] In the absence of any good demographic studies, this is only an assumption. Marten (1969) shows an increase in adults between 1689 and 1780 in one of the Calenberg districts. Mauersberg (1938, pp. 152–161) gives scattered figures from four parish registers that indicate lower death rates in the eighteenth century.

TABLE 6
Household Composition in 1766

Number of relatives		Possible relationship to household head	Number of households			
Over age 14	Under age 14		Calenberg		Göttingen	
Two or more	One or more	Parents and/or unmarried brothers and sisters	10%	(89)	5%	(62)
More than two	None					
Two same sex	None					
One male and one female	None	Retired parents	9%	(87)	5%	(63)
One	One or more	Widowed parent and child(ren)	4%	(33)	2%	(23)
One	None	Widowed parent	20%	(190)	20%	(260)
None	None	Nuclear family only	56%	(521)	67%	(880)
None	One or more	Young relative	1%	(11)	2%	(30)

tices changed in the partible region of Göttingen, the household organization of the two regions continued to have a strong differential
impact on the social distribution of the population. According to the
model, impartible inheritance restricts population growth not only by
preventing the formation of new households but also by maintaining
high rates of celibacy and out-migration of non-heirs. The mechanism
for this in Calenberg was not to keep non-heirs celibate in the household (in 1689 only 6% of the households included adult unmarried
siblings). Instead, it was to push the non-heirs out of their family and
into other households where they were employed as farm servants, and
as long as they stayed in these positions they were not allowed to
marry. In the impartible region 17% of all the males over 14 in 1766
were unmarried sons at home and 14% were servants in other households; in the partible region 24% were at home and only 6% were
servants elsewhere (Table 7). This difference is even more pronounced

TABLE 7
Distribution of Population by Age and Sex in 1766

| | Calenberg | | | | Göttingen | | | |
	Male		Female		Male		Female	
Household heads	893	(48%)	936	(47%)	1239	(55%)	1353	(53%)
Children over 14	314	(17%)	225	(11%)	537	(24%)	486	(19%)
Servants	258	(14%)	195	(10%)	141	(6%)	192	(7%)
Relatives over 14	247	(13%)	364	(18%)	197	(9%)	360	(14%)
Lodgers over 14	160	(8%)	264	(13%)	119	(5%)	186	(7%)
Total adults	1872	(100%)	1984	(100%)	2233	(100%)	2577	(100%)
Children under 14	869	(73%)	886	(80%)	775	(64%)	1013	(68%)
Children over 14	314	(27%)	225	(20%)	537	(36%)	486	(32%)
Total children	1183	(100%)	1111	(100%)	1512	(100%)	1499	(100%)

[a]Children of household heads at home

in some lists prepared in 1745 for recruitment purposes, in which the
peasants were asked how many of their unmarried sons were living at
home, and what those who had left home were doing.[9] In the impartible region only one-third of the sons over 14 were living at home, and
nearly half (45%) were away as servants; in the partible region half the
older sons were at home, and only 14% were servants elsewhere (Table
8).

[9] These lists are in NSSA, Hann. 74 Münden C 1341 and Hann. 74 Calenberg A viii Nr.
11.

TABLE 8
Location of Peasants' Sons in 1745

	Calenberg[a]		Göttingen[b]	
Total sons				
Sons under 14	57%	(1032)	56%	(1054)
Sons over 14	43%	(785)	44%	(819)
Total sons	100%	(1817)	100%	(1873)
Sons over 14				
At home	33%	(260)	50%	(409)
Servants elsewhere	45%	(349)	14%	(116)
In the army	21%	(166)	29%	(238)
Out of the country	1%	(10)	7%	(56)
Total	100%	(785)	100%	(819)
Sons at home				
Under 14	80%	(1032)	72%	(1054)
Over 14	20%	(260)	28%	(409)
Total	100%	(1292)	100%	(1463)

[a] Villages in the Amt Calenberg only.

[b] Villages in the Amt Münden only.

With partible inheritance, all the children have a claim to the land; when they are ready to marry each may claim a portion and move out of the household. The father and the mother can delay retirement until either of them dies or until the youngest child is ready to marry. This considerably reduces the probability of having two co-resident couples, and means that both the head couple and the children remaining in the household will, on the average, tend to be older. In Göttingen, one-third of all the children living with their parents in 1766 were over 14; in Calenberg it was only one-fourth. Similarly, in Göttingen twice as many families (20%, versus 10% in Calenberg) had *only* children over 14 in the household. Thus the inheritance system made an important difference in the lives of the children. In the partible region, young adults stayed at home until they received a piece of property in order to marry; in the impartible region, young teenagers left home to support themselves as servants on other farms.

Although most of the results are consistent with the two models relating inheritance, household and family structure, and population growth, there are a number of problems that have not really been solved. The most bothersome is the difficulty of actually demonstrating that the fragmentation of holdings was a result of the inheritance practices. It is possible that the new households in Göttingen were established as a result of land clearings, or that they were composed of cottagers dependent on some rural industry such as linen weaving. They account for the smaller increase in households in the impartible region, and must certainly account for some of the new households in the partible one. Inheritance patterns alone cannot explain all the variation in household organization and population growth in these two regions, but they certainly explain enough to warrant serious consideration in demographic research.[10]

REFERENCES

Arensberg, Conrad, & Kimball, Solon (1968). *Family and Community in Ireland.* 2nd ed. Cambridge, Mass.: Harvard University Press.

Berkner, Lutz K. (1972). "The Stem Family and the Developmental Cycle of the Peasant Household: An Eighteenth-Century Austrian Example," *American Historical Review,* Vol. 77, pp. 398–418.

Berkner, Lutz K. (1976). "Inheritance, Land Tenure and Peasant Family Strucure: A German Regional Comparison," in J. Goody, J. Thirsk, & E. P. Thompson, eds., *Family and Inheritance in Rural Western Europe, 1200–1700.* Cambridge: Cambridge University Press.

Berkner, Lutz K., & Mendels, Franklin F. (forthcoming). "Inheritance Systems, Family Structure, and Demographic Patterns in Western Europe (1700–1900)," in Charles Tilly, ed., *Historical Studies of Changing Fertility.* Princeton, N.J.: Princeton University Press.

Borries, Grafen von (1864). "Die Bauerhöfe," in *Beiträge zur Kenntniss der landwirtschaftlicken Verhältnisse im Königreiche Hannover.* Vol. 1. Hanover: Klindworth.

Brandt, Alexandre de (1901). *Droit et coutumes des populations rurales de la France en matière successorale.* Paris: Librairie de la Société du Recueil général des lois et arrêts.

Burchard, Max, & Mundhenke, Herbert, eds. (1940–1972). *Die Kopfsteuer-beschreibung der Fürstentümer Calenberg-Göttingen und Grubenhagen von 1689.* 13 vols. Hanover, then Hildesheim: August Lax.

Cole, John W., & Wolf, Eric R. (1974). *The Hidden Frontier: Ecology and Ethnicity in an Alpine Valley.* New York: Academic Press.

Davis, Kingsley (1963). "The Theory of Change and Response in Modern Demographic History," *Population Index,* Vol. 29, pp. 345–366.

Easterlin, Richard A. (1976). "Population Change and Farm Settlement in the Northern United States," *Journal of Economic History,* Vol. 36, pp. 45–75.

Gagan, David P. (1976). "The Indivisibility of the Land: A Microanalysis of the System of Inheritance in Nineteenth-Century Ontario," *Journal of Economic History,* Vol. 36, pp. 126–141.

Grossmann, F. (1900). "Provinz Hannover," in Max Sering, ed., *Die Vererbung des ländlichen Grundbesitzes im Königreich Preussen.* Vol. 2. 4 vols. Berlin: Perey.

---

[10] For two very promising recent applications of inheritance models to population change see Easterlin (1976) and Gagan (1976).

Habakkuk, H. J. (1955). "Family Structure and Economic Change in Nineteenth-Century Europe," *Journal of Economic History*, Vol. 15, pp. 1–12.

Hajnal, J. (1965). "European Marriage Patterns in Perspective," in D. V. Glass & D. E. C. Eversley, eds., *Population in History*. London: Edward Arnold.

Hallam, H. E. (1958). "Some Thirteenth-Century Censuses," *Economic History Review*, 2nd ser., Vol. 10, pp. 340–361.

Homans, George (1941). *English Villagers of the Thirteenth Century*. Cambridge, Mass.: Harvard University Press.

Marten, H.-R. (1969). *Die Entwicklung der Kulturlandschaft im Alten Amt Aerzen*. (*Göttinger Geographische Abhandlungen*, Pt. 53, Göttingen: E. Goltze.

Mauersberg, Hans (1938). *Beiträge zur Bevölkerungs- und Sozialgeschichte Niedersachsens*. Hanover: Schaper.

Petersen, William (1960). "The Demographic Transition in the Netherlands," *American Sociological Review*, Vol. 25, pp. 334–347.

Sering, Max, ed. (1899–1910). *Die Vererbung des ländlichen Grundbesitzes im Königreich Preussen*. 4 vols. Berlin: Perey.

Tilly, Charles, ed. (forthcoming). *Historical Studies of Changing Fertility*. Princeton, N.J.: Princeton University Press.

Wittich, Werner (1896). *Die Grundherrschaft in Nordwestdeutschland*. Leipzig: Duncker and Humblot.

Wrigley, E. A. (forthcoming). "Fertility Strategy for the Individual and for the Group," in Charles Tilly, ed., *Historical Studies of Changing Fertility*. Princeton, N.J.: Princeton University Press.

The Civil Code and Nuptiality: Empirical Investigation of a Hypothesis*

ALBERT I. HERMALIN
University of Michigan

ETIENNE VAN DE WALLE
University of Pennsylvania

The Malthusian model of fertility is a nuptiality model. Early and universal marriage leads to population growth, and to misery when the population hits the ceiling of subsistence. The preventive checks of virtuous celibacy and late marriage are the road to economic salvation for the individual if not for society. Although passion between the sexes will tend to sway individuals from this narrow path, institutions such as the unequal subdivision of private property will fortunately set limits to the ability to marry. Communal tenure and schemes aimed at diffusing the property of land and housing to the lower classes, however, would lead to a lower level of living by stimulating nuptiality. Malthus (1951) was specifically applying this model to France:

> On the effects of a great subdivision of property, a fearful experience is now making in France. The law of succession in that country allows but a small portion of a father's property to be disposed of by will, and the rest is equally

* This chapter reports preliminary—and somewhat tentative—results from research funded in part by the Rockefeller and Ford Foundations' Program in Support of Population Policy Research in the Social Sciences, Humanities, and Law. Professor Lutz Berkner provided helpful comments on an earlier version of this chapter. Susan Etter was a valuable research assistant and J. Michael Coble aided very capably with computer programming.

71

divided among all the children without distinction of age or sex. . . . It is universally allowed that a division of property to a certain extent is extremely desirable. . . . But if such a law were to continue permanently to regulate the descent of property in France, if no modes of evading it should be invented, and if its effects should not be weakened by the operation of an extraordinary degree of prudence in marriage, which prudence such a law would certainly tend to discourage, there is every reason to believe that the country, at the end of a century, will be quite as remarkable for its extraordinary poverty and distress, as for its unusual equality of property [pp. 376–377].

The "fearful experience" consisted of the inheritance provisions of the Civil Code, promulgated in 1804. These provisions would lead to a fragmentation of the land, and since the prospect of a plot of land, however small, would encourage marriage and the birth of more claimants for portions of the patrimony, Malthus foresaw economic disaster. Escape from the quandary might become possible if (1) the law were evaded, or (2) prudential marriage prevailed despite the incentive of property.

As a footnote to the present argument, we should add that prudential behavior *within* marriage, i.e. contraception, might have offered another logical solution. Malthus rejected the idea, but some of his neo-Malthusian successors advocated it. Le Play suggested that the decline of fertility in France was a consequence of the egalitarian philosophy of the Revolution, and that interference by the State in the area of testamentary freedom led to smaller families in order to avoid the morselization of holdings (Spengler, 1938, chap. 8). This theory seems to be disproved by the fact that fertility had declined before the enactment of the Civil Code in several areas of France. Furthermore, fertility almost invariably declined within 50 years after the time when Le Play was writing, even in parts of Europe where the French Civil Code was not accepted.

It has been pointed out (e.g., Worms, 1917; Bloch, 1955) that not all the customs of the Old Regime were less egalitarian than the Civil Code. Le Play had a schematic vision of primogeniture as the traditional norm. He attributed to the whole population of France in the Old Regime a form of testamentary devolution that prevailed in some of the noble customs—although by no means in all (Meyer, 1972). The systematic inventory of the old customs by Jean Yver (1966) makes it clear that a wide range of situations prevailed among the common people prior to the standardization imposed by the 1804 Civil Code.

We are interested here in the effect of inheritance rules—and the effect of their radical change as an act of policy—on nuptiality. We assume that the Malthusian model, which relies on nuptiality for the regulation of population growth, had some relevance at the end of the Old Regime in France. We also assume that the operation of this model was influenced by the nature of the customs regulating the transmission of property, and that the Civil Code represented enough of a break in this regulation to exert a pressure on nuptiality. To test these assumptions, we will use the available information on traditional inheritance customs in conjunction with estimates of nuptiality at the beginning of the nineteenth century. But we shall first briefly present our methods for the study of nuptiality at the beginning of the century and our preliminary results. We shall then discuss the nature of the legal information on successions. In the last section of the chapter we shall look at the model used to link inheritance and nuptiality, and we shall present an empirical application of that model to the data at hand.

NUPTIALITY

In contrast with inheritance customs and practices, nuptiality is a readily quantifiable variable. We shall now describe the methods we used to estimate indices of nuptiality in 1806, the time of the first usable French census. (The reader who is not interested in demographic analysis may go on to the next section.) Keep in mind that we hoped to find that the nuptiality differentials in 1806 corresponded roughly to the inheritance customs prior to 1804 (date of the Code's promulgation) and that the nuptiality changes of the nineteenth century were related to the impact of the new law on inheritance.

We have presented elsewhere a series of departmental indices of nuptiality covering the period 1831–1901 (van de Walle, 1974). French census statistics before 1851 are scanty. There were censuses referring to 1801, 1806, and 1821, although these were taken locally at widely varying dates, with unstandardized methods. Information was collected on marital status, but age is not available. The reconstruction of the population by age for the beginning of the century, a by-product of our reconstruction of the fertility and nuptiality history of the departments, becomes more and more unreliable as one goes back in time, and omits marital status prior to 1831. The vital registration contained virtually no information on marriages. We believed there was no way of reconstructing nuptiality at the beginning of the century, until Jacques Dupâquier drew our attention to a set of data in the French National Archives: the distribution of deaths by age and marital status, by department, for the period from 1806 to 1852. The gaps in this material were filled either by interpolating or by resorting to additional data in the archives or in the published record. A full discussion of this material and our methods must be given elsewhere. What follows here is a brief report on research in progress. Our results are provisional.

The main obstacle to the conversion of the proportions of deaths by age and marital status into an age distribution of single, married, and widowed persons at a given date is the fact that mortality strikes differentially according to marital conditions. Let us consider women aged 50, for example. Their chances of dying are higher if they are single than if they are married, and the proportion of single female deaths at age 50 is higher than the proportion of living women who are single. Fortunately, there is an elegant way of estimating the latter from the deaths of single women over 50, classified by age, provided few first marriages occur after that age. That condition is satisfied in most female populations and it means that women who were single at age 50 will die single, no matter what their age at death will be. All we need to do then, to estimate the proportion single at 50 in a live population at a given time, is to record the marital status of its 50-year-olds, whenever they die. We add the single deaths in the cohort born in 1756–1760 (i.e., the deaths at ages 50 to 54 during the years 1806–1810, at 55 to 59 during 1811–1815, and so on until we reach the deaths at ages 95 to 99 during 1851–1855). We divide this total number of single deaths by the total number of deaths in that cohort at the same ages during the same years. The result is the proportion of the population single at 50 in 1806.

This computation yields a remarkable result for France as a whole, and with a few exceptions, for the French departments: The female proportions ever married in 1806 are extremely similar to those recorded by midcentury censuses. For 86 departments, the correlation between proportion ever married (by age 50) for those born in 1756–1810 with those born in 1806–1810 is .79. The mean for the earlier cohort is 87.2%, compared to 88.4% for the later cohort. Chasteland and Pressat (1962) have shown that this proportion has remained remarkably stable in France well into the twentieth century. The regional differences were not negligible: between 95.2% in Seine-et-Marne and 77.9% in Cantal for the cohort of women born 1806–1810. But these differences were already established for women born in 1756–1760 who were 46–50 years old in 1806, though of course there were some changes.

On a gross level, then, it appears that the Civil Code had little influence on this aspect of nuptiality. (We will examine this matter in more detail in a later section.)

Another important dimension of nuptiality is age at marriage. To compute this for 1806, we first determined what numbers of the population over age 50 (distributed by age according to the reconstruction mentioned earlier) had been married, using the percentage never married. This number, subtracted from the total ever married (i.e., married plus widows) according to the 1806 census, gave the number ever married under 50. We used Coale's age patterns of marriage (Coale, 1971) to determine the parameter k that would yield the number ever married under 50. Coale has shown that most patterns of marriage can be described by three parameters: C, the proportion married over 50; k, a horizontal scale factor expressing the pace at which people contract first marriage in comparison to a model schedule; and a_0, the beginning of the marriage curve, which for our purpose can be fixed at 15. Since both C and a_0 are known, our computations can be described as the determination of the age of first marriage that will produce the total number of married women enumerated in 1806, with the age structure estimated for that date.

At this stage of our research, the quality of the inputs is crucial, since the age of marriage (or k) will incorporate an error term, possible either in the data from the census or from the vital registration of deaths, or in the reconstructed population by age. The French official statistics of the time are not worthy of much confidence, and no result can be accepted unless it has been confirmed by an independent source. In the instance of C, (i.e., the proportion married over 50), such a confirmation is provided by the midcentury censuses. It cannot be an accident that our value for 1806 corresponds closely, in department after department, to the value 50 years later. But ages at marriage computed in the way just described are often very different from those computed for later in the century. Sometimes they are higher and sometimes lower. We would expect some change, if only because of the influence of the Civil Code, but some of the changes are simply too large to be the result of anything but bad data. A criterion is required to discriminate between genuine changes in the age at marriage, and garbled results. We have decided to accept as reliable those data where the estimated proportion single at ages 20–24 falls within 10 percentage points of the proportion of single deaths at the same ages for the period 1806–1815. This choice is based on the fact that the ratio of these proportions is close to one for France later in the century, a finding reflecting the absence of marked differentials in mortality by marital status among young adults. The period 1806–1815 is close enough to the time that concerns us; data from 10 years are necessary to reduce random fluctuations.

Table 1 gives a series of indices of nuptiality for the 39 departments that appear to have reliable estimates of the age at first marriage in 1806 according to the chosen criterion. Three indices of nuptiality are given:

TABLE 1
Indices of Nuptiality for 1806 and 1851, Selected Départements of France

Département	Inheritance code	Percent ever married aged 46-50		Age at first marriage		I_m	
		1806	1856	1806	1851	1806	1851
Allier	4	89.4	93.7	25.5	22.9	.508	.604
Alpes (Hautes-)	5	88.3	85.2	27.5	25.1	.449	.497
Ardennes	2	90.5	92.0	25.4	23.9	.510	.584
Ariège	5	83.5	84.6	24.8	24.4	.501	.501
Aude	5	89.1	93.7	22.2	22.5	.626	.604
Calvados	2	81.9	85.2	26.1	24.6	.450	.509
Cher	4	86.4	93.6	25.4	23.4	.492	.597
Côtes-du-Nord	1	84.8	78.6	24.9	26.5	.481	.409
Doubs	0	81.9	82.4	26.4	26.6	.443	.444
Finistère	1	86.7	87.1	24.3	24.9	.521	.466
Gers	5	86.0	88.5	25.0	23.6	.516	.581
Indre	3	93.0	93.8	24.4	23.4	.559	.594
Isère	5	87.6	88.0	24.0	25.5	.532	.486
Landes	5	87.4	90.0	24.4	25.3	.529	.505
Loir-et-Cher	3	93.7	93.9	25.8	24.1	.503	.591
Loire	4	85.9	86.5	25.4	25.5	.481	.492
Loire-Inférieure	1	85.6	84.9	25.0	26.7	.495	.446
Loiret	3	89.1	92.2	25.0	24.0	.509	.584
Lot	5	85.7	91.0	24.3	24.7	.543	.538
Lozère	5	80.6	82.4	27.1	25.7	.415	.464
Maine-et-Loire	2	86.6	88.5	25.9	25.8	.470	.502
Manche	2	83.7	83.8	28.7	26.6	.382	.430
Marne (Haute-)	3	89.2	89.8	25.6	24.6	.505	.559
Mayenne	2	81.7	83.5	28.2	25.9	.380	.454
Nièvre	4	83.4	94.6	21.7	23.0	.592	.615
Orne	2	87.4	86.6	28.0	25.1	.423	.518
Puy-de-Dome	4	85.8	88.1	24.5	24.3	.521	.526
Pyrénées (Hautes-)	5	79.4	79.7	23.8	26.4	.504	.434
Saône (Haute-)	0	90.2	86.2	25.7	25.8	.500	.468
Sarthe	2	90.0	90.9	27.6	24.3	.440	.554
Seine-Inférieure	5	88.0	88.9	26.5	25.8	.467	.483
Sèvres (Deux-)	1	91.4	91.6	27.8	25.1	.451	.554
Somme	3	86.6	89.5	26.3	23.8	.469	.562
Tarn-et-Garonne	5	90.8	90.1	23.3	22.2	.595	.628
Var	5	91.6	90.5	24.0	23.5	.571	.588
Vendée	1	87.5	89.7	26.7	25.3	.462	.528
Vienne	2	89.0	91.9	24.8	23.8	.536	.583
Vosges	3	87.2	86.0	25.4	25.6	.488	.483
Yonne	3	91.5	95.0	26.1	23.7	.496	.610
France	0	87.2	88.4	24.1	24.4	.533	.526

the proportion single at age 50, the age at first marriage, and the proportions married at the fecund ages, weighted by a standard fertility schedule. The latter index, I_m, described elsewhere (Coale, 1969), has been used extensively in the Princeton study of the European fertility decline. Table 1 provides these indices at two successive dates, together with our score of the department on the scale of inheritance customs. The data from Table 1 constitute in part the empirical evidence that we used to test our model relating nuptiality and inheritance customs. We have also used, in addition to the data in Table 1, data for about 40 other departments on percentage ever married as of 1806. For later years, we have information on all three indices of nuptiality for 82 departments (van de Walle, 1974), as well as data on other characteristics that will be described in detail subsequently.

INHERITANCE

We now turn to our data on inheritance customs prior to the Civil Code. By providing fairly simple legal criteria, Yver (1966) has provided a key to the understanding of Old Regime customs of inheritance in France. Although the results of legal systems may be tempered in real life by subtle adaptation mechanisms, Yver's categories lend themselves to a crude ranking on a gradient from a high to a low degree of partibility. Map 1 illustrates our awkward attempt to make a complex story look simple.[1] One obvious problem is that Yver mapped custom areas, whereas we use the departments as units, in order to correlate the legal categories with the demographic information collected in the administrative units existing after 1800.

Map 1 shows the departments with scores from 1 to 5 indicating our interpretation of how their pre-Revolution inheritance customs fall in a continuum from perfect egalitarianism (score of 1) to unmitigated preferential treatment of one child (score of 5). (Some areas marked zero were not surveyed by Yver.) Egalitarian systems mostly prevailed in the west of France, with Normandy and Brittany as typical examples. These customs determined the division of property equally among the children (among boys only in Normandy). The father had no right to bequeath important property in a will; whatever he had given to a preferred child before his death must return to the patrimony to be shared—the so-called *rapport forcé*. At the other end of the spectrum, there were rare customs of primogeniture; the most remarkable was in the Pays de Caux, an area corresponding somewhat to Seine-Inférieure on our map. For the present purpose, however, most of the areas marked as most restrictive (score of 5) are south of the Loire River, in the area of written law where inheritance was ruled by the father's full freedom to write a testament. In addition to these extremes, there is an important area including the customs of Orléans and Paris, where heirs

[1] The main source of Map 1 is Yver's own "sketch" published as an appendix to his book (1966).

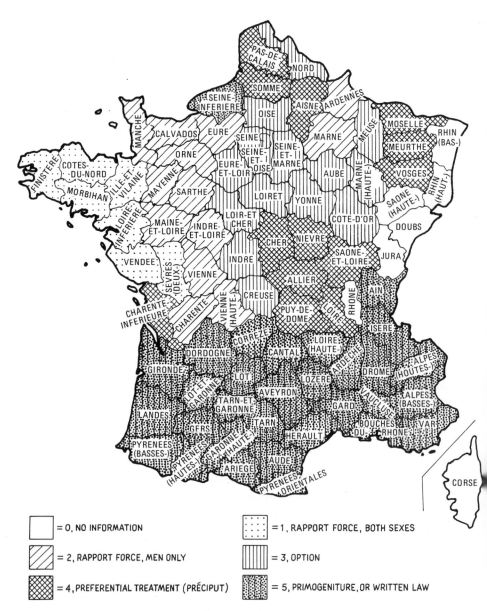

Map 1. Departments of France by inheritance code. Code definitions: 0: no information; 1: *rapport forcé*, both sexes; 2: *rapport forcé*, men only, or attenuated partible inheritance; 3: option; 4: preferential treatment (*préciput*); 5: primogeniture, or written law.

had the option of retaining the advances and gifts made during the life of the deceased or bringing them back to the succession to be divided again in equal parts. (Of course, a child who had really been favored would opt for the status quo, and would surrender his right to a smaller share.) Finally, there were the customs typified by Burgundy, which prevailed in the Civil Code. These customs allowed the father to set a preferential part aside for one child (the size of that part varying according to custom) before the rest of his property was divided equally among the claimants. In the Civil Code, the proportion that could be disposed of freely by the father depended on the number of children; it was one-third when there were two children and one-fourth when there were three or more children.

Within the complex French inheritance patterns, there are additional factors that have a bearing on the division of property. We can do little more here than indicate some of the major dimensions. In most areas, property left intestate was divided equally among descendants, regardless of the discretion possible through testamentary succession. Thus differences among areas in equality of division would depend not only on legal provisions but on the relative frequency with which wills were utilized. As example, Berkner and Mendels (forthcoming, citing LeRoy Ladurie, 1961) state that, even in the area of written law in southern France where testaments were more likely, "often the peasants did not bother to leave a will, which meant that property was divided evenly among the children [p. 5]." Another factor that tended to reduce regional differences was the principle of *légitime*, which guaranteed each child a fraction (often one-half) of what he or she would have received through intestate inheritance (Giesey, 1975). This provision, operating in areas of customary and of written law, set an absolute limit on the degree to which one child could be advantaged.

In many areas of customary law, the rules governing a father's freedom of disposition varied by the nature of the property. A major distinction here was between real property (*immeubles*—"immovables") and personal property (*meubles*—"movables"). *Immeubles* included not only land and buildings, but also sums received as perpetual annuities in exchange for land or money (*rentes foncières* and *rentes constituées*). Such transactions were quite common in the eighteenth century (Giesey, 1975, pp. 3, 17). Another factor affecting the ability to favor one heir was the classification of real property as *propres*, property previously inherited, or *acquets*, property acquired by an individual. Only a limited proportion of property previously inherited could be disposed of freely. On the other hand, little restriction was placed on the disposition of acquired property, within the overall limits of the *légitime* described earlier.

These aspects of property take on significance as one moves from the provisions of law or custom to a consideration of actual practice. Attempts to favor one child could take place during a father's lifetime through a sizable marriage endowment or other gifts, but the success of this approach depended on the provisions for including these items in the estate at the time of division, as described in Yver's classification (1966). An alternative approach would be to convert inherited property into acquired property, by sale or exchange, since there was greater freedom to dispose of the latter.

We touch on these complexities of French succession to emphasize that despite Yver's scholarly achievement, our classification of departments based on his work must be regarded as a very approximate measure of the variations in degree of partibility that characterized France during the Old Regime. A more definitive measure must await systematic analysis of actual inheritance documents left behind by courts and notaries. As one attempt to gauge the sensitivity of our results to this classification, we employ in a later section an alternate typology given by Brandt (1901). This classification is based on the agricultural survey of 1866, plus Brandt's own research, and divides the departments as of 1866 according to the dominant mode of transmission of rural property. Brandt's typology was used by Berkner and Mendels (forthcoming) to study the association between inheritance patterns and demographic characteristics. Our analysis will permit comparison with their results as well as an examination of alternate classifications of partibility.

THE APPROACH

Our model starts with the proposition that people want to get married. To do so they require a material basis, which includes a place to live and a means of livelihood. It follows logically that they *will* get married, provided dwellings and jobs are available. We assume, on the basis of these premises, that the extent of nuptiality reflects the availability of a material basis of marriage. There are, of course, rich bachelors and impoverished—jobless, landless and even homeless—grooms. On the whole, and all other things being equal, the proportions ever married and the age at marriage will be influenced by the ways in which the new generation gains access to worldly possessions.

In peasant societies, access to land may be important, although one may presume that nonagricultural jobs, the use of someone else's land as a tenant or sharecropper, or even a salaried job as a farmhand could be sufficient to support a family. We are assuming that owning a house is as important as title to agricultural land. Acquiring at least some of what we have referred to as *immeubles* (real or unmovable property) is a serious precondition of marriage, and inheritance is an important way of acquiring such goods. Inheritance laws, then, may have various demographic consequences.

Ceteris paribus, a partible system of inheritance should lead to high nuptiality, low out-migration, and nuclear family structure; an impartible system should be associated with low nuptiality, high out-migration, and complex household structure (Berkner & Mendels, (forthcoming); Habakkuk, 1955). In a partible system, division of property among the children facilitates marriage and the creation of separate households within the community. In an impartible system, the favored heir can marry and co-reside with the parents, but the other children must seek employment opportunities and marriage elsewhere, both within and outside the community; often they can remain in the parental household while celibate.

Straightforward tests of these associations are difficult for a number of reasons. In the first place, as we have noted previously, inheritance systems are not simply partible or impartible but exist at varying degrees of partibility. Due to their complexity and possible modification in practice, the systems are difficult to classify with great accuracy. Beyond this, there are many factors that can mask the postulated relationships; up to this point, we have assumed such factors to be constant. These factors fall generally into two classes, economic and demographic. If the economic base supporting the population were to increase continuously, then (1) moderate population growth could occur without deterioration of living conditions, (2) jobs might be available in increasing numbers, and (3) restrictive inheritance rules would exert no pressure toward high rate of celibacy and late marriages. This might be the case in a frontier economy, where younger sons and their wives move out of the paternal sphere and settle on their own new land. Similarly, in nineteenth century Europe, the growth of an urban economy could compensate for the lack of opportunities in the villages. Inversely, even the most liberal system of partible inheritance will not promote marriage if so much subdivision has already occurred in the past, and if the population has grown so impoverished because of earlier fragmentation, that the future generation cannot be accommodated on property inherited from the current generation. Since interest often centers on the relation of inheritance rules to the size of *landholdings*, it is well to realize that the transmission of property may have little effect on the land tenure system. A peasant may farm land belonging to several owners, or inversely, several *fermiers* or sharecroppers may subdivide the exploitation of a large tract owned by one landlord. Berkner and Mendels (forthcoming) show how specific land tenure arrangements and the proportion of land under leasehold may influence the degree to which land is subdivided, since some tenure systems prevented subdivision and in many cases inheritance rules did not affect leaseholds. Berkner and Mendels also illustrate how settlement restrictions and the type of agriculture in an area act to limit further subdivision of the land.

In addition to these aspects of social and economic structure, demographic factors play a role in the working out of the effects of an inheritance system. If there was quasi-universal marriage and no population growth, due to low fertility and/or high mortality, the inheritance pattern would have little effect on nuptiality, migration, or household structure; opportunities for land and dwellings would be relatively abundant, and privileged heirs would not be unduly favored in the competition for them. Further consequences of the demographic setting will be developed later when the model to be tested is specified.

In the face of such complexities, it is important to be clear about the structure of the analysis to be presented. We are attempting to detect whether the change in inheritance practices embodied in the 1804 Civil Code had demographic consequences, particularly with respect to nuptiality. We have proceeded by analyzing the relationship between inheritance pattern and demographic characteristics in a series of areal cross-sections starting early in the nineteenth century, using departments as the unit of analysis. Throughout the analysis, we have kept each department's inheritance pattern fixed in the pre–Civil Code class determined by Yver (1966). The first step was the determination of the relationship between inheritance and nuptiality prior to the effect of the Civil Code. This served as a baseline. We then proceeded to examine the persistence of this relationship at successive points after enactment of the Civil Code.

If inheritance patterns influenced nuptiality and if the Code did bring about more uniform practice, the baseline relationship would have vanished or diminished over time. On the other hand, if the baseline relationship remained the same, this would be taken as evidence that the pre-Code classification of inheritance patterns continued to exert an influence. Although multiple adaptations and readjustments were expected, we hoped that the effect of inheritance customs on nuptiality would be perceptible and that any nudge exerted by the Civil Code would show up. There were certainly accommodations to the new law in the subdivision of property but there may also have been demographic adaptations. We claim no precision. The effect of legislation on demographic behavior is a topic of recurrent interest. A negative finding—i.e., that laws had no discernible effect on nuptiality—may not be less interesting than a positive one.

The limitations of this approach are worth stressing. We have no direct measurement of whether inheritance practices did or did not change as a result of the Code; nor should our results be taken as evidence that the French generally complied with or evaded the new body of law. This should be studied directly. (As we shall see later, there are some indications that changes in inheritance practice did occur over the period studied, but not necessarily in the direction countenanced by the Code.) Furthermore, our unit of analysis, the department, is probably too highly aggregated for optimum results; within a given department there may be considerable heterogeneity in a number of the social and economic variables that bear on the relationship between inheritance and nuptiality. Analyses of the type undertaken here need to be complemented by data based on individuals and by detailed case studies of smaller aggregates, as exemplified by Berkner's comparison of two villages (this volume). Despite its shortcomings, areal analysis is consonant with the form in which many hypotheses about differentials in demographic rates are stated. The use of a large number of units permits a multivariate analysis and hence control of more factors than is possible in a delimited case study.

THE DEVELOPMENT OF THE MODEL

Let us first assume that the relationship between inheritance and nuptiality is straightforward and that no other variables intervene in the process. Table 2 presents the means of the demographic variables thought to be influenced by the inheritance pattern at select points in the nineteenth century, for departments according to Yver's scale (1966) and for two possible dichotomies of this scale. In addition to its substantive implications, this table points out aspects and limitations of our data that need to be kept in mind by the reader.

1. In studying nuptiality, we distinguish two dimensions—age at marriage and the proportions who ever marry. The singulate mean age at marriage (SMAM) and the proportion of specified birth cohorts married by ages 46 to 50, respectively, are used as the measures of these two dimensions. Since the latter measure is available for only a few time points, we also make use of the index of nuptiality (I_m) used in the Princeton fertility studies. This index is a standardized proportion married, with as numerator the weighted sum of the number of women married in each age group, and as denominator the weighted sum of all the women in each age group.[2] The index of nuptiality is affected by both age at marriage and proportions marrying. For the data presented, I_m is more highly correlated, negatively, with SMAM at each time point;

[2] The weights in each instance are the age-specific fertility rates of married Hutterite women. The choice of the standard resulted from the fact that the Hutterites use no contraception and have the highest fertility on reliable record.

TABLE 2
Mean of Nuptiality, Migration, and Household Size Variables by Inheritance Pattern[a] for French Départements

| | | Inheritance pattern | | | | | Classification I | | Classification II | |
		1	2	3	4	5	Partible 1,2	Impartible 3,4,5	Partible 1,2,3	Impartible 4,5
Nuptiality										
Singulate mean age at marriage	1806	25.7	26.8	25.5	24.5	24.7	26.4	24.9	26.1	24.7
	1831	25.9	26.9	24.3	24.0	24.5	25.3	24.4	24.8	24.4
	1856	26.0	24.0	23.6	23.5	24.2	24.7	23.9	24.2	24.1
	1866	26.4	24.0	23.5	23.5	24.3	24.8	24.0	24.3	24.2
Proportion ever married of birth cohorts of	1756–1760	.86	.88	.90	.88	.86	.88	.88	.88	.87
	1806–1810	.85	.90	.91	.90	.88	.88	.89	.89	.88
	1811–1815	.87	.91	.92	.92	.90	.90	.91	.91	.90
Index of Nuptiality, Im	1806	.48	.45	.50	.52	.52	.46	.52	.48	.52
	1831	.46	.52	.56	.52	.51	.50	.53	.52	.52
	1856	.46	.57	.59	.55	.54	.53	.55	.55	.54
	1866	.46	.57	.59	.56	.54	.53	.56	.56	.54
Migration rate	1806–1831	-.008	-.033	-.041	-.044	-.061	-.024	-.052	-.031	-.057
	1831–1846	-.002	.006	-.006	-.002	-.013	.003	-.009	-.001	-.010
	1846–1856	-.005	-.008	-.021	-.024	-.011	-.006	-.016	-.013	-.014
	1856–1881	-.057	-.034	-.039	-.045	-.069	-.042	-.057	-.041	-.064
Household size	1866	4.44	3.61	3.63	3.96	4.04	3.90	3.92	3.78	4.02
N for 1806[b]		5	8	7	5	12	13	24	20	17
N for other years[c]		7	13	15	11	30	20	56	35	41

[a] Yver's 5 point scale, shown in Map 1. Classifications I and II are dichotomies created by collapsing the scale in two ways, as indicated.

[b] These N's refer only to singulate mean age at marriage, 1806, and Im, 1806.

[c] These N's apply to most of the other rows. In a few cases, the number of départements actually used may differ by 1 or

it is, however, quite highly positively correlated with proportions ever marrying as well (except for 1806). Again with the exception of 1806, SMAM and proportion ever marrying show a high negative correlation with one another.

2. The earliest time point available for study at present is 1806, and that year will serve as a baseline. Though the Civil Code was enacted at about that time, it is unlikely that the relationships we are studying would have responded so quickly to the new inheritance provisions. A more serious limitation with regard to this choice of baseline is the possibility that the marital patterns of 1806 were atypical of earlier practices as a result of the excess male mortality and the conscriptions that took place during the Napoleonic wars.

3. The migration rates used are for females and were computed from the migration indexes prepared by van de Walle (1974, pp. 199–202) using 1846 as a reference year. Only four time periods are presented.[3] Table 2 indicates that both the partible and impartible areas generally had out-migration (or negative rates). That there is more out- than in-migration comes about because the departments that contain the largest cities (Paris, Lyons, and Marseilles) have been excluded, and these are of course areas of high in-migration.

4. For household complexity, we have available only the average size of household, and that only for a single year, 1866. Though our measure is affected by the presence of children (and therefore by fertility), Parish and Schwartz (1972, Appendix Table B) show a correlation of .89 between household size and the number of adults per household in 1876.

5. Given that the areas exist at various degrees of partibility, the question of grouping arises when one desires the convenience of a simple dichotomy. In Table 2, we present two classifications. In the first, Classification I, the departments coded as "option" (scale point 3) are combined with scale points 4 and 5 as impartible; in the second, Classification II, the "option" areas are grouped with scale points 1 and 2 as partible. It is difficult on *a priori* grounds to choose between the two possibilities, since much depends on whether the "option" arrange-

[3] The four time periods are 1806–1831, 1831–1846, 1846–1856, and 1856–1881. The reconstruction of the female population of nineteenth century France provided for each department over time a set of migration indexes (defined as the ratio of the reported population to the population computed by the balance of births and deaths). For these computations, the 1846 reported population was used as a starting point in determining the denominator. These ratios served to calculate net migration estimates for the periods specified. Note that only female net migration estimates are available and these may not be good indicators of the male migration ratio. As Berkner and Mendels (forthcoming) have noted, the effect of migration on nuptiality depends in part on the extent to which migration is sex-selective.

ment did indeed lead to one heir's being favored. Richard's (1976) review of the evidence indicates little tendency to utilize the option, so that combining these departments with the more strictly partible ones (as in Classification II) seems preferable. It also has the virtue of producing close to equal numbers of each class. Though we will focus this initial discussion on Classification II, note that the two methods of division do lead to nontrivial differences on many of the variables.

Turning to the substantive implications of Table 2, we focus first on the relationship between inheritance and nuptiality. Looking first at the proportions ever married and the index of nuptiality, and the detailed Yver scale, we note generally a curvilinear pattern, with lower nuptiality levels for scale points 1 and 5 (mostly Brittany and the southern area of written law respectively) and higher levels at the intermediate scale points. The dichotomy according to Classification II indicates, at best, slightly more frequent marriage in the partible areas. In both types of areas, the proportions increased quite consistently throughout the nineteenth century (though not in the departments of Brittany, scale point 1, considered alone).

In discussions of the relationship between partibility and nuptiality, little distinction is usually made between frequency of marriage and age at marriage. Insofar as an impartible system allows a favored heir to marry in expectation of an inheritance, one might hypothesize a younger age at marriage in the impartible areas. The pattern by detailed level of partibility is rather irregular, the only notable feature being the consistently higher average age for scale point 1. According to Classification II, there is a slight tendency for younger age at marriage in the impartible areas, and this difference is augmented if Classification I is employed.

With respect to average household size, the detailed scale again shows a curvilinear pattern with larger average size occurring at scale points 1 and 5, and the impartible areas having a larger average than the partible, according to Classification II. For migration, there is a fairly clear tendency for the impartible areas to show greater out-migration than the partible, as hypothesized in the earlier discussion.

The data of Table 2 are, in effect, the zero-order relationships between inheritance pattern and the demographic consequents. It remains to be seen whether the general absence of sharply different levels may be due to the operation of the various factors that may possibly mask the posited relationships. Unfortunately, we have measures of only a few of these factors, and even these are not available for each time point. The general model of interest is shown in Figure 1, where

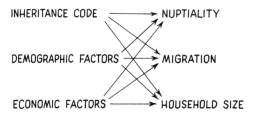

Figure 1. General model: Schematic of broad factors affecting nuptiality, migration, and household size.

the dependent variables are seen as influenced by the inheritance pattern and by economic and demographic factors. Because of the limitations of the data, our major emphasis will be on the demographic factors that need to be controlled.

The basic model used, therefore, is as shown in Figure 2. In this model, we focus on the relative influence of the inheritance code, and marital fertility and expectation of life, both suitably lagged, on the various measures of nuptiality. In addition, since the pace of migration preceding the date of interest can affect nuptiality, we will, on occasion, introduce migration as an independent variable. Finally, since the opportunities for marriage should affect the subsequent migration rate, we will also consider a model in which migration is dependent on nuptiality as well as on inheritance, marital fertility, and expectation of life.

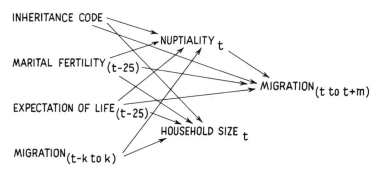

Figure 2. Basic model: Schematic of influences of inheritance code and specified demographic factors on nuptiality, household size, and migration (with time lags indicated by subscripts).

The choice of lagged values of marital fertility and expectation of life merits some discussion. We noted earlier that opportunities for marriage are in part a function of the size of the cohort that reaches marriageable age. This size is determined by both fertility 25 years earlier and intervening mortality (applicable to the younger age groups).[4] The use of an index of marital fertility, I_g,[5] rather than overall fertility, aims at reflecting the relative number of adult siblings *per family* in the marriageable age span. Thus we hoped to achieve an adequate surrogate of both the overall pressure on a department's resources to provide dwellings and economic opportunities for newly forming families and the pressure on resources within the household to provide for children wishing to marry. In an impartible area, we expect the favored heir to marry early and the other siblings to marry much later, if at all. The average age at marriage over all the siblings will clearly depend on the number of nonfavored sibs, as well as the specific ages at marriage. Even in a truly partible area, a large number of sibs may delay marriage so that the average age at marriage is greater, because the amount received by each may be too small to allow new family formation; time will elapse while additional resources are sought. Our basic model thus views the pressure on both community and family resources as a function of the number of adult children, and this pressure as affecting frequency and age at marriage. Family size, therefore, should be controlled in studying the relationship of inheritance to nuptiality.

A strong inverse relationship between the index of marital fertility and the level of nuptiality for France has been noted (van de Walle, 1968). In addition, Lesthaeghe and van de Walle (1976) have pointed out that the relationship is even stronger when the marital fertility measure is lagged behind that of nuptiality. Much of the emphasis concerning this phenomenon has been placed on whether the increases in nuptiality preceded the decline in marital fertility or vice versa, and on the mechanisms involved. This is not our focus of interest but the model specified in Figure 2 justifies the introduction of this relationship as a statistical control in studying the relationship of inheritance pattern to nuptiality. The argument advanced does give precedence to the level of marital fertility and suggests that the social and economic constraints in

---

[4] Since we do not have a more precise measure, we use estimates of expectation of life at birth, but these estimates are highly correlated with the levels of infant mortality. The mortality of parents also affected the age at marriage of heirs and the inheritance system. If the parents were long-lived, children who had to await their inheritance married late. (Under such circumstances, parents often made *inter vivos* gifts.)

[5] I_g is a legitimate fertility index in which the numerator is the number of legitimate births in a department and the denominator is a weighted sum of the number of women married in each age group; the weights are the age-specific fertility rates of married Hutterites. The indexes used here are based on births over a 5-year period, so a value of I_g lagged 25 years should capture the relative size of those aged 23–27, inclusive.

TABLE 3
Mean of Fertility, Expectation of Life, and Income Measures by Inheritance Pattern for French Départements

| | Inheritance Pattern | | | | | Classification I | | Classification II | |
	1	2	3	4	5	Partible 1,2	Impartible 3,4,5	Partible 1,2,3	Impartible 4,5
Fertility									
CBR, 1801–1805	32.86	27.73	32.13	33.77	33.22	29.52	33.03	30.64	33.37
Ig, 1831	.725	.494	.499	.591	.565	.575	.552	.542	.572
Ig, 1841	.675	.449	.473	.550	.535	.528	.522	.504	.539
Ig, 1856	.614	.400	.437	.497	.498	.475	.482	.459	.498
Ig, 1866	.648	.404	.423	.494	.501	.489	.479	.461	.499
Ig, 1881	.677	.403	.410	.448	.490	.499	.460	.461	.481
Expectation of life, born:									
1801–1805	33.0	37.3	31.7	33.2	37.7	35.8	35.2	34.0	36.5
1826–1830	35.9	42.0	38.0	36.2	40.1	39.9	38.8	39.1	39.0
1836–1840	40.2	44.8	40.7	39.0	39.6	43.2	39.8	42.1	39.4
1851–1855	40.7	45.7	42.2	41.4	40.3	44.0	41.0	43.2	40.6
Income									
Landed income 1821	40.1	51.2	56.2	48.2	50.7	47.3	51.7	51.1	50.0
Landed income 1851	52.0	78.3	82.9	72.3	65.6	69.1	71.6	75.0	67.4
Income in ag. occ. 1864	782.4	1022.1	1222.1	1043.0	888.7	938.2	1008.3	1059.9	930.1
Income in non-ag. occ. 1864	392.6	475.6	479.3	482.2	408.2	446.6	441.8	460.6	428.1
Income per head, 1866	367.0	489.8	516.6	451.2	421.0	446.8	452.5	476.7	429.1
N	7	13	15	11	30	20	56	35	41

family formation were important mechanisms in bringing about the observed relationship between marital fertility and nuptiality. Table 3 shows the level of marital fertility by inheritance pattern. As observed with nuptiality, the relationship is curvilinear, with high values of I_g at scale value 1 as well as 4 and 5, and lower levels for the areas ranking intermediate on partibility. As a result, the two dichotomies shown give different implications. The first suggests little difference in marital fertility by partibility whereas the second indicates higher marital fertility in the impartible areas to a modest degree. Table 3 also presents data by inheritance pattern for some of the other independent variables used in the analysis.

TESTS OF THE MODEL

In this section we shall present the results of testing the basic model depicted by Figure 2. Subsequently, where available, the effect of adding economic variables, as indicated by Figure 1, will be shown. The method of analysis is linear multiple regression. The inheritance code is used here as an interval scale with the values indicated on Map 1; larger values of the code represent greater degrees of impartibility.[6] The other variables entering the analysis were defined in the previous section.

Table 4 shows the relative influence of the inheritance pattern and the demographic variables (marital fertility, expectation of life, and migration) on the various measures of nuptiality. The standardized regression coefficients or beta values, their t values, and the coefficient of determination (R^2) are shown, with and without migration as an independent variable.

The first available date for our measure of marital fertility, I_g, was 1831, and this means that we could not introduce an appropriately lagged value of this variable for the regressions of 1806 and 1831. For both these regressions we used the only available surrogate, the crude birth rate (CBR) of 1801–1805. The CBR of 1801–1805 is correlated .29

---

[6] The inheritance code is at most an ordinal scale. The effect of using it as an interval scale was tested by comparing the results obtained from introducing it as a dummy variable with those results obtained from the interval scale assumption on a number of linear regressions. In some cases, the amount of variance explained in the dummy variable approach was not significantly greater, at the 5% level, than the interval assumption for some of the regressions; but it was significantly greater in others. In all cases, however, the additional variance explained was very small, and we decided to use the interval scale assumption, since it gives a simpler and more interpretable structure to the models.

TABLE 4

Standardized Partial Regression Coefficients of Inheritance Code and Demographic Determinants of Nuptiality: France, 1806-1881 (t-statistics in parentheses)[a]

	Basic model without migration					Basic model with migration				
	Year					Year				
	1806	1831	1856	1866	1881	1806	1831	1856	1866	1881
Dependent variable: index of nuptiality (Im)										
Inheritance	.390	.214	.021	-.056	.070	N.A.	.215	.019	-.062	.080
	(2.75)	(1.84)	(.40)	(1.05)	(.97)		(1.79)	(.37)	(1.18)	(1.08)
Fertility	-.336	-.151	-.943	-1.00	-.920		-.150	-.953	-1.024	-.898
	(2.24)	(1.22)	(17.09)	(17.98)	(11.12)		(1.15)	(16.10)	(17.14)	(9.91)
Exp. of life	-.302	-.470	-.358	-.363	-.229		-.469	-.363	-.378	-.222
	(2.05)	(3.87)	(6.48)	(6.25)	(2.64)		(3.52)	(6.43)	(6.34)	(2.53)
Migration							.001	-.027	-.059	-.047
							(.01)	(.48)	(1.09)	(.61)
R^2	.46	.18	.80	.82	.68		.18	.80	.83	.68
N	37	78	76	74	74		78	76	74	74
Dependent variable: singulate mean age at marriage (SMAM)										
Inheritance	-.360	-.292	-.164	-.044	-.151	N.A.	-.285	-.161	-.035	-.164
	(2.47)	(2.47)	(2.50)	(.76)	(2.12)		(2.35)	(2.45)	(.60)	(2.25)
Fertility	-.387	-.026	.853	.964	.914		-.014	.867	.994	.886
	(2.51)	(.21)	(12.40)	(15.69)	(11.17)		(.11)	(11.75)	(15.10)	(9.90)
Exp. of life	.207	.311	.338	.403	.245		.326	.344	.421	.236
	(1.37)	(2.53)	(4.90)	(6.27)	(2.86)		(2.42)	(4.90)	(6.41)	(2.73)
Migration							.036	.037	.074	-.061
							(.29)	(.53)	(1.24)	(.81)
R^2	.43	.16	.69	.79	.68		.16	.70	.79	.69
N	37	78	76	74	74		78	76	74	74

TABLE 4 *Continued*

Dependent variable: proportion ever married (PEM)

Inheritance	-.126 (1.14)	-.025 (.36)	-.190 (2.41)	-.024 (.34)	-.213 (2.76)
Fertility	.177 (1.51)	-.800 (10.88)	-.834 (10.05)	-.791 (10.02)	-.910 (10.53)
Exp. of life	-.382 (3.34)	-.533 (7.24)	-.593 (6.84)	-.529 (7.04)	-.639 (7.41)
Migration	N.A.	N.A.	N.A.	.024 (.32)	-.186 (2.38)
R^2	.25	.65	.61	.65	.64
N	80	76	74	76	74

[a]Values for inheritance code were taken from Map 1. Other independent variables are defined as follows:

1806: Fertility = crude birth rate, 1801-1805; Exp. of life = female expectation of life at birth, born 1801-1805.

1831: Fertility and Exp. of life, same as for 1806; Migration - migration rate, 1806-1831.

1856: Fertility = Ig, 1831; Exp. of life = female expectation of life at birth, born 1826-1830; Migration = migration rate, 1846-1856.

1881: Fertility = Ig 1856; Exp. of life = female expectation of life at birth, born 1851-1855; Migration = migration rate, 1856-1881.

with the I_g of 1831; the CBR of 1826–1830 is correlated .65 with I_g of 1831. This suggests that the CBR of 1801–1805 may be a fair surrogate of contemporaneous I_g but a poor approximation of the unmeasured I_g existing 25 years prior to our 1806 baseline date. In addition, the CBR is influenced by the proportions married at each age as well as marital fertility (and the age structure). This further weakens the usefulness of the CBR as an independent determinant of nuptiality. These further limitations in the baseline regression, along with the problems arising from the unsettled conditions of that time, must be kept in mind. The earliest expectation-of-life data are for 1801–1805, but this presented less of a problem, since regional levels and differentials of mortality were, in all likelihood, changing rather slowly at that time.

Our discussion of Table 4 will take up each of the measures of nuptiality in turn and focus first on the basic model excluding migration. For the index of nuptiality (I_m) as dependent variable, the baseline regression indicates that impartibility is positively and significantly associated with nuptiality, contrary to expectations.[7] The magnitude of the association tends to decrease with time and is not statistically significant at any other date.[8] From this pattern alone we would have the rather surprising conclusion that prior to the Civil Code impartibil-

---

[7] Throughout this chapter we have used a 5% level of significance. Where the direction of influence is hypothesized and a one-tailed test is appropriate, conditions that occur mainly with the relations involving the inheritance code, a t statistic of 1.67 or greater is needed for the number of units employed in most analyses ($N = 70$). Where direction is not hypothesized, a t statistic of 2.00 or more is required for this level of significance.

[8] Many of our independent variables are indexes or approximate interval scales (like the inheritance code). So, in presenting the results of the multiple regressions, we have chosen to show the standardized partial regression coefficients rather than the nonstandardized. The standardized coefficients may be interpreted as the amount of change in standard deviation units in the dependent variable associated with a one-standard-deviation change in the independent variable; the nonstandardized coefficients measure change in terms of the original units of each variable.

A standardized coefficient is equal to the nonstandardized coefficient multiplied by the ratio of the standard deviation of the independent variable to the standard deviation of the dependent. The standardized coefficients may differ across regression equations, even when the nonstandardized coefficients agree. This has led some to caution against comparing standardized regression coefficients across equations (Schoenberg, 1972, p. 4). Blalock suggests that standardized coefficients are "appropriate if one wishes to measure the *actual* amount of impact that each variable has on the other in a given population [1967, p. 675; italics in original]," whereas the unstandardized form is more appropriate for describing causal structure. Since at various points we were interested in comparing effects across years, we have been attentive to possible differences in the trends presented by the nonstandardized coefficients. We found in this case that the trends discussed were essentially similar from both types of coefficients. The choice of coefficient, of course, has no effect on level of significance.

ity fostered nuptiality and that the effect of the Civil Code was to diminish this influence strongly. Before embracing this view, we should recall that the index of nuptiality incorporates both the dimensions of age at marriage and frequency of marriage. For 1806, I_m is much more associated with age at marriage; and it is probably this dimension that is reflected in the 1806 regression coefficient. There is a negative relationship between fertility and nuptiality from 1831 on, and the relationship is particularly strong for the three most recent dates for which a lagged value of I_g was available. This is in keeping with the expectation that a high density of adults would depress nuptiality. The only reversal of this pattern is for 1806 and this reversal is due without doubt to the nuptiality component of the CBR, 1801–1805, used as the fertility measure. The regression coefficients for expectation of life were large and statistically significant at each date, and in the direction hypothesized: Higher expectation of life led to lower levels of nuptiality.

The regressions with singulate mean age at marriage are more easily summarized. At every point, greater impartibility was associated with earlier age at marriage. The relationship is statistically significant for each year except 1866 and there is some tendency for the magnitude of the coefficient to decrease over time. For the three most recent years where a lagged value of marital fertility is available, there was a strong positive relationship with age at marriage, as expected, if a greater density of young adults adversely affects marriage probabilities. For the two earlier years, where the weak CBR measure was used as the fertility surrogate, the results were in a contrary direction, and again most likely due to the nuptiality component in this measure. As hypothesized, higher expectation of life was associated with later age at marriage at each date. Note that throughout we have used female age at marriage, and, insofar as the differential between age of groom and bride varies across departments, analyses based on males might differ from those shown.

Measures of the proportion ever marrying were available for only three of the time points. For each one, the hypothesized relationship of greater impartibility to smaller proportions marrying was found, though the coefficient was significant only for 1866. As before, the effect of fertility for 1856 and 1866 was in keeping with the model posited; higher marital fertility led to lower proportions married. The results for expectation of life were also in keeping with the model at each of the three points.

TABLE 5
Standardized Partial Regression Coefficients of Inheritance Code and Demographic Determinants of Migration and Household Size: France, 1806-1881

Independent variables[a]	Dependent Variable: Migration						
	1806-1831			1831-1846		1856-1881	
Inheritance	-.184	-.273	-.194	-.114	-.169	-.207	-.240
	(1.70)	(1.54)	(1.77)	(1.00)	(1.44)	(1.98)	(2.20)
Fertility	-.310	-.405	-.295	-.320	-.325	-.476	-.304
	(2.69)	(2.15)	(2.52)	(2.64)	(2.71)	(4.32)	(1.56)
Exp. of life	-.425	-.374	-.456	-.354	-.295	.098	-.030
	(3.78)	(2.15)	(3.77)	(2.98)	(2.41)	(.89)	(.23)
S.M.A.M.			-.247		-.188		-.202
			(1.27)		(1.70)		(1.07)
P.E.M.			-.080				
			(.71)				
R^2	.27	.31	.28	.19	.22	.24	.25
N	80	37	80	80	80	74	74

	Dependent variable: household size	
	1866	
Inheritance	.100	.105
	(1.25)	(1.30)
Fertility (Ig 1841)	.731	.750
	(8.68)	(8.25)
Exp. of life (1836-1840)	-.072	-.060
	(.82)	(.67)
Migration (1846-1856)		.047
		(.57)
R^2	.60	.60
N	74	74

[a]Independent variables are as defined in footnote, Table 4.
For 1806-1831, see Table 4 footnote for 1806. S.M.A.M. = singulate mean age at marriage, 1806; P.E.M. = proportion ever married, born 1756-1760.
For 1831-1846, see Table 4 footnote for 1831. S.M.A.M. = singulate mean age at marriage, 1831.
For 1856-1881, see Table 4 footnote for 1856. S.M.A.M. = singulate mean age at marriage, 1856.

The linear regression equation used accounted for a high proportion of the variance in the nuptiality measures for 1856, 1866, and 1881, ranging from 61 to 82%. The model explained less than 20% of the

variance for 1831, and the results for the baseline year were intermediate, with a range of 25 to 46%.

Our model up to this point used only fertility and mortality as the
independent variables determining the pressure of population on resources, and therefore influencing nuptiality. Out-migration, however,
could have relieved the pressure of numbers, and was therefore introduced as an independent variable; these results are also given in Table
4. In almost every case the coefficient for migration during the preceding period was neither statistically significant nor of large magnitude;
the coefficients for the other variables in the model remained virtually
unchanged and there was no gain in the proportion of variance explained. Only in 1866, for the dependent variable proportion ever
married, did there appear to be a statistically significant negative relation between the level of in-migration and this aspect of nuptiality.
Given that this is the only significant effect and that the migration
variable here refers to the period from 1846 to 1856, it is probably best
not to attach any particular importance to it.

Table 5 presents the results of using migration, this time as a dependent variable over the three specified periods. Household size in 1866
was also included in the model. For migration, two versions of the
model presented in Figure 2 are shown. In the first, migration was
viewed as dependent on the inheritance pattern and the antecedent
variables—fertility and expectation of life. In the second version, one of
the dimensions of nuptiality, as of the start of the period, was added.
The first set of coefficients in Table 5 indicated that impartible areas
were associated with greater out-migration, as predicted, but only the
coefficient for 1856–1881 was significant at the level used here.[9] Higher
fertility and expectation of life led to greater out-migration, which is the
hypothesized effect of a greater density of young adults. These effects
were quite strong and generally significant. Opportunities for marriage
tended to reduce out-migration (i.e., lower age at marriage was associated with less out-migration), but the coefficients were not significant and adding the variable raised the proportion of variance explained only slightly.

This suggested that the basic model used to account for nuptiality
also accounted for migration, without postulating an additional independent effect from nuptiality to migration. When the antecedent fertility and mortality variables were omitted, we observed a more sizable
effect from nuptiality to migration in two out of the three periods:

[9] For migration during 1806–1831, the inheritance code was significant under the 1.67
criterion (see note 7) for two of the equations shown but not for the third.

Standardized Partial Regression Coefficients of Inheritance Code and Singulate Mean Age at Marriage on Migration (*t* statistics in parentheses)

	Dependent variable: Migration		
	1806–1831	1831–1846	1856–1881
Inheritance code	−.438	−.329	−.269
	(2.52)	(3.00)	(2.51)
SMAM	−.194	−.231	−.438
	(1.11)	(2.10)	(4.10)
R^2	.16	.13	.22
N	37	80	74

Of the independent variables used with household size, only the earlier level of marital fertility was strongly and significantly related, as expected from the nature of the dependent variable. The sign of the coefficient of the inheritance code was in keeping with the hypothesis of more complex household structure in impartible areas, but it failed to reach significance at the 5% level.

We noted earlier the potential importance of economic factors in the relationship between inheritance and nuptiality. Our ability to test this with the available data was limited. Table 6 shows the effect of introducing income measures at a few select points. For 1831 and 1856, we added to the demographic model measures of landed income for 1821 and 1851, respectively. For the 1831 nuptiality measures, this income variable had a significant effect in the expected direction—higher income was associated with a higher index of nuptiality and lower age at marriage. In addition, the coefficients for the other variables were little changed from their values in the basic demographic model, as shown in Table 4. Thus the income variable was an additional and sizable determinant of nuptiality. For 1856, however, income was significantly related only to the index of nuptiality and in a direction contrary to expectation. That is, higher income was associated with lower levels of nuptiality. We have no adequate explanation for this except to note the possibility that we might have been using a poor measure of the economic conditions existing in an area over the period relevant to nuptiality decisions. As before, the addition of the income variable had little effect on the size of the coefficients of the other independent variables.

For 1866, we had three possible income measures based on 1864: (1) income per person employed in agricultural occupations, (2) income per person employed in nonagricultural occupations, and (3) total income per head (Delefortrie & Morice, 1959). Since the last measure used total

TABLE 6
Standardized Partial Regression Coefficients of Economic and Demographic Determinants of Nuptiality: France 1831, 1856, 1866 (t-statistics in parentheses)

Independent variables[a]	1831 Dependent variable		1856 Dependent variable		
	Im	SMAM	Im	SMAM	PEM
Inheritance	.142	-.235	.001	-.148	-.024
	(1.42)	(2.07)	(.03)	(2.25)	(.34)
Fertility	-.089	-.056	-1.083	.963	-.796
	(.82)	(.46)	(14.55)	(10.03)	(7.52)
Exp. of life	-.476	.331	-.387	.362	-.530
	(4.32)	(2.64)	(7.07)	(5.13)	(6.80)
Landed income, 1821 or 1851	.524	-.357	-.192	.140	.008
	(5.89)	(3.54)	(2.70)	(1.54)	(.083)
Migration	-.021	.052	-.004	.020	.025
	(.21)	(.44)	(.07)	(.29)	(.32)
R^2	.45	.28	.82	.70	.65
N	78	78	76	76	74

	1866								
	Full Model			Economic Model I			Economic Model II		
	Im	SMAM	PEM	Im	SMAM	PEM	Im	SMAM	PEM
Inheritance	-.052	-.061	-.207	.100	.226	.012	.130	-.238	.033
	(.99)	(1.16)	(2.64)	(.92)	(2.25)	(.10)	(1.40)	(2.54)	(.30)
Fertility	-.995	.946	-.918	--	--	--	--	--	--
	(16.32)	(15.50)	(10.12)						
Exp. of life	-.388	.439	-.638	--	--	--	--	--	--
	(6.60)	(7.47)	(7.31)						
Migration	-.107	.184	-.207	.142	-.063	.062	-.020	.031	-.058
	(1.82)	(3.12)	(2.36)	(1.15)	(.52)	(.46)	(.20)	(.29)	(.46)
Agric. income 1964	.094	-.147	-.036	.361	-.384	.141	--	--	--
	(1.58)	(2.49)	(.41)	(2.96)	(3.28)	(1.06)			
Non-ag. income, 1964	.051	-.161	.073	.004	-.119	.036	--	--	--
	(.88)	(2.78)	(.84)	(.04)	(.97)	(.26)			
Income per head	--	--	--	--	--	--	.642	-.618	.404
							(6.11)	(5.83)	(3.22)
R^2	.84	.84	.64	.19	.25	.04	.40	.39	.14
N	74	74	74	74	74	74	74	74	74

[a]Independent variables are as defined in Table 4 footnote.

population in the denominator, it could be correlated with other determinants of population size, such as the index of marital fertility (I_g) of 1841. This was confirmed, as the following table shows. The table also shows that income per head was highly correlated with the agricultural income measure and that both agricultural and nonagricultural income had only modest correlations with I_g:

Intercorrelation among 1864 Income Measures and I_g, 1841

	Ig	Income per capita	Nonagricultural income
Agricultural income	−.41	.84	.41
Nonagricultural income	−.18	.44	—
Income per capita	−.68	—	—

Taking into account this pattern of intercorrelations, the "full model" in Table 6 using both demographic and economic determinants employed agricultural and nonagricultural income as its economic variables. Both these measures had significant effects in the expected direction only on the singulate mean age at marriage. The coefficients of the remaining variables were little changed from what they had been before the economic variables were added (compare with Table 4). The only shift of note is that the effect of migration on nuptiality was somewhat stronger when the economic variables were taken into account.

Table 6 also presents the results, as Economic Model I, of omitting the fertility and expectation-of-life variables from the regression equation. This increased the coefficients of agricultural income noticeably, but the model as a whole did not perform so well as the demographic model presented in Table 4, if we use the proportion of variance explained as criterion. Lastly, what is termed Economic Model II in Table 6 substituted income per head for the other two economic measures. The coefficients for this income measure were large and significant; the model performed better than Economic Model I but still not as well as the demographic model. The improvement was probably due to the high correlation of income per head and marital fertility, previously noted, so that the coefficients for this income measure may have been reflecting in part the effect of prior fertility. When the demographic variables were included with income per head, the coefficients for this economic measure were no longer significant. (This regression equation is not shown in Table 6.)

Finally, we looked briefly at the effect of including economic variables when migration and household size were the dependent variables. The results are shown in Table 7. For migration during 1831–1846, the addition of "landed income, 1821," had little effect whether or not fertility and expectation of life were included in the model. For migra-

TABLE 7
Standardized Partial Regression Coefficients of Economic and Demographic Determinants of Migration and Household Size: France, Select Years (t-statistics in parentheses)

Independent variables[a]	Dependent variable: migration				
	1831–1846		1856–1881		
Inheritance	-.329	-.170	-.192	-.212	-.172
	(2.99)	(1.43)	(1.95)	(2.07)	(1.77)
SMAM 1831 or 1856	-.211	-.169	-.337	-.266	-.252
	(1.80)	(1.40)	(3.37)	(2.30)	(2.32)
Fertility	--	-.319	--	--	--
		(2.62)			
Expectation of life	--	-.301	--	--	--
		(2.43)			
Landed income, 1821 or 1851	.055	.047	--	.349	.208
	(.48)	(.42)		(3.07)	(1.79)
Non-ag. income 1864	--	--	.405	--	.332
			(4.10)		(3.14)
R^2	.13	.22	.37	.31	.40
N	80	80	74	74	74

	Dependent variable: household size	
	1866	
Inheritance	.082	.064
	(1.08)	(.89)
Fertility (Ig, 1841)	.674	.484
	(7.68)	(4.92)
Expectation of life, 1836–1840	-.035	-.044
	(.41)	(.55)
Migration, 1846–1856	.157	.179
	(1.85)	(2.31)
Income per head, 1864	--	-.462
		(4.66)
Agricultural inc., 1864	-.253	--
	(2.97)	
Non-Ag. income, 1864	-.092	--
	(1.10)	
R^2	.66	.70
N	74	74

[a]For definition of variables, see Table 5 footnotes.

tion during the period 1856–1881, however, both income variables employed had significant effects in the expected direction, higher income being associated with more in-migration or less out-migration.

The income variables also had a significant effect on household size, with higher income associated with lower household size. The coefficient of prior marital fertility was reduced when income per capita was used as the economic variable; this was due to the collinearity previously noted. For both migration and household size, the inferences concerning the role of inheritance remained unchanged with the addition of income to the regression equation.

To summarize, a fair evaluation of the hypothesis that the inheritance provisions of the French Civil Code affected demographic behavior would be the verdict used in French jurisprudence—"not proven." Focusing on nuptiality, Table 4 shows that as of 1806, our baseline, the inheritance code was significantly related to the proportion married, I_m (though not in the direction expected), and the age at first marriage, but not to the proportion *ever* married. In the succeeding years studied, the inheritance code ceased to be related to I_m and generally maintained its significant relation to age at marriage, although with decreasing coefficients. For 1866, inheritance was significantly related to proportion ever married. Thus, at best, there is only weak confirmation of the hypothesis, though mitigating circumstances exist. In particular, it is possible that the weaknesses associated with the baseline year understate the importance of inheritance prior to the Code.

CHANGES IN INHERITANCE PRACTICES AND THE EFFECT OF ALTERNATE MEASURES

Our strategy of analysis has been to keep fixed the inheritance code as it existed in the Old Regime, according to Yver's (1966) classification. We expected to find that, as the departments moved to a uniform set of inheritance practices in keeping with the Civil Code, the baseline relationship between inheritance and nuptiality diminished over time. However, this is not the only kind of change in inheritance practices that would vitiate the initial relationship. Any pattern that makes the Old Regime classification less predictive of demographic behavior would produce the same result. In particular, changes in inheritance practices in directions not countenanced by the Code could also lead to weak relationships unless these changes were incorporated into the classification scheme.

The question of the effect of the Civil Code on inheritance practices is best addressed directly through studies that establish both the law and the actual practices in the Old Regime and the practices in effect after the Civil Code. As discussed in the section on inheritance, description of legal traditions may not reveal the net result of their operation in real life.

A number of studies of inheritance practices in nineteenth century France have been conducted; research into this question continues. The available studies indicate both perseverance and change in inheritance practices, with the direction of change sometimes surprising in light of the Civil Code. In many areas, the new legislation seems to have left its mark from the start. But Bourdieu (1962) shows that primogeniture survived in Béarn at least until World War I, despite the Civil Code. Elsewhere the evolutions were subtle and varied. In Brittany, large-scale adoption of the *bail congéable,* a form of land tenure transmitted to only one son, may have served to override the inflexibility of the inheritance rules and to avoid excessive fragmentation (Benoiston de Chateauneuf & Villermé, 1843, pp. 98–105).

We indicated in an earlier section that Brandt (1901) presented an alternate classification of the inheritance practices of the departments according to the dominant mode of transmission of rural property. Brandt attempted to distinguish those departments where rural property tended to be divided in kind among the heirs from those departments where the landholder attempted to transmit the land to only one heir. In addition, there is a small residual category that Brandt identified as having mixed practice. Brandt's categories did not distinguish partible and impartible areas in the legal sense of Yver's classification; rather, they represent an effort to capture the actual land transfer patterns. Departments in which transfer of land to only one child took place could still be in compliance with the Civil Code, provided suitable payments of money or other property were made to the remaining heirs. Brandt's study is valuable because it showed that even under the Civil Code there could be variation in practice on this important dimension. Brandt's classification shows a number of points of similarity and difference with that of Yver. In general, the areas Brandt denoted as maintaining the land parcels intact or as having mixed practice are the areas in southern France coded 5 on Map 1. The remaining departments, coded 1 to 4 on Map 1, were generally classified by Brandt as dividing the property in kind. (For convenience we will refer to Brandt's category of dividing the property in kind as partible, and undivided transmission as impartible, though the difference in meaning to be attached to these words as against their earlier usage should be kept in mind.) The exceptions are as follows:

1. A number of departments in southern and western France coded 5 in Map 1 (impartible) were coded as partible or mixed by Brandt.

2. Three of the departments in Brittany, coded 1 (partible) in Map 1 were classified as impartible by Brandt.

The departmental differences in points 1 and 2 seem consonant with the inheritance practices noted in the detailed studies cited earlier. It will prove instructive, therefore, to examine the effects of using Brandt's classification on the results obtained. We approached this in two ways: first, we compared the correlations obtained by Berkner and Mendels (forthcoming) using Brandt's classification, with those based on Yver (1966), and we tried to account for the differences; second, we substituted Brandt's classification in place of Yver's in our basic multiple regression model and compared the differences.

Berkner and Mendels (forthcoming) have made use of Brandt's classification together with data on farm fragmentation and migration by Goreux (1956), data on household complexity by Parish and Schwartz (1972) and the nuptiality and fertility data used here, to study the association between inheritance practices and demographic characteristics. Their correlations appear in the first column of Table 8. Column 2 presents the correlations based on Yver's scale values as shown with Map 1. The two sets of correlations differ sharply. The correlations in column 1 appear to confirm the hypotheses set forth earlier in this chapter. Impartibility based on Brandt's classification was associated with lower nuptiality, higher rates of out-migration, and greater household complexity. (It was also associated with higher marital fertility but the question of the relation of inheritance to fertility has not been a focus of this chapter.) On the other hand, the correlations based on Yver's classification (column 2) were of small magnitude and sometimes in a direction contrary to that hypothesized.

In column 3 we present the results obtained by a simple adjustment of Yver's scale to bring it into closer conformity with Brandt's. We were interested in isolating the chief factor that accounted for the different implications about the relation of inheritance to demographic behavior reached by using each classification system. In column 3, the seven departments coded 1 in Map 1 have been given a scale value of 4, and the correlations have been recomputed with this new scale. This rough adjustment tends to capture some of the differences between Yver and Brandt noted previously. The seven departments coded 1 by Yver are the five departments of Brittany and two proximate departments to the south (Vendée and Deux-Sèvres). The thrust of the adjustment then is to reclassify Brittany from partible to impartible. (In so doing, we have gone beyond Brandt, who classified only three of the departments in Brittany as impartible.) The results of the adjustment are quite striking, as the correlations in column 3 are now very similar to those in column 1 and sharply different from those in column 2, with the exception of migration. The correspondence is all the more striking when it is noted that different numbers of departments were used in the correlations of column 1 versus columns 2 and 3, and that some of the demographic characteristics were measured quite differently.

This analysis dramatically demonstrates that the results of ecological correlations, based as they often are on a small number of units, can be highly sensitive to changes in values of a few cases. In Table 8, the reclassification of the seven departments sharply alters the inferences, on the zero-order level at least, that one would make about the relation of inheritance to demographic behavior. The magnitude of the shift is

TABLE 8
Correlation between Inheritance Pattern and Demographic Characteristics According to Method of Classification of Départements

Correlation between inheritance and	Brandt Dichotomy (1)[a]	Yver Scale (2)[b]	Adjusted Yver scale (3)[c]
Index of nuptiality (Im) 1856	-.32	.05	-.24
Index of marital fertility (Ig) 1856	.37	.04	.37
Migration[d] 1856-1881; 1866-1886	-.41	-.19	-.25
Household complexity[e]	.57 .46	.11	.41
N	67	76	76

[a]Column 1:   Based on Brandt classification with partible areas coded 0 and impartible and mixed départements coded 1 (Berkner and Mendels, forthcoming).

[b]Column 2:   Based on Yver's 5 point classification shown with Map 1.

[c]Column 3:   Original Yver Scale   Adjusted Yver Scale
                       1   =   4
                       2   =   2
                       3   =   3
                       4   =   4
                       5   =   5

[d]For correlations with Brandt dichotomy, migration rates were those for 1866-1886 by Goreux (1956), used by Berkner and Mendels (forthcoming). For the other correlations, the migration rates 1856-1881 developed in this paper were used.

[e]For correlation with Brandt dichotomy, the top figure is adults per household and the second figure is marital units per household, 1856, developed by Parish and Schwartz (1972), used by Berkner and Mendels (forthcoming). For the other correlations, average household size (i.e., population per household) in 1866 was used.

due in large part to the rather distinctive demographic profile of Brittany, as shown in Tables 2 and 3. Keeping in mind that the departments coded 1 represent Brittany and two nearby areas, note first that Brittany's marital fertility was consistently far in excess of the other regions and that, over time, its level of nuptiality became substantially lower than the rest of France. In 1806, one or another of the categories was as low as or lower than Brittany on each measure of nuptiality, but by 1831, Brittany's distinctive nuptiality became clear and the differences widened with time: Brittany's average age at marriage increased while that of the other areas was decreasing; the proportion married and the index of nuptiality remained constant there while they tended upward in other areas. Brittany was also distinctive in the average size of its household, due in part, no doubt, to its high level of marital fertility. Only in migration was its demographic behavior well in accord with that occurring in other departments. The details provided in Tables 2 and 3 help make clear the reason for the sharp differences that result according to whether Brittany is classified as partible or impartible.

Although there is some doubt about the extent to which the old custom of Brittany tolerated—or even encouraged—undivided transmission to one heir, here we interpret the discrepancy between Yver and Brandt as the outcome of the evolution of inheritance practices during the first part of the nineteenth century. Though we are handicapped by the lack of earlier data, we hypothesize that under its egalitarian inheritance provisions Brittany's high level of marital fertility led to excessive fragmentation of holdings. The continuation of high fertility, under these circumstances, acted to restrict nuptiality and eventually led to the wider adoption of land-use arrangements that would minimize further fragmentation and constrain the opportunities for marriage.

We turn now to our second approach for gauging the effect of the difference in inheritance measures. Here we have substituted the Brandt scale in our basic model given in Figure 2 and Table 4, and compared the two multiple regression results for 1856. The following table shows key zero-order correlations entering into the regressions:

Selected Correlations Entering into Regressions

	Brandt scale versus	Yver scale versus
Index of nuptiality, 1856	−.19	.05
SMAM, 1856	.14	−.19
Percentage ever married, 1806–1810 cohort	−.37	−.02
Expectation of life (1826–1830)	.11	.08
I_g (1831)	.27	−.06

TABLE 9

Standardized Partial Regression Coefficients of Inheritance Code and Demographic Determinants of Nuptiality: France, 1856 Showing Effect of Alternate Measures of Inheritance Pattern[a] (N = 76)

	Inheritance pattern	
Independent Variable	Yver scale (1)	Brandt scale (2)

Dependent variable: index of nuptiality, Im

Inheritance	.02	.11*
Exp. of life, 1826-1830	-.36*	-.38*
Ig, 1831	-.94*	-.98*
R^2	.80	.81

Dependent variable: singulate mean age at marriage, SMAM

Inheritance	-.16*	-.14*
Exp. of life, 1826-1830	.34*	.36*
Ig, 1831	.85*	.91*
R^2	.69	.68

Dependent variable: proportion ever married, 1806-1810 cohort

Inheritance	-.02	-.12
Exp. of life, 1826-1830	-.53*	-.51*
Ig, 1831	-.80*	-.76*
R^2	.65	.66

*$|t| \geq 1.95$

[a]Definitions of inheritance patterns:
  (1) Regression uses full Yver scale. See Map 1 for definition.
  (2) Regression uses full Brandt scale: 1 = partible; 2 = mixed; 3 = impartible.

The two sets of correlations are quite different, as we would expect from Table 8.[10] The partial regression coefficients resulting from the use of the Brandt scale, however, are very close to those obtained from the Yver regressions, as Table 9 indicates. The main factor operating to produce the similarity in effects is the stronger correlation between Brandt's classification and the measure of marital fertility, which in turn is highly correlated with nuptiality. Thus, the inferences one would draw about the effect of inheritance on nuptiality, based on the

[10] The correlations given in the first column of the text table differ from those given in the first column of Table 8 for the following reasons: Table 8 uses a smaller number of more rural departments; it dichotomizes Brandt's three-point scale; and the dates of some of the covariants are different.

multiple regressions, are quite similar for each of the measures, at least for 1856. Though it would be of interest to repeat the analysis for other years using Brandt's classification, it is not clear how much earlier than midcentury the practices delineated by him can be assumed to hold.

The important methodological point arising from the comparison is that without a model that specifies the key interrelationships, one can be highly misled about the role of inheritance in nuptiality. Inferences based on zero-order correlations alone assume either that no other variable is affecting nuptiality or that the effects of other determinants are independent of the effect of inheritance. This is not likely to be the case. Of course, nothing in our results confirms the particular model utilized and further research into the process will undoubtedly lead to improved specifications.

SUMMARY AND CONCLUSIONS

The central question motivating this chapter has been whether the inheritance provisions of the French Civil Code of 1804 had subsequent effects on nuptiality in France. Our major analysis involved two assumptions:

1. That the original inheritance practices for the time and place studied did have consequences for nuptiality.
2. That the enactment of the Code did narrow the range of inheritance patterns observed in France.

On the basis of these assumptions, we reasoned that the relationship between inheritance and nuptiality based on the pre–Civil Code classification of inheritance laws should diminish with time after 1804 as the new set of practices became more uniformly adopted. Our tests of this hypothesis were inconclusive; but in general, the hypothesis does not appear to be supported by the data. For our baseline year 1806, the relationships between inheritance and the various measures of nuptiality were not clear-cut. Only with age at marriage was there a significant effect in the expected direction, and this effect was generally maintained at successive time-points with only slight diminution. Adding to the ambiguity is the possibility that limitations of data and the unsettled conditions of the period may have affected the observed inheritance–nuptiality relationship in 1806.

We noted instances where practices contrary to the spirit, if not the letter, of the Code were maintained or even augmented in the nineteenth century. To the extent that the provisions of the Civil Code were evaded, one would not expect them to have an effect on nuptiality. However, one must guard against facile extrapolation from these instances to an assumption of widespread evasion, for there is evidence through petitions seeking relief and adjustments in the Code itself that there was enforcement and compliance as well (Brandt, 1901, p. vii). Clearly, more complete documentation is needed to ascertain the extent and nature of the adoption of the inheritance provisions of the Code.

Our analyses tend to support the assumption that inheritance practices had some demographic consequences—at least on age at marriage, and perhaps, in certain periods, on migration. However, the case of Brittany reminds us that this is not necessarily a simple cause-and-effect relationship. There, the continuation of high marital fertility may have led to the adoption of a land-use system at sharp variance with the earlier egalitarian practice. Thus, as noted by Berkner and Mendels, we must view the inheritance system "not only as a cause but also as a result of demographic change [1972, p. 4]."

Thus, we emerge with the somewhat paradoxical conclusion that, though the Civil Code as a body of law had little discernible effect on nuptiality during the period studied, previous inheritance customs and practices did continue to exert an influence on a number of demographic characteristics.[11] This may be because the effects of the Code were not particularly dramatic. In areas in which property was divided prior to the Civil Code, this process could, of course, continue—unless fragmentation had gone so far, as in Brittany, that adaptations were made. In formerly impartible areas, land could still be passed on undivided under the Code, provided that adequate compensation was given to the other heirs. In addition, the provision of the Code enabling the father to dispose of a share freely still allowed one heir to be favored.

Comparison of Yver's legal classification with Brandt's survey of property transmission shows, with the exceptions previously noted, generally high concordance in that the formerly partible departments were to a large extent the areas where division was made in kind (i.e., division of land took place); the formerly impartible areas generally were the departments where an attempt was made to transmit the holdings to one child. Aiding the process was the fact that local tribunals played a large role in enforcing and interpreting the Code, and presumably they were guided in part by the customs with which they were familiar.

---

[11] It is possible that the Civil Code did have more of an effect on demographic characteristics other than those tested here—for example, marital fertility. This is not amenable to investigation with the models specified here, which treat both inheritance customs and marital fertility as exogenous determinants, among others, of nuptiality.

We have attempted throughout this study to stress the complexities involved in studying the relationship of inheritance to demographic behavior. In the first place, we have called attention to the variations that exist among the ideal types of partible and impartible; secondly, we have noted the important distinction between law and custom on one hand and practice on the other. In addition, we have shown the necessity of placing both inheritance practices and demographic behavior within the context of a broader social–economic system, by pointing out the many variables that can impinge on their interrelation. We do not claim to have developed a fully adequate model of the pertinent variables, and limitations of data have prevented us from taking into account many of those of which we are aware. Nevertheless, the models we have tested do indicate the importance of prior demographic conditions, since both earlier marital fertility and expectation of life generally had strong effects on nuptiality and the other dependent variables. We have interpreted these prior variables as capturing the pressure on community and family resources needed for marriage. Economic characteristics were also important in a number of instances, but at least those available to us seemed of secondary importance to the demographic setting.

This analysis also raises a number of methodological points. Hypotheses relating inheritance and nuptiality need to specify the dimensions of nuptiality at issue. We have found, for example, that impartibility can be associated both with earlier age at marriage and lower proportions ever married. The use of an overall index of nuptiality affected by both dimensions may thus be a poor operational definition for this type of study. Another methodological difficulty is apparent from the high degree of clustering of inheritance patterns by region shown in Map 1. Insofar as the inheritance code delineates quite distinct regions of France, it will be difficult to dissociate from the effect of inheritance any regional effects not captured by the independent variables utilized.

For the period under study, inheritance and nuptiality are two important foci of the social fabric. As Berkner and Mendels note in summing up the views of many who studied this period, "The basic peasant goals are to maintain the family property intact while providing for one's old age [forthcoming]."[12] Counterposed to these goals are the desires of young adults to marry and to gain access to sufficient resources for this purpose. The mutual adjustment of these goals is mediated only in part

---

[12] See, however, Richards (1976), who holds that insufficient attention has been given to the desire to avoid jealousy among heirs and to provide for the needs of all family members.

by the inheritance system. "The inheritance system sets limits, creates problems and opportunities and evokes certain types of behavior which conform to it or avoid its consequences. Inheritance laws and customs are things that the peasant must deal with in planning a strategy which will reach his goals; they do not determine the goals or the strategy [Berkner & Mendels, 1976, p. 13]." In the analysis presented here we claim only little headway against this complex and dynamic system, but the matter seems worthy of further pursuit in its potential for illuminating the intersection of demographic behavior with legal, social, and economic forces.

REFERENCES

Benoiston de Chateauneuf, L. F., & Villermé, L. R. (1843). "Rapport d'un voyage fait dans les cinq départements de la Bretagne," *Mémoires de l'Académie des sciences morales et politiques*. Vol. 4, 98–105.

Berkner, Lutz K., & Mendels, Franklin F. (1972). "Legal Variables, Family Structure, and Fertility in Western Europe," Mimeographed. Prepared for presentation at the Seminar on Early Industrialization, Fertility, and Family, Institute for Advanced Study, Princeton University.

Berkner, Lutz K., & Mendels, Franklin F. (forthcoming). "Inheritance Systems, Family Structure and Demographic Patterns in Western Europe (1700–1900)," in Charles Tilly, ed., *Historical Studies of Changing Fertility*. Princeton, N.J.: Princeton University Press.

Blalock, H. M., Jr. (1967). "Path Coefficients versus Regression Coefficients," *American Journal of Sociology*, Vol. 72, No. 6, pp. 675–676.

Bloch, Marc (1952). *Les Caractères originaux de l'histoire rurale française*. Paris: A. Colin.

Bourdieu, Pierre (1962). "Célibat et condition paysanne," *Etudes rurales*, Vol. 5–6, pp. 32–135.

Brandt, Alexandre de (1901). *Droit et coutumes des populations rurales de la France en matière successorale*. Paris: Librairie de la Société du Recueil générale des lois et arrêts.

Chasteland, Jean-Claude, & Pressat, Roland (1962). "La nuptialité des générations françaises depuis un siècle," *Population*, Vol. 17, pp. 215–240.

Coale, Ansley J. (1969). "The Decline of Fertility in Europe from the French Revolution to World War II," in Samuel J. Behrman, Leslie Corsa, & Ronald Freedman, eds., *Fertility and Family Planning: A World View*. Ann Arbor: University of Michigan Press.

Coale, Ansley J. (1971). "Age Patterns of Marriage," *Population Studies*, Vol. 25, pp. 193–214.

Delefortrie, Nicole, & Morice, Janine (1959). *Les revenus départementaux en 1864 et 1954*. Paris: Armand Colin.

Giesey, Ralph E. (1975). "National Stability and the Hereditary Transmission of Political and Economic Power." Paper presented at the Fourteenth International Congress of Historical Sciences, August 1975, San Francisco.

Goreux, L. M. (1956). "Les migrations agricoles en France depuis un siècle et leur relation avec certains facteurs économiques," *Etudes et Conjoncture*, Vol. 11, pp. 327–376.

Habakkuk, H. J. (1955). "Family Structure and Economic Change in Nineteenth Century Europe," *Journal of Economic History*, Vol. 15, pp. 1–12.

Lesthaeghe, Ronie, & van de Walle, Etienne (1976). "Economic Factors and Fertility Decline in France and Belgium," in Ansley J. Coale, ed., *Economic Factors in Population Growth*. London: Macmillan.

Malthus, Thomas (1951). *Principles of Political Economy*. 2nd ed. New York: Augustus M. Kelley.

Meyer, Jean (1972). *La noblesse bretonne*. Paris: Flammarion.

Parish, William L., & Schwartz, Moshe (1972). "Household Complexity in Nineteenth Century France," *American Sociological Review*, Vol. 37, pp. 154–173.

Richards, Edward W. (1976). "The Stem-Family Model of Inheritance Strategy in Modern French History and Historiography." Paper presented at the Twenty-second Annual Meeting of the Society for French Historical Studies, April 1976, Rochester, N.Y.

Schoenberg, Ronald (1972). "Strategies for Meaningful Comparison," in Herbert Costner, ed., *Sociological Methodology*. San Francisco: Jossey-Bass.

Spengler, Joseph J. (1938). *France Faces Depopulation*. Durham, N.C.: Duke University Press.

van de Walle, Etienne (1968). "Marriage and Marital Fertility," *Daedalus*, Vol. 97 (Spring), pp. 486–501.

van de Walle, Etienne (1974). *The Female Population of France in the 19th Century*. Princeton, N.J.: Princeton University Press.

Worms, René (1917). *Natalité et regime successoral*. Paris: Payot.

Yver, Jean (1966). *Egalité entre héritiers et exclusion des enfants dotés—Essai de géographie coutumière*. Paris: Sirey.

Primonuptiality and Ultimonuptiality: Their Effects on Stem-Family-Household Frequencies*

E. A. HAMMEL

University of California, Berkeley

KENNETH W. WACHTER

Harvard University

A central problem of historical demography, and indeed of sociologically sensitive demography in general, is the way systems of cultural rules and sets of demographic rates influence one another to produce the observational detritus that goes by the name of census. It is this empirical residue, like the fossilized bones of a once-fleshy beast, that the historian confronts and from which he must seek to infer the meatier ôutlines of reality. The problem, of course, is but a special case of the general—the interaction of ideology, environmental constraint, and behavior.

A typical example of the historical demographic problem is the interplay of cultural rules and demographic rates in the production of stem-family households—households in which there are two (or more) conjugal units, each of which stands only in a genealogically lineal relationship to every other.[1] A household containing two married couples, one

---

* This chapter was originally prepared for the conference, "Behavioral Models in Historical Demography," held in Philadelphia, 24–26 October 1974, under the sponsorship of the Mathematical Social Sciences Board.

[1] Actually, we use a slightly less restrictive definition in this analysis so as not to truncate unfairly the frequency counts that might be reached by other systems of definition. See the later text.

parental and the other a married child and spouse, would qualify as a stem-family household; with the addition of a married grandchild, the household would still remain a stem-family household. Such households are often thought to have been extremely important in the social life of European peasants. Indeed, the symbolic evidence for their presence, in testaments, in literature, in the normative statements of peasants and of admiring scholars themselves reared in smaller households, would lead one to expect their near-universality. On the other hand, the empirical evidence for their presence in many censuses (particularly those of Britain) is often very weak.

In an earlier paper, we and our associates (Hammel, Hutchinson, Laslett, & Wachter, 1974) reviewed the historical and demographic evidence to see whether particular demographic regimes might not be responsible for the disparity between cultural expectation and observed behavioral reality. The existence of stem-family households is in part a function of the temporal overlap of the married lives of parents and children. If life expectancy is low and age at marriage late, this overlap will be smaller than if life expectancy is high or age at marriage is early. We used demographic rates thought broadly representative of those prevailing in southern rural England around 1700. We also employed a system of cultural rules designed to maximize the occurrence of stem-family households, carrying the suggestions from the literary evidence to their logical extreme. We found that the observed proportion of stem-family households in real English historical populations before 1800 was very much smaller than that one might expect under such rates and with such a system of cultural rules. Therefore, we concluded that either (1) the system of cultural rules cannot have been as strongly favorable to stem-family-household formation as the maximal system postulated, or (2) there were some as yet unknown impediments to the realization of the expected proportions. That research continues. In addition to the investigation of how a particular, historically appropriate set of demographic rates interacts with a particular system of cultural rules, work is underway on the effects of systematic variation in demographic rates (Wachter, forthcoming). This chapter deals with yet another facet of the investigation: the effects of different systems of cultural rules, in combination with the same set of demographic rates, on the formation of stem-family households.

The tool for this (and similar) investigations is computer microsimulation. A population of notional individuals is established (consisting of course of a series of electronic records in a computer), and the individuals of this population "experience" demographic events in a stochastic way, that is, according to the principles of random selection.

The occurrence of demographic events is governed by sets of rates fed to the computer and by the use of random numbers, so that although events occur randomly to individuals they do so at rates appropriate to certain categories of persons (for example, categories of age and sex) and in such a way that the ultimate actual rates of occurrences come as close as possible to the input governing rates. The occurrence of sociological events, where these are not preempted by the governing vital rates, are mechanistically determined by invariant rules. Thus, for example, marriages are governed by the vital rates in a stochastic process, but postmarital residence is governed by invariant logical rules.

The kinds of demographic events occurring in the simulations are birth of a child, marriage, and death. Birth rates are monthly age-specific rates by age of mother. Marriage rates are also monthly age-specific; the occurrence of a marriage is governed by the age of the woman, but the marriage cannot take place unless a male of suitable age is found. The suitability of males, by age, is relative to the age of the female and is also specified as a parameter. Death rates are monthly age- and sex-specific. The birth rates are marital-status-specific, as are marriage rates (remarriage is possible), but death rates are not marital-status-specific. An option for parity-specific birth rates was available but was not used; similarly, an option for polygyny was available but was not used. In its purely demographic aspects, the microsimulation program can be tested against predictions from mathematical population theory. In tests for bias in which stationarity was specified in the rates, and for 100 independent runs for 250 years with a starting population of 500 persons, the actual mean person-years lived was within 1% of the calculated expected value.[2] The cultural rules for household formation cannot be tested in such a way, but we will spell them out later so that they can be examined in detail.

The notional population established for a simulation can be an artificial one, constructed on the basis of the age and sex distribution appropriate to a model life table of particular specifications. It can also be constructed out of an actual historical population on the basis of census records. Of course, if it is constructed out of a historical popula-

[2] Full details will be found in Hammel, Hutchinson, Wachter, Lundy, and Deuel, *SOCSIM: A Demographic–Sociological Microsimulation Program* (1976). The SOCSIM program was originally based on POPSIM (closed model), developed by D. G. Horvitz and associates. The major programming was done by Hutchinson with the assistance of Lundy and Deuel, under the supervision of Hammel and Wachter. The program employed in this analysis does not include divorce or migration. Arguments concerning the irrelevance of migration for the problem at hand are found in Hammel *et al.* (1974).

tion, it very rapidly ceases to be one (indeed it does so at the first occurrence of a demographic event), for the exact events occurring in a demographic simulation are not the exact events occurring to a population that existed in the past. They are only statistically similar, and then only in the long run and on the average. The demographic rates selected for a simulation are specified either according to the demographic problem being investigated—that is, on theoretical grounds—or in a way that approximates rates thought to prevail in some historical population.

It needs to be stressed very much that the results of a microsimulation are like experimental results in a laboratory.[3] When physicists bombard nuclei they are not replicating the universe but only simulating parts of it in an artificial set of circumstances. From their experimental results they not only generalize in a logical sense but also extend to sets of conditions thought—perhaps only hoped—to be similar. If it were not for this, Newtonian mechanics would still be restricted to the billiard table, or even to that scholar's orchard. Because the processes under investigation are so complicated and subject to random fluctuation, an experiment (simulation) must be repeated many times to determine both its central tendency of result and the variation between the results of individual experiments. The more experiments performed (under conditions as nearly identical as possible but nevertheless statistically independent), the more stable are the estimates of the true values of central tendency and of variation.

This notion of replication to achieve a stable estimate has equally important implications for the interpretation of historical data. A given historical observation, let us say a single household census list from a single community at a point in time, is but one observation out of many theoretically possible for the class of communities of which the one is thought representative. In the absence of some notion of expectable variability, acceptance of the single observation as actually typical of the class of communities could be quite misleading. Historians or ethnographers seldom have many such observations, and the reliability of their generalizations is consequently less than it might be if they had more. Thus, to compare the results of a large series of simulation runs with a very few historical instances may well be to make the wrong kind of comparison, for in the sense of experimental reliability the results of the simulation runs are more dependable than the direct historical

---

[3] Similar arguments on the nature of microsimulation as experiment are found in Hammel *et al*. (1974). See also Dyke and MacCluer (1973), Johnston and Albers (1973), and MacCluer (1973).

evidence. This rather bizarre proposition must of course be taken with proper qualification, namely that the simulations are a better guide to reality if and only if reality is governed by the conditions of the experiments.

Put in another way, the result of a large series of simulations is a more reliable way of estimating the nature of interaction between specified variables than is observed historical reality when the values of those variables for the historical situation can often only be inferred. In the case at hand, one can specify a particular demographic regime and a particular set of cultural preferences about postmarital residence, and go on to ask what the results of the interaction of rates and rules are. In the historical situation, although the actual census counts give a very clear picture of household composition, one cannot be certain that the picture is at all representative of a type of community, and one can know only with great difficulty what the demographic rates and cultural rules were. Computer microsimulation cannot help the historian find out what household composition was like at a particular time and place, but it can help him to evaluate his inferences about the conditions he assumes led to the empirical conditions he observes. It can also help him appreciate the amount of purely random variation he might expect under relatively constant demographic and social conditions.

What follows then, is an exploration of a theoretical problem—what is the effect of a change in sociological rules, under a single demographic regime, on household composition? We are of course aware that the effect of the rule changes may differ depending on the particular demographic regime and that this chapter is only a partial exploration of the problem.

For purposes of comparison with earlier work, the demographic regime selected here is one thought broadly appropriate to southern England in the period about 1600–1700, for medium-sized rural communities. We pick these rates not to replicate the particular conditions of Pifflewimple-by-the-Fen because it is quite unlikely that we shall ever know enough about the demographic rates at any Pifflewimple to reproduce them accurately. We have taken ballpark estimates for birth and death rates and have done some ad hoc adjustment for the marriage rates. The monthly birth rates are given in Table 1, for six age ranges, separately for married and unmarried women. The marital fertility rates are based on a family reconstitution of Aldenham for 1600–1649 by the Cambridge Group for the History of Population and Social Structure; the illegitimate rates are guesses.

The input marriage rates and the observed proportions in the experiment are shown in Table 2A. The rates are monthly probabilities of

TABLE 1
Monthly Birth Rates

Marital status	Age						
	17-19	20-24	25-29	30-34	35-39	40-44	>44
Married	.036500	.033200	.02600	.026100	.019000	.009200	.000055
Unmarried	.001011	.000671	.000521	.000522	.000381	.000181	.000005

marriage for women for seven age ranges, separately for single and widowed persons. These rates are not themselves based directly on estimates from historical data, since family reconstitution, yielding no measure of person-months lived at risk of marriage, gives no estimates of marriage probabilities. Instead, the rates are chosen with the aim of producing observed proportions of ages at first marriage (Table 2B) to match proportions from historical data, in this case data from the village of Aldenham for 1600–1649 from the files of the Cambridge Group for the History of Population and Social Structure. In a separate investigation, simulation has been used to identify a set of marriage rates that, given the death rates, would generate the desired distribution of ages at marriage. The solution is not unique. Several different sets of rates could yield the same distribution of ages. But for the household experiments, the distribution of ages at first marriage and not the marriage rates are the critical parameters, since the age at marriage and the temporal overlap of the married lives of parents and children are the demographic features that impinge upon stem-family household prevalence. Thus our roundabout definition of marriage probabilities is well suited to our purposes.

The death rates are taken from Sully Ledermann (1969) Reseau 103, Q = 350, adjusted so that the monthly death rates for males and females in the first month of life are .105226 and .092222, respectively, and in the next 11 months are .010057 and .008757, respectively. The expectation of life at birth under these rates is 38.212 for males and 40.15 for females. The rates are appropriate to those observed for individuals aged 0–15 for Colyton in the 1600s, in a general way.

The input population used in this experiment is drawn from an actual historical listing, that of the parish of Ealing, near London, in 1599. This listing is the earliest available for England giving households and ages, although the age distribution is badly bunched and challengeable. We used it for conceptual convenience and general historical relevance, and also because the idea of a completely artificial population is sometimes difficult to explain. On the other hand, we have found that using an actual historical listing puts us out of the frying pan and into the fire, because we must then justify why the "real" input population no longer looks "just like Ealing" after a few years of simulation. We repeat that there is no intent to replicate an actual historical population but rather to investigate the processes that affected it.

The input population undergoes simulation, under the rates and rules specified, for a period of 150 years; it is this simulation of 150 years that is the basis of the experiment. The 150-year simulation, based on the same initial population, is carried out 100 times, each time

TABLE 2A
Monthly Marriage Rates for Women.

Marital status	Age								
	15-17	18-19	20-24	25-29	30-34	35-39	40-44	45-49	>49
Single	.001500	.003300	.009900	.008300	.004500	.003200	.003800	.000900	0.
Widowed	.002400	.005200	.015000	.008300	.002200	.001600	.001600	.000900	0.

TABLE 2B
Proportions of Women's First Marriages by Age Group

Marital status	Age					
	15-19	20-24	25-29	30-34	35-39	>39
Primonuptial	.156	.472	.220	.074	.039	.035
Ultimonuptial	.156	.465	.249	.079	.042	.039

using an independent series of random numbers in the stochastic process, so that the 100 different simulations are statistically independent. The 100 simulations constitute a statistical sample we can examine in the usual way to estimate means, ranges, and variances for the usual measures of demographic process. The means should of course come reasonably close to the input rates, but the ranges and variances are totally new information difficult or impossible to obtain except by simulation.

Table 3 gives the estimates of these measures for the 100 terminal populations of the experiment. It does so *twice,* for this experiment consisted of two simulation samples, each under a different set of cultural rules about postmarital residence. There are some differences between these two samples as far as the achieved demographic rates are concerned, differences to which we will address ourselves briefly later. Our intent is to examine the effects of two different sociological rule systems on household formation, whether these effects are direct or are mediated by demographic shifts themselves caused by alteration of the sociological rules.

Up to this point we have not clarified what is meant by a set of sociological or cultural rules. Some of the procedures in the simulation have a cultural or sociological component but are treated in the context of the demographic simulation itself, that is, stochastically. The monthly probabilities of marriage for women of different ages and different marital statuses of course have a sociological component. The suitability of males as spouses for females of particular ages is also a sociological matter but treated within the demographic simulation routines. The limits established for this experiment were quite broad, with an age difference in either direction allowable up to 20 years, but a desired mean of husband aged 2 years older than the wife.

Other sociological rules in the simulation are not treated stochastically but as invariant decision rules dependent on particular observed conditions. These rules are not intended to replicate the true pattern of preferences that the actors in a society might have in their minds. It would be just as dangerous for us to do this in microsimulation as it is for historians or ethnographers to do it after a scanning of their observations of actual household composition. Our rules are much more like the ethnographer's description of what people actually do decide under defined circumstances.

Of course, people do not always make just the same decisions under identical circumstances, so that our rules share the defect of determinism with the kinds of generalizations usually drawn by ethnographers and historians. Further, we ought to note that historians and

TABLE 3
Demographic Results of 100 Simulations

	Primonuptial				Ultimonuptial			
	Mean	SD	Minimum	Maximum	Mean	SD	Minimum	Maximum
Total population	698.01	126.5	413	1025	750.88	117.5	482	1159
Crude birth rate	.02786	.00105	.02550	.03006	.02829	.000891	.02625	.03065
Crude death rate	.02471	.00053	.02356	.02627	.02467	.000534	.02305	.02594
Crude growth rate	.00315	--	.00023	.00581	.00361	--	.00075	.00667
Male mean age at death	34.70	1.26	32.47	37.70	34.26	1.17	30.85	37.13
Female mean age at death	36.46	1.21	33.48	39.04	36.03	.97	33.84	37.63
Number of households	116.47	20.30	77	155	161.43	24.12	107	242
Women's mean age at first marriage	24.8	.31	24.0	25.6	24.9	.24	24.3	25.6
Age of husband minus age of wife in years	5.26	.65	3.72	6.71	4.86	.70	2.88	6.46

ethnographers seldom really observe people making decisions, or if they do, they have very few instances from which to generalize. What they usually observe are the results of decision-making processes that are themselves unobserved, and what they offer as rules of decision making are logical statements that would result in a distribution of results very much like the one observed, if they had indeed been used by the actors in a society. Such sets of rules may or may not be a unique solution to the generation of the desired distribution. Our rules in this simulation share all these defects. They have the virtue, however, of being quite specific—specific enough to be challengeable point by point, inasmuch as one cannot execute a fuzzy statement on a computer.

We use two sets of rules affecting residence in households. The first of these is designed to maximize the occurrence of stem-family households. The key to such maximization lies in the mechanisms of inheritance of the headship of households, so that some lineal descendant under the head is a presumptive heir, retains that position of presumptive heir regardless of the vagaries of demographic events, and has enhanced probabilities for reestablishment of the stem should it need to be repaired after a death. For these reasons, sons and daughters are both privileged to inherit, whether they are the children of the head or the head's stepchildren. (This provision would ensure an heir even if a household were without a child of the privileged sex in a unisexual inheritance system. There are some residual exceptions to this in the experiment, but they are not important.) The presumptive heir to headship is designated on his or her marriage and is the first child to marry. In this, the rule system differs from the ordinary primogenitural system, in which the firstborn child is the designated heir. It is, thus, primonuptial. We take this option in order to avoid situations in which, because of the stochastic nature of the simulation, the firstborn child might not be the first to marry and the overlap of the married lives of parent and child might not be fully maximized. Of course, we could have written (programmed) rules according to which the firstborn child had to be the first to marry, or, if that child were to die before marriage, the oldest surviving child had to be the first to marry. Such a rule system might seriously affect the demographic routines themselves, and we have not elected it, leaving that problem for later investigation.

The rules of postmarital residence permit only one married child (or grandchild) in each generation to co-reside with the head, whether the head is married or widowed. Others who marry must leave to found new households or to join their spouse in the spouse's natal household, if the spouse is permitted to remain in that household. While the head of the household lives, the married co-residing child (or grandchild, if the household lacks surviving intermediate parents) is the presumptive heir. If the presumptive heir is widowed, his or her status as presumptive heir is retained even if no children have been born to the marriage, and he or she is eligible for remarriage at the prevailing age-specific rates. In this way, the stem can be repaired and continued. If the head of a household is widowed but not superannuated, the probability of marriage is enhanced. This provision for rapid remarriage of the head is ethnographically sensible and operationally important, for it allows household formation rules to influence demographic events. We do this rather than simply pass headship on to any existing presumptive heir, because in this way a full stem family is re-created. We shall give these rules in somewhat more detail later in the chapter.

At marriage, a decision must be taken on postmarital residence. If neither the bride nor the groom is head of household and neither is presumptive heir already by virtue of a previous marriage, we ask whether the groom is eligible to become a presumptive heir by virtue of being the child or stepchild of the head of his natal household and also by virtue of the absence of any existing presumptive heir in that household. If he is ineligible for either reason he must leave. We perform the same check for the bride. If both must leave, they found a new household. If only one must leave, that one joins the other in the other's natal household. If neither must leave we move the one in whose natal household there would remain the larger number of potential presumptive heirs (that is, unmarried children or stepchildren or grandchildren of the head), to the household of the one in which fewer of these would remain. If an equal number would remain in both, the woman joins the man. In this way we maximize the actual and potential number of stem-family households.

A presumptive heir may marry only a person who is neither head of a household nor another presumptive heir. In this way, the number of potential stem-family households is increased by their enforced separation; two potential stem-family households cannot merge to form one. Two persons already heads of households may marry, merging their households, but not if both households already contain presumptive heirs. Any person who moves into a household is accompanied by all his or her never-married children, including any illegitimate children of a woman. If a man joins a woman who is already head of household and he is not, he becomes head. When any of these shifts of residence occurs we check to see whether any existing head in the household to which the newly married couple moves is either unmarried, or a widow over 45 or a widower over 60; in each of these cases the newly married male becomes head. We prohibit marriages between siblings or half-siblings and between any co-residents of the same household, for to permit such marriages might prevent other households from achieving stem-family organization by restricting marriages between households. (Considerations of bourgeois morality did not enter into this programming decision.)

At the birth of a child we simply add the child to the household of the mother. At death, we remove the deceased from the household. If the deceased was the head of the household, a new head must be found, and under some circumstances the marriage chances of the new head will be altered by his or her assumption of the headship. Unmarried (single or widowed) males who become head have their eligibility as grooms enhanced; they become the most desirable males in the marriage market. Unmarried (single or widowed) women who become heads have their next demographic event set to marriage; if they are under 15 their search for a groom begins in that year.

If the deceased head had been living alone or with one other person, no elaborate rules are needed, for if there were no survivors the household ceases to exist, and if there was one, he or she becomes head. If there was more than one survivor, the procedure is more complicated. If the deceased head was married, he must have been a male (since married women are not heads), and the headship passes to his wife if she is less than 45. If the deceased head was unmarried or married to a woman older than 45, a more elaborate search for an heir is necessary. The priority of succession follows:

1. An ever married son, stepson, grandson, or stepgrandson, or husband of a daughter or stepdaughter
2. An ever married daughter, stepdaughter, or wife of son or stepson
3. The oldest son or stepson over age 18
4. The deceased head's widow, even if over age 45
5. The oldest daughter or stepdaughter over age 18
6. The oldest male over 18, regardless of kin relationship
7. The oldest female over 18, regardless of kin relationship
8. The oldest male
9. The oldest female

These procedures ensure that an heir will be found. Priority is given to married lineal male descendants or stepdescendants or to married lineal female descendants' husbands or widowers. Then it passes to widowed lineal female descendants or widows of lineal male descendants, then to unmarried adult male lineal descendants, then to the elderly widow, then to any adult female lineal descendant, then to any adult male, to any adult female, to any male, and finally to any female, ordered by age. The procedures maximize the potential for stem-family-household formation, not only for individual households but also for the population.

There is one alternative kind of rule that might increase stem-family-household proportions even more, and that is to restrict marriage to those persons who become presumptive heirs. That is, once one member of a junior generation in a household married and became presumptive heir, all remaining persons could be denied the opportunity to marry. That rule would of course greatly decrease the number of nuclear households in the population and thus increase the proportion of stem-family households. It would, however, wreak such havoc with the marriage rates and thus the birth rates, since the latter are marital-status-specific, that we have not ventured into that variation of the experiment.

The foregoing describes the primonuptial pattern. The second half of the experiment is based on ultimonuptial rules, in which it is the last child to marry, rather than the first, who stays with the parents to form the stem-family household. The rules for the ultimonuptial simulation are exactly the same as those for the primonuptial, except for the following: When a marriage occurs we check both the groom and bride to see if either lives in a household that contains a sibling or half-sibling of any age, or a grandchild of the head or stepgrandchild of the head older than 12, or any ever-married person other than the head, head's spouse, or parent or step-parent of the head. If any one of these is found, a potential heir is assumed to exist. If an heir is found in both households, the bride and groom found a new household. If a potential heir is found in the bride's but not the groom's, she moves to his household. If a potential heir is found in neither household she also moves to his household. If a potential heir is found in his household but not in hers, he joins her.

The rules for classfying households resulting from the simulations are as follows:

1. Nuclear households (NUC) are those containing only one conjugal pair with or without children, or one parent–offspring unit. No other kinsmen outside these pairs are found.
2. Extended households (X) are those including only one of the kinds of pairs noted under NUC but also including one or more persons not a member of one of those pairs or of any other such pair.

3. Multiple households (M) are those containing more than one of the kinds of pairs noted under NUC.
4. Special households (SPEC) are those containing more than one person but no pairs of the kinds noted under NUC.
5. Solitary households (SOL) are those containing only one person.
6. *Other* (O) is a flag to indicate the presence in a household of a person who is unrelated to the head.

Some subtypes are also defined:

2a. Extended lineal households (XLN) are those in which the additional person not a member of a pair is lineally related to the head of the household.
2b. Extended lateral households (XLT) are those in which the additional person not a member of a pair is laterally related to the head of the household.
2c. Extended lateral-down households (XLTD) are those in which the additional person not a member of a pair is both lineally and laterally related to the head of the household, as, for example, a nephew to his uncle the head.
3a. Multiple lineal households (MLN) are those in which the constituent pairs stand only in lineal relationship.
3b. Multiple lateral households (MLT) are those in which the constituent pairs stand only in lateral relationship.
3c. Multiple lateral-down households (MLTD) are those in which the constituent pairs stand simultaneously in lineal and lateral relationship, as, for example, a married nephew to his uncle the head. MLTD does not mean the conjugal unit of the head plus a conjugal unit of a lateral relative plus the conjugal unit of a lineal relative (see the following text).

Many of these types can occur in combination. NUC can be combined with Other, as can SPEC. SOL of course cannot be combined. X and M households can occur in varying combinations. For example, a household could be MLN, XLN, and MLT simultaneously if it consisted of a widowed parent plus two married sons, and a married grandson. It would be MLN because of the lineal link between the grandson and his parent, lateral because of the link between the two brothers, multiple because of the presence of more than one conjugal unit, and extended lineal because of the presence of the widowed parent. The possibility of multiple classification makes the counting of households cumbersome, because some types of combinations are unique or extremely rare. Here we will not count the households themselves but rather the principles that go into their formation. The household just described would therefore be counted three times, once for each type of principle (MLN, XLN, and MLT). Very little inflation of the count is involved, about 11% in the primonuptial runs and about 3% in the ultimonuptial runs. Table 4 gives the distribution of households for the primonuptial and the ultimonuptial simulations, by type of organizational principle. For easier comparison it is also summarized by giving the total of all extended households, of all multiple households, and the sum of all occurrences of XLN, MLN, and MLTD, since these could all be construed as stem-family households.

The first question to be settled on looking at Table 4 is how there could occur any households demonstrating a principle of MLT or MLTD when the organizational rules for postmarital residence disallow the co-residence of married siblings. These households all result from the occasional presence of sisters or nieces (or perhaps sometimes aunts) of the head who have one or more illegitimate children and thus form a parent–child pair, which is counted as a conjugal remnant by the classification program. The second question is how there could occur any persons unrelated to heads of households, thus producing the appearance of the organizational principle, Other. These households all result from the truncation to Other of occasionally overflowed alphanumeric strings describing very complex kinship relationships. They are thus artifacts of the kinship–algebraic routines in the program and should be ignored.

The outstanding result of the experiment, visible in Table 4, is the dramatic decrease in the proportions of complex household forms produced by the relatively minor shift from primonuptial rules to ultimonuptial rules. Proportions of stem-family households drop from 46 to 21%. The proportion of multiple households is cut by three-fifths. The proportion of extended households is cut by a third. The proportion of multiple lineal (MLN) households, which contain at least two intact conjugal family units, is reduced from 36 to 14%. Corresponding to these decreases in complex households, there is an increase in nuclear households from 38 to 68%. This trade-off is the trade-off one would expect, but its scale is so large as to be surprising. Both sets of rules we have used are patterns that would come under the general heading of stem-family household patterns in discussions of historical cases. But the experiment shows that the plausibility of interpreting a historical listing as evidence for stem-family preferences hinges altogether on specifying what variant of stem-family household formation one has in mind.

TABLE 4
Results of Simulation after 150 Years

Principles of organization	Primonuptial			Ultimonuptial		
	Mean (%)	SD (%)	Mean number	Mean (%)	SD (%)	Mean number
NUC	37.9	3.9	49.34	67.5	3.8	112.68
XLN	9.1	2.9	11.79	6.5	1.8	10.81
XLT	9.4	3.1	12.05	6.2	2.2	10.28
XLTD	3.4	1.8	4.33	1.2	.9	2.00
MLN	36.4	4.3	47.31	14.2	3.1	23.57
MLT	1.0	.9	1.32	.7	.7	1.23
MLTD	.4	.6	.48	.2	.3	.29
Other	.1	.3	.13	<.1	.1	.02
SPEC	1.0	.9	1.29	1.2	1.0	1.88
SOLE	1.3	1.1	1.62	2.3	1.4	3.71
All extended	21.7	--	28.17	13.9	--	23.1
All multiple	37.9	--	49.11	15.8	--	25.1
"Stem" = XLN + MLN + MLTD	46.0	--	59.58	20.9	--	34.7

Figure 1 shows histograms of the distributions of proportions of nuclear households for the two samples of 100 primonuptial and 100 ultimonuptial simulations. The sampling distribution of the proportions is evidently reasonably bell-shaped about its mean, so that only 1 in 20 of the samples would be expected to give a proportion more than twice the standard deviation from the mean proportion. For the historian, this means that a village of around 500 people with a proportion of nuclear households between 30 and 46% is not incompatible with a hypothesis of household formation behavior along primonuptial lines, whereas 59 to 75% nuclear fits ultimonuptial assumptions. From this observation an incidental point worthy of note emerges. Even discounting demographic differences between a pair of villages, a contrast of as much as 10% in nuclear proportions is entirely likely to arise from chance alone and to merit no attention or explanation. Such information about variances in village statistics, usually unavailable from historical data alone, is a major benefit from the simulation approach.

Comparing the primonuptial and ultimonuptial simulations, the patterns of ages at death and at first marriage are very similar, as indicated by Table 3. Therefore the shifts in proportions of household types ought to be regarded largely as a function of the diminution of overlap of the married lives of parents and children *as co-residents*, achieved by the change in postmarital residence rule, granting the right of co-residence to the last, rather than to the first, child to marry.

Since simple households tend to be at least slightly smaller than complex households, we expect the mean household size in the ultimonuptial sample, where there are more nuclear households, to be slightly smaller than in the primonuptial sample, as indeed it is, 4.65 versus 5.99. A paradox seems to lurk here, for in both samples a family with N children ought ultimately to result in N households. Of course in the ultimonuptial case the household that contains the presumptive heir of a family remains multiple for a shorter period of time, due to the shorter overlap in married lives of parents and heir, but for as long as this household is nuclear it is nuclear and large, so the mean household size should not be depressed. Where do the "extra" nuclear households arise? The answer lies in the times that the households formed by members of a given family are created in the primonuptial and ultimonuptial cases. The marriage of the first child to marry results in a new nuclear household under the ultimonuptial rules. The second marriage produces a new household under both rules. The marriage of the last remaining child in the family redresses the balance, for it results in no new household under ultimonuptial rules but in one more under

Percent of all Households which are Nuclear

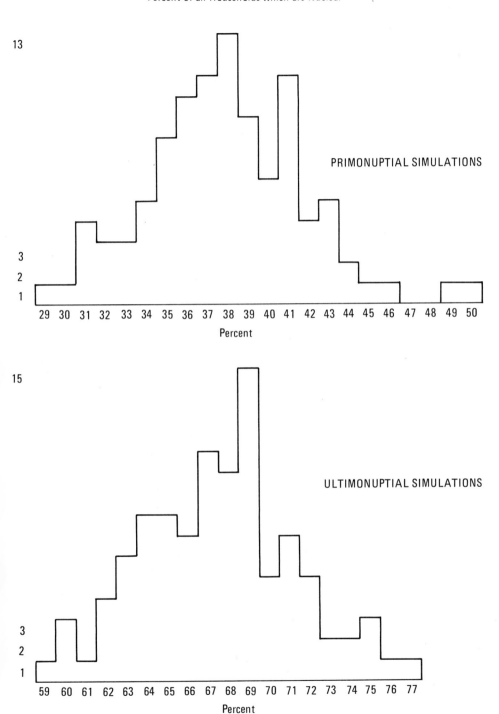

Figure 1. Percentage of all households that are nuclear.

primonuptial rules. However, there is always some probability that the last remaining child in a household will fail to marry, so that the balance will never be redressed. That eventuality is rare in the ultimonuptial case, where the child would be heir and would become head and would have enhanced marriage chances, but it is less rare in the primonuptial cases, where the deficiency occurs. Furthermore, at the end of any simulation (or at any other time) there will be marriageable but not yet married children in some households. Among these prospective brides and grooms will be those whose marriage and departure would have redressed the excess of nuclear households established for the ultimonuptial case early in the household cycle. Thus, termination of observation leaves the most productive stretch of the family cycle in hiving off children into independent households within the set of observed data in the ultimonuptial simulations but outside the period of observation in the primonuptial case.

The smaller mean household size partly accounts for the mean of 161 households in the ultimonuptial sample as compared with only 116 in the primonuptial sample. The other half of the story is the greater total mean population under ultimonuptiality, 750 compared to 698. But this greater population is itself a puzzle, since the demographic rates specified for the two batches of simulations are the same. The difference is a large one, unlikely to occur by chance alone, being more than three times the standard error of the estimates. How could a difference in rules of inheritance lead to such a visible demographic change?

The answer presumably lies in the way household structure and the rules for household formation interact with the enhanced marriage chances of unmarried and widowed heads of households. The rules provide that widows under age 45 are immediately remarried if they are heads of households. Widowhood and remarriage are extremely common. Out of 900 marriages in an ultimonuptial simulation, 300 on average are of widows. Furthermore, these remarriages take place in a marriage market in which husbands tend to be a good deal older than their wives. Daughters who are married and living with their fathers under a primonuptial system will have an average age closer to that of their father than daughters who are married and living with their fathers under an ultimonuptial system, since the co-resident married daughters tend to be elder daughters under the former and younger under the latter. Since the husbands of co-resident daughters tend to be older than their wives by about the same amount under both rule systems, those husbands will also be closer in age to their wives' fathers in the primonuptial system than in the ultimonuptial system. Thus, if the husband of the co-resident daughter should die, the father is more likely to have died already in an ultimonuptial system, being rather older than his son-in-law. The death of the husband of a co-resident daughter who is herself under 45 means a much higher likelihood that the daughter will become head and thus immediately remarry. Since the fertility of married women is higher than that of unmarried women, her remarriage maintains her exposure to risk of pregnancy more consistently than under a primonuptial system. In the latter, the father would be less likely to have died and would remain head, his daughter not inheriting the headship until his death, and thus having her remarriage subject to the marriage rates appropriate to her age range, unenhanced by assumption of headship. Her exposure to risk of pregnancy would be diminished. Further it should be noted that under an ultimonuptial system the "last child to marry" may fail to marry at all before the death of the head but would become head on the head's death. If the "last child to marry" were a daughter, she would immediately marry on assumption of headship. She would thus be exposed to the risks of pregnancy appropriate to married women sooner than she might be under a primonuptial system, where she would not become head, that position having been taken by an older sibling who married earlier. Both of these situations—that of the co-resident daughter whose husband dies, and that of the junior daughter who becomes head while still single—differentiate the exposure to risk of pregnancy of women in the two rule-systems, leading to higher completed fertility in the ultimonuptial system.

We must repeat that this experiment, like most, is artificial. We would not expect real populations to behave in exactly this way. Nevertheless the experiment is instructive. We see from it that a strong rule system produces a much greater frequency of stem-family households than we are accustomed to observe even in societies purported to have strong rule systems favoring such households. Second, we see that what is apparently only a minor perturbation of the rule system, a shift from primonuptial to ultimonuptial, so markedly affects the temporal coexistence of parents and children that it halves the frequency of stem-family households. Finally, we see that the interactions of demographic rates and sociological rule systems can be very subtle, leading to entirely unanticipated results. Of course, all these results would be likely to be muted in reality, but, for example, to the extent that widows or single women who were heads of households had *some* greater probability of remarriage than widows or single women who were not heads, the same effects should be observable. It is the subtlety of interactions that we wish to demonstrate, and the stylized nature of the simulation experiment throws that subtlety into sharpest relief.

REFERENCES

Dyke, Bennett, & MacCluer, Jean W., eds. (1973). *Computer Simulation in Human Population Studies*. New York: Academic Press.

Hammel, E. A.; Hutchinson, D.; Laslett, P.; & Wachter, K. W. (1974). "Demographic Rates and Complexity of Households: A Simulation Experiment Evaluating Demographic Constraints on Stem-Family Household Formation." Paper presented at the Conference on Microsimulation and Related Mathematical Tools for the Study of Historical Social Structure, 8–10 July 1974, held at Cambridge University under the auspices of the Cambridge Group for the History of Population and Social Structure and the British Social Science Research Council.

Hammel, E. A.; Hutchinson, D.; Wachter, K. W.; Lundy, R.; & Deuel, R. (1976). *SOCSIM: A Demographic–Sociological Microsimulation Program Operating Manual*. Research Series #27. Berkeley: University of California, Institute for International Studies.

Johnston, Francis E., & Albers, Morris E. (1973). "Computer Simulation of Demographic Processes," in M. H. Crawford & P. L. Workman, eds., *Methods and Theories of Anthropological Genetics*. Albuquerque: The School of American Research and University of New Mexico Press.

Ledermann, Sully. (1969). *Nouvelles Tables-Types de Mortalité*, Cahier 53, Institut National d'Étude Demographiques. Paris: Presses Universitaires de France.

MacCluer, Jean W. (1973). "Computer Simulation in Anthropology and Human Genetics," in M. H. Crawford & P. L. Workman, eds., *Methods and Theories of Anthropological Genetics*. Albuquerque: The School of American Research and University of New Mexico Press.

Wachter, K. W., ed. (forthcoming). *Quantitative Studies in Historical Social Structure* (tentative title). New York: Academic Press.

Deaths, Marriages, Births, and the Tuscan Economy (ca. 1300–1550)

DAVID HERLIHY

Harvard University

For the period of the late Middle Ages, and in particular for the fifteenth century, the region of Tuscany in northern Italy possesses probably the richest documentation, illuminating demographic patterns and movements, extant anywhere in western Europe. To be sure, there are numerous gaps and interruptions. The picture of Tuscan behavior recoverable from these records is in the style of *chiaroscuro:* Some parts of the picture are brilliantly illuminated, whereas others remain in obscurity or darkness. In spite of the interspersed shadows, the picture retains coherence, and it must also attract for its venerable age.

In this chapter I shall review, insofar as the sources permit, deaths, marriages, and births; their basic (or at least their most visible) characteristics; and their interrelationships in Tuscany, from about 1300 to 1550. As guides in this analysis, I shall use several theoretical models, which have been proposed to explain the interrelationships of these vital events.[1] No attempt will be made to develop alternative econometric models, or even to propose formal corrections for those already in the field. My purpose is only to assess how well the observed behavior of this historic population corresponds with the models' theoretical assumptions and predictions, thereby to contribute to the dialog between theoreticians and observers, among sociologists, demographers,

---

[1] These models are described in econometric notation and discussed at length by Ronald Lee (1973, 1974, forthcoming).

economists, and historians, upon which progress in historical demography principally depends.

The surviving records so powerfully shape and limit our view of behavior in late medieval Tuscany that we must initially, if rapidly, explore the contours of the available documentation. The records fall into two principal categories: registrations, or primitive efforts to record and measure vital events and movements; and surveys, which illuminate the composition of the Tuscan population at fixed times.

REGISTRATIONS

Even before secular governments took an active interest in population changes, Tuscan churches were making sporadic efforts to record vital events. As almost all Tuscans were Christians, the birth of almost every baby was quickly followed by his or her baptism. The conferral of baptism was the prerogative of certain ancient churches called *pievi* (from *plebes*, "peoples"), which included numerous subordinate parishes, extending over wide areas of the countryside or embracing entire cities. Thus, the *pieve* of San Giovanni included all the urban parishes of Florence and even a few immediately outside the city walls.[2] This high measure of centralization in the administration of the sacrament facilitated the keeping of baptismal records.

By at least the 1330s, the presiding priest (*pievano*) at the baptistry of San Giovanni at Florence was keeping count of baptisms by setting aside a black bean or a white bean, to mark the baptism of a boy or girl respectively. Sometime between 1336 and 1338 he reported to the chronicler Giovanni Villani that very year between 5500 and 6000 babies were baptized at his font (Villani, 1823, Vol. 6, p. 184). This use of beans as counters shows evident curiosity regarding total baptisms and births, but it may also imply that no register of the baptized was yet being maintained.

In this complex society, registration of baptisms was rapidly acquiring civil as well as religious significance. The Lord, it could be assumed, would know His own, but the city government wanted also to know its own—those who could claim its citizenship by birth and who enjoyed the fiscal and social benefits attendant upon urban residence. Not only did baptism in the city give proof of residence, but it also gave

[2] In 1427, the total population of the *pieve* of San Giovanni was 44,068 persons, of whom 37,146 (84.3%) lived within the walls of Florence and 6922 lived in the immediately surrounding countryside.

proof of age, which brought with it certain obligations and certain prerogatives. Probably as much for civil as for religious reasons, by the later fourteenth century Tuscan baptistries, especially in the cities, were keeping full registers of those baptized. The register typically included the name of the baptized baby and the name, occupation, and residence of the father. Even illegitimate, orphaned, or abandoned babies were registered. Residence in the city was a social advantage, and these last unfortunates needed every benefit they could claim. The earliest extant register of baptisms apparently dates from the year 1379, and is found at Siena (Lastri, 1775, p. 9).[3] Similar registers are reputedly extant for Pisa (from 1457), Volterra (from 1544), for portions at least of the Florentine countryside (from 1490), and for the city of Florence (from 1451). In 1775, the Florentine scholar Marco Lastri published the totals of this last register by month and by year, and according to sex, from 1451 to 1774. The sex ratio of the baptized babies is a normal 104, and the total number of yearly baptisms stands in reasonable ratio with the size of the urban population whenever it is known (36.6 baptisms per 1000 urban residents, for example, in 1767). The registrations, in other words, seem reasonably complete; at least there are no obvious omissions. This lengthy, uninterrupted series of registered baptisms in the city of Florence has not attracted, to my knowledge, the thorough modern study it richly deserves. (See Somogyi, 1950.) The other Tuscan baptismal registers rest, for all we know, in nearly total oblivion.

Churches and religious institutions were also in advance of secular governments in recording deaths. The religious congregation was a fellowship that extended over generations as well as classes, and the very logic of its existence demanded that memory be preserved of dead brethren, that their names be recorded, and that prayers be offered for their souls. The monastic necrology is nearly as old as monasticism, but, curiously, only late in the Middle Ages does the year of death, as well as the day, become worthy of record. Many laymen wished to be buried in monastic cemeteries and many made donations to the monks to obtain that favor. The monks in turn kept records of the deaths and burials of their lay benefactors, sometimes including their names with those of deceased monks, sometimes listing them in separate necrologies.

---

[3] For a more recent survey of these early registers, see Corsini (1974, p. 648–699). There exists a listing of births in the city of Florence from 1428 to 1435; see *Archivio di Stato di Firenze* (henceforth, ASF), Manoscritti 496, for a seventeenth century copy of this listing. However, only male births are registered, and apparently only the babies born into prominent families, as the yearly totals of births never surpass 200, when a figure of 500 would be expected.

At Florence, the two oldest and richest of the surviving necrologies are associated with the Dominican convent of Santa Maria Novella. One gives the names of deceased friars; the other, those of the laymen buried in the convent's cemetery. The first lists 602 dated deaths of Dominican friars from 1225 to 1504; it is one of the oldest such necrologies to survive (Orlandi, 1955). The second necrology is even larger, recording the names of 1758 deceased laymen from the late thirteenth century until the sixteenth century (Ildefonso di San Luigi, 1777, pp. 123–203). Numerous other Florentine and Tuscan monasteries and convents—and, from the fifteenth century, hospitals—possess similar necrologies, but all begin from later years and all are unpublished and virtually unstudied.[4]

What can these exclusively urban and obviously partial lists of burials offer to historical demography? Clearly, the number of entries reflects not only the prevailing death rate, but the size of the convent (which is not always known) and its appeal as a place for committing one's body, in life or in death, to God. Still, the influence of long-term changes in the size of the religious community or in its popularity can be minimized by appropriate statistical techniques. What remains is a respectable record of the yearly fluctuations of deaths within the city, which can especially reveal the dates and the relative severity of the many epidemics that flailed the urban population over the course of the late Middle Ages, into modern times. I shall presently return to an analysis of this record of deaths.

Beginning about 1376–1378, the government of Florence was itself seeking to keep a comprehensive count of all deaths and burials within the city.[5] Urban undertakers were allegedly overcharging poor families in burying their dead. The commune could not countenance this violation of Christian charity, and it doubtlessly feared the hygienic consequences of numerous, unsupervised burials. Moreover, the officials in charge of public health wished to be alerted at the earliest signs of approaching plague, which the undertakers would be among the first to see. Finally, the provisioning of adequately cheap food for the city required some knowledge of the size of the urban population, which deaths continuously affected. From 1376–1378, two communal agencies kept two separate but nearly equal registrations of burials within the

---

[4] On the value of these necrologies for demographic history, see the brief but discerning comments of G. Parenti (1943–1949, pp. 294–296). The lists of the deceased in the Florentine hospital of Santa Maria Nuova, for example, have survived from 1470.

[5] On these registrations, see the comments of Parenti (1943–1949). Parenti did not, however, examine the earliest surviving registrations (before 1451), perhaps because of their disordered state in the Florentine archives.

city of Florence: the Guild of Spice Merchants, which supervised the undertakers, and the Office of Foodstuffs (*Grascia*), which was responsible for ensuring adequate provisions in the city. All urban undertakers were required to report all deaths to the notaries of each of these two agencies. The notaries in turn entered the name of the deceased, the date of the death (and sometimes the apparent cause) into so-called "Books of the Dead," *Libri dei morti*. Time, however, has not treated these two series gently. Those redacted by the Guild of Spice Merchants survive only from 1451; the series kept in the Office of Foodstuffs begins in 1385, but contains extended interruptions (1413–1422; 1431–1438; 1450–1456) and many separate pages are missing from the volumes.[6]

The reporting of burials seems to have been reasonably comprehensive in the early fifteenth century. From 1424 to 1430, for example, the avaerage yearly number of burials within the city, based on interpolated estimates for complete years, is 1456.[7] As the city of Florence possessed somewhat more than 37,000 inhabitants in 1427, this would represent a credible death rate of 39.1 persons per 1000. But the quality of the reporting deteriorates after 1450, when the number of reported burials reaches ludicrous levels. During the terrible epidemic of 1527, which allegedly claimed 25,000 lives within the city, the number of reported burials is only 463 (Parenti, 1943–1949, Table 1, p. 284).

Marred by numerous gaps and deteriorating quality, the official Books of the Dead still give a vivid picture of mortality at Florence, particularly during the great epidemics (more than 10,000 burials were reported during the plague of 1400). Children are usually identified among the dead, and the registrations thus provide a crude way of assessing the impact of these devastating epidemics on the different age levels of the population. We shall come back for a second look at these *Libri dei morti*.

In gathering data on marriages, the Florentine churches and the government itself were lethargic. The blessing of a priest in church was still not strictly required for a legitimate marriage, and the government was more interested in the gains or losses of citizens than in their marital status. Still, at least from the 1370s, the Florentine government did attempt to supervise marriages within the city. Its aim was the enforcement of sumptuary laws, which limited the number of guests

---

[6] ASF, Arte de' Medici e Speziali, reg. 244 ff. "Hic est liber sive quaterna continens in se notificationes mortuorum [ASF, *Grascia*, reg. 186 ff]."

[7] To compensate for missing pages in the poorly preserved registers, a daily average of burials for each year, based on surviving registrations, was calculated, and then multiplied by 365. The yearly average of reported burials in the surviving registrations is 1103.

and the food they could be served at weddings. The cooks of the city were obligated to report all weddings, the number of guests, and the dishes consumed, to the notary of the Guild of Spice Merchants. Incongruously, from 1385 until 1389, the notary entered these descriptions of Florentine marriages into the Books of the Dead. (In 1385, for example, 38 marriages were recorded; in 1386, 21.) After 1390, the listing of those married disappears from among those buried, probably for the reason that reports of marriages were by then being collected in a separate register. The chances are good that this register has survived, and may someday be discovered amid the unexplored riches of the Florentine archives.

The Forentine government was also concerned about the continuing and considerable inflation in dowries, which injured the public interest by obstructing marriages and allegedly ruining families with several nubile daughters. Apparently in 1432, the Florentine government established a special "dowry fund" (*Monte delle doti*).[8] The heads of urban households invested a certain sum in the fund at the birth of a daughter; when the girl married, this sum was returned to the family, together with substantial interest, in order to constitute the major part if not the totality of her dowry. A similar system of purchasing government securities in anticipation of dowry payments functioned also at Genoa (Heers, 1961, p. 148). The administration of this dowry fund required that records be kept of the births of Florentine girls, the sums deposited in their names, and the dates of their marriages, their entries into convents, or their deaths. Such a register survives; Professors Anthony Molho, of Brown University and Julius Kirshner of the University of Chicago, have recently undertaken its systematic analysis, and the results of their work should tell us much about marriages at Florence in the fifteenth century.[9]

Not only churches and governments, but private families too, recorded vital events. From the later thirteenth century, many heads of families, at Florence in particular, kept personal memoirs, usually called *ricordi*, in which they entered events of importance to their households, including the deaths, marriages, and births of family members. (See Bec, 1967; Lugli, 1909.) Along with a few statistics, these writers also provide abundant comment on the feelings and behavior of families as they confronted issues touching on life and death. These observations

[8] This is the date given in *Giovanni Rucellai e il suo Zibaldone*, Vol. 1: *Il Zibaldone quaresimale* (Perosa, 1960, p. 48). According to Giovanni Rucellai, an investment of 50 florins yielded 100 florins in only 5 years.

[9] The register was discovered by Professor Molho in the still largely uncataloged deposit of the Monte commune, in the ASF.

often clarify patterns of behavior and motivations that are otherwise only dimly discernible in the partial statistics.

The historian can thus collect some statistical series, recording vital events in Tuscany from the late Middle Ages, but only through strenuous efforts and often with disappointing results. The skein of data is frequently threadbare or disrupted, and is concerned almost exclusively with the cities. Much richer sources for historical demography, preserved in Tuscan archives, are the surveys, which afford what the registrations do not, a complete picture of all segments of Tuscan society in the late Middle Ages.

SURVEYS

In the thirteenth century, the Tuscan territory was divided among numerous free communes, all of which were striving to expand their fiscal resources. For a variety of purposes—to count the number of hearths in their territories, or to determine the number of salt consumers, grain consumers, or able-bodied males in their populations—these communes were conducting extensive surveys from at least the early thirteenth century. Good runs of surveys have survived from the small towns and territories of Pistoia, San Gimignano, and especially Prato, and these give us insight into population movements in Tuscany even before the Great Pestilence of 1348. (For Pistoia, see Herlihy, 1967; for San Gimignano, Fiumi, 1961; for Prato, Fiumi, 1968.)

The political integration of Tuscany under Florentine rule led eventually to the integration of these fiscal surveys. Here the great monument is the *Catasto* of 1427–1430, which recorded all persons and all belongings in all lands then subject to the Florentine government. It included some 60,000 households, containing 260,000 persons, who in turn possessed taxable assets worth more than 15 million gold florins. One unique advantage offered by the *Catasto* is the full illumination of sectors of the population, notably peasants and the poor, who are notoriously difficult to investigate through other sources.

The *Catasto* of 1427 represented the supreme effort and achievement of Florentine administration in the late Middle Ages.[10] Florence was

[10] On the history of Florentine fiscal surveys, see especially Elio Conti (1966). Data from the entire *Catasto* of 1427, and from samples of later surveys, have been edited into machine-readable form by the present author in collaboration with Mme Christiane Klapisch of the Ecole des Hautes Etudes, VI. Section, Paris. The work of collecting the data and the subsequent analysis have been supported by the National Science Foundation in America and by the Centre National de la Recherche Scientifique in France.

never again able to achieve a similarly comprehensive survey of persons and possessions in its entire territory. The government did, however, take several subsequent, partial surveys of the capital city (1430, 1433, 1458–1459, 1469–1470, and 1480) and of its own immediate countryside or *contado* (1458–1460, 1469–1471, and 1487). In 1495 Florence abandoned the making of *Catasti* altogether, in favor of a much simpler, and far less revealing, system of assessment based on real property alone (the *Decima della Repubblica*). Finally, in 1552 the government took a census of the population then inhabiting what had become the Grand Duchy of Tuscany. This census has survived for the city of Florence, but we have only the summary totals for the population settled in the other Tuscan territories.[11]

In this chapter I shall make use of data from (1) the entire survey of 1427, (2) 10% samples of two subsequent surveys of the city of Florence (1458 and 1469 respectively) plus one survey from the Florentine countryside (1470); and (3) the published totals of the Grand Ducal census of 1552.

Tuscan surveys, in sum, give remarkably full pictures of the population and its structure at certain moments in time. The movements in vital events that shaped the structure are considerably less apparent. The documentation, in other words, supports cross-sectional analysis of the Tuscan community better than it does the time-series analysis of vital movements. Still, the excellent view afforded of variation within the community has considerable value, even in the study of changes over time. The censuses and surveys show clearly that Tuscans were not uniform in their demographic behavior. Certain factors, which I shall call environmental, also influenced that behavior, more or less as independent variables. It is important to recognize the presence of these environmental factors. Apparent changes in aggregate behavior, for example, may represent, not uniform changes across the entire population, but a shift of numbers from one sector into another. What then were the chief environmental factors that affected demographic movements in Tuscany from the late Middle Ages?

RESIDENTIAL ENVIRONMENT

The most consistent (or at least the most visible) factor in influencing demographic behavior was *residential environment*, that is, the physical

[11] For the urban population, see Battara (1935). E. Repetti gives, commune by commune, the number of families and inhabitants throughout the Florentine domains, according to this census, which he dates 1551 (1843, pp. 566–577). For the dating of the census we are following Battara (1935, p. 3).

location of the individual or his household, in countryside, small town, large town, or metropolis. The Tuscan community of 1427 can be divided into four residential environments—the large metropolis of Florence, with a population of more than 37,000 in 1427; the six secondary cities (Pisa, Pistoia, Arezzo, Prato, Cortona, and Volterra), average population of 4383; 15 small towns, average population of 1654 persons; and the countryside. This division, like all divisions, can reflect only imperfectly the range of economies and communities found in Tuscany in 1427. The category of *countryside*, for example, embraces villages in the high mountains, where people supported themselves by harvesting chestnuts and tending sheep, and suburban hearths more industrial than agricultural in economic activities. Still, the major, though not the exclusive, support of the rural population was peasant agriculture.

Of all vital events, marriage and the relationships created by it leave the deepest, most stable, and most visible imprint in the surveys. Table 1 shows certain salient features of marriage in Tuscany, across these four environments, in the year 1427. To reduce somewhat the burden of

TABLE 1
Tuscan Marriages, 1427

	Florence	Six cities	Fifteen towns	Florentine countryside
		A. Men		
Average age first marriage	30.0	27.4	26.4	25.6
Percentage married (adults)[a]	47.6	58.9	62.8	66.8
Percentage widowed	4.0	3.6	3.2	3.4
Percentage permanent bachelors[b]	11.8	8.4	6.0	5.4
		B. Women		
Average age first marriage	18.0	17.9	17.9	18.6
Percentage married (adults)	53.2	56.6	61.2	64.9
Percentage widowed	25.1	23.8	20.7	18.0
Percentage permanent spinsters	5.8	5.4	2.5	2.0

[a] Men age 13 and over and women age 12 and over are considered adults.
[b] Men and women in the age range 48-52 who appear in the survey with no indication of ever having married are regarded as permanent bachelors and spinsters respectively.

calculations, only those resident in the Florentine *contado,* and not those in the other rural areas of Tuscany, have been included as representative of the rural population. In calculating the average ages at first marriage, I have followed the methods developed by J. Hajnal (1953).

Residential environment strongly affected how both men and women approached marriage and remarriage, but the behavior of the two sexes was quite diverse. For men, residence in the metropolis of Florence is associated with delayed first marriage and with a high percentage (11.8) of permanent bachelors in the male population. In rural areas, on the other hand, men were considerably younger at first marriage, and more of them married. The urban environment, in other words, either discouraged men from marrying or it attracted from other areas young men intent on remaining single; the rural environment acted on the behavior of males in an exactly contrary fashion. This contrast in the male approach to marriage probably reflects basic contrasts in the urban and rural economies. Within the cities, the merchant, professional man, and even the artisan had to master a trade and accumulate resources before he could marry. In rural areas, on the other hand, the young man had first to marry, before he could assume the cultivation of a farm in his own right and name. As the Russian economist A. V. Chayanov (1966) has argued, the basic unit of labor in the peasant economy is more truly the family rather than the individual, and the peasant household head could not function without a wife and eventually children. Put another way, for males within the city, marriage followed upon economic independence; for males within the countryside, it was prerequisite for it.

The ages at first marriage for women did not vary widely across the four environments, but it was slightly higher in rural areas than in the metropolis. Cultural factors operated here—urban males probably preferred young, presumably pure and unspoiled girls for their brides. Moreover, the young girl in the peasant home contributed more in an economic sense to her household than did her counterpart in the city. Peasant families were consequently not as eager as urban parents to rid themselves of economically burdensome daughters.[12] And the peasant groom probably preferred a somewhat older, stronger bride, who could help him in his labors.

Remarkably, however, this pattern of behavior was reversed in regard to second and subsequent marriages. In all environments, men who had waited long before taking a first bride remarried almost at

[12] The Florentine matron Alessandra Strozzi, for example, lamented the presence in her household of her daughters, whom she viewed as exclusively consumers. "For it's true, alas, that as long as there are girls at home, nothing is done that isn't for them." Cited in Lauro Martines (1974, p. 23).

once following the death of their wives. Widowers are consequently few in all four environments. Frequently, the widower was left with small children, and a new wife was considered essential for their proper training. And the factors that delayed first marriages for men no longer operated upon them in later life. Widows, on the other hand, usually did not remarry quickly and many did not remarry at all. The urban environment in particular, as it obstructed first marriages for men, so also discouraged remarriage for women, or it attracted from the countryside widows who were not eager to take another mate. The widow could live alone, successfully and comfortably, within the city, and she did not need a male to help her with heavy agricultural labors. The high dowry, which strained the resources of her family when she married, was returned to her at her husband's death, giving her a measure of economic independence she had never known before. Many women relished that independence.[13] Widows consequently proliferated within the urban environment; one out of every four adult women was widowed at Florence in 1427.

Contrasts in marriage patterns inevitably generated contrasts in the character and structure of the Tuscan hearth. Table 2 summarizes some of the salient differences in Tuscan households across the four environments. (Here, the category of countryside includes all rural areas, not only the Florentine *contado*.)

TABLE 2
Tuscan Households, 1427

	Florence	Six cities	Fifteen towns	Countryside	Totals
Households	9821	6724	5994	37226	59765
Persons	37245	26315	24809	175840	264210
Average size	3.79	3.90	4.14	4.72	4.42
Married heads	5725	4315	4233	28859	43132
Percentage	58.3	64.2	70.6	77.5	72.2
Male heads, single and widowed	2586	1281	969	4988	9824
Percentage	26.3	19.0	16.2	13.4	16.4
Female heads, single and widowed	1510	1128	792	3380	6810
Percentage	15.4	16.8	13.2	9.1	11.4

[13] The sixteenth century writer, Lodovico Dolce, claimed that some women rejoiced at the death of their husbands, "As if a heavy yoke of servitude had been lifted from their backs." "Non m'è ascoso, che alcune donne . . . . non che elle s'attristino, ma s'allegrano della morte de' loro mariti non altramente, che se fosse loro scosso dal collo un grave giogo di servitù [Dolce, 1560, p. 68]."

Two comments seem appropriate here. Men and women within the city did not have to marry in order to serve as head of a hearth or household. Only slightly more than one out of two household heads were married in the city of Florence in 1427, as opposed to more than three out of four in the countryside. Moreover, the complex category of *countryside* obscures to some extent the true importance of marriage in the peasant economy. For example, in one Florentine rural quarter, Santo Spirito, where a system of peasant agriculture based on family farms enjoyed a particular prominence, 5868 out of 6678 households, or 87.9%, were headed by married couples in 1427. Single or widowed persons rarely headed a family farm. Secondly, urban households were poor producers of children, for several reasons. The tendency for men to delay first marriage and for women to avoid remarriage limited the span of years men and women spent within the married state. This also limited the number of children the urban woman was likely to bear in the course of her life. There is further evidence of widespread contraceptive practices within urban marriages.[14] Fundamentally, in order to function economically, most urban residents needed children no more than they needed mates. Children were valued workers on the family farm, but they added little to the economic capacities of the urban household. In the city, children, like a mate, were a reward for economic success; in the countryside they were a means of attaining it.

SOCIAL ENVIRONMENT

The second major factor that affected behavior is *social environment*—the status a family held. This is roughly if imperfectly measured in the surveys by the total taxable wealth the household possessed.

Within cities, wealth tended to reinforce the urban pattern of marriage and household structure just described. The rich urban male was older at first marriage than his poorer neighbor. At Florence in 1427, among males in households with more than 400 florins in total assessment, the average age at first marriage was 31.1 years; for men from households with no taxable assets, the comparable age was 27.7 years. The percentage of presumed permanent bachelors (men still single in the age category 48–52) was high among the rich (10.2%) and especially low among the destitute (7.7%). The richest girls, on the other hand,

[14] St. Bernardine of Siena in the early fifteenth century claimed that of every 1000 marriages, 999 were of the devil, because of such practices. For further comment, see Herlihy (1969, p. 1350).

were younger at first marriage (18.0 years) than the poorest bride (18.4 years). The urban rich characteristically sought to divest themselves of daughters while retaining sons.

Within marriage, however, the wealthy Florentine wife was considerably more prolific than her destitute neighbor. At least she was distinctly more successful in bringing her children through the critical early years of life. In the richest Florentine homes there were 873 children age 0–4 per 1000 women age 13–47, but there were only 648 children per 1000 women in households with no taxable assets.[15] By this measure, the poor women of the city were the least successful childbearers, or child-rearers, in the entire Tuscan community. In contrast, wealthy urban wives rivaled peasant women in the numbers of children in their families.

Delayed first marriage for men, but high fertility within marriage, gave to the wealthy urban household a larger average size and a more complex structure than that found among the poor. The wealthy household typically contained numerous children and some lateral relatives of the head, chiefly males waiting to marry. Among the wealthy, brothers also tended to keep their patrimony undivided for some years after the death of their father, and joint households are consequently common in the highest levels of urban society. The less advantaged lived with few children in small households that rarely show lateral extension. Here, the nuclear family enjoyed an overwhelming predominance.

However, within the city, it took substantial increments in wealth before fortune showed a visible correlation with behavior. If we regress the average wealth of Florentine households upon the number of their members, then for each additional member there corresponds an increment in average wealth of 489 florins. In a sample rural area (the quarter of Santa Croce in the Florentine countryside) the corresponding increment for each additional household member is only 13.7 florins.[16] At Florence, high marital fertility and large and complex households

[15] This range of ages, 13–47, was selected because of the early age at first marriage for Florentine women. Also, because of the tendency to round ages, it was preferable not to place a preferred age (15 or 45) at the margins of the interval.

[16] The households were grouped according to the number of members they possessed, from 1 to 12 and over, and the average wealth was calculated for the households in each of the 12 categories. The number of members was considered the independent variable, the average wealth the dependent variable, and the values, 489 and 13.7, represent the slope of the regression line for the urban and rural households respectively. The coefficients of correlation are also very high for both groups—.872 in the city of Florence and .914 in the rural quarter of Santa Croce.

were thus characteristic of the patriciate, not of the low or middle classes.

In rural areas, wealth similarly tended to reinforce the influences flowing from the residential environment, but with a significant exception. (See, for example, Klapisch & Demonet, 1972, for the relationship of wealth and household characteristics in one part of Tuscany.) The rich peasant tended to be younger at first marriage than men in general in the rural population (22.5 as opposed to 26.5 years). In the countryside, as in the city, the rich also presided over distinctly large and complex households. However, because of the marked differences in marriage patterns, wealthy households in the city show a slightly greater tendency toward lateral extension; the rich rural households are characteristically extended in a generational direction.[17] The substantial *paterfamilias* in the city often counted a brother among the members of his household; his counterpart in rural areas would more likely discern married sons and grandchildren.

The relationship between wealth and behavior is not, however, linear in the countryside. The principal deviation from a linear relationship is found among those households possessing no taxable assets. This category included many sharecroppers (*mezzadri*), who were in fact peasant cultivators, working family farms on behalf of urban landlords. The landlords usually provided seeds, fertilizer, animals, and even loans to ensure the productive cultivation of the farm. In spite of the dearth of taxable property, the *mezzadri* more nearly resemble the prosperous, independent peasants than they do the small property owners who stood above them on the scale of wealth. Many small owners did not possess sufficient land for the support of a family, and they had to supplement their income through employment in countryside or city. The limited resources they commanded hampered marriage and reproduction.[18] The *mezzadri*, in contrast, resemble the prosperous peasants in their demographic behavior; like them, they tended to marry earlier and to support larger families than their propertied, but

[17] Although Florentine urban households in 1427 were smaller and generally simpler than those of the countryside, 17.17% of them, as opposed to 16.84% in the countryside, show some lateral extension (i.e., they included a brother or sister of the household head). Among the urban households, 11.45% included more than two generations, versus 26.26% in the countryside.

[18] For example, in rural households with no taxable assets, the child-to-woman ratio is 845 per 1000; it is only 771 in households having from 1 to 25 florins in taxable wealth, and 765 in households having 26 to 50 florins. In those prosperous rural households having from 201 to 400 florins in assessment, the ratio is 861. Households in the assessment category of 26 to 50 florins also show the lowest percentage of any category of married males.

still poor neighbors. In the countryside, association with a family farm, rather than wealth directly, seems to have been the decisive factor in influencing demographic behavior.

Tuscan people thus approached marriage, reared their children, and lived out their days under a complex web of influences. The same factor—wealth, or access to resources, for example—might have different effects upon behavior across different residential environments, encouraging marriage in the countryside but discouraging it in the city. The same amount of wealth, which might be associated with large, prolific families in rural areas, could be the mark of tiny domestic units in the city. In seeking to unravel this web of unfluences, in examining the separate strands, the researcher must recognize how subtly and how intricately they are interwoven.

Against this background, we may now consider the relationships of vital movements in Tuscany from the late Middle Ages.

DEATHS AND MARRIAGES

I shall take deaths as the point of departure, because of the extraordinary role mortalities, principally attributable to plague, played in shaping the structure of the population. From 1424 to 1430, for example, the Florentine undertakers listed the apparent cause of death for the 7718 bodies they buried. No major plague struck Florence in these years, although the city endured two comparatively mild attacks in 1424 and 1430. Still, 41.3% of all deaths were specifically attributed to plague. Even in the absence of a major epidemic, two out of five Florentines were buried with the mark of the plague upon their bodies.[19]

The very power of the late medieval epidemics also gives to deaths high visibility in the chronicles and in the partial necrologies and registrations. Marriages are not so easily monitored, as we almost completely lack registrations. In studying marriages in relation to deaths, we must primarily rely on the comments of chroniclers, the observed behavior of certain individual Florentine families, and partial data on the ages at first marriage, before and during periods of epidemics.

According to contemporary observers, the major epidemics acted as powerful stimuli to marriage among the survivors. A French chronicler,

---

[19] ASF, Grascia, reg. 188. To identify plague victims, the notary scribbled *di segno* ('with the mark') in the margin to the right of the burial entry, and added a large *P* in front of the name.

Jean de Venette, described the reaction of the population to the Great Pestilence of 1348 in the following terms:

> After the cessation of the epidemic . . . the men and women who survived married each other. There was no sterility among the women, but on the contrary fertility beyond the ordinary. Pregnant women were seen on every side. Many twins were born and even three children at once . . . [Birdsall, 1953; cited in Bowsky, 1971, p. 17].

The plague apparently swept away inhibitions against marrying. One English chronicler remarks how, after the plague of 1361, women shamelessly took as husbands "both strangers and other weaklings and cowards," and did not hesitate to marry those of lower social station.[20]

Examination of the marital behavior of the ancestors of Giovanni Morelli, a Florentine merchant who has left us a rich set of memoirs, allows us to perceive how the plagues encouraged marriage (1956, pp. 138–142). Giovanni's eldest uncle, also named Giovanni, did not marry until he was past age 40. One reason for the delay was apparently the survival of his father, who, in these favored years before the Black Death, lived until 1347, when Giovanni was 38 or 39. Significantly, Giovanni took a wife "because he was the eldest [son]" in 1349, 2 years after the death of his father and 1 year after the Great Pestilence of 1348. It took another pestilence to allow any of his brothers to marry. The plague of 1363 carried off Giovanni and two other brothers, sparing the youngest brother, Pagolo, the father of our author. Pagolo was now free, even obligated in the interest of family survival, to take a wife, as he did in January 1364. Without the intervention of pestilence and death, Pagolo would have been much older at marriage, if indeed he could have married at all.

The Florentine family memoirs rather characteristically show a flurry of marriage arrangements in the years following major epidemics. Matteo di Niccòlo Corsini, for example, was probably married in 1364, following the epidemic of 1363, as the first of his 20 children was born in 1365 (Petrucci, 1965, *passim*). His daughter Francesca and his son Giovanni were both married in 1401, following the plague of 1400, and another daughter in 1403. Giovanni in turn arranged the marriage of one daughter in 1418, following the plague of 1417, and another in 1425, following the plague of 1424.

---

[20] J. F. D. Shrewsbury, in *A History of Bubonic Plague in the British Isles* quotes the *Polychronicon*: "foeminae . . . sumpserunt maritos tam extraneos quam alios imbellices et vecordes, purodoric [sic] non parcentes . . . se cum inferioribus copulare [1970, p. 128]."

For patrician families, frequent marriages in the wake of epidemics doubtlessly sprang from conscious policy. The patricians desperately wanted male heirs (but not too many heirs); the death of a father or older married brother, enabled—even required—younger males to marry, lest the lineage expire. But even among the less advantaged classes, massive deaths opened up numerous basic jobs and career opportunities, which gave to younger men the economic independence needed for marriage.

Deadly epidemics, high mortalities, and shortened expectations of life consequently exerted downward pressures on the ages of first marriage, especially for men. For the period before the Great Pestilence of 1348, there are few hard figures, but we do have some striking comments on Florentine marriage practices.

Giovanni Morelli, writing about 1400, describes how Florentines approached marriage in both the past and the present. In the twelfth and thirteenth centuries, before the onslaught of the great epidemics, Florentines allegedly survived well and lived a long time—"ed erano di buona e forte natura e viveano assai [1956, p. 111]." Forty years of life, Morelli claims, was equivalent to only 26 to 30 years passed in his own days—"era tenuto questo tempo [d'anni quaranta o circa] come sarebbe tenuto uno di venzei insino a trenta anni [p. 111]." But long life was accompanied by late marriage and low fertility within marriage. The usual age of first marriage for men in the twelfth and thirteenth centuries was, in Morelli's estimation, 40 years, and he tells his reader not to be surprised, as this was the custom. In olden times Florentine girls married between the ages of 24 and 26, whereas his own contemporaries were reluctant to wait until the fifteenth year before arranging their daughters' marriages (p. 207).

The impression that men at least were older at first marriage in the thirteenth century than in the middle and late fourteenth century was widely shared. A chronicler from Rimini, writing in 1354, notes that males in the time of Emperor Frederick II (d. 1250) delayed marriage until age 30, and he obviously found this delay remarkable: "Cum autem matrimonia eorum fiebant erant quasi annorum xxx [Battagli da Rimini, 1913, p. 10]." The Florentine domestic chronicler, Lapo di Giovanni Niccolini, who wrote in the early fifteenth century, notes with similar surprise that three of his male ancestors, who lived in the thirteenth century, postponed marriage until age 40, and then only one of them took a wife—"e 3 figliuoli maschi, e ciascheduno passò l'età di 40 anni, e niuno ebbe moglie, se non uno [Bec, 1969, p. 57]." What could these authors have known about the social customs that prevailed a century and more before they were writing? They did not view the distant past entirely through clouds of legends, but they could take advantage of the traditional practice of maintaining and preserving family archives, which they assiduously consulted. Their comments deserve respect.

From the late fourteenth century, surviving surveys can be used to estimate average ages at first marriage. In 1371, within the city of Prato, admist a plunging population, the average ages at first marriage were only 24.5 years for men, and 15.9 years for women. These are lower ages than those found in any subsequent year, in any Tuscan community so far studied. The Tuscan population, at Prato and elsewhere, stabilized at low levels from approximately 1410. By 1427, the ages of first marriage in the city of Prato had advanced by $1\frac{1}{2}$ years for women and $2\frac{1}{2}$ years for men. The Tuscan population remained largely stable in size until approximately 1460, when it once more began to grow at moderate rates. By 1552 the population was larger by two-thirds over what it had been in 1427. The waning ferocity of epidemics, the increased longevity of Tuscans, and the growing population now exerted upward pressures on ages of first marriage. Within the city of Florence, the age of first marriage for men moved from 30.0 years in 1427 to 30.5 in 1458 to 31.4 in 1480; for women the comparable age advanced from 17.9 years in 1427 to 19.5 in 1458 to 20.8 in 1480. A similar advance is discernible in rural areas, where for men, the average age at first marriage passed from 25.5 years in 1427 to 27.7 in 1470, and for women from 18.4 years to 21.0. In the late fifteenth century, as in the thirteenth, the Tuscan community seems to have been intent on slowing or stopping its further growth through forcing its young to delay their marriages.

DEATHS AND BIRTHS

In encouraging marriages, the high levels of mortality in the late Middle Ages also encouraged births. Presumably, the younger persons who were allowed to marry in the wake of the epidemics would be more fertile than the older couples they replaced. But our sources also affirm that the epidemics directly enhanced the fertility even of married women. The chronicler Jean de Vinette, previously cited, claims that after the Great Pestilence of 1348 women were "fertile beyond the ordinary [cited in Bowsky, 1971, p. 17]." We need not credit his assertion that many more twins and even triplets were born after the Great Pestilence, but clearly his impression was of a world swarming with babies. Giovanni Morelli relates that Florentine women in the period before the great epidemics, in spite of their good health and long lives, bore in the course of their days usually only four or six children. One of his own contemporaries, Lorenza, wife of Matteo di Niccòlo Corsini, bore 20 babies in 24 years, from 1365 to 1389 (only five survived childhood) (Petrucci, 1965, p. 82). Another Tuscan writer remarks how fertile the women of Florence became after the plague of 1400: "At that time many women became pregnant; it's a long time that they weren't making babies [Cigliotti, 1937, p. 197]."[21]

Massive deaths stimulated births principally because they included a heavy toll of children. The Sienese chronicler Agnolo di Tura relates in *Cronache senesi* (p. 55) how in 1348 he buried all five of his children with his own hand (cited in Bowsky, 1964, p. 17). In killing children the epidemics also destroyed a principal reason why parents might have exercised restraint in further procreation.

The register of baptisms for the city of Florence, beginning in 1451, allows us to observe how the number of births fluctuated in periods of known plague. Table 3 illustrates the fluctuations in the number of baptisms at Florence, for 4 years before and for 4 years after epidemics. These plagues did not follow exactly the same chronological pattern.

TABLE 3
Plagues and Baptisms in the City of Florence[a]

Year 0 = Years from plague	1457		1479		1497		1527	
	Baptisms	Index	Baptisms	Index	Baptisms	Index	Baptisms	Index
-4	2046	100.0	2536	100.0	2548	100.0	2899	100.0
-3	2100	102.6	2512	99.1	2760	108.3	2885	99.5
-2	2100	102.6	2539	100.1	2565	100.7	3342	115.3
-1	2207	107.9	2664	105.0	2468	96.9	3377	116.5
0	1882	92.0	2126	83.8	2136	83.8	2645	91.2
1	1781	87.0	2215	87.3	2269	89.1	1777	61.3
2	2058	100.6	2337	92.2	2578	101.2	3148	108.6
3	2105	102.9	2412	95.1	2704	106.1	3208	110.7
4	2206	107.8	2515	99.2	2871	112.7	2070	71.4

[a] From Marco Lastri, *Richerche dell' antica e moderna popolazione della città di Firenze per mezzo dei registri di battesimi del Battistero di San Giovanni dal 1451 al 1774* (Florence, 1775).

[21] "In questo tempo [1400] sono ingrossate molte donne, che è gran tempo non ne feceno fanciulli. . . . "

Usually, the plague appeared in autumn, and reached its peak virulence in the late summer and autumn of the following year; the years given in Table 3 represent the period of maximum mortalities, as shown in the necrologies. But the plague lingered over several years in the late 1490s, from 1496 to 1499.[22] In terms of severity, the epidemic of 1527, which claimed more than 25,000 lives, was probably the worst to strike the city since 1348.[23] To judge from the deaths of friars at Santa Maria Novella, the plague of 1479, which claimed 15 friars, was more severe than that of 1497, which took 9 friars, or 1457, which killed only 3.

In all these plague years, baptisms, and presumably births, fell by an average of more than 12%. Many families were doubtlessly fleeing Florence, and some babies were consequently born and baptized outside the city. The drop in baptisms was still greater in the year following the epidemic—more than 18% on the average. This is attributable to the many disrupted marriages in the wake of the high mortalities, the necessary delay in arranging new unions, and probably also the common fear that sexual intercourse during plagues heightened the risk of infection. In the murderous epidemic of 1527, the drop in births the following year was especially severe. But thereafter, the number of baptisms and births rebounded, to equal or surpass the levels maintained in the years immediately preceding the plague. The most remarkable recovery is that which followed the most severe of the epidemics—that of 1527. In spite of the reduction of the total population by probably one-third, the crop of babies born in 1529 and 1530 was nearly as large as the numbers born each year from 1523 to 1526. (The sharp drop of births in 1531 primarily reflects political disturbances, notably the siege of the city by the forces of Emperor Charles V. This siege lasted almost an entire year, from October 1529 to August 1530.)

This feat of producing babies is more remarkable when we consider that the epidemics were not lenient on young adults of childbearing age. By count of burials made in the epidemic of 1400, the number of children (*pueri, puelle*) among the deceased increased by a factor of 12.2 over the average of the previous 3 years.[24] The number of deceased

[22] According to Luca Landucci, pestilence was already noticed in the city in 1495 but grew worse in 1496 and 1497. See Landucci (1883, pp. 116, 127, 154–155).

[23] This is the estimate of a contemporary, Lionardo Morelli (1783, p. 248). Morelli was, however, writing in October, 1527, before the plague had entirely abated.

[24] Based on the burials listed in the *Libri dei morti* for the years 1397–1399, the average number of buried children was 236.67 per year, of widowed women 109, and of married women 189. During the plague of 1400, the burials of children were 2894; of widows, 260; and of married women, 985. It should also be noted that the burials recorded in 1400 probably represented only one-half the true number of deaths, which contemporaries estimated to be 20,000.

widows, presumably older women, grew by a factor of only 2.2. The epidemics spared the aged. But the deaths of married, presumably younger, women, multiplied during the epidemic by a factor of 5.2. Young married women were not cut down by plague in the same measure as children, but their ranks were substantially thinned. The plague of 1497 allegedly made particular inroads into the numbers of household heads between 20 and 50 years of age: "e nota che moriva tutti capi di case da 20 anni insino in 50 e non fanciuli [Landucci, 1883, p. 155]."

The powerful stimulus that high mortalities exerted on births introduced marked distortions into the age structure of the total population. In taking only moderate tolls among the mature and the aged, the epidemics allowed the community to accumulate relatively large numbers of older persons. In 1427, 14.6% of all Tuscans were age 60 or over. The ranks of younger adults were thin in comparison, but they were also prolific in producing babies, at least in the immediate wake of epidemics. A staggering 15.8% of all Tuscans were age 4 or younger in 1427 (a plague had struck Tuscany in 1423 and 1424). These proportions do not correspond well with the distributions to be expected theoretically for stable populations, for any assumed birth rates and death rates. (For stable population rates, see Coale & Demeny, 1966.) Although the Tuscan population of 1427 might be considered stationary in the sense that its total size does not seem to have varied significantly for some two decades, it was still being molded by highly variable rates of mortality and fertility.[25] And the characteristic effect of these fluctuations was to leave the population with disproportionately large numbers of the very old and very young.

DEATHS AND DEATHS

Are cyclical movements discernible in the occurrences and recurrences of plague? The two necrologies of Santa Maria Novella, the family memoirs listing deaths, and the partial registrations of burials give us a means of identifying the years of plagues within the city of Florence and also the relative seriousness of an epidemic. In collaboration with Perry Gluckman and Mary Pori, formerly of the staff of the Center for Advanced Study in the Behavioral Sciences at Stanford, California, I subjected the composite record of deaths in the city of Florence from 1275 to 1500 to *spectral analysis*, which is essentially a means of search-

[25] Based on the reported burials in the city of Florence from 1424 to 1430, the death rate varied from 16 per 1000 in 1427 to 100 per 1000 in 1430 when an epidemic struck the city.

ing for cycles in time-series data. The proper application of spectral analysis requires that the observed values (in this case, counts of burials) be transformed, in order to distribute the values symmetrically about zero and in order to remove long-term (i.e., noncyclical) trends. The results of the analysis showed the presence of a principal cycle with a period of approximately 43 years, and secondary cycles showing periods of approximately 32, 25, and 15 years respectively.

As this analysis was based on only a part of the extant data (we were unable to include unpublished necrologies and other archival records), the analysis must be regarded as experimental. It does, however, suggest some hypotheses.

The mortalities engendered by the late medieval epidemics were to some extent age-specific. The most numerous victims were children and young adults; mature people who lived through one or more epidemics were not likely to fall victim to a later pestilence. The immediate impact of epidemics was to "age" the population, which also obviously came to consist of persons who had experienced and survived the plague. For this reason, the population possessed a certain immunity from the early recurrence of another major epidemic.

The population also rebounded from its terrible losses in distinctive ways. The massive deaths raised fertility levels among the survivors, which in turn led to the formation of a large cohort of babies relative to the total population in the years immediately following the epidemic. This large cohort seems visible in the age pyramid of 1427, with 15% of the population less than 5 years of age. With time, this swollen cohort moved up the scale of ages. From approximately age 15, the girls in the cohort would begin to marry, and these girls would reach their maximum fertility (their mean age of motherhood) at approximately age 26. (This was the mean age of mothers with babies less than 1 year of age in the city of Florence in 1427.) However, the girls had to find husbands within a much older and far smaller age cohort of males. Consequently, many girls would be unable to marry, and this would lower the gross rate of reproduction for the cohort as a whole. By age 30, the young men in the enlarged cohort would be marrying in large numbers, and since they selected much younger brides, they would have no difficulty finding wives. As a group, these men would reach their maximum rate of reproduction (their mean age of fatherhood) at approximately age 40, which was the mean age of fatherhood in the city of Florence in 1427. It appears, in other words, that the large cohort, generated in response to the mortalities of a major plague, would be most actively reproducing itself (of course with the aid of women found in younger cohorts) approximately 40 years later, and at that time would be making its most substantial additions to the total population. This was likely to create another "baby bubble" and set it moving up the scale of ages, but it would also give the population large numbers of young people and increase its vulnerability to another major epidemic.

It is worth noting that the baptisms of the year 1456, preceding the plague of 1457, were the highest recorded for any year since the start of the series in 1451; baptisms for 1478, preceding the plague of 1479, were similarly the highest yet recorded; those of 1494, preceding the lingering epidemic of 1495–1499, were similarly the highest yet attained; and the baptisms of 1526, preceding the most devastating of the period's epidemics in 1527, were the highest in the entire register from 1451 to past 1600. Plague cycles, in other words, may have been influenced by basic cycles in the patterns of marriage and reproduction, observable at Florence in the fifteenth and sixteenth centuries.

HEARTHS

These vital movements necessarily affected the hearths or households in the Tuscan community, but they were not the exclusive determinants of the total number or of average size. In periods of population changes, the number of hearths shows relative inertia, reflecting those changes only belatedly and sometimes not at all. Average household size is much the more sensitive variable, as it responds immediately to variations in the total population. At Prato, for example, the population in both city and countryside declined between about 1290 and 1325 by an estimated 15.2%, but the number of hearths contracted by only 6.7%.[26] Simultaneously, however, these Pratese hearths were shrinking. Those in the countryside, for example, fell during this period from an average size of 5.6 persons to one of 4.7 persons. Most remarkably, at Florence itself, the population grew from 37,000 in 1427 to 59,000 in 1552, but the number of urban hearths showed a slight decline, from 9780 to 9771. Average household size, which increased from 3.79 persons in 1427 to 5.66 in 1552, was here not simply the initial but the sole indicator of population growth.[27]

Inertia in the total number of households partially reflects the manner in which the community both suffered losses and recovered from them. The epidemics rarely wiped out entire families, but they left in their

[26] The total population fell from an estimated 26,474 to 22,453; the number of hearths declined from 5637 to 5256. These estimates are based on data in Fiumi (1968).

[27] In calculating average household size at Florence, institutions and other forms of artificial households are not included in the calculations.

wake numerous small, truncated households, lacking sexually active partners and incapable of natural growth. At Florence in 1427, the most common type of household, comprising 20% of all households, contained only a single person. So also, if births increased, the babies would be initially received into existing families; only when these new members reached maturity would they begin to establish households of their own and thus increase the total number of hearths.

A problem, however, remains. At Florence, between 1427 and 1552, the considerable growth in the population never led to an increase in the number of hearths; the enlarged numbers of Florentines were entirely absorbed within the established households. In this, however, Florence was not typical. The city of Verona in northern Italy in its own demographic history offers a sharp contrast to the Florentine experience. Between 1425 and 1502, Verona nearly tripled in size, growing from approximately 14,225 inhabitants to 42,000 (Herlihy, 1973, p. 103). Predictably, the growth in its initial phases primarily affected the average size of the urban households, not their total number. Between 1425 and 1456, when the population grew by nearly 50% (to 20,800), the number of hearths increased by only a little more than 5% (from 3866 to 4078). But the average size of households jumped from 3.68 persons to 5.20. Thereafter, the continued growth in population led to the formation of new households, which increased by 80% between 1456 and 1502 (from 4078 to 7042), whereas average household size remained relatively stable (increasing from 5.20 to 5.89 persons). At Verona, but not at Florence, sustained population growth eventually led to an increased number of hearths.

How can we explain these differing patterns of growth in the two Italian cities? The answer seems to lie in the simultaneous—and contrasting—performances in the economies of the two communities. Florence was not a vigorous participant in the general European boom of the late fifteenth and sixteenth centuries. Rather, it was clearly losing the preeminence it had once enjoyed as one of Europe's industrial and financial capitals. Verona, Venice, and the region of the Veneto, on the other hand, enjoyed marked prosperity, drawing benefit from the growing trade across the Alps with southern Germany. Facing a sluggish economy, young Florentines, who traditionally sought their fortunes in commerce and banking, now also confronted a dearth of career opportunities. This discouraged the young men from leaving home at an early age or from leaving home at all. In retaining these young men, the Florentine urban household grew progressively larger in size and more complex in structure across the late fifteenth and sixteenth centuries.

Two other, economically parasitic groups also registered remarkable expansion at Florence: domestic servants and religious. Servants and slaves seem to be relatively few in Florentine households in 1427, but by 1552 they constituted 16.7% of the entire urban population (Battara, 1935, p. 80).[28] Of the urban households, 42% possessed at least one domestic, and one citizen maintained a staff of 57. The religious included 441 friars and an extraordinary 2786 nuns—6.51% of the total urban population (Battara, 1935, p. 20; Fiumi, 1968, p. 153). The throngs of nuns indicate how difficult it was to marry at Florence in the middle sixteenth century. It is also not unfair to state that these numerous servants of men and of God included many Florentines who could not find more productive employment.

At Florence and everywhere, the number of hearths within the community was a function of its economic resources—specifically the number of family farms in the rural areas and the number of what I shall call *basic jobs* in the city—jobs that were productive enough to allow the holder to support a family. The close relationship of hearths to economic resources and their exploitation helped stabilize the number of hearths even during periods of demographic decline or growth. In periods of decline, the state, landlords, and employers strove mightily to keep hearths occupied—which is to say, farms cultivated and basic jobs filled—lest their own revenues in taxes, rents, or profits should decline. Through offering low rents, high wages, or favorable terms, they recruited younger sons, younger brothers, servants—persons who might otherwise have stayed for longer or for indefinite periods in their households of origin or employment. Wages, for example, increased by three or four times between 1344 and 1415, as the Florentine population was falling by more than half.[29] To the extent that these efforts were successful, the number of hearths would hold relatively steady, but their average size would fall.

Conversely, in periods of population growth, if the number of available farms or of basic jobs did not also grow, the increased population would be largely or entirely absorbed into the existing households.

[28] This percentage was among the highest in Italy. In 1563 at Venice only 7.7% of the population were domestics, and only 10.7% at Bologna in 1587.

[29] See the entries under "De salariis debitis famulis et similibus," (Masi, 1348/1934, pp. 161–164). Also see the revision of the same entries in *Statuta populi et communis Florentiae,* Vol. 2, pp. 267–270 (Freiburg, 1778). The first list of salaries dates from 1344, and its revision from 1415. The yearly wages of a *famulus masculus*, 'male servant,' increased from 12 to 36 pounds. The yearly wages of a squire (*ragazzus equi vel ronzini*) increased from 12 to 48 pounds. These increases do not, however, take into consideration the steady debasement of the Florentine silver pound, which fell in relation with the gold florin by about 44% in this period.

Many younger sons or brothers would remain at home; some might be allowed to marry, but the new joint family would still live on the resources of a single household. We call these households *impacted*, as the population increment was turned inward and distributed among the established hearths. Eventually, this impacted structure would generate strong pressures restraining or stopping further demographic expansion, particularly through delaying or preventing the marriage of the young. This pattern seems to summarize the Florentine experience in the late fifteenth and sixteenth centuries.

REFLECTIONS

We are now prepared to examine several models of population dynamics, estimating the relationships of demographic and economic movements over time. (For a full description of these models, see Lee, 1973, 1974, forthcoming.)

Constant Fertility (CF)

The Tuscan evidence strongly indicates that fertility was not constant but was highly variable and sensitive to both environmental and temporal factors.

Constant Population (CP)

The Tuscan experience confirms the basic assumption here that fertility will fluctuate up or down as does mortality. However, given the power of the late medieval epidemics, perfect equilibrium between deaths and births could not be readily achieved. There is, after all, no theoretical limit to death rates (unless it be 1000 deaths per 1000 persons in the community), but there are obvious biological limits to birth rates. The plague further slowed recovery by taking large tolls from among the young adults, who were the potential mothers and fathers. To judge from baptisms, the community was able to maintain a stable yearly crop of babies even in the face of the most horrendous losses. But even this impressive feat could not produce a quick return to former levels of population size.

Given these unequal vital balances, the Tuscan population from about 1300 to 1550 was not at all constant but shows considerable variations in size. The mechanisms described by the model operated imperfectly. Viewed another way, the equilibrium of constant population envisioned by the model could be achieved across a whole range of levels, depending on the severity of epidemics and the success of the population in responding to them. And the equilibrium, once achieved, was easily disturbed.

Mortality Dependent Equilibrium Wage and Constant Equilibrium Wage

Wages were sensitive to mortality levels, and rose strongly in response to the plunging population of the fourteenth century. The high wages helped recruit superfluous members of established households, who in turn cultivated farms and assumed basic jobs. The families they established refilled or replaced deserted hearths. High wages thus generally encouraged demographic recovery. The Mortality Dependent Equilibrium Wage offers a more realistic model of the actual Tuscan experience than the Constant Equilibrium Wage, as the latter assumes that fertility can compensate perfectly for variations in mortality. This need not be so, and was not so amid the terrible epidemics of the fourteenth century.

There are, however, conceptual difficulties in applying the concept of an equilibrium wage to the Tuscan economy. For reasons already mentioned, the cities tended to run a demographic deficit over time in relation to the countryside, and had constantly to generate immigration from rural areas through offering higher wages. Under such conditions, no equilibrium wage could be reached for the community as a whole, as immigration would then cease and the system could no longer function. The traditional city was, in other words, typically short of labor, and typically forced to bid for it at higher rates than did the rural villages. In 1415, for example, wet-nurses within the city of Florence received a salary of 4 pounds per month for caring for a baby in their homes; those within 12 miles of the city received 3 pounds; and those beyond 12 miles only 2.5 pounds.[30] These environmental variations in wage levels rendered the demographic effects of changing wages particularly complex, even paradoxical. The rustic immigrant into the city could well earn higher wages but would probably acquire a smaller family than his brother who remained back home in relative need; the urban environment was hostile to marriage and to procreation. It is, in other words, difficult to apply the same estimation of behavior to what Chayanov (1966) considered, in our opinion rightly, to be two economies.

[30] These are the maximum wages allowed according to the Statutes of 1415. See the *Statuta populi et communis Florentiae*, Vol. 2, pp. 267–270.

Fixed Hearths

The number of hearths within the community does show relative stability, but that number was not fixed "by convention." Rather, it mediated the influence land and resources exerted upon demographic behavior.

I would argue that the number of hearths set the equilibrium level, or rather, the range of levels, across which the Tuscan population fluctuated, while displaying the close interactions between mortality and fertility assumed in the preceding two models. The same number of hearths could, for example, contain populations of remarkably different sizes. The Florentine population grew by more than 50% between 1427 and 1552, but the number of its hearths increased not at all.

Still, to sustain demographic expansion, the community eventually needed additional hearths, which required in turn either the opening of new lands or the creation of new basic jobs in industry or commerce. Florence in the sixteenth century was unable to achieve this; its urban households consequently grew large and impacted, and this generated forces that blocked its further growth.[31] The more dynamic economy of Verona was able to generate additional jobs, and this substantially raised the limits upon its expansion. A city probably one-third Florence's size in the fourteenth century, Verona equaled or surpassed the Tuscan capital by the middle sixteenth century. In other words, within certain limits, the fluctuation in the size of the Tuscan population reflected interactions among mortality, wages, and fertility, as the models depict. But sustained growth in the population was contingent on an increment in the number of hearths, which required in turn an increase in the number of farms or jobs. Without economic growth there could be no sustained demographic growth.

One other factor is of importance here: the distinctive character of the urban household. Cities generally acted as a brake upon demographic growth, as the urban environment discouraged marriages and procreation. This seems primarily to reflect the low economic value of women and children within the urban household. Much in contrast with rural areas, the urban wife and child made little substantial contribution to the productivity of their household and to the wealth of the city. But if this is true, then it follows that any change in the economic functions and value of women and children within the urban households would have profound social and demographic repercussions. Students of historical demography, even those primarily interested in aggregate

---

[31] In spite of its stable population, the average size of the Florentine household was one of the largest in Italy. See Battara (1935, pp. 80–81).

movements, should not neglect the microanalysis of households and of the changing economic functions of their members, especially women and children, especially within cities.

Limited land, limited jobs, limited hearths, and limited economic functions for the urban wife and child combined to halt demographic growth in Florence by the middle sixteenth century, and surely contributed to the city's decline from the heights of cultural leadership it once so brilliantly held. The story does not have a cheerful ending. Still, in allowing us to view so closely how they behaved, the Florentines of these past centuries richly deserve our admiration and gratitude.

REFERENCES

Battagli da Rimini, Marcha di Marco (1913). *Breviarium italicae historicae*, ed. Aldo Francesco Massera. Rerum italicarum scriptores, n.s., Vol. 16, Pt. 3; Città di Castello.

Battara, Pietro (1935). *La popolazione de Firenze alla metà del '500*. Florence:

Bec, Christian (1967). *Les marchands écrivains, affaires et humanisme à Florence* (1376–1434). Paris and The Hague: Mouton. P. 492.

Bec, Christian, ed. (1969). *Il libro degli affari proprii di casa de Lapo di Giovanni Niccolini de' Sirigatti*. Paris.

Birdsall, Jean, Trans. (1953). *The Chronicle of Jean de Venette*. New York: Records of Civilization, Sources and Studies, No. 50.

Bowsky, William M. (1964). "The Impact of the Black Death upon Sienese Government and Society," *Speculum*, Vol. 39, p. 17.

Bowsky, William M. (1971). *The Black Death. A Turning Point in History?* New York: Holt. P. 128.

Chayanov, A. V. (1966). *The Theory of Peasant Economy*, ed. Daniel Thorner, Basile Kerblay, & R.E.F. Smith. Homewood, Ill.: R. D. Irwin. P. 317.

Cigliotti, G. C., ed. (1937). *Cronache di ser Luca Dominici*. Pistoia: Pacinotti. P. 274.

Coale, Ansley, & Demeny, Paul (1966). *Regional Model Life Tables and Stable Populations*. Princeton, N.J.: Princeton University Press.

Conti, Elio (1966). *I catasti agrari della repubblica fiorentina e il catasto particellare toscano (secoli XIV–XIX)*. Rome: Instituto storico italiano per il medio evo.

Corsini, C. A. (1974). "Nascite e matrimoni," *Le fonti della demografia storica in Italia*. Vol. 2. Rome: Comitato italiano per lo studio dei problemi della popolazione.

Dolce, Lodovico (1560). *Dialogo de M. Lodovico Dolce della istituzione delle donne*. 4th ed. Venice: Gabriel Giolito de Ferrari. P. 80.

Fiumi, E. (1961). *Storia economica e sociale de San Gimignano*. Florence: Olschki. P. 372.

Fiumi, E. (1968). *Demografia, movimento urbanistico e classi sociali in Prato dall' etá comunale ai tempi moderni*. Florence: Olschki. P. 687.

Hajnal, H. (1953). "Age at Marriage and Proportions Marrying," *Population Studies*, Vol. 7, pp. 111–136.

Heers, Jacques (1961). *Gênes au XVe siècle. Activité économique et problèmes sociaux*. Paris.

Herlihy, D. J. (1967). *Medieval and Renaissance Pistoia. The Social History of an Italian Town, 1200–1430*. New Haven and London: Yale University Press. P. 297.

Herlihy, D. J. (1969). "Vieillir à Florence au Quattrocento," *Annales: Economies, Sociétés, Civilisations*, Vol. 24, pp. 1350.

Herlihy, D. J. (1973). "The Population of Verona in the First Century of Venetian Rule," in John Hale, ed., *Renaissance Venice*. London: Faber and Faber. Pp. 91–120.

Ildefonso di San Luigi (1777). *Delizie degli eruditi toscani*. Vol. 9. Florence: Cambiagi. P. 372.

Klapisch, Christiane, & Demonet, M. (1972). *"A uno pane e uno vino:* la famille toscane au début du XVe siècle," *Annales: Economies, Sociétés, Civilisations*, Vol. 27, pp. 873–901.

Landucci, Luca (1883). *Diario fiorentino dal 1450 al 1516 di Luca Landucci, continuato da un anonimo fino al 1542*, ed. I. del Badia. Florence: G. C. Sansoni. P. 377.

Lastri, Marco (1775). *Ricerche dell'antica e moderna popolazione della città di Firenze per mezzo dei registri de battesimi del Battistero di San Giovanni dal 1451 al 1774*. Florence.

Lee, Ronald (1973). "Population in Pre-Industrial England, An Economic Analysis," *Quarterly Journal of Economics*, Vol. 88, pp. 582–607.

Lee, Ronald (1974). "Estimating Series of Vital Rates and Age Structures from Baptisms and Burials: A New Technique, with Applications to Preindustrial England," *Population Studies*, Vol. 28, No. 3 (November).

Lee, Ronald (forthcoming). "Models of Preindustrial Population Dynamics with Applications to England," in Charles Tilly, ed., *Historical Studies of Changing Fertility*. Princeton, N.J.: Princeton University Press.

Lugli, V. (1909). *I trattasi della famiglia nel Quattrocento*. Bologna and Modena.

Martines, Lauro (1974). "A Way of Looking at Women in Renaissance Florence," *Journal of Medieval and Renaissance Studies*, Vol. 4, p. 23.

Masi, Gino, ed. (1348/1934). "De salariis debitis famulis et similibus," *Statutum bladi reipublicae florentinae*. Milan: Biblioteca di testi medievali.

Morelli, Giovanni di Pagolo (1956). *Ricordi*, ed. Vittore Branca. Florence: F. Le Monnier. P. 553.

Morelli, Lionardo (1783). "Secunda cronica di Lionardo Morelli," *Delizie degli eruditi toscani*, ed., Ildefonso di San Luigi. Vol. 19. Florence: Gaetano Cambiagi.

Orlandi, Stefano, ed. (1955). *"Necrologio"* di *S. Maria Novella. Testo integrale dall' inizio (MCCXXV) al MDIV*. 2 vols. Florence: Olschki. P. 1422.

Parenti, G. (1943–1949). "Fonti per lo studio della demografia fiorentina: I Libri dei morti," *Genus*, Vols. 6–8, pp. 294–296.

Perosa, A., ed. (1960). *Giovanni Rucellai e il suo Zibaldone*, Vol. 1: *Il Zibaldone quaresimale*. London: Warburg Institute. P. 219.

Petrucci, Armando, ed. (1965). *Il libro di ricordanze dei Corsini (1362–1457)*. Rome: Fonti per la storia d'Italia.

Repetti, E. (1843). "Stato e movimento della popolazione . . . di ciascuna comunità della Toscana e della Romagna granducale a quattro epoche diverse," *Dizionario geografico fisico storico della Toscana*. Vol. 5. Florence: Repetti. Pp. 566–77.

Shrewsbury, J. F. D. (1970). *A History of Bubonic Plague in the British Isles*. Cambridge: University Press. P. 661.

Somogyi, S. (1950). "Sulla mascolinità delle nascite a Firenze dal 1451 al 1474," *Rivista Italiana di Economia Demografia e Statistica*, Vol. 4, pp. 460–470.

Villani, Giovanni (1823). *Cronica di Giovanni Villani*. Vol. 6, Book 11. Florence: Magheri. P. 285.

The Influence of Economic and Social Variables on Marriage and Fertility in Eighteenth and Nineteenth Century Japanese Villages*

SUSAN B. HANLEY

University of Washington

Among the Japanese there were fundamental similarities in the cultural condi-
tioning of, and the individual motivations in, the limitation of family size in
the Tokugawa and the modern worlds. The pressure of numbers on subsistence and the misery of poverty do not explain the control of fertility in the
industrial society; they did not explain the abortion and the infanticide of the
agrarian society [Taeuber, 1958, p. 33].

The population of Japan from the 1720s to the 1840s as seen in the
national aggregate figures grew very slowly. For some periods, the
growth rate was negative. The traditional explanation has been that
Japan's population was "stagnant" because of the recurrent and wide-

* This chapter is a shortened version of a chapter to be published in Susan B. Hanley
and Kozo Yamamura, *Economic and Demographic Change in Preindustrial Japan, 1600–1868,*
copyright Princeton University Press. I am indebted to Professor Hayami Akira for help
in obtaining and for guidance in the use of the *shūmon-aratame-chō*, the documents used
in this study; to Professor Naitō Jirō for making available the documents for Numa; and to
Professors John W. Hall and Taniguchi Sumio for their kind assistance in the study of
Okayama. I would also like to thank the Foreign Area Fellowship Program and the
East–West Population Institute, Honolulu, for financial support for collecting the data and
analyzing it by computer. The responsibility for the contents, however, is solely mine.

spread famines and the resulting practices of abortion and infanticide resorted to by desperate, poverty-stricken peasants.[1] But though periodic famines and ensuing epidemics contributed to the slow population growth in the eighteenth and nineteenth centuries, they by no means account for it, even in the regions in which the worst famines occurred.[2] Evidence of abortion and infanticide also exist, but again, the increasing body of evidence on the growth in the economy and improvements in the standard of living in most of the country makes it difficult to explain the motivation in terms of acts of desperation by families struggling for survival.[3] Yet an analysis on the village level of fertility, mortality, and life expectancy in central and western Japan indicates an average completed family size of three children, one that cannot be explained by high death rates.[4]

Why then was the family size small? And if couples were deliberately limiting the number of children they had, was it in response to conditions that made it physically impossible to raise more children, or were they perhaps responding to positive incentives, such as trying to raise

[1] Takahashi Bonsen, the most prominent proponent of this view, attributed the "slowness of the rate of population increase . . . partly to frequent famines and the outbreak of diseases, but the major reason was birth control, that is, abortion and infanticide were flourishingly practiced [Takahashi, 1936, p. 50]." Takahashi's evidence—and he provided painstaking documentation—is drawn, however, almost exclusively from the Tōhoku region and from domains in the Kantō, two of the regions that suffered most severely from the periodic famines.

[2] Evidence on the exaggeration of the famine statistics from the domain of Morioka, which is considered to have been among the hardest hit, can be found in Yamamura (1973).

[3] An overview of major studies appearing in the 1960s that document this growth can be found in Hanley and Yamamura (1971). The American scholar who pioneered in documenting premodern economic growth and a rise in the living standard in the villages is Thomas C. Smith. (See Thomas C. Smith, 1958, 1959, 1969.)

[4] See Hanley (1974) for a study of the same set of villages analyzed here. The leading historical demographer in Japan is Hayami Akira, Professor of Economics at Keio University, who has published several dozen articles on Japan's premodern population plus a prizewinning book (Hayami, 1973a). For articles in western languages, see Hayami (1966–1967, 1968, 1972, 1973b).

It should be noted that the studies of Hayami and Hanley with regard to village population during the second half of the Tokugawa period (eighteenth and nineteenth centuries) are generally mutually supporting though carried out on different areas. For example, in his study of Yokouchi village in central Japan (Shinano province), Hayami found that "from 1671–1725 married women who survived until age 45 with their husbands had 6.5 births if the women married between 15–20, 5.9 if married at 21–25, and 1.5 if at over 26. From 1726–75 they averaged 4.2 births if married between 15–20, 3.4 if at 21–26, and 3.0 if at over 26. And after 1776, women averaged 3.6–3.8 births whenever they married. I think this was due to the practice of birth control [1967–1968, English summary].

their standard of living or protect family assets? In this chapter I will analyze the influence of various social and economic variables on fertility in four villages in western Japan, all of which had average family sizes of about three children. Despite the obvious impossibility of uncovering the motivation of these villagers, it is possible to examine the results of their actions affecting fertility and to isolate how behavior differed according to the economic situation of both families and villages.

For the microdata necessary for this study, information on fertility was obtained from the *shūmon-aratame-chō* (religious investigation registers)[5] from three villages in Okayama, one of the most economically advanced domains in Tokugawa Japan. A fourth village from Mikawa province in western Japan yields data for a 15-year period covering one of the worst famines in Japan. The data permit comparisons of fertility between villages with different economic conditions and within a village over time. For Fujito of Okayama, fertility can be analyzed also by families categorized by landholding size.

Four major hypotheses are presented here: (1) Families sought to rear an optimum-size family of about three to four children, depending on the village and period in time. Rather than passively accept as many or few children as were born to them, families controlled the number of children raised, not only through limiting births, but by adopting children if they could not have as many as they wanted or by giving out excess children for others to adopt. Women who suffered the loss in infancy of desired children often bore more than the average number of children in an effort to achieve desired family size. (2) Fertility patterns indicate that birth control, including abortion and infanticide, was being practiced within marriage to a considerable degree even in areas

[5] The *shūmon-aratame* or religious investigations were begun in the early seventeenth century as a means of controlling Christianity. Every person was required to be registered at a temple or shrine, and the resulting records are very similar in form to the scattered population surveys dating from the same century. Although the original function was lost, the registrations were continued and formed the basis for the national population surveys that were carried out periodically from the 1720s. Listings in the registers were by household. Though the form and contents varied somewhat by area, each household entry usually contained the temple to which each member belonged, the names of the family head and male and unmarried female family members, the position of each person in the household with relation to the head, any official village position held by a member, the number of servants or employees, and often any cattle holdings. Other information was noted where applicable—in particular, marriages, births, deaths, adoptions, and the destination of any individual who left the village and reason for leaving. In most places ages were also recorded, although the age at first registration varied by domain; the most common practice was to list a child for the first time in the next registration after he was born, which would be early in the calendar year after the one in which he was born.

that were developing economically and during periods of economic growth. This is indicated by the very low average age of women at last birth. The sex ratios of lastborn children also suggest that some sex-selective infanticide was being practiced. (3) Fertility was regulated not only within marriage, but perhaps more importantly, by varying the age at which persons were permitted to marry and the proportion of the population allowed to marry. Delaying marriage for women shortened their childbearing years. Also, the number of childbearing couples within a household was usually limited to one. In times of poor economic conditions, the number of marriages within a village would drop, and thus the number of children would decline although marital fertility remained fairly constant. In a period of an expanding economy, younger brothers who would normally leave home or remain unmarried were permitted to marry and remain in the village. This response to economic conditions was fairly rapid, within 5 to 10 years at most. (4) Famines had a minimal effect on the social and household structure of all the villages studied here, even those that experienced a rise in the death rate. Any vacuums created by death and disease were quickly adjusted for through marriages, births, and the adoption of people of all ages, but the need for such adjustments was in most cases minimal.

Several additional hypotheses are advanced from an analysis of the data from Fujito. The first is that household size tended to remain constant over generations unless the economic conditions of the household changed drastically. In other words, the size of each household tended to fluctuate very closely around the mean of its size over time, despite changes in the life cycle of the head of the family and changes in who was head.

A second hypothesis is that size of landholding seems to have had very little visible influence on the demographic behavior of a family. If anything, there was an inverse relationship between the size of the holding and the size of the family. Families with large holdings tended to limit their heirs in order to prevent the dispersion of their wealth, but families with little or no land were often not dependent on the land for their livelihood or had few family assets to protect.

These hypotheses were posited after a study of the Okayama villages. Here quantitative data will be provided to demonstrate that these hypotheses hold for the three Okayama villages. Using the data from Nishikata in Mikawa, testing will be begun to determine whether these hypotheses are valid for other areas in Japan.

To test these hypotheses, I will analyze the fertility patterns and the actions Japanese took to control their family sizes in relationship to the circumstances and conditions that may have influenced this regulation. The four villages studied are as follows:

1. Fujito, a farming village that seemingly had economic problems in the late eighteenth century but a growing economy in the nineteenth. (For a case study of this village, see Hanley, 1972.) It was located in the southernmost district of Okayama on a major route from the castle town, the administrative center of the domain, to Shimotsui, a major port on the Inland Sea. The village became involved in the cotton industry, and in the nineteenth century the weaving of cotton cloth formed an important by-employment in the village. Also, the arable land in the village increased by about 20% in the early nineteenth century through reclamation. Data are available for this village for 42 years during the period 1775–1863. In this period the population of the village grew from just under 600 persons to slightly over 700.

2. Fukiage, a fishing village on the Inland Sea that grew rapidly in the eighteenth century as its neighbor, Shimotsui, became a port on the shipping circuit from western Japan to Osaka. Thirty-one registers, scattered throughout the two centuries from 1683 to 1860, still exist for this village. The population of this village tripled, increasing from 308 in 1685 to 932 in 1860.

3. Numa, a landlocked farming village that showed a nearly stable total population of a little over 300 from 1780 to 1871, a century during which data exist for 33 years. Although it was located in the plains area on the road to the castle town, Numa did not have the opportunities for economic expansion that either Fujito or Fukiage had.

4. Nishikata, a farming village adjacent to Mikawa Bay off the Pacific coast and next to a post station on the Tokaido, the most traveled road in Japan. Records exist for this village for the crucial famine years of the 1780s, and although they cover only 15 years, they are continuous from 1782 to 1796. Nishikata's population dropped during this period from 271 to 248, around 9%.

EVIDENCE OF EFFORTS TO CONTROL FAMILY SIZE

Crude birth- and death-rate averages in much of western Japan were so low in the Tokugawa period as to be suspect without a thorough examination of the sources from which they were compiled. The mean death rates for each village ranged within the narrow limits of 20 and 23 per 1000, and the birth rates showed a low of 18.5 for Nishikata and a high of 26 for Fukiage (see Table 1). The rates are lower than modern

TABLE 1
Crude Birth and Death Rate Averages (per thousand)[a]

	Crude birth rate averages	Crude death rate averages		Crude birth rate averages	Crude death rate average
Fujito -- 1794-1863			*Fukiage -- 1693-1860*		
1794-1799 (N = 4)[b]	20.2	20.5	1693-1700 (N = 5)	31.0	15.9
1800-1804 (N = 5)	15.4	16.8	1702-1712 (N = 5)	26.3	21.1
1805-1810 (N = 5)	22.3	17.0	1727-1741 (N = 3)	31.9	30.8
1825-1829 (N = 5)	25.2	20.5	1773-1781 (N = 3)	25.4	24.6
1830-1834 (N = 5)	33.1	29.0	1791-1801 (N = 3)	26.0	20.3
1835-1841 (N = 3)	23.3	25.8	1821-1826 (N = 3)	18.4	19.4
1844-1848 (N = 5)	28.5	21.6	1854-1860 (N = 3)	19.4	22.2
1850-1857 (N = 4)	28.6	26.4			
1859-1863 (N = 3)	18.3	19.2			
Nishikata -- 1782-1795			*Numa -- 1785-1871*		
1782-1786 (N = 5)	19.9	14.5	1785-1803 (N = 7)	24.9	--
1787-1791 (N = 5)	18.6	29.2	1814 (N = 1)	23.9	--
1792-1795 (N = 4)	16.7	26.9	1819-1832 (N = 13)	19.3	22.8
			1860-1871 (N = 10)	15.7	16.6
Mean of means					
Fujito (N = 39)	24.2	21.8			
Fukiage (N = 25)	26.0	21.5			
Numa (N = 31)	19.6	20.1			
Nishikata (N = 14)	18.5	23.3			

[a]From S. B. Hanley, "Fertility, Mortality, and Life Expectancy in Pre-modern Japan," *Population Studies*, 28, 1(March 1974), p. 131.
[b]N = number of years in each period for which data are available.

birth and death rates because infant deaths in the first few hours and days after birth were not recorded. The shortest life span recorded in any of the villages was 3 weeks. Nevertheless, because these rates were compiled from a study of individuals over time, there is little doubt that they indicate the general magnitude of births and deaths in these villages (see Hanley, 1974).

Such low birth rates naturally resulted in a small number of children recorded as ever born to couples and a small number of children raised. The number of children ever born averaged from just under three to between three and four for all the villages. Although the average was around three, the modal number of children born was sometimes only two, as was the case for Fukiage between 1773 and 1801 and Fujito for women who married after 1841 (see Tables 2 and 3).

The number of children recorded as ever born to a woman does not,

TABLE 2
Distribution of Completed Family Size in Fujito for Families with Children

Number of children	Number of families by number of children ever born	Number of families by number of children who survived
Women aged 23-44 in 1794 (Cohort Group D)[a]		
0	-	1
1	5	9
2	8	10
3	16	10
4	15	17
5	5	4
6	3	4
7	2	0
8	1	0
Average	3.53	3.11
Women who married 1825-1841 (Cohort Group G)		
0	-	3
1	11	15
2	4	13
3	17	21
4	19	16
5	15	6
6	8	2
7	2	0
8	0	0
Average	3.72	2.76
Women who married after 1841 (Cohort Group H)		
0	-	0
1	10	13
2	16	18
3	8	10
4	9	11
5	8	6
6	8	1
Average	3.22	2.69

See Appendix for explanation of Cohort Groups.

however, necessarily represent the number of children she raised. In-fant and child mortality was frequently high. Because of an epidemic of some disease to which children were particularly susceptible, and also because of the practice of letting children be adopted by others, women in Fujito who married between 1825 and 1841 on the average saw one child less than the number they bore survive, or 2.76 instead of 3.72. No one in the village had more than six children survive in any of the three periods shown in Table 2.

Appendix to Table 2
Cohort Groups for Fujito

Sample size

---

34   A) Those married women who had reached age 39 but no more than 55 by
         1775 (or 39 by 1778).

20   B) Women of childbearing age but less than age 39 who appeared in the
         records only in 1775-1778.

34   C) Childbearing women aged 18-38 in 1775 (or 18 by 1778) who could be
         identified in the 1794 records.

56   D) Married women aged 23-44 in 1794 and who were married prior to
         1794 (but who did not appear in the 1775-1778 records).

51   E) Women whose marriages were contracted between 1794-1810. This
         group includes six women whose marriages were terminated prior to
         1810.

42   F) Married women aged 31-45 in 1825 who did not appear in records
         prior to that year.

80   G) Women who were married between 1825-1841. This cohort group has
         been further divided into eight classes by the *kokudaka* size of
         the household in which each woman lived.

62   H) Women who were married (or who bore children without recorded
         husbands) after 1841 but who reached age 44 or whose marriage had
         terminated in or prior to 1863. This cohort group has been further
         subdivided into eight classes by the *kokudaka* size of the house-
         hold in which each woman lived.

44   I) Women who were married or bore children without recorded husbands
         after 1844 but who were still of childbearing age and married in
         1863.

- -

Kokudaka Classes

I   Households with no recorded landholdings

II   Households holding land assessed at one *koku* or less

III   Households holding land assessed at from 1-3 *koku*

IV   Households holding land assessed at from 3-6 *koku*

V   The remaining households consisting of the following groups:

        1) Households containing ten or more members for the
            entire period under observation
        2) Households holding land assessed at from 6-10 *koku*
        3) Households holding land assessed at more than ten
            koku (only the Hikasa and Hoshijima lines were in
            this category from 1825-1863, the period for which
            the classifications were made)
        4) Households which changed *kokudaka* classes from 1851-
            1863, most often switching between the 1-3 and 3-6
            kokudaka classes.

TABLE 3
Distribution of family size in Fukiage and Numa

Number of children	Number of families by number of children ever born	Number of families by total number of children at any one time
Fukiage 1773–1801		
0	24	15
1	25	27
2	51	50
3	42	51
4	38	38
5	15	13
6	10	12
7	2	3
8	2	0
Average	2.73	2.82
Numa 1814–1832		
0	7	4
1	7	9
2	15	18
3	14	15
4	16	14
5	4	5
6	2	0
Average	2.69	2.63
Numa 1860–1871		
0	3	2
1	3	4
2	5	3
3	13	13
4	3	6
5	0	0
6	0	0
7	1	0
Average	2.89	2.61

But, although the size of many families was diminished through death and adoption, other families made up for losses through the birth of additional children or adoption. Thus in Fukiage, in the period 1773–1801, 24 families, or nearly one-eighth of the sample, had no children of their own, but only 15 families raised no children (see Table 3). The distributions of families by the number of children born to them and the number raised are very similar, but these totals in fact cloak the actions on the part of families to ensure that they raised the number of children they desired. Since, for example, as many as 25% of the children born to women married between 1825 and 1841 in Fujito died while very young, some of these families adopted children in order to obtain the family size they wanted.

Adoption was a common method of regulating family size in premodern Japan, and even until World War II. In the four villages studied here, persons of all ages were adopted, even some elderly women after the Tempō famine of the 1830s. But the most common adoptions were of children above age 2, who became adopted sons and daughters, and of young men who married daughters of families without male heirs, took up residence with the family, and became family members, receiving the family name and usually succeeding the head. Adoptions were so widely practiced that in Numa, in the years between 1860 and 1871, there were more adoptions recorded than marriages. The ratio of adoptions to marriages varied by village and by period (see Table 4), but it was never very low and frequently was over 50%.

The widespread custom of adoption can be considered one of the major reasons the premodern Japanese were able to limit family size in a society in which the continuation of the family line was of the utmost importance both economically and socially. This well-known practice of samurai families was even more frequently used by peasant families, at least in the village of Fujito. Of 105 families for whom records exist for at least two or more generations, 56 families, or 53%, adopted heirs in order to continue the family line. This is easily twice the rate of adoption found for the *hatamoto* class of samurai (Yamamura, 1974). And this percentage may well be an underestimate, as there was a tendency to drop the term *adopted* within a few years of the event, particularly after an adopted son succeeded to the headship of a family.

In addition to ensuring the continuation of family lines, the system of adoption created an outlet for excess sons in a family that was already assured an heir. The custom of adoption was so widely accepted that at least two families in Fujito permitted their younger sons to leave home or become adopted, and when subsequently their own heirs died, the families took in adopted sons to succeed the head rather than have their own children return. The importance of the family name and the continuation of the line in Japan has long been stressed by anthropologists, but what is a crucial difference between Japan and, for example, India is that in Japan any male in the family, whether adopted or not, is eligible to become head, to carry on the family name and business, and to say prayers and care for the tablets of deceased family members.[6]

[6] For a discussion of "ancestor worship" and the care of tablets for the dead, see Robert J. Smith (1966).

TABLE 4
Incidence of Adoption Compared to Marriage

	Be adopted in	Be adopted out	Total no. adoptions	Marry in	Marry out	Total no. marriages	Adoptions as percentage of marriages
			Fujito				
1775-1810 (15)[a]	12	8	20	54	58	112	17.9
1825-1841 (13)	24	23	47	54	44	98	48.0
1844-1863 (12)	31	24	55	51	41	92	59.8
			Fukiage				
1693-1741 (13)	11	7	18	56	40	96	18.8
1773-1860 (12)	71	45	116	65	54	119	97.5
			Numa				
1880-1832 (22)	14	14	28	67	57	124	22.6
1860-1871 (10)	29	25	54	23	24	47	114.9
			Nishikata				
1782-1796 (15)	13	10	23	20	16	36	63.9

[a]Number of years during the period for which there are data.

The practice of adoption ensured continuity to families and gave a certain stability to the village, but it was not a practice with built-in rigidities. Adoption was no more irrevocable than marriage, perhaps less so. An adopted son was theoretically to leave his own family behind and become part of the new family just as a bride did—thus the symbolic burning of straw behind a bride to indicate her permanent departure from her old home—but in reality people returned home when things did not work out. Thus in Nishikata in the 15 years under survey, there were 13 adoptions into Nishikata families and 10 out, for a total of 23, compared to 36 marriages. During the same period 16 persons who had been adopted out returned home. Adoptions seem to have been somewhat more successful in Fujito and the incidence increased over time. In the 15 years for which there are records before 1810, 12 persons were adopted out and 8 in. In contrast, from 1825 to 1863, in a total of 25 years for which there are records, 57 people were adopted in and 47 went out, with the average number of adoptions per year double that of the earlier period. Only one person came back from an unsuccessful adoption in the first period and six in the second. The highest incidence of adoption in Fujito occurred in the 1840s and 1850s, just after the Tempō famine and ensuing epidemics. The effect of a series of poor harvests could also be the reason for the high rate, especially of unsuccessful adoptions, in Nishikata where the records cover the Temmei famine years.

BIRTH CONTROL THROUGH ABORTION AND INFANTICIDE

Datai–mabiki (abortion and infanticide) are commonly used as a phrase by Japanese historians, but the older of the two practices is undoubtedly *mabiki*, which means "to thin out" and usually refers to the thinning of plants. The infanticide in the Tohoku region during the Temmei famine of the 1780s is legendary; in the domain of Nambu the bodies of scores of dead children wrapped in straw mats were reported seen floating down one river (Takahashi, 1936, pp. 121–122). Fear of the results on the tax revenue of the widespread use of these methods to limit children caused administrators in many areas to issue regulations banning these practices and to effect measures to see that the prohibitions were more than exhortatory. Many domains required pregnant women to be registered, and some provided monetary incentives for bearing children.

Various methods of abortion seem to have been well known, and if the numerous regulations and bans against them are any testimony, they were widely used. A common method seems to have been to apply continuous pressure to the belly or to vibrate it until abortion was induced. The practice of inserting a stick-like object into the head of the uterus had been perfected by the mid-seventeenth century and was used by professionals—usually midwives—from this time on. Many names exist for the medicines used to induce miscarriages, which were sold as "menstrual medicine" (*gekkei yaku*).[7] The most common of these was a mercurial compound, and one can imagine the possibly serious side effects. In 1646 the Shogunate banned public advertisement of these within the city limits of Edo (Tokyo), and in 1667 it became illegal to perform abortion in the city. Nevertheless, various subterfuges were used and the business continued (Honjō, 1930, p. 116). Nearly two centuries later, in 1842, an Edo magistrate ruled that "those who unwarrantedly perform abortions out of their own private wishes, both men and women, would be driven out of Edo for a distance of ten *ri* in all directions."[8]

Not all the methods for abortion had the efficacy of those used by the professionals in Edo. In Okayama there were a number of beliefs about how to terminate pregnancy that undoubtedly had little effect. To induce abortion, Okayama women used to cauterize the navel with moxa, or brew the seeds of the white morning glory and drink the resulting tea. They tried eating carp before they were 2 months pregnant, and they massaged the belly vigorously. Abortion was considered most likely to be successful if attempted in odd-numbered months. If all of these methods failed, they might try jumping from a "high place" in the seventh or eighth month of pregnancy (Nishijima, 1969, pp. 241–242).

After a child was born or aborted, women often tried to prevent future pregnancy. It was thought effective to drink a bowlful of salt water every night before going to bed. Urinating immediately after intercourse was supposed to prevent conception. Women also resorted to religion; many made bottomless sacks out of cloth and dedicated them to nearby shrines to prevent pregnancy. And one might name the last child Sué (the last) if a girl or Tomekichi (*tome* means "stop") if a boy. That this last practice was rarely effective is attested to by the number of children in Okayama who bore these names but who had one or more younger brothers and sisters.

Although qualitative evidence on the practices of abortion and infanticide can be found in numerous sources, it is more difficult to assess to what extent these practices were prevalent and what effect they had on population growth. Takahashi tends to attribute declines in population to these practices and increases in population to the effectiveness of countermeasures (1936, pp. 100, 102). However, there are certain statis-

---

[7] The various methods of abortion used are vividly described in Takahashi (1936, pp. 27–31).

[8] Kōjiruien, Hōgibu 12, Ijutsu 3, 882–83.

tical tests that can be carried out to determine whether methods of birth control were being practiced to an extent that affected population patterns.

First, we can examine the average span of childbearing in our four villages (see Tables 5 and 6). The average age at first birth tended to coincide with the average age at marriage in each village because it was not uncommon for a marriage to be legally registered only after the bride became pregnant or had borne her first child, and because even where this was not the case, women tended to bear their first child within a year or two of marriage. From this evidence it would be difficult to conclude that women were limiting their family size by

TABLE 5
Average Age at First and Last Birth in Fukiage, Numa, and Nishikata

Period	Average age first birth	Sample size	s	Average age last birth	Sample size	s
Fukiage						
1683–1712	23.1	67	3.4	37.4[a]	82	4.1
				37.3[b]	61	0.4
1773–1801	22.7	80	3.4	37.6	126	4.6
				37.5	107	4.9
Numa						
1814–1832	24.0	32	2.5	33.0	33	5.9
				35.5	25	4.7
1860–1871	22.7	18	3.4	33.1	14	4.8
				34.0	13	3.4
Nishikata						
1782–1796	21.1	7	1.7	32.4[c]	26	4.3
				33.3[d]	13	5.3

[a] The first figures for Fukiage and Numa are for women who were married to age 44 or whose marriages ended earlier due to the death of either spouse. The divorced and childless have been omitted.

[b] The second figures for Fukiage and Numa are based on the same group of women as the first but with all women eliminated whose marriages terminated before the women reached age 43 or whose daughters may have borne the last child listed.

[c] The first average is for women who were between ages 18 and 38 in 1782.

[d] The second average is for women who were at least 39 but no more than 55 in 1782.

TABLE 6
Average Ages at First and Last Births in Fujito by Cohort Group and Kokudaka Class

Average ages at first and last birth by cohort group

	First birth	s	Last birth	s
A)	--	--	36.0	4.9
B)	21.5	2.8		
C)	23.0	4.4	35.9	5.1
D)	24.6	4.1	34.3	4.5
E)	24.4	4.6		
F)	26.5	4.2	36.6	4.4
G)	22.8	3.0	33.1	6.0
H)	23.1	4.8	31.8	6.5
I)	22.3	3.6		
Total	23.6	4.3	34.1	5.7

Average age at first birth for women by Kokudaka class for cohort groups G and H

	G	s	H	s
I	25.3	3.3	25.3	2.9
II	22.4	2.6	25.9	6.5
III	22.0	2.7	24.3	6.0
IV	22.4	2.9	21.2	2.9
V	23.2	2.8	21.5	4.0
Total[a]	22.8	3.0	23.0	4.8

Average age at last birth of women who bore five or more children

	Age	s	Sample size
A)	39.5	3.6	8
C)	39.4	2.5	13
D)	38.8	2.1	12
E)	37.1	3.3	8
F)	38.8	3.5	11
G)	38.3	3.1	24
H)	35.8	3.0	17
Total[a]	38.1	3.3	93

[a]The total averages are weighted averages.

delaying the birth of their first child. And this practice has not been common even in the twentieth century.

The average age at last birth, however, indicates that women in these four villages stopped having children on the average many years before they became incapable of bearing them. The highest average age at last birth, 37, is for Fukiage, the village in which the population grew the most rapidly. The lowest averages, around 33, were for Numa and Nishikata. Even with the elimination of the women whose marriages terminated before age 44 due to the death of either spouse, the averages stayed virtually the same. Thus it is clear that the low average age was not caused by early widowhood or a high maternal death rate. It is possible, of course, that general malnutrition and poor health caused early menopause, but a life expectancy in these same villages not dissimilar to that in western Europe and the United States in the nineteenth century makes this possibility seem unlikely. If so, one must conclude that women were taking measures of some kind to prevent the births of unwanted children either after the desired family size had been reached or after they had reached an age at which it was no longer considered "proper" to bear children.[9]

Women could prevent unwanted additional births either by abortion of infanticide, among other methods, but if they were using infanticide as a major method, it is possible that a preference for one sex would create an abnormal sex ratio among children in the village, especially among the last-born children. At the margin women may have kept children only if they were of the preferred sex, most likely boys because they would grow up to be economic assets, unlike girls who married and left home.

An examination of the sex ratios of all children born to and living with their mothers in Fukiage, Numa, and Nishikata (Table 7) reveals that despite a sex ratio of 1.21 in Numa during the decade 1860–1871, we fail to reject the null hypothesis that these samples do not come from a normal universe. That is, we can say with 95% confidence that these samples could have come from a universe in which the sex ratio was 1.04. The sex ratios of children born in Fujito have been divided into 19 groups: 9 cohort groups and 5 subgroups categorized by landholding size of the mother's household for two of the cohort groups (see the appendix to Table 2). Because of the small size of many of the groups,

---

[9] It was not considered proper for a mother and her daughter-in-law to be bearing children at the same time. In Tosa at least, often the child of the older woman was not allowed to live. Information on social pressures in Tokugawa Japan against having large families can be found in Tsuge (1936).

BLE 7
x Ratios of All Children Born to and Living with their Mothers During Periods
r Which Data Exist

llage	Sex Ratio	Average number of children	Sample size Children	Mothers
kiage (1683-1730)	1.15	3.69	468	127
ma (1814-1832)	1.05	3.02	178	59
ma (1860-1871)	1.21	2.44	117	48
shikata (1782-1796)	1.18	2.98	131	44

even with sex ratios of .56 and 1.42, we fail to reject the same null hypothesis (see Table 8). In only one group is it statistically probable that families were using *mabiki* to weed out undesired girls. This is the sample of 100 mothers married between 1825 and 1841 whose households held land assessed between 3 and 6 *koku*.[10] However, when the groups were aggregated, a sex ratio of 1.24 was obtained for the total of 1336 children. This sex ratio is outside the 95% confidence interval, thus indicating that women were consciously behaving in such a way as to raise more male children than female.

If we test the sex ratios of only last-born children, we find that the sex ratios for Numa show a bias in favor of girls, but the samples are small (Table 9). The sex ratios for Nishikata and Fukiage are high, between 1.4 and 1.8, whether samples include only women who were married to age 44 or also women whose marriages ended earlier. Again, the size of the samples precluded rejecting the null hypothesis that women were not practicing sex-selective infanticide. However, for Fujito, not only is the sex ratio of 1.70 for last-born children of women in Group H (who married after 1841) outside the 95% confidence range, but so is the sex ratio of 1.40 for the total, the 355 last-born children for whom we have information. Thus we can conclude that in Fujito women tended to keep only males when they had reached a point where they felt they had had enough children, and that this behavior influenced the sex ratios of children ever born. It is hypothesized here that such behavior was prevalent in other villages also, given the large number of samples in which the sex ratio is much greater than 1.04, and that this can be shown statistically when larger samples can be obtained.

[10] Land was usually discussed in terms of its estimated (or official) assessment of rice output. One *koku* was approximately 5 bushels.

TABLE 8
Sex Ratios of Children Born in Fujito by Cohort Group and Kokudaka Class of Mother

Group		Sex ratio (M/F)	Sample size
A		1.28	139
B		.96	45
C		1.36	137
D		1.26	203
E		1.23	132
F		1.00	132
G	I	.56	25
	II	.77	39
	III	1.00	52
	IV	2.23^a	100
	V	1.04	57
Total for G		*1.21*	*273*
H	I	.92	23
	II	.92	23
	III	1.07	29
	IV	1.35	73
	V	1.42	46
Total for H		*1.20*	*194*
I		1.38	81
Total for all groups		1.24^a	*1336*

[a]Indicates the sex ratio is outside the 95 percent confidence interval.

There is support in the literature on Tokugawa Japan for the conclusion that women tended to keep only male children at the margin, making the decision whether or not to keep the child immediately after it was born. In Tosa, a domain in southern Shikoku, families in some communities were laughed at and mocked if they had more than three children, and thus it became customary to raise only two boys and one girl. Killing a baby at birth was so prevalent that it became the custom not to congratulate a family on the birth of a child until it was learned whether or not the child was to be raised. If the answer was negative nothing was said; if positive, the usual congratulations and gifts were offered. If a woman bore a child after being divorced, the child was often killed so it would not prove a hindrance to a second marriage (Tsuge, 1936). Sekiyama states that the idea that a family should be small was widely held throughout Japan, by the samurai and townsmen as well as by farmers (1958, p. 301).

TABLE 9
Sex Ratios of Last-Born Children

Village	Sex ratio	Sample size
Fukiage (1683-1730)		
I[a]	1.41	82
II[b]	1.36	104
Numa (1814-1832)		
I	.83	22
II	.90	40
Numa (1860-1871)		
I	.67	10
II	.85	24
Nishikata (1782-1796)		
I	1.83	17
II	1.50	30
Fujito		
A	1.20	33
B	2.60	18
C	1.75	33
D	1.45	54
E	1.15	43
F	1.00	38
G	1.30	76
H	1.70*	60
Total for Fujito	*1.40**	*355*

[a]Mothers who lived with their husbands to age 44.

[b]Mothers married to age 39 or whose marriages ended prior to that age due to the death of either spouse.

*Indicates the sex ratio is outside the 95 percent confidence interval.

POPULATION CONTROL THROUGH THE REGULATION OF MARRIAGE

Although it is highly probable that many couples were controlling fertility within marriage, fertility within the village as a whole was certainly being limited by customs that restricted marriage to certain individuals and shortened the span of marriage for those who did marry. First, a large number of women in the childbearing ages were unmarried. The twenties are considered the most fertile years for women, but of a sample of 21 years from the four villages, the percentage of women married in the 20–24 age group was under 40% in 13 of these years (see Table 10). In fact, the fluctuations in the percentage of women married in this age group are more revealing of the actions affecting fertility taken by the villagers in response to economic conditions than any other statistics compiled. Although the total percentage of women married who were aged 15–44 tended to be around 60% for the 21 samples, the percentage in the 20–24 age group ranged from 14.3 to 81.8%. And even though the total was affected by the unintentional disruption of marriage through death, nearly all the unmarried women aged 20–24 had never been married.

The two extremes of this range come from Numa, where nearly 82% of the 20–24 group and 73% of all women aged 15–44 were married in 1780. The percentage for the total steadily dropped through the following century, reaching 44% in 1871 when only 14.3% of the 20- to 24-year-olds were married. Less than 30% of the 20- to 24-year-olds were married in 1801 but nearly 56% were married in 1831. Two factors can be seen at work here. First, the village seems to have been at its maximum population in the late eighteenth century; thereafter the total population of the village ceased to grow. For this zero population growth to be achieved, the number of marriages permitted within the village had to be gradually reduced on a long-term basis, hence the steady but gradual decline in the percentage of women married. But short-run economic conditions also affected marriages. There seems to have been a recession in the villages of Okayama around the turn of the nineteenth century, and persons who would otherwise have married either postponed marriage or remained single. In Fujito and Fukiage the percentages of women in the 20–24 age group were also at a low; all were in the 20–30% range around 1800. However, from the 1820s on, conditions improved, and more marriages were contracted. In the 1830s the percentage of 20- to 24-year-old women married rose to over 50% in Numa and Fujito, probably partly in response to the increase in by-employments, which began to boom at this time.

It should be noted, however, that although the percentage of women never married was higher than it is today, large numbers of Tokugawa women were not forced to remain single for life. The percentages of women aged 30–39 who were married were usually over 80%; these figures should not be misconstrued as representing percentages ever married, since by this age many women had been divorced or widowed. But having the highest proportions married in the thirties when fewer children were born—witness the early age at last

TABLE 10
Percentage of Women Married by Age Groups

| | Fujito | | | | | | | | Fukiage | | | | | |
Age groups	1775	1794	1810	1825	1837	1844	1863	1683	1702	1730	1773	1801	1821	1860
15-19	7.7	4.5	0.0	0.0	6.1	13.0	2.6	26.3	0.0	7.1	3.2	6.3	9.8	5.9
20-24	38.5	20.0	32.0	44.4	53.6	38.2	47.6	37.5	21.0	50.0	38.9	21.9	34.1	45.5
25-29	81.3	84.2	66.7	70.6	75.0	70.8	62.1	100.0	92.3	72.0	71.4	57.1	70.3	43.8
30-34	92.9	82.6	84.6	96.1	91.7	78.9	64.0	71.4	81.8	83.3	75.6	75.6	76.3	53.8
35-39	93.3	100.0	72.7	77.8	94.1	84.2	88.2	60.0	76.0	88.5	74.1	86.1	75.0	75.0
40-44	83.3	90.0	73.6	93.3	72.4	73.3	87.5	90.0	70.0	84.2	84.6	85.7	79.3	61.5
Total	56.9	59.7	49.1	63.0	57.6	56.0	52.6	57.5	56.6	62.2	56.6	55.3	55.0	47.2
Total no. of women	109	124	112	127	139	134	154	73	106	148	182	190	225	176

| | Numa | | | | | Nishikata | |
Age groups	1780	1801	1831	1861	1871	1782	1796
15-19	9.1	0.0	5.0	7.1	0.0	27.3	0.0
20-24	81.8	29.4	55.6	40.0	14.3	50.0	25.0
25-29	66.7	84.6	66.7	37.5	50.0	60.0	55.6
30-34	100.0	90.0	80.0	80.0	77.8	69.2	90.9
35-39	100.0	90.9	90.0	83.3	50.0	85.7	80.0
40-44	83.3	100.0	85.7	83.3	90.0	66.7	62.5
Total	72.6	61.6	56.2	51.7	43.9	57.6	60.4
Total no. of women	62	73	73	60	66	59	48

childbirth—and comparatively few in the early and mid-twenties obviously had the effect of reducing births considerably. The high average age at first marriage is well known as one of the most effective means of reducing fertility in Europe; it seems to have been equally effective in Japan. Again, this was not a custom introduced in the late Tokugawa period as a short-term measure for reducing births; in Fukiage in 1683 only 37.5% of the women aged 20–24 were married, but 100% of women aged 25–29 were living with husbands.

The selection of who was to marry and who was to remain single was not random. It clearly can be seen to have had an economic basis. And if not motivated by their own economic considerations, people found constraints to their behavior in government regulations. Despite the efforts of various domains to increase their populations, domain administrations can be held partly responsible for slowing population increases through the setting up of legal barriers blocking the establishment of new families. The primary examples of such regulations in Okayama were the regulations involving the transfer of land. The purpose of these regulations was to encourage farming on a scale that would generate the maximum amount of tax income. The first regulation in Okayama against the parceling of land was issued in 1656 (Taniguchi & Shibata, 1955, p. 53). Subdividing land was to be prohibited except in cases where land was acquired through the ending of a family line or where large tracts of land were to be given out to a number of people (Otake, 1962, p. 155). The prohibitions against the alienation of land were gradually relaxed, however, as they proved unworkable in the long run, and by 1715 it was legal to pawn land for 10 years.[11] But the regulations against willing land to more than one heir were not relaxed; in 1798 it was ruled that a family had to have at least 3 *tan* (.74 acre) in order to establish a branch line.

The regulations limiting the subdivision of land meant that in the case of small farmers only one son could inherit. Any other sons had to remain as subordinate family members or leave and find employment elsewhere. The effect of this regulation was to limit the number of marriages, usually to one per household per generation, as large families created a burden on the household both economically and socially. The logic from the domain administration's point of view was to prevent the parceling of land to the point that the tax rate would have to be lowered to permit mere subsistence and to obviate famine relief. However, by this very policy they encouraged small families.

[11] The Okayama regulations on alienation of land and on the establishment of branch families are discussed in Taniguchi (1964), especially pp. 131 ff., 200 ff.

The effect of the government regulations can be seen in the village registers (see Table 11). The number of childbearing couples in each household tended to be limited to one or none and the number of households grew only slowly over time. On the average, most households contained one woman in the childbearing ages, but nearly a third of these were unmarried. The custom of restricting marriage to the main line of descent is evidenced in Table 12. Very few of the women classified *wives* were married to men other than a head, his father, his son, or his grandson. The highest percentage was 4%, and the years in

TABLE 11
Average Number of Households Containing Married Women in the Childbearing Ages in Percentages

Year	Number of households	Percentage with wives 15-44	Average number women 15-44 per household in percentage
Fujito			
1775	110	56.4	.99
1794	111	66.7	1.12
1810	111	49.5	1.01
1825	112	71.4	1.13
1837	119	67.2	1.17
1844	118	63.6	1.14
1863	132	61.4	1.17
Fukiage			
1683	65	64.6	1.12
1702	78	76.9	1.36
1730	134	68.7	1.10
1773	190	54.2	.96
1801	210	50.0	.90
1821	240	51.7	.94
1860	255	32.5	.69
Numa			
1780	58	77.6	1.07
1801	63	71.4	1.16
1831	70	58.6	1.04
1861	69	44.9	.87
1871	73	33.7	.90
Nishikata			
1782	67	52.2	.88
1796	68	42.6	.71

TABLE 12
*Percentage of Population which is Comprised of Wives of Persons Other Than in Main
Line of Descent[a]*

Fujito		Fukiage		Numa		Nishikata	
Year	Percentage	Year	Percentage	Year	Percentage	Year	Percentage
1775	2.85	1683	0.0	1780	4.15	1782	.36
1794	2.83	1702	3.77	1801	3.72	1789	0.0
1810	2.47	1730	1.82	1831	3.66	1796	0.0
1825	4.08	1773	.96	1861	2.22		
1837	4.07	1801	.88	1871	1.27		
1844	3.28	1821	1.19				
1863	2.28	1860	.87				

[a]Wives other than those of head or his father, son, or grandson.

which high percentages occurred were years of a growing population and expanding economic opportunities in the villages involved. On the other hand, after the Temmei famine no one in Nishikata was married to anyone not in the main line of descent. Thus only one son could count on inheriting from his father, and the others either had to leave the village to work elsewhere or remain at home, unmarried and subservient to a brother.

Some of the excess males were adopted into other families as sons or sons-in-law, but many chose to leave the village to work elsewhere on contract. More often than not it was the younger son who had to leave, but not always. Both the *shūmon-aratame-chō* and the legal records of the Tokugawa period indicate that quite frequently a son other than the eldest inherited the family assets, often because of a quarrel with the head or behavior that would not permit the family to let the eldest succeed to the headship (see Henderson, 1974). That only one brother was usually allowed to marry and stay within the family is exemplified by the case in Fujito in which the wife of the oldest brother died and another woman was brought into the family, but this time the younger son married, the eldest remaining a widower.

THE EFFECT OF FAMINES ON FERTILITY

Even if one is to accept the evidence presented thus far that families in Tokugawa villages were following various customs in an effort to limit fertility, it might still be argued that famines played a crucial role in limiting the growth of population either in certain periods or in the long run. Thus one would expect to find famines negating the effect of positive growth rates during normal periods or periods of abundance. Therefore we shall examine changes in fertility and in demographic behavior affecting fertility during and immediately after the years considered to be among the worst famine years in Japanese history.

Table 13 gives the total population figures and the crude birth and death rates for Fujito between 1828 and 1850 and for Nishikata for 1782–1795 inclusive. The highest death rate for either of these villages occurred in Fujito in 1832 when 23 people, most of them children under age 10, died in the fourth month. This occurred prior to the Tempō famine, which was considered at its worst in 1836–1837, although there were several years of bad harvests. The death rate did jump to 30 per 1000 in Fujito in 1837 and to 36 and 47 per 1000 in Nishikata in 1787 and 1788 respectively. But by 1841 the death rate was under 15 per 1000 in Fujito, and in 1790 in Nishikata the death rate was back to 15 per 1000. It is impossible to tell how much suffering and illness existed in these two periods from the death rates alone, but clearly these "famine" years did not result in the economic or social dislocation seen after recurrences of the plague in Europe.

It is more difficult to decipher the results of the famines in the birth

TABLE 13
Crude Birth and Death Rates During Nationwide Famine Years for Nishikata and Fujito

	Fujito				Nishikata		
Year	Population first of year	Birth rate	Death rate	Year	Population first of year	Birth rate	Death rate
28	600	28.3	23.3	1782	271	18.5	18.5
29	610	21.3	14.8	1783	270	22.2	18.5
30	617	45.4	22.7	1784	269	11.2	7.4
31	636	29.9	15.7	1785	274	11.0	7.3
32	647	24.7	57.2	1786	273	36.6	29.3
33	620	27.4	22.6	1787	278	25.2	36.0
34	625	35.2	24.0	1788	274	11.0	47.4
35	634	31.5	28.4	1789	264	26.5	26.5
37	638	18.8	39.2	1790	264	11.4	15.2
41	612	29.4	14.7	1791	269	14.9	22.3
44	637	18.8	31.4	1792	268	7.4	37.3
45	628	43.0	20.7	1793	251	43.8	19.9
46	643	14.0	24.9	1794	260	11.5	30.8
47	645	31.0	20.2	1795	250	4.0	20.0
48	649	37.0	12.3				
50	669	32.9	32.9				

rates. The population of Nishikata was so small that there tended to be almost cycles in the birth rate since the average interbirth interval was 3 years. Birth rates were low in Fujito during the 1840s, compared to the years immediately preceding and following, but this was also a period in which the percentage of women in the childbearing years who were married had begun to fall. It seems likely that the poor harvests caused a period of financial retrenchment after the rapid growth of the 1820s— hence fewer marriages—rather than that women, due to their weakened physical condition, were less capable of bearing children.

This is not to minimize the effects of the two famines, even on these two villages in central Japan. The crude death rates by approximately 5-year averages (Table 1) were higher for Fujito in the 1830s than the mean for the total 42 years for which there are records. The death rate in Nishikata jumped from 14.5 to 27 per 1000 during the 1780s. And although famines had little apparent effect on fertility, an analysis of the registers family by family indicates a higher incidence of dislocations than were to be found in normal times. These dislocations include increased deaths, the adoption of a variety of people other than direct heirs, and a fall in the number of people who migrated to work. Nevertheless, when considering the long-term effect on fertility during the last century of the Tokugawa period, in Fujito at least we cannot conclude that the Tempō famine did anything more than slightly accelerate the existing trend.

There are no registers extant for Fujito between 1778 and 1794, but

TABLE 14
Estimated Percentage of Women of Childbearing Age who Bore Children in Fujito, 1775-1800[a]

Year	Percentage	Percentage	Year
1775	11.6	1788	21.3
1776	15.6	1789	21.3
1777	15.7	1790	19.4
1778	25.9	1791	20.0
1779	9.8	1792	22.1
1780	6.6	1793	14.3
1781	21.9	1794	22.4
1782	10.6	1795	18.5
1783	14.1	1796	15.4
1784	21.7	1797	19.2
1785	12.2	1798	13.7
1786	5.4	1799	8.3
1787	16.0	1800	12.2

[a]Sample was drawn from Cohort Groups C and D.

using the information obtained from the registers before and after this period, which covers the Temmei famine, we can attempt to determine any changes in fertility during the famine years. In Table 14 an estimate has been made by year of the percentage of women known to have been married and in the childbearing years who did in fact bear children in any given year. The estimates are only approximations for the years for which there are no registers; it was necessary to calculate backward from the 1794 records. Thus all women and children who dropped out of the records before 1794 have been excluded. Despite these omissions, particularly of children who died in infancy, in the 5 years from 1788 to 1792 nearly 20% of the women in the sample bore children who were still alive in 1794. Certainly marital fertility does not seem to have been affected by the Temmei famine in Fujito.

THE INFLUENCE OF VILLAGE AND FAMILY ECONOMIC CONDITIONS ON FERTILITY IN FUJITO

An analysis of family size over the 90-year period for which data are available in Fujito suggests the hypothesis that, whatever the fluctuations in fortune for the village as a whole, the relative position of each family within the village changed little. The average family size (here defined as household minus servants), obtained by dividing the total population by the number of households, was 5.5 for the entire period. The mean and mode were close in value; in 1775, 43% of the families had either five or six members (exclusive of servants). Although there was a greater spread in terms of family size in the later years, the modal class was either five or six for most years until 1856, when it changed to four.

The relatively constant mean in family size over the period was largely due to the small fluctuation in the number of family members around the mean in each household. In short, a family in which the modal and/or mean number was five tended to return to this number whenever the number of members either exceeded or fell below five. This was true for families of any size. This tendency has been statistically tested by calculating the coefficient of variation for each household over time (see Table 15). Only those families that could be identified over a span of time were used in the sample, which included 87 families identified from at least as early as 1825 and found in the registers until the end of the period under observation.

Of the 87 families, 24 had a coefficient of variation of less than .25; 50 had a coefficient of variation of less than .33; and 80 had a coefficient

TABLE 15
Coefficient of Variation for Changes in Family Size Over Time by Household in Fujito, 1775-1863

House-hold	$\bar{x}$	σ	$\sigma/\bar{x}$	House-hold	$\bar{x}$	$\sigma/\bar{x}$	σ	House-hold	$\bar{x}$	σ	$\sigma/\bar{x}$
1	5.36	0.99	.185	30	5.00	1.29	.258	59	6.09	2.35	.386
2	9.19	2.96	.322	31	7.20	2.05	.285	60	12.50	0.88	.070
3	4.58	1.07	.234	32	5.48	2.00	.365	61	5.53	2.69	.487
4	5.30	1.40	.264	33	4.69	1.17	.249	62	7.66	2.49	.325
5	5.58	1.77	.317	34	4.29	1.45	.338	63	6.72	2.97	.442
6	4.46	1.51	.337	35	3.57	1.75	.490	64	3.86	2.44	.633
7	5.67	1.12	.198	36	2.86	2.47	.864	65	3.15	0.76	.241
8	9.05	1.84	.203	37	6.36	1.72	.271	66	5.73	1.55	.271
9	4.83	2.06	.427	38	4.79	2.05	.428	67	4.05	1.36	.336
10	6.73	1.30	.193	39	5.91	2.03	.344	68	5.70	0.95	.167
11	5.86	1.02	.174	40	6.57	1.64	.249	69	5.23	1.17	.224
12	4.39	0.62	.141	41	1.07	3.91	.366	70	5.73	1.88	.328
13	5.56	1.47	.264	42	8.26	4.03	.488	71	2.93	1.19	.407
14	5.07	0.94	.185	43	7.81	1.79	.229	72	7.38	2.78	.377
15	7.22	3.09	.428	44	5.36	1.62	.302	73	4.18	1.14	.273
16	3.63	1.83	.504	45	4.27	1.59	.373	74	4.97	0.31	.062
17	7.65	2.34	.306	46	8.69	2.54	.292	75	4.03	1.27	.316
18	6.67	2.57	.385	47	4.56	1.36	.298	76	6.03	1.59	.264
19	7.12	0.87	.122	48	7.00	1.65	.236	77	5.27	2.03	.385
20	5.62	1.23	.219	49	7.84	2.44	.311	78	7.05	1.97	.279
21	7.12	3.30	.464	50	5.46	1.66	.304	79	4.13	1.42	.344
22	5.26	2.20	.418	51	16.76	2.49	.149	80	1.92	1.30	.677
23	7.62	3.31	.434	52	6.10	1.84	.302	81	7.08	2.79	.394
24	4.81	1.16	.241	53	6.01	1.91	.318	82	5.53	1.67	.302
25	7.73	2.29	.296	54	3.43	0.31	.090	83	2.37	1.20	.418
26	3.59	1.85	.515	55	3.61	1.21	.335	84	2.69	1.54	.572
27	3.93	2.88	.733	56	6.83	1.85	.271	85	3.56	1.71	.480
28	4.53	1.51	.333	57	11.67	1.57	.135	86	4.50	1.27	.282
29	7.55	2.91	.385	58	5.66	1.35	.239	87	4.51	1.41	.312

less than .50. These findings lead to the conclusion that the variation in the annual population of each family was small. It is suggested here that the reason for this was that the fixed base of each household tended to change relatively little over time, and any changes were shared by other households, thus necessitating each household to maintain the same number of members—the optimum economically—in order for the household to maintain its position within the village. That the fixed capital base in terms of land tended to remain constant is evidenced in the fact that of the 142 women in Cohort Groups G and H, only 8, from seven households, came from families who changed landholding class from 1851 to 1863.

We find, then, in Fujito a pattern of families controlling the size of their households, primarily through controlling family size, in order to maintain as far as possible a constant, maximum size given their individual labor requirements, income, and desire to perpetuate the family line. If land is the primary fixed asset in Fujito, we should then expect to find differences in the number of children born and raised according to the size of landholding. For Fujito it is possible to examine fertility among women who have been divided into groups according to the size of landholding of the households in which they lived. *Nengumai toritate sanyō-chō* or Records of Rice Tax Computation are available for 6 scattered years during the nineteenth century. These records provide a breakdown in units of *koku* of the landholdings of individuals within the village. Because the population records exist for every year from 1825 to 1835 and nearly every other year after that until 1863, women from these registers were divided into two cohort groups and then further subdivided into five *kokudaka* classes. (See the appendix to Table 2 for a complete description of these.) Cohort Group G consists of women who were married between 1825 and 1841, whereas Group H is comprised of women who were married or who bore children without recorded husbands after 1841 but who reached age 44 or whose marriages had terminated prior to 1863. The *kokudaka* classes range from no landholdings (Class I) to 3–6 *koku* (Class IV), and a miscellaneous category of the large landholders, those who switched classes, and so on (Class V).

In Table 16, we find for Cohort Group G that the average number of children in the completed family size recorded for each *kokudaka* class is within 0.2% of the mean for the entire cohort group, which was 3.5. For Cohort Group H, however, Class III, comprised of women from households holding land assessed at 1–3 *koku*, had an average of only 2.6 children; Class V, including women from the largest landholders and households containing 10 or more members, had an average of 4.2

TABLE 16
Average Number of Children in the Completed Family in Fujito by Cohort Group and Kokudaka Class

Cohort group	Number of children	Class	G	H
A	3.5	I	3.6	3.3
C	4.0	II	3.5	2.9
D	3.6	III	3.5	2.6
E	2.9	IV	3.7	3.5
F	3.5	V	3.4	4.2
G	3.5	Total[a]	3.5	3.4
H	3.4			

[a]The total averages are weighted averages.

children, though the mean for the entire cohort group was still 3.4. Returning to Table 6, we see that the average age at first birth was just over 22 for Cohort Group G as a whole and close to it for most of the classes within it with the exception of women who came from families holding no land at all who married on the average at 25. For Cohort Group H, though, the average age at marriage tended to fall as the amount of land held by the brides' families rose. Thus women from families with larger fixed assets married at just over 21 whereas those from families with extremely little or no land married at over 25.

If we turn to sex ratios of children born to these two cohort groups (Table 8), we find that only for women married between 1825 and 1841 into families with 1–3 *koku* of land (G, IV) is the sex ratio of all children so distorted at 2.23 (sample of 100) that we can conclude that sex-selective infanticide was being carried out. But if we look at the sex ratios of last-born children (Table 9), we can say with 95% confidence that the sex ratio of 1.7 for Cohort Group H does not come from a universe in which the sex ratio is unity. The sex ratio of lastborns for Group G is 1.3, but we cannot statistically reject this group as having come from a normal universe. Thus it seems highly likely that these two cohort groups and others were practicing "postpartum birth control" to some extent.

Families may have used still a third method for reducing family size in addition to abortion and infanticide. This might be either intentional or inadvertent lack of care for children, which might show up in higher

TABLE 17
Incidence of Infant and Child Mortality in Fujito by Kokudaka Class

Class	Number children	Number died age 10 or less	Percentage died
For children born to women married 1825-1841 (Cohort Group G)			
I	25	10	40
II	39	7	18
III	52	18	35
IV	8	3	38
V 1)	110	23	23
2)	26	5	19
3)	10	1	10
4)	13	3	23
Total	283	70	25
For children born to women married after 1841 (Cohort Group H)			
I	23	2	9
II	23	2	9
III	29	4	14
IV	17	3	18
V	101	21	21
Total	193	32	17

infant and child mortality figures for some groups (see Table 17). For Cohort Group G, fully 25% of the children registered died before the age of 10, in part due to the epidemic of 1832. The percentages of children dying before 10 vary by *kokudaka* class, reaching as high as 40%, but even this 40% who came from landless families can be assumed to be within the same universe as the total, using a 95% confidence interval. The percentages are lower for Cohort Group H (a total of 17%) but if anything the death rates rose in direct relation to size of landholding. But we cannot say from these percentages that any one group faced statistically higher infant and child mortality rates than did any other.

Two conclusions can be drawn from the foregoing comparison of fertility by landholding class: First, despite slight variations, such as the age at marriage of women married after 1841, it is difficult to discern major differences in fertility among women from various landholding classes in Fujito ranging from the poorest to the few wealthy families. This lends credence to the idea that the Japanese limited their families across the board and that they raised only wanted families. Making the decision whether to raise a child before or immediately upon birth is less economically and socially wasteful than limiting families through careless attention to children already being raised.

Second, the behavior of families to maintain optimum family size over time no matter whether the family was large or small, combined with the fact that fertility control did not vary significantly by landholding class, leads to the conclusion that the fixed capital base of land was possibly not the determining economic factor in optimum family size in many cases. One would expect to find this situation only in a society in which land was not the only or the most important asset. Thus families with no land but thriving businesses would find it profitable to maintain large families in order to have available a ready supply of labor in a labor-short economy, whereas a family with holdings in the modal class and few possibilities of by-employments might have found it necessary to limit children to two in order to maintain or improve the standard of living.

Demographic behavior witnessed in the *shūmon-aratame-chō* indicates that the small fluctuation over time in family size was not coincidental. That families were almost certainly limiting the number of children they raised has already been discussed. But there is also evidence that families tried not to permit their numbers to fall below a certain optimum size, a size determined by the conditions within each household. For example, in the same year that a family lost an adult member, it would replace this member with another adult of the same sex. This was frequently accomplished by taking in a bride for a son in the same year that an adult daughter married out of the family. Adoption was frequent as a means of reducing the size of some families and increasing the size of others. The effect of attempts to maintain a stable family size are most apparent in the years following the Tempō famine when adoptions of people of all ages, even elderly women, were common.

There were many economic reasons why the optimum family size was on the average small in Fujito. First, the amount of arable land available to the village remained constant during the last century and a half of the Tokugawa period with the exception of the 1820s and 1830s, when possibly 20% was added to it through reclamation. With a limitation placed on the amount of cultivated land, each additional person in a family meant a lowering of the per capita income for that family. This may well indicate why the groups of people who seemed to be practicing infanticide in this village were those with relatively small amounts of land. On the other hand, the groups with the lowest sex ratios among their children and the largest families were those with no land or less than 1 *koku*. It is clear from other village records that these families were not dependent on agriculture for their living and preferred large families in order to maintain a stable labor force necessary for their businesses. These families permitted brothers, sons, and even cousins to marry and remain within the family.

Even in families in which the economic base was not fixed, there was an economic incentive for them to limit the proportion of dependent or consuming members relative to those in the labor force. Particularly in the nineteenth century, when by-employments became common in Fujito, an additional adult in a family might bring in more income than he consumed, thus raising per capita income in the family; an additional child, however, could only lower it. We find that the proportion of the population in the working ages (15–64) in Fujito was always well above 60, as it was for six other villages studied. The major change that took place in Fujito was a substitution of young children for the elderly in the mid-nineteenth century, but this shift did not change the proportion of the population in the working age groups. Thus all villages studied to date, regardless of population pattern, had percentages of persons in the working ages favorable to average productivity and similar to those in the industrialized nations of the twentieth century.[12]

Not only poorer families dependent on limited amounts of land had incentive to limit family size; so also did the rich. Large landowners had sufficient land to permit the establishment of branch families by younger sons, but to do so would dissipate their wealth. Thus we find that although the large landowners in Fujito tended to marry younger than did the average villager, they had on the average no more children. The number of these families is too small to make any statistics compiled from them statistically significant, but still there is not a single example of a large family among them.

By the early nineteenth century all evidence points to growth in the economy not only of Fujito, but of the domain of Okayama as a whole. Yet there is no evidence of a major change in population patterns or demographic behavior beyond the brief period of an increase in families and the number of children born during the 1820s and 1830s. Thus all increases in family income from weaving and other by-employments went toward increasing per capita income and hence raising the standard of living in the village. Furthermore, the changes taking place in the village economy permitted men to leave relatively

---

[12] See Spengler (1968). In contrast to the Japanese and modern industrial pattern, the countries of Africa, Asia, and Latin America today have percentages well below 60.

poorly paid work, such as daily farm labor, to go into business or commerce. Unmarried adults and some heads of families could leave home and become well-paid workers in the salt and cotton industries. If the villages of twentieth century Japan are any indication, a rise in the standard of living and increases in the goods consumed among some families must have created incentive if not pressure for the other families to achieve the same goals. Exactly what these villagers of late Tokugawa Japan were thinking can never be known, but their demographic behavior taken with their economic activity resulted in a rise in their standard of living as represented by an increased consumption of material goods.

CONCLUSION

Based on the statistics on the behavior of families from these four villages in Tokugawa Japan, and if the analyses of the data are correct, we can conclude that families were consciously regulating their size, usually to limit it but sometimes to raise it to the optimum number of members. The methods used included adoption; permitting marriage only when sufficient income was available; regulating the age at first marriage, especially for women; and probably abortion and infanticide. Through a relatively high age at marriage and hence first birth and a short span of childbearing—about 12 years on the average—marital fertility was reduced to no more than about three children who lived long enough to be registered. Total fertility was reduced still further through the custom of letting only the successor to a household marry. Thus a rather large proportion of the village population had to remain single or leave home, and if we add to this group the childless (ranging from 5 to over 10%) and reductions due to infant and child mortality (in Fujito around 20% from the 1820s on), the zero population growth rate of the late Tokugawa period is not difficult to comprehend.

Why the Japanese in the Tokugawa period were so carefully limiting their numbers and how they were able to achieve these results throughout so much of the country remain more of a puzzle than the results of their population control. Clearly famines were the cause of neither the slow population growth nor the practice of abortion and infanticide in these four villages. Even during period of growth in Fujito and Fukiage fertility did not vary significantly from that in Numa and other villages during famines or poor harvest years.

The reasons for the government regulations involving the partibility of land are obvious, just as are the reasons for the measures to prevent abortion and infanticide in regions suffering population decline through famines and lack of economic opportunities. But just as keeping the labor force at an optimum must have benefited the government, so must it have benefited the villagers themselves to maintain the highest possible marginal productivity of labor.[13] Although economic growth during the last century and a half of the Tokugawa period was slow by modern standards, the slow increases in productivity and output combined with a low to zero rate of growth in the population enabled villagers to increase their standard of living considerably from the eighteenth to the nineteenth century. By foregoing large families, the people of Okayama were able by the mid-nineteenth century to enjoy the luxury of travel for pleasure and they were able to imitate the life-style of townsmen, with incense, fans, perfumes, hair oil, and cosmetics available for purchase in their own villages. And, perhaps most important, a 2-year-old had a life expectancy similar to that enjoyed in the West in the same period, although modern industrial technology was not to be introduced into Japan for several decades to come.

REFERENCES

Hanley, Susan B. (1972). "Toward an Analysis of Demographic and Economic Change in Tokugawa Japan: A Village Study," *Journal of Asian Studies*, Vol. 31, No. 3 (May), pp. 515–537.

Hanley, Susan B. (1974). "Fertility, Mortality, and Life Expectancy in Pre-modern Japan," *Population Studies*, Vol. 28, No. 1 (March), pp. 127–142.

Hanley, Susan B., & Yamamura, Kozo (1971). "A Quiet Transformation in Tokugawa Economic History," *Journal of Asian Studies*, Vol. 30, No. 2 (February), pp. 373–384.

Hayami Akira (1966–1967). "The Population at the Beginning of the Tokugawa Period," *Keio Economic Studies*, Vol. 4, pp. 1–28.

Hayami Akira (1967–1968). "Shūmon-aratame-chō o tsūjite mita Shinshū Yokouchi-mura no chōki jinkō tōkei [The Demographical Aspects of a Rural Village in Tokugawa Japan, 1671–1871]." Sangyō Kenkyūsho Shirizu No. 202 [Series No. 202 of the Institute of Industrial Research]. Tokyo: Keio Gijuku Daigaku Sangyō Kenkyūsho.

Hayami Akira (1968). "The Demographic Analysis of a Village in Tokugawa Japan: Kando-shinden of Owari Province, 1778–1871," *Keio Economic Studies*, Vol. 5, pp. 50–88.

Hayami Akira (1972). "Size of Household in a Japanese County Throughout the Tokugawa Era," in Peter Laslett, ed., *Household and Family in Past Time*. Cambridge: Cambridge University Press.

Hayami Akira (1973a). *Kinsei nōson no rekishi jinkō-gakuteki kenkyū* [A historical demographic analysis of Tokugawa farming villages]. Tokyo: Tōyō Keizai Shimpōsha.

[13] That increases in output were not being taxed away is documented in a number of case studies. For a study in English, see Thomas C. Smith (1958).

Hayami Akira (1973b). "Labor Migration in a Pre-Industrial Society: A Study Tracing the Life Histories of the Inhabitants of a Village," *Keio Economic Studies*, Vol. 10, No. 2, pp. 1–17.

Henderson, Dan Fenno (1974). " 'Contracts' in Tokugawa Villages," *Journal of Japanese Studies*, Vol. 1, No. 1 (Autumn), pp. 51–90.

Honjō Eijirō (1930). *Jinkō oyobi jinkō mondai* [Population and population problems]. Tokyo: Nihon Hyōronsha.

Nishijima Minoru (1969). *Edo jidai no sei seikatsu* [Sex life in the Tokugawa period]. Tokyo: Yuzankaku.

Otake Hideo (1962). *Hōken shakai no nōmin kazoku* [Farm families in a feudal society]. Tokyo: Sōbunsha.

Sekiyama Naotarō (1958). *Kinsei Nihon no jinkō kōzō* [The population structure of Tokugawa Japan]. Tokyo: Yoshikawa Kōbunkan.

Smith, Robert J. (1966). "Ihai: Mortuary Tablets, the Household and Kin in Japanese Ancestor Worship," *Transactions of the Asiatic Society of Japan*, 3rd ser., Vol. 9 (May), pp. 83–102.

Smith, Thomas C. (1958). "The Land Tax in the Tokugawa Period," *Journal of Asian Studies*, Vol. 18, No. 1 (November), pp. 3–19.

Smith, Thomas C. (1959). *The Agrarian Origins of Modern Japan*. Stanford, Calif.: Stanford University Press.

Smith, Thomas C. (1969). "Farm Family By-employments in Preindustrial Japan," *Journal of Economic History*, Vol. 29, No. 4 (December), pp. 687–715.

Spengler, Joseph J. (1968). "Demographic Factors and Early Modern Economic Development," *Daedalus*, Vol. 97 (Spring), pp. 433–446.

Taeuber, Irene B. (1958). *The Population of Japan*. Princeton, N.J.: Princeton University Press.

Takahashi Bonsen (1936). *Datai mabiki no kenkyū* [A study on abortion and infanticide]. Tokyo: Chūō Shakai Jigyō Kyōkai Shakai Jigyō Kenkyūjo.

Taniguchi Sumio (1964). *Okayama han* [The domain of Okayama]. Tokyo: Yoshikawa Kōbunkan.

Taniguchi Sumio, & Shibata Hajime (1955). "Kinsei ni okeru kazoku kōsei no henshitsu katei [The process of change in family composition during the Tokugawa Period]," *Bulletin of the School of Education*, Okayama University, No. 1.

Tsuge Takeshi (1936). "Nōson mondai no ichi to shite no mabiki ni tsuite [Concerning infanticide as one of the problems of farming villages]," *Keizai-shi Kenkyū*, Vol. 15, No. 2 (February), pp. 15–32.

Yamamura, Kozo (1973). "Toward a Reexamination of the Economic History of Tokugawa Japan, 1600–1867," *Journal of Economic History*, Vol. 33, No. 3 (September), pp. 509–546.

Yamamura, Kozo (1974). *A Study of Samurai Income and Entrepreneurship*. Cambridge: Harvard University Press.

Childbearing and Land Availability: Some Evidence from Individual Household Data

R. M. McINNIS

Queen's University

There has been a resurgence of interest in the pattern of nineteenth century U.S. birth rates associated with recency of settlement and the density of population in relation to agricultural land. Children were considerably more numerous in relation to women of childbearing age in newly and thinly settled frontier regions than in older, longer settled areas. The continuously declining birth rate in the United States over the course of the nineteenth century has been attributed to the working out of a cross-sectional relationship that can be observed at any time during the century: As unused land was taken up and a smaller proportion of the nation's population lived on the agricultural frontier, the lower fertility ratios characteristic of the more densely populated, longer settled regions came to prevail. Of course this is not claimed to be the only reason birth rates fell—yet it is a mechanism that appears to account for a significant part of the overall decline.

The importance of this pattern was first emphasized by Yasuba (1962), but for several years the pattern attracted little further attention. In an extensive review of U.S. population before 1860, Potter (1965) reemphasized the central role of urbanization and industrialization but waved aside Yasuba's research without actually evaluating it. More recently, a number of writers have taken up Yasuba's line of investigation. Forster and Tucker (1972), using modified measures of land availability and somewhat more sophisticated statistical techniques than Yasuba, have reinforced the empirical validity of Yasuba's main point—that fertility ratios varied systematically with the density of settlement in relation to agricultural land. The reaffirmation of this pattern and its importance to understanding the trend of fertility over the nineteenth century is most associated, though, with the work of Easterlin, who called attention to the significance of the phenomenon in an early paper (1971). He has subsequently reported on a research project designed to explore this fertility pattern and to gain a deeper understanding of it. In two recent papers (1975, 1976) Easterlin has emphasized the two aspects of the phenomenon on which this chapter concentrates—the need to determine that it is a phenomenon of individual human behavior and not just an outcome of the selection of individuals most likely to be found in frontier areas, and the need to develop and test hypotheses that might explain the phenomenon.

Here, I will report on an investigation (carried out in cooperation with and parallel to Easterlin's research on the United States) of the same fertility pattern as it appeared in nineteenth century Canada. Researchers had found indications that the phenomenon was not unique to the United States; in a number of European countries, birth rates tended to be noticeably higher in more recently settled districts where land was relatively more abundant. Demeny (1968), in particular, notes a relationship of that sort in Hungary. Canada seemed to be an obvious place to look for a parallel to the U.S. pattern. Moreover, relatively good data were available to support a more intensive investigation.

This work is based on evidence for Upper Canada, the English-speaking western half of pre-Confederation Canada that is now the southern part of the province of Ontario. In the middle of the nineteenth century this area had one of the highest birth rates in the world. Upper Canada's fertility ratio was higher than that of both French-speaking Roman Catholic Lower Canada (widely renowned for its high birth rate), and neighboring U.S. states such as Ohio and Michigan. The whole of Upper Canada had been quite recently settled and was preponderantly rural. There were only five towns of more than 5000 population. Fertility ratios varied widely, though, across the 55 counties of Upper Canada. They ranged in 1852 from fewer than 700 children under 5 years of age per 1000 women 15–49 in the earliest settled counties along the St. Lawrence River and in the Niagara Peninsula to well over 1000 in those frontier counties to the northwest that were then being settled for the first time. Although the average fertility ratio was falling, the geographic pattern remained consistent over the census years 1852, 1861, and 1871. In all 3 census years there was a strong, inverse correlation between county fertility ratios and the density of population in relation to the maximum acreage of land ever cultivated in each county (taken as a proxy for the potentially cultivable area).

The relationship at the aggregate, county level of fertility with a number of variables including land availability, degree of urbanization, and the proportion of a county's population adhering to the Roman Catholic faith was reported in detail in an earlier paper (McInnis, 1972). It is sufficient to recall here that the pattern of variation in fertility in Upper Canada reflected closely the one being increasingly emphasized in literature on the United States, and that, of the several variables investigated at the aggregate level, an index of land availability had the strongest statistical association with fertility ratios.

Two important questions remain. To what extent does the higher fertility in more land-abundant situations show up at the individual household level so that we may have some assurance that it is not just a compositional matter? If we can indeed show that it is a behavioral matter—an outcome of the actions of individual households—what evidence can we assemble in support of one or another hypothesized explanation? The empirical evidence presented here is drawn from a sample of individual household records from the manuscript enumerations of the Canadian census of 1861. The nature of that sample and the way in which it was developed for the purposes of this study will be reviewed later. The data indicate that the higher fertility in frontier areas was not merely an outcome of population composition. The data also offer the possibility of an attempt to take a few preliminary steps in the direction of sorting out the possible causes of the geographical pattern of fertility. With that in mind I will review in the next section some theorizing about the determinants of family size to see what might be suggested about the way households would behave in circumstances that vary with the availability of land and the relationship of frontier agricultural communities to the national economy.

MODELS OF CHILDBEARING IN RELATION TO LAND ABUNDANCE

Why might families in land-abundant, newly settled frontier situations tend to have more children than families in long-settled areas of relatively scarcer land? The class of explanations that I will examine here draws on economic theory and reflects a particular view of the household as a rational, decision-making unit seeking to maximize its material well-being under different sets of external circumstances. This is certainly not the only way one might view households. However, it is one that has been developed into a rich body of theory. More important, among the most obvious circumstances that differ between rural households in long-established and newly settled areas are those affecting their economic life. In particular, the ease with which the essential asset needed to produce a livelihood—a farmstead—can be obtained is likely to influence strongly the number of children desired.

In the literature on the economic theory of human fertility, children are seen in the dual role of producer goods and consumer goods. The value of children as producer goods—assets that augment the household's ability to produce income—has long been recognized, especially for farm families. Recent developments in the economic analysis of family size decisions (Becker, 1960; Mincer, 1963; Schultz, 1969; Schultz & Nerlove, 1970; Willis, 1973) have placed a much greater emphasis, though, on the role of children as consumer goods. It is surely commonplace that people in the greatest variety of situations have children, at least in part, for the direct pleasure and enjoyment that they afford. To incorporate this into the analytical model has been both more novel and more apropos of twentieth century North America. We should expect it to play a part in influencing the actions of nineteenth century farm families as well.

The demand for children as consumer goods, like the demand for all such goods, depends on the household's income and the relative price of the good. It is generally presumed that children should be "normal" goods and hence should be demanded in greater numbers as income rises. Since the crude empirical relationship between income and fertility is almost always a negative one, the principal challenge of economic models of fertility has been to show how other factors account for this crude relationship in spite of a "normal," positive partial relationship of fertility to income. Wealth, in the broadest sense, from which current income is derived, is taken to be the appropriate constraint in the most developed models. As we shall see, though, the principal element of farm wealth is improved land, which households in older settled areas have in greater abundance. So, we are faced with the usual situation where the crude empirical relationship is one where the less wealthy (frontier) households have the larger families. One matter that I wish to investigate using the Canadian census data is whether, within given settlement areas (holding other influences on childbearing constant), a positive partial relationship of childbearing to wealth is found.

The recent literature on fertility analysis emphasizes strong, negative relative price effects as the influence overriding the effect of increased wealth. Higher prices of child-related goods and a higher opportunity cost of mother's time are claimed to make the relative price of children (of given quality) higher to households with higher income. One of the most striking situations in which this occurs, and the one that perhaps gets the most emphasis in the literature, is in the comparison between urban and rural households. My concern here is entirely with farm households. Most of the factors affecting the relative prices of children that get discussed in the literature have by definition been made uniform. What we have to ask is why farmers in older settled regions might be thought of as facing a higher relative price of children than farmers in frontier districts. Obvious answers do not spring readily to mind but one very tentative suggestion may be made.

An important distinction between farm households in the two sets of circumstances is that in the newly settled areas the infrastructure of the market system has not yet been fully developed. In the early years of settlement, frontier districts are only weakly integrated with the market system. This is the real meaning of the economic isolation of the frontier. Pioneer farms were highly self-sufficient not by choice but because the market system was not yet fully and efficiently organized. High transport costs and the absence of a fully organized set of institutions for the distribution of goods assure that some material goods will be virtually unavailable, or if available only at extraordinarily high prices. That in effect lowers the relative price of children. Children, and the food and shelter that children require, are locally produced and relatively cheap. Other goods that have to be imported have high prices and intermittent supply. Many services get marketed locally only after settlement has proceeded for some time and the community has attained the market size needed to support their profitable pursuit of such activities.

The foregoing situation may be a particularly striking feature of recently settled frontier communities, but it probably persists in varying degree over much longer periods and across a wide variety of densities of settlement. Some years ago T. W. Schultz (1953) proposed a general theory of agricultural development based on the premise that the market system itself was an urban–commercial construct that functioned most efficiently in cities and their environs. The more remote from the urban–industrial nexus a rural community might be, the less well it would be integrated into the market system and the less efficiently the price system would work. The chief difficulty will lie in satisfactorily capturing this spatial feature of the market system in the form of variables sufficiently independent of other factors to be analytically useful.

It is not only that the variety of material goods to be bought on the market is cheaper and more abundant in longer and more thoroughly developed communities. There is also a greater complexity of interpersonal relationships that compete for the housewife-and-mother's time and thereby raise the relative price of children.

Easterlin (1971) attempted to redirect attention from relative prices to the income variable and the feedback that it might have on the formation of preferences. He argued that individuals' preferences, specifically for material goods vis-à-vis children, are influenced by the incomes of their parents at the time these individuals were growing up and forming their tastes. The children of frontier farmers, whose experience was of a rather meager and unsophisticated material standard of living, would tend to take over farms developed to the point where they could support both modest expectations of consumption of material goods and large numbers of children as well. Young people coming into possession of farms in older settled areas would have greater aspirations as to the consumption of material goods but not proportionately greater income-producing assets. They could achieve the standards of material comfort to which they aspired only by allocating fewer resources to children. The main suggestion coming out of this theory is that the second generation settlers in new areas are the ones most likely to have the largest families. Although Easterlin has continued to emphasize this general line of argument in his more recent writings on the socioeconomic theory of fertility, he has not pursued it in his discussions of historical fertility patterns in the United States (1975, 1976).

We should consider the role of children as producer goods, contributing to the income of farm households. There is little question that children can play a more significant role of this sort in agricultural communities than in towns and cities. What is of direct concern here, though, is how the marginal productivity of child labor might vary in relation to settlement densities. It is not enough to note that the marginal product of labor generally and child labor in particular will be higher the greater the abundance of land. It is not raw land but the capital value of improved land that combines with labor to produce agricultural output, and improved land is less abundant in the more recently settled districts. Moreover, children may be relatively less useful to the demanding tasks of frontier agriculture, where particularly strenuous jobs to which they are less able to contribute predominate. A counterargument may be that children maintain their high value by undertaking the more menial chores and freeing adult labor for the strenuous tasks of clearing land of trees and breaking soil. At least for the particular circumstances of Upper Canada this argument is not so persuasive, since the frontier districts were heavily given over to wheat production and were notably deficient in the livestock, poultry, and other aspects of farming in which children's labor was most valuable.

It is questionable then, whether a good argument can be made to the effect that the value of children's labor would have been greater in the more newly settled areas. The issue becomes one to be decided on empirical grounds, although that may prove difficult. The skeptical view expressed here is shared by Easterlin (1976), who introduces a bit of empirical evidence that casts doubt on any supposedly higher productivity of child labor in frontier districts.

Children also would have contributed to parents' economic security in old age. Especially in a regime of high mortality, it might have been necessary to have a good number of children to be reasonably assured that some of them would be around to supply care and support in one's old age. The level of care and support would in turn depend on the ease with which a man's sons could obtain farmsteads in the immediate locality, and that would have been greater in land-abundant, frontier areas. However, the level of care and support in old age that a farmer could claim would also be strongly affected by the value of the asset he could pass on to his prospective heir. The farm itself would be particularly important, especially since it could be passed on with more strings attached. The asset value of that farm, with fewer acres of land cleared, would be less in the frontier areas.

In addition, farmers may have been concerned not only for their own but for their children's future welfare. An important objective of the farm household may be to provide an appropriate inheritance to the children. There have been many references in Eruopean history to this "inheritance" motive and to suggestions that the difficulties met by parents in providing a suitable legacy for their children may have been an important incentive to reduce the number of offspring. It is still not obvious, though, how this might work differentially between frontier and longer-settled areas. In his most recent paper, Easterlin (1976) has explored the idea, but, as his commentator points out, he does not have much to go on. If, as Easterlin argues, a farmer endeavors to pass on to his children an inheritance of the value he himself received, the second generation of farmers in the frontier areas, who may have inherited a relatively low-valued, mainly unimproved farm, may be the ones most inclined to have many children in the belief that they are not obliged to pass much on to them. On the other hand the farmer who has migrated to settle on the frontier might be relatively less concerned about the need to provide a legacy for his children because farmsteads can be obtained so cheaply. The main prediction that the inheritance motive may yield is that eventually, as areas become heavily populated and land more scarce, parents who are concerned for the future well-being of their children may wish to limit the size of their families. In its present state the theory has little to offer as to when in the settlement process this concern might begin to have real effect.

The possible importance of noneconomic influences on childbearing should not be excluded. The most commonly cited of these is the influence of urbanization through its effect on attitudes and preferences. Little has been done, though, to work out how this operates at the behavioral level. Two other ideas, however, deserve mention. One is that "family" values may get reinforced by the isolation of life in frontier areas. This may be little more than the sheer loneliness of the pioneer housewife, driven to surround herself with a large family. A second, but not entirely unrelated idea, is that the relative isolation of households in less densely settled areas may significantly increase the general riskiness of life. In this circumstance of greater risk the family is the one institution that can be relied on. Surrounding oneself with a large family is a rational response to the generally hazardous and risky life of the more isolated settler. As a community grows up, people are able to depend upon the community at large and even institutions organized specifically to shoulder some of the risk of life.

The theoretical discussions of fertility, in their present form at least, turn out to be less fruitful of reasons why households in more recently and less densely settled areas should have more children than they are of reasons for other types of differentials. A few ideas do emerge, though, that have a bearing on the kind of patterns observed in nineteenth century rural fertility. With a full recognition that considerably more work needs to be done on the theoretical front, and also with modest expectations about the possibilities of extracting from limited empirical data results that might sharply differentiate between alternate hypotheses, let us turn to the empirical evidence for Canada.

THE UPPER CANADA FARM SAMPLE–1861

With the sorts of issues in mind that were discussed in the foregoing section, I assembled a body of data on childbearing and other aspects of Canadian households of 1861. The manuscript enumerations of the census of 1861 were chosen because they were readily available and because they offered a wide selection of demographic and agricultural variables. A stringent budget and the preliminary exploratory nature of the project dictated a rather small sample of about 1200 farm households. Within the limitations imposed, every attempt was made to maximize the usefulness of the sample. For that reason a sample was designed in which a small, random selection of individual households whose heads declared their occupation to be farmer was drawn within each of a much larger number of randomly selected localities. This was a stratified, two-stage random sample. Upper Canada's 300-odd townships were organized into six strata of differing dates of initial settlement. A random selection of townships was made within each of these strata, so that 150 townships in all were selected. Then, in the second stage, a handful (eight) of farm households was randomly selected from within each township. The agricultural census was then searched to match farm data with household data.

For each individual in each household a number of potentially important demographic characteristics were recorded—sex, age, relationship to head of household, birthplace, religious affiliation, and occupation. For each household there was also information on the type of dwelling, the size and characteristics of the farm holding, and a long list of variables that pertain to farm operation. In many ways this represents a wealth of data, but from the point of view of the issues raised here, it is quite limited. Variables that might be directly useful to the analysis of fertility are scanty. Apart from indicators of the wealth of the farm, these variables had to be developed from outside sources. The easiest to incorporate, and all that are developed for the present analysis, are characteristics of the township within which the farm is located. A second limitation is that it was not really possible to develop entirely satisfactory measures of household fertility.

In the Canadian census of 1861 there was nothing corresponding to the "own children" questions or childbearing histories of more recent censuses. The children listed are those of the male head of household, not necessarily of his current wife, and they are surviving children still residing in the household. The number of children of the head of household represents an accumulation of past childbearing, influenced by conditions that may have changed over time or as a consequence of migration. For all its weaknesses, this measure is the most direct and most comprehensive that can be derived from these data.

A more current measure of childbearing, and one that might be more likely to reflect directly the influences on the household at the time of the 1861 census, would be the number of young children. This measure is also less susceptible to systematic variations in the age at which more mature children leave the home. In this study, "Young" children were defined to be under 5 years of age. This measure would be most satisfactorily studied for quite specific age-groups of women. The sample is too small, however, to tabulate statistically reliable mean numbers of children under 5 for narrowly specified age groups of mothers. Fortunately, close examination of the sample evidence indicates that the common pattern in Upper Canada at that time was for women to continue bearing children up to a very late age. Consequently, from the small sample at hand we do not lose many observations because households with older wives have no children under 5 years of age. Out of 1200 households with wives of all ages (and including a few in which there were no wives), fully 770 had at least one child under the age of 5.

Several other possible measures of fertility were investigated, including the inferred ages of women at the birth of their oldest surviving child, the inferred ages of women at the birth of their youngest surviving child, and the length of the interval between penultimate and last child. The technical and interpretative problems associated with such measures preclude their inclusion in the short space available here. Only one additional measure is considered—the frequency of children per year of the span between the oldest and the youngest child. Actually the age span was increased by 1 year to provide for the inclusion of women with only one child born within the year, and only households with wives no older than 40 were selected, so as to minimize distortion from the exclusion of older children who might have left the household. The study of birth intervals is quite common in demographic analysis. The concept is that families that want fewer children space them more widely. In the particular historical setting under study, though, this measure may be of doubtful usefulness. The data from the sample suggest that in nineteenth century Upper Canada it was more common for women to bear children at relatively short and quite even intervals and then to cease abruptly, presumably when the desired size of family had been attained (or more than attained?). One presumes that the widespread technique of family limitation was simply abstinence from sexual intercourse when no more children were desired. That certainly is the most common picture that emerges from the sample of households examined here. A second reason for doubt about the usefulness of the frequency-of-childbearing variable is that it is disturbed by the deaths of children. One of the really serious gaps in the information we have about Upper Canada in the third quarter of the nineteenth century is an almost complete lack of knowledge of rates and systematic differentials in infant and childhood mortality. They were high enough to be a seriously complicating factor in any quantitative analysis. It is difficult to be convinced in principal, though, that child mortality would have been higher in the more remote and probably less well-off frontier areas than in the longer developed, more densely populated districts where diseases might be more readily communicated.

The main economic characteristic of the household that is considered is the size and status of the farm. The value of the farm is the best available overall indicator of family wealth. The Canadian census, unlike that in the United States, did not return data on personal property. The value of the farm was to a considerable degree a reflection of both the size of the farm and the extent to which the occupied land had been brought under cultivation; the latter tended to be more important. In the regression analysis of the next section, in place of the single variable "asset value of the farm," farm size and the proportion of farm area improved are introduced separately, in the event that they reflect different influences upon household decisions.

Two important cultural variables are available for each member of each household: religious adherence and country of birth. There might be a supposition that Roman Catholic households and perhaps those of the more Fundamentalist Protestant persuasions would have been more pronatal than Anglicans or Presbyterians. Unfortunately, place of birth within Upper Canada for the native born was only sometimes recorded, but country of birth was always shown. The adult population included a high proportion of immigrants and there may be reason to suspect differences between English, Irish, and Scottish ethnic groups. There are other variables for each household that might be thought of as influencing fertility—literacy, school attendance of children, complexity of family organization, type of dwelling—but these do not exhibit enough variability to hold any promise.

As has already been noted, the sample was designed to permit the exploitation of locality variables in addition to individual household variables. The former relate to the township within which the household was located. The most straightforward of these locality variables was built into the design of the sample whereby townships were initially stratified according to the periods of approximately a decade in length during which they were first settled. The stratification of the sample had been introduced to ensure sufficient representation of the smaller number of recently and more sparsely settled townships. Settlement had first begun in Upper Canada with the influx of the United Empire Loyalists in the 1780s and had reached its peak rates in the 1830s and 1840s. The last townships were being opened for settlement in the decade preceding the census of 1861.

A second locality variable of direct and obvious concern is the relative abundance of uncultivated land. Alternative ways of specifying land availability were experimented with. The index used here is a relatively simple one. It is the ratio of improved acreage in 1861 to the maximum ever of improved acreage (occurring in most cases early in the twentieth century) in an area that for each township consisted of the township itself and all contiguous townships. Individual townships were themselves too confined an area and counties were inappropriate units, especially since many of them tended to be elongated in shape in the direction of the moving frontier of settlement; in many cases townships in remote corners of counties were very badly described by the situation for the whole county. This index is lower the greater the amount of nearby land still available to be brought under cultivation.

Two additional locality variables were devised to attempt to capture different aspects of the influence of urbanization. Simply to look at the proportion of a township's population that might be classed as urban did not seem very persuasive. Towns of 500 or 1000 persons are not very urban in the sense that term is used in most discussion of fertility. Only a half-dozen townships contained centers of more than 5000. To the extent that the concern was with the cultural and attitudinal influence of real cities, a better alternative seemed to be to focus on the distance from each township to such an urban center. The index used is admittedly rather mechanical, and owes its inspiration to some degree to the "gravity" and "potential" concepts developed by geographers. A number of large and presumably influential cities in both Canada and the United States were identified and the distance measured from each to every township in the sample. The "urban influence" on the farms in each township, then, was computed by summing each city's population weighted by the reciprocal of the square of the distance from that city to the rural locality.

A final locality variable is intended to reflect, in an admittedly crude way, the degree of integration into the market system and the range of nonfarm goods and services locally available. This is measured by the town and village population within a fairly easy day's travel distance. Specifically this was taken to be the size of the nonfarm population within the township and an area 8 miles in each direction from the township boundaries. For the most part, that nonagricultural population would owe its existence to the provision of those goods and services characteristic of more fully developed communities or brought in from outside the community.

The data from the Upper Canada Farm Sample and the locality variables constructed in conjunction with the sample were utilized in two general ways. First, census data were retabulated to relate measures of childbearing to the other variables discussed. Second, individual household data were used to make statistical estimates of the parameters of functional relationships that attempt to express hypothesized causal influences on childbearing.

Both approaches have very apparent limitations. The sample is small and cross-tabulations quickly run into cells too small to be statistically reliable. No more than a few categories of any variable can be specified, so that tabulations can reveal only a limited amount of the variation in childbearing that occurs in relation to any of the selected explanatory variables. On the other hand, linear regression analysis at the microlevel is typically unable to account for any appreciable fraction of variability. At the household level purely random elements tend to dominate. Moreover, the relationships we seek to explore are only weakly specified in the variables available for regression analysis. Nevertheless, since little has been done to use individual household data to explore the relationship between fertility and land availability or recency of settlement, the Canadian evidence developed here is examined in a preliminary way in the following two sections.

CHILDBEARING IN OLD AND NEW AREAS

In this section the evidence of the Upper Canada Farm Sample is examined in a relatively simple way by comparing tabulations of farm and household data for three groupings distinguished by the timing of initial settlement. This is admittedly a coarse way of using evidence; however, the sample is too small to permit separation into more than three groupings. Nevertheless, some bold patterns of differences emerge between townships initially settled before 1815 (Area I), townships initially settled between 1815 and 1842 (Area II), and the last-settled group of townships, settled between 1843 and 1860 (Area III).

The census data do not provide refined measures of childbearing, so we have to infer patterns from rougher, indicative measures. A variety of measures is presented in Table 1. The best-known and most straightforward indicator is the fertility ratio—the total number of children under 5 years of age per 1000 women aged 20–49 years. Childbearing at ages less than 20 was at such low rates that women 20–49 years make a more suitable denominator here than the more conventional 15–49. The fertility ratio can be calculated from published census data for the townships in the sample, as well as directly from the sample itself—thus giving a check on the reliability of the sample. The fertility ratios from the published census, shown as line 1 of Table 1, are for the entire rural population, including villages, not just for the farm popula-

TABLE 1
*Indicators of Childbearing in Different Settlement Period Areas of Canada West,
1861*[a]

		Settlement-Period Area		
		I	II	III
1.	Children under 5 per thousand women 20-49 (from published census)	660	858	950
2.	Children under 5 per thousand women 20-49 (upper Canada farm sample)	645	878	940
3.	Number of children per household	3.9	4.4	4.1
4.	Number of children per household where wives are 40-54 only	4.1	5.1	4.7
5.	Number of children under 5 years of age, per household, wives under 45 only	.92	1.10	1.11
6.	Average number of persons per household	6.1	6.4	6.2
7.	Percent of households with no children	11.4	8.0	7.8
8.	Percent of households with fewer than 4 children	49.6	46.4	47.2
9.	Percent of households with more than 6 children	13.0	16.0	21.6
10.	Inferred mean age of wife at birth of first child (women less than 45 only)	22.8	22.5	23.0
11.	Inferred mean age of wife at birth of youngest child (women 45-64 years)	41.8	43.7	41.1

[a]Line 1 from Census of Canada, 1861; lines 2-11 from Upper Canada Farm Sample,
1861.

tion. The fertility ratios from the sample (line 2) are for farm households
only and so are not exactly comparable to those of line 1. The two sets of
numbers are in fact in close agreement, suggesting that the sample,
small though it may be, provides a reliable reflection of the characteristics of the population. Two points of considerable interest arise from an
examination of these fertility ratios. One is that the farm population
evidently did not have higher fertility than either the village and other
rural nonfarm population in either old or newly settled districts. Second, the larger difference in fertility appears to have been between the
oldest settled region and the other two. Between Area III and Area II the
difference was of a much smaller order. Broadly speaking, the three
settlement areas correspond to generations, with Area III consisting
entirely of migrant heads of households. Area II contained many migrants but had a large number of second-generation families. Area I had

predominantly third-generation families. What the fertility ratios of Table 1 hint at, and what is supported by evidence to be discussed later, is that the major downward adjustment of fertility came between the second and the third generations and not more immediately after first settlement.

The average number of children per household (line 3) is lower in Area I than in either of the newer areas by an amount that is statistically significant. The smaller number of children per household in the most recently settled area (III) may result from a greater proportion of younger households in the frontier districts. It is more pertinent to compare average numbers of children only for households that have completed childbearing. At the time we are considering, completion of childbearing occurred at a relatively late age, by which time older children would have begun to leave home. Therefore the measure becomes seriously biased downward. The problem is alleviated somewhat by the fact that in *all* areas women continued to bear children into their forties. The small size of the sample does not permit us to focus on a very narrow age group. Line 4 presents what may be a fair compromise, the average number of children in households where the wife is 40–54 years of age. It mirrors the pattern of the overall average number of children per household (line 3) but in a rather more pronounced way. Area I is differentiated from both of the other, more recently settled areas by a decidedly lower number (of children). Area III, the most recently settled, had a smaller number than Area II, but still well above Area I.

The average size of household (line 6) did not vary significantly between settlement areas. This is because households in Area I tended to have more persons other than husband and wife and children. Complex households, containing grandparents, other relatives, and hired help, although not common anywhere in mid-nineteenth century Canada, were much more likely to be found in the older settled areas than in the frontier.

In lines 7 through 11 of Table 1, several additional indicators of childbearing are examined, largely to test their consistency with the pattern already discussed. Childlessness (line 7) was significantly more frequent in Area I. On the other hand, there was no systematic variation in the frequency of small families—those with less than four children (line 8). The proportion of households that might be described as having large families (more than six children) was substantially higher in Area II than Area I and even higher in Area III, the most recently settled area. This is one of the few measures for which Area III was sharply distinguished from Area II. In most cases the main difference was between the oldest settled district (I) and the rest of the region. There is no appreciable difference between settlement areas in the inferred ages at which women bore their first (surviving) child (line 10). This suggests that frontier women were not having larger families because they married and began childbearing at a younger age. On the other hand, women old enough to have completed childbearing appear to have borne their last child at an older age on average in Area II than in Area I. The inferred age of completion of childbearing is lower again in the most recently settled region, in part because the effects of variations in age composition have not entirely been removed from the comparison.

The historical census sample data do not provide enough information for a fully satisfactory age standardization of fertility ratios between settlement areas. The effect of area differences in the age composition of women can be examined in a rough way and should be looked at; there is a common suspicion that the observed variations of fertility ratios by recency of settlement is largely a matter of greater concentrations of women of peak childbearing ages in the frontier areas. Table 2 shows that in mid-nineteenth century Upper Canada there was neither a systematic nor a significant difference in the average ages of wives of farm household heads across settlement areas. Wives of heads were younger, on the average, in Area II but not in the most recently settled

TABLE 2
Age Characteristics of Women by Settlement-Period Areas, Canada West, 1861[a]

	Settlement-Period Area		
	I	*II*	*III*
Mean age of wife of head of household	34.7	31.7	34.5
Percentage of all women 20-49 aged:			
20-24	24.73	26.89	17.5
25-29	20.29	18.02	26.0
30-34	15.00	17.91	23.8
35-39	15.52	14.72	14.6
40-44	12.36	11.93	9.3
45-49	12.10	10.53	8.5
	100.00	*100.00*	*100.0*

[a]From Upper Canada Farm Sample, 1861.

area. How this came about is suggested by the age distributions of all women (not just wives of household heads) in the three areas, also shown in Table 2. The settlement frontier (Area III) had fully half of all women 20–49 years of age in the 25–34 year bracket, whereas the other two areas had only 35–36% of women in that age group. Both Areas I and II had proportionally more 20–24-year-olds, many of whom at this time would not have been married, and more women over the age of 40.

The incidence of children under 5 by age of wife of household head for the whole sample is shown in Table 3. The sample was divided into

TABLE 3
Number of Children Under Five Per Household, by Age of Wife of Head of Household[a]

Age of wife	Children under 5 per household
Less than 20	1.08
20–24	1.54
25–29	1.87
30–34	1.97
35–39	1.66
40–44	1.12
45–49	.71

[a]From Upper Canada Farm Sample, 1861.

age groupings so small that the difference cannot be shown to be statistically significant, and the ratios appear to vary over age groups rather less, perhaps, than might have been expected. Nevertheless, the ratios show a consistent and creditable pattern, and the data of Tables 2 and 3 tempt us to ask what the differentials in fertility ratios between settlement areas would have been if the incidence of children per household by age of wife had been constant across space and only the age distribution of women differed. The result is interesting. In index form, if the fertility ratio of Area I equaled 100, age composition alone would have raised the fertility ratio of Area III to 108, but that of Area II to only 101. In fact the fertility ratio of Area II was 36% above that of Area I; this cannot be accounted for by differences in the age composition of the adult female population. On the other hand, the difference in fertility ratio between Area III and Area II (from Table 1, line 2) might have been accounted for entirely by the greater concentration of Area III women in the highest childbearing ages.

The foregoing suggests that two processes have been at work. Indeed, the frontier areas have been selective of women closer to peak childbearing ages and that does account for a part of the higher fertility observed in frontier regions. However, that is the lesser element and tends to account for the excess of fertility of very recently settled areas over recent but somewhat longer-settled regions (Area II in the present analysis). The main difference in fertility level, though, is between Areas II and III together and the oldest settled region, and that difference is not a product of a difference in the age composition of women.

Let us turn now to variables measuring possible influences on differential childbearing by settlement area. Recency of settlement would be associated with a number of characteristics of farming and of the organization of rural society that should have a bearing on fertility of the population. Frontier area farms are less well developed, have a smaller accumulated investment in cleared land, and are more remote from markets for farm products and sources of supply of nonagricultural goods that have to be purchased. A number of these differences are brought out in Table 4.

The farm of 100 acres predominated in Upper Canada in 1861. However, the average size of farm was larger in areas of more recent settlement. This was more because of a considerably lower frequency of small farms—subdivisions of standard 100-acre lots—than because of a higher frequency of 200-acre or larger farms. The wealth of a farm is to be gauged more by the cleared and improved acreage rather than by the overall size of the farm. Improved acreage as a percentage of occupied

TABLE 4
Social and Economic Characteristics of Settlement-Period Areas, Canada West, 1861[a]

		Settlement-Period Area		
		I	II	III
1.	Average size of farm in acres occupied	104.4	107.7	116.0
2.	Farm progress--ratio of improved to occupied farm acreage	61.8	48.1	24.0
3.	Average declared value of farm in dollars	2643	1890	1238
4.	Land utilization index	65	50	26
5.	Nearby town and village population (in hundreds of people)	196.4	112.5	32.2
6.	Urban influence	80.1	13.3	7.3

[a]From Upper Canada Farm Sample, 1861.

acreage (line 2) declines sharply as we pass from Area I toward Area II and the frontier Area III. This measure is used in the subsequent analysis and called, for short, an index of farm progress. It corresponds very closely to the stated value of farms (line 3). Both measures, though, differentiate Area III from the other two settlement areas, which is the reverse of the pattern of fertility. Of course the average farm value of farm progress varies in the opposite direction to the fertility differentials by settlement area, so that there is no suggestion here of the positive wealth elasticity of household demand for children posited by microeconomic theory. However, I will consider in the next section whether there is any indication that within settlement areas individual households with larger and more improved farms also tend to have larger numbers of children.

The emphasis in the literature on the relationship of birth rates to density of settlement has been on the availability of still unsettled farmland. That is captured in line 4 of Table 4 by the index of land utilization (explained on p. 212), which shows that only half the land area eventually cultivated in Area II was under cultivation in 1861, and in Area III only a quarter. In the oldest settled area 65% of land ever cultivated was already under the plow. Two of the other indices described in a foregoing section are shown in lines 5 and 6 of Table 4. These are the town and village population within a regular wagon haul of the farm and an index of the influence of large urban centers, diminished by distance from them. The latter is especially interesting because of the way in which it differentiates Areas II and III collectively from Area I. Although a lack of town and village organization is clearly an aspect of the very frontier of settlement, it does not differ to quite the same degree between Areas I and II. However, all but the oldest settled area are relatively remote from the influence of large urban centers. That indicates in part their remoteness from the most fully developed market centers, but it also is suggestive of other influences involving urban attitudes and cultural influences upon human behavior.

Such a simple comparison of general attributes of farm households grouped into three broad settlement areas is inadequate to push very far into the examination of reasons for the decline of fertility with increasing density of settlement. The evidence presented so far tends to confirm that a similar pattern existed in mid-nineteenth century Canada to what has been observed for the United States and it has pointed to a few suggestive aspects of that pattern. To get any greater discrimination between possible sources of the widely observed pattern of birth rates a more refined analysis has to be undertaken. The following section reports on a regression analysis at the individual household level of childbearing variables for farm households in different circumstances with respect to period of settlement and other variables discussed here using the 1200 farm households of the Upper Canada Farm Sample.

A REGRESSION ANALYSIS OF CHILDBEARING IN RELATION TO LAND AVAILABILITY AND RECENCY OF SETTLEMENT

Studies of the behavioral factors determining patterns of fertility in historical periods must eventually get down to the level of the individual household where decisions about family size are actually made. The most readily available technique for sorting out influences of variables on each other at the individual household level is linear regression analysis. There is ample precedent for this in, for example, the work of Schultz (1969), Willis (1973) and much research that is just now appearing in print. Here I will report on a first set of experimental regression results using the Canadian data described earlier. It should be made clear in advance, though, that our expectations ought to be modest. Other research endeavoring to analyze fertility in this way has met with only qualified success. The limitations on what can be done are quite severe. The absence of rural–urban differentials in a sample of entirely farm households removes by definition some of the most powerful influences emphasized by theory. We have already seen that part of the variation in childbearing patterns is compositional and will not be revealed at the level of the individual household. There remains a substantial amount of variability at the household level, but much of it may be random disturbance. It is a common problem in cross-sectional microanalysis for there to be a large element of random noise and a low fraction of overall variability for which even very complex regression relationships are able to account.

Three dependent variables are considered. I have indicated that one serious limitation of the historical census manuscripts is the inability to derive from them very refined measures of fertility. Some of the difficulties met here could be overcome by an expansion of the sample to provide a large number of households within particular categories, but much of the problem stems from the limitations of the rather simple census questionnaire used a century ago. The dependent variables examined here are the number of children of the head of household in each household, the number of such children under 5 years of age, and the frequency of childbearing, measured as the number of surviving children born per year between 1 year before the birth of the oldest child and the year of birth of the youngest child. The birth interval, or the frequency of childbearing, has been commonly used in demographic research, especially where it is expected that family limitation is accomplished by the wider spacing of children. In the Canadian population of 1861, it is more likely that family limitation would have been accomplished through either later marriage or an earlier cessation of childbearing than by variations in spacing; so this third variable is least expected to give interesting results.

The use of the number of children under 5 years of age as a dependent variable raises special problems. The variable takes on discrete values of 0, 1, 2, 3, and in a very few cases 4. More than half of all households in which the wife is age 50 or less have one child under 5 years of age. Another quarter have no young children. Most of the rest have two children. Given such a distribution it would be very difficult to make the assumption required by the method of least squares, that the random disturbance term is normally distributed. Nor does any plausible distribution for which an estimator can be derived spring readily to mind. The solution adopted here is very much of a second-best sort.

Instead of the number of children under 5 years of age, just the existence of any number of children under 5 is noted. The dichotomous or "dummy" dependent variable can be associated with a symmetrical distribution of the disturbance term, a distribution that may be considered to be approximately normal. If the actual number of children under 5 is used as the dependent variable, the fit of the regression equation is improved—R^2 goes up. But one is left in a quandary as to how to evaluate the significance of the regression coefficients.

Three categories of explanatory variables were used. Age of wife of household head was introduced as a control since the fertility indicators were measures that changed systematically with age. Secondly, religious and birthplace characteristics of the household were introduced as additive dummy variables. Five religion and seven birthplace categories were recognized. A dummy variable took on the value of 1 if the head of the household was Roman Catholic, Anglican, Presbyterian, or Methodist. All four religion variables were 0 if the household was one of the approximately 10% with some "Other" religious affiliation. All birthplace variables were 0 for households whose head was born in Upper Canada. A dummy variable took on a value of 1 for each of these birthplaces: Lower Canada, England, Ireland, Scotland, United States, and Other.

These dummy variables were used primarily to prevent household characteristics that might have a systematic influence on a household's preferences for children from obscuring the partial relationship of hypothesized influences to the childbearing variables. No real hypotheses were entertained about birthplace and religious influences. As will be seen, however, some significant influences do emerge.

A third group of variables is made up of those drawn from hypotheses about the determinants of fertility. The economic theories of childbearing stress wealth and price influences. The sample included data on the main item of household wealth, the value of the farm itself. This is strongly influenced by two other variables, the size of the farm in acres occupied, and the investment made in clearing the farm—or farm progress (measured by the ratio of improved to occupied acreage). The two components of farm value were separately introduced into the regression equation. The issue of concern here is whether, with a substantial number of controls on other characteristics, rural households exhibited the positive relationship of childbearing to wealth that economic theory would lead us to suppose.

In this, as in all studies of the determinants of family size, there are no direct measures of the relative price of children. Earlier in the chapter I discussed the implications for the relative price of children of the availability of a wide range of other goods and services. The number of people living in the nearby towns and villages, producing and handling nonfarm goods and services, was proposed as a rough indicator of a lower price of nonfarm goods. The variable used here is simply the total town and village population (measured in hundreds of people) within 8 miles of the nearest boundary of the township in which the household is located. This is a "locality" rather than a household level variable and assumes the same value for each household in the same township.

The census sample data contain several household variables that might imply variations in relative prices of children, but they do not appear to be readily usable. Nonfarm occupations representing employability outside the household; existence in the household of persons other than family members, who might cheapen the cost of child care; and specialized forms of agriculture that might put a higher value on children's services all occur with such low frequency as to offer no statistical explanatory power. School attendance by children in the family is difficult to interpret; moreover, it does not seem to vary much by settlement area.

The principal explanatory variables that can be investigated at this stage are the period of first settlement of the township in which the household is located and the index of land utilization—the ratio of improved land in 1861 to maximum land ever improved for an area of the township and all contiguous townships. Neither of these offers much prospect of discriminating between alternative versions of the economic model and they might even be interpreted to reflect the social isolation and family orientation of the recently settled, land-abundant frontier. For whichever reason, though, we expect measures of childbearing to be positively associated with period of settlement (the scale running from earlier to more recent) and inversely related to the index of land utilization.

To attempt to capture the indirect influences of urbanization, an index (described earlier)—the weighted sum of large city populations where the weights are the inverse of the squared distances from each city to the township in which the household is located—is introduced with the expectation that childbearing should be inversely related to it. The higher the value of the index, the larger or more nearby are major urban centers and hence the lower we might expect fertility to be.

The regression equation was estimated in this form:

$$CH = \alpha_0 + \alpha_1 \frac{1}{X_1} + \alpha_2 \frac{1}{X_2} + \ldots \beta_1 D_1 + \beta_2 D_2 + \ldots + \epsilon$$

where CH is the number of children or the frequency of childbearing, the X's are the explanatory variables other than the D's, the dummy variables that take on a value of 0 or 1 (since 1/0 would raise great difficulties and 1/1 makes no difference), and ϵ is a random disturbance term that is assumed to be normally distributed. The functional form was selected as a means of introducing a degree of curvilinearity without resorting to a logarithmic transformation. The zero values of variables, such as number of children, are meaningful and should be retained in the analysis. The curvilinearity is implied by the natural ceiling on the dependent variable. As that limit is approached a proportionate increase in the independent variable can only induce a smaller and smaller rise in the dependent variable. The specification used is about the simplest that captures this implied curvilinearity. However, it makes the interpretation of the regression coefficients somewhat more complicated. The reader has to keep in mind the reversal of signs imposed by the specification. If childbearing is hypothesized to be negatively related to L, the index of land utilization, it shows up as having a positive coefficient for $1/L$.

The results of this regression analysis are summarized in Table 5. As might have been expected, these results are somewhat mixed. One of the most notable general features is that the estimated relationships differ according to which dependent variable is selected. Not surprisingly, though, age of mother always turns out to be significant, in the predicted direction. Recalling that the explanatory variables were en-

TABLE 5
Estimated Regression Coefficients[a]

Dependent variable	Number of children (1)	Frequency of childbearing (2)	Dummy for children under 5 years (3)
Explanatory variables			
Age of mother	*-3.99*	*.26*	*.016*
Farm size	*-3.92*	*(-.27)*	*(.000)*
Farm progress	*-2.05*	*-.26*	*(.000)*
Period of settlement	*(.24)*	*(-.03)*	*(-.002)*
Town and village population	*(-18.98)*[b]	*-4.13*	*(.000)*
Land utilization	*(-3.24)*	*(-1.01)*	*.015*
Urban influence	*2.69*	*.37*	*.278*
Dummy Variables			
Religion of head			
Roman Catholic	*(-.17)*	*(-.02)*	*(.015)*
Anglican	*-.74*	*-.19*	*-.185*
Methodist	*(-.02)*	*(-.06)*	*(.007)*
Presbyterian	*-.53*	*-.08*	*-.076*
Birthplace of head			
Lower Canada	*(.59)*	*(.06)*	*.115*
England	*(.32)*	*-.07*	*(-.015)*
Ireland	*.53*	*(.02)*	*(-.003)*
Scotland	*.61*	*(-.03)*	*(.069)*
U.S.	*(-.45)*	*-.10*	*-.029*
Constant term	*4.07*	*.51*	*.832*
R^2	*.08*	*.05*	*.120*
F statistics	*5.33*	*3.33*	*8.51*

[a]Coefficients which are significantly different from zero at the .95 level are in italics. Coefficients that fail to pass that significance test are enclosed in parentheses.

[b]Coefficient would be significant at the .90 level.

tered into the regression equation as reciprocals so that their signs are the reverse of the measured relationship between childbearing and the variable in its ordinary form, we find a negative coefficient for age of mother, indicating that the older the woman the larger the number of children. On the other hand, both the mean interval between children and the existence of children under 5 in the household are associated negatively with age of mother and hence positively with the reciprocal of the variable.

The number of children is greater the higher the level of household wealth, as indicated by both farm size and progress. The inclusion of older children in the dependent variable, though, suggests that some reverse causality may be getting picked up here since farmers with older sons would have the labor available to clear more land. Neither of the farm wealth variables has a significant relationship with the number of children under 5. But farms with a larger proportion of their land under cultivation tend to have children born at more frequent intervals.

The relative abundance of unused land—the variable that most closely captures the relationship that spurred this investigation in the first place—comes through with mixed results. It does not reveal a significant partial relationship with either the number of children per household or the frequency of childbearing. When a more current measure of childbearing, "children under 5," is analyzed, a statistically significant association emerges, but it is not strong—the difference in land utilization between Areas I and II would, of itself, account for only 2% of the difference in the fertility measure between the two areas.

The "urban influence" and "town and village population" variables were introduced in an attempt to capture different aspects of the lack of urbanization and remoteness in more recently settled areas. The accessible town and village population would reflect the extent of nearby nonagricultural development and the extent of market organization. It performs badly as an explanatory variable. In the only case in which it has a statistically significant coefficient, the sign is the reverse of what was expected *a priori*. On the other hand the more narrowly conceived effect of urbanization in the sense of the economic and cultural influence of large cities, even at some distance, as measured by the index of urban influence used here, shows up in all three equations to have a significant downward influence on childbearing. The average value of the reciprocal of the urban influence index for Area I is .012, an amount .063 less than the average value for Area II. A change of that magnitude, the regression coefficient tells us, would reduce the probability of there being children under 5 in the household by .0175, or 35% of the actual difference between Areas I and II.

Little will be said about the dummy variables for religious affiliation and birthplace. They were introduced mainly to provide controls for cultural factors about which we do not have well-articulated theoretical expectations. Lower fertility was clearly associated with Anglican or

Presbyterian religion. Scottish and Irish birthplace of head was associated with large numbers of children in total. However, the probability of there being young children in the household was significantly raised if the head were born in Lower Canada or lowered if he were born in the United States. These variables influenced differences between households in the measures of childbearing but would have little influence on variations in fertility by settlement area since religion and origin characteristics of the population did not vary much across regions. The one origin group that was heavily concentrated in a particular settlement area—the U.S.-born in the oldest settled districts—was not sufficiently numerous for its lower fertility to have an appreciable downward influence on Area I fertility.

Overall, the regression analysis adds very modestly to our understanding of the determinants of childbearing in nineteenth century North American farm households. A number of variables are found to have a statistically significant influence on the selected fertility measures. Together these are able to account for from 5 to 12 % of the variability between households in the measures of childbearing. This is not especially gratifying, yet it is not out of line with typical results of regression analysis at the microlevel. The main disappointment is that the regression analysis, which it should be reiterated is the result of a preliminary exploration of this data body, did not throw much light on the behavioral basis for the widely observed gradient of fertility ratios in relation to recency of settlement and land abundance. What did emerge is that the timing of initial settlement alone is not the relevant factor. When other influences are taken into account the period-of-settlement variable never has a statistically significant coefficient.

As was expected, an abundance of nearby, uncultivated land affects the probability of there being young children in the household. However, the magnitude of its influence is small and it does not consistently affect other childbearing variables in the same way. The strongest result obtained is that fertility falls as larger cities develop sufficiently close by for there to be a real influence of urban life and culture. The behavioral basis for that remains insufficiently explored, however.

More substantial results may be obtained in further research if better articulated childbearing variables can be developed. Although the historical census data are particularly limited in that regard, some improvement may be obtained by enlarging the sample so that the analysis can be focused on more narrowly defined groupings by age and other characteristics. The idea of using locality variables may be extended also to develop variables that more precisely capture the influences hypothesized by theory. There are also refinements that can be made in the specification of the regression relationship, such as the use of "logit" analysis in place of the dummy dependent variable. Extension of the research along lines such as these may increase the likelihood that a more satisfactory explanation can be found for the really remarkable variations in fertility across areas of different settlement dates, which must stand out as one of the most prominent features of the demography of nineteenth century North America.

REFERENCES

Becker, Gary S. (1960). "An Economic Analysis of Fertility," in Universities-National Bureau of Economic Research, *Demographic and Economic Change in Developed Countries*. Princeton, N.J.: Princeton University Press.

Demeny, Paul (1968). "Early Fertility Decline in Austria-Hungary: A Lesson in Demographic Transition," *Daedalus*, Vol. 97, No. 2, pp. 502–522.

Easterlin, Richard A. (1971). "Does Human Fertility Adjust to the Environment," *American Economic Review: Papers and Proceedings*, Vol. 61, No. 2, pp. 399–407.

Easterlin, Richard A. (1975). "Farm Production and Income in Old and New Areas at Mid-Century," in Richard K. Vedder & David C. Klingaman, eds., *Essays in Nineteenth Century Economic History*. Athens: Ohio University Press.

Easterlin, Richard A. (1976). "Population Change and Farm Settlement in the Northern United States," *Journal of Economic History*, Vol. 36, No. 1, pp. 45–75.

Forster, Colin, & Tucker, G. S. L. (1972). *Economic Opportunity and White American Fertility Ratios, 1800–1860*. New Haven, Conn.: Yale University Press.

Leet, Don R. (1975). "Human Fertility and Agricultural Opportunities in Ohio Counties: From Frontier to Maturity, 1810–1860," in Richard K. Vedder & David C. Klingaman, eds., *Essays in Nineteenth Century Economic History*. Athens: Ohio University Press.

McInnis, R. Marvin (1972). "Birth Rates and Land Availability in North America in the Nineteenth Century, With Special Reference to Ontario." (Mimeographed. Kingston, Canada: Queen's University.) Paper presented to the annual meeting of the Population Association of America, April 1972, Toronto.

Mincer, Jacob (1963). "Market Prices, Opportunity Costs and Income Effects," in *Measurement in Economics, Studies in Mathematical Economics and Econometrics in Memory of Yehuda Grunfeld*. Stanford, Calif.: Stanford University Press.

Potter, J. (1965). "The Growth of Population in America, 1700–1860," in D. V. Glass and D. E. C. Eversley, eds., *Population in History*. London: Edward Arnold.

Schultz, T. Paul (1969). "An Economic Model of Family Planning and Fertility," *Journal of Political Economy*, Vol. 77, No. 2, pp. 153–180.

Schultz, T. Paul, & Nerlove, Marc (1970). *Love and Life Between the Censuses: A Model of Family Decision Making in Puerto Rico, 1950–1960*. Santa Monica, Calif.: RAND. RM-6322-AID.

Schultz, T. W. (1953). *The Economic Organization of Agriculture*. New York: McGraw-Hill. (See especially chaps. 9 and 10.)

Willis, Robert J. (1973). "A New Approach to the Economic Theory of Fertility Behavior," *Journal of Political Economy*, Vol. 81, No. 2, Supplement, Pt. 2, pp. 514–564.

Yasuba, Yasukichi (1962). *Birth Rates of the White Population in the United States, 1800–1860*. Baltimore, Md.: Johns Hopkins.

American Fertility Patterns
since the Civil War

PETER H. LINDERT

University of Wisconsin–Madison

The history of fertility in the United States presents the social scientist with a fascinating set of puzzles. There is, first, the long and fairly steady decline in the birth rate, by 60% or more, from 1800 or earlier to the middle of the 1930s. The initial level was extraordinarily high, a fact commonly attributed to the availability of land in a frontier nation. Part of the puzzle is how so great a decline in birth rates was achieved. There was no trend toward postponement of marriage. The median age of marriage for women, and the share of them never marrying, could not have risen enough before 1890 to account for the extent of observed birth reduction. Since 1890, when national census data on marriage began, marriage has become slightly more prevalent and has occurred at earlier median ages for women. We can only speculate from what little we know of the vast prehistory of contraception that couples turned mainly to withdrawal and abstinence until the use of condoms became widespread in the late nineteenth and early twentieth centuries (Himes, 1936, Chaps. 8, 13).

The question of *why* birth restriction came to be practiced more and more has seemed less troubling. We have come to expect declining birth rates as the land fills up and as modernization brings a shift from agriculture toward the cities, declining infant mortality rates, rising incomes, more schooling, and advances in the technology of contraception. It seems natural enough that couples in more modern settings have higher goods aspirations and better information about known contraceptive techniques. It is interesting to note the similarity in the long-run trends in birth rates for all major classes of American society.

To be sure, some classes at times reduced their fertility faster or slower than the rest of the nation. Southern white fertility, for example, dropped less than that of other regions between 1870 and 1900, and the birth rate of native-born New England women failed to drop at all between the 1860s and the 1920s (Spengler, 1930, Table 19). The black birth rate dropped somewhat faster than the white rate between 1880 and 1920, and since 1960, but rose relative to the white rate between 1920 and 1960. Yet the overall record shows an impressive similarity in the extent of the great decline up to the 1930s. The ratio of rural to urban fertility, the ratio of black to white fertility, and the rankings of different regions by fertility changed little.

The same negative relationship between fertility and modernization prevails, of course, in modern cross-sections as well as for the trends: Fertility is lower among more educated, urban, affluent, and better-informed couples. One can still wonder why such couples do not manage to gratify their modern consumption desires out of their higher incomes while having the same average number of children that others have, rather than fewer children on the average. In general, though, this question has not been posed, the implicit answer being that tastes and relative child costs must somehow differ so strongly in the cross section that having fewer children is the average outcome for higher-status couples.

The inverse relationship between fertility and modernization variables has not carried over into recent time-series patterns. Birth rates vary positively with income over the business cycle. This potential contradiction might be resolved in either of two ways. First, it could be argued that the positive cyclical pattern is but an adjustment in the timing of births (and marriages) with no implications about family sizes over the longer run. The other possible resolution is to strike income from the list of modernization variables that reduce fertility. Income, perhaps, encourages births, whereas everything else that grows with income in the long run and in the cross section—education, urban residence, and so forth—reduces births.

This entire line of reasoning seemed to receive a setback from the long baby boom extending from the end of World War II into the early 1960s. Fifteen years or more was a long time for temporary catching-up by returning soldiers and their wives. The tactic of again distinguishing between income and contemporaneous modernization variables might have seemed attractive were the facts less unkind. The baby boom was not just a national response to improvements in income combined with little change in the usual correlates of income. The exodus from agriculture and the rise of young adults' education, for example, proceeded faster than ever. To make matters worse, fertility rose fastest among the urban and the most educated.

A new set of fertility patterns seemed to take over around 1965. Incomes continued to grow as rapidly as they had from the late 1940s to the late 1950s, but the growth in the schooling of young adults decelerated. Fertility fell off sharply, matching the mid-Depression lows in the early 1970s. The fertility differentials by race, income, and religion narrowed. The differentials by education converged by some measures of period fertility but not by others.

Of all these patterns the one that has seemed most difficult to fit into a single model has been the postwar baby boom, and on this front an attractive explanation has been offered by Richard Easterlin (1968), Chaps. 4, 5; 1973). The swings in national fertility between the Depression and the present seem to fit neatly into a model of tastes that gives a central role to the consumption standards that young adults have inculcated from the households in which they were raised. Armed with this hypothesis, one can explain the postwar baby boom by noting that the young couples of that era found their income prospects much brighter than those they had known, or their parents had talked about, in the Depression. Given a tendency to raise children in a manner affected by their own upbringing, they felt they could afford several. The couples of prime childbearing age after 1965 felt the opposite: Raised in postwar prosperity and then faced with a job market flooded with young applicants, they felt pressure to postpone or prevent childbearing.

The reconciliation hinging on the relationship of prior consumption standards to current prospects for young couples has not yet met all potential criticisms. In particular, there remains an objection to the role it gives to current income, voiced earlier by Ansley Coale. Coale (1960) doubted that income-related explanations of the postwar baby boom could explain why no such boom occurred in the 1920s:

> [T]he interpretation of the baby boom as the natural consequence of prolonged prosperity is hardly more tenable than the earlier interpretation of the (slight revival of the birth rate in the later) 1930's as momentary. The next earlier period of notable prosperity in the United States—the 1920's—was a period of sharply falling fertility. In fact, as Dudley Kirk ([1960], pp. 243–246) points out, the depressed 1930's produced *more* births by far than one would expect on the basis of an extrapolation of the trend of the prosperous 1920's [pp. 5, 6].

Easterlin shared Coale's concern about the 1920s, and endeavored to reconcile that experience with his model of postwar behavior with several references to special influences on rural, native urban, and foreign-born urban fertility (1968, pp. 82, 89, 92, 99–100). His reconciliation failed to convince Alan Sweezy, who criticized it and renewed Coale's skepticism (Sweezy, 1971, pp. 258–260). Sweezy also found the Easterlin model incapable of explaining the striking tendency of fertility to rise more among couples with more education and higher husband's job status during the baby boom (Sweezy, 1971, pp. 260–262). World War II and the subsequent prosperity were accompanied by a dramatic reduction in income inequalities, with those in the bottom income and educational classes gaining considerable ground. If prosperity relative to past family incomes set off the baby boom, why was not the boom more characteristic of less educated couples than of the more educated?

To the historian accustomed to savoring history's infinite variety, the problem of reconciling these patterns may seem artificial. The social scientist who tries to fit a wide range of experiences to a single theory is off on the wrong quest, he may argue. The simplest way out of the seeming contradictions is to recognize that there may be no unifying theme to it all. Fertility is a complex matter, so why not just offer different careful explanations for different episodes? The supply of plausibly relevant variables will always exceed the number of patterns to be explained, and the task of the demographic historian might rightly be to decide which of several long listings of influences best fits each unique experience.

The subject matter of human fertility is such that this stress on historical uniqueness will always command respect. Yet it is important to avoid giving up on the generalizing hypotheses. There are indeed common themes, common models, that fit broad ranges of the history of fertility. By identifying the explanatory power as well as the limits of these generalizations, the demographic historian can offer a considerable service to others who think they care little about history. A wider public has come to realize that population growth has profound long-run effects on the social positions of age groups, on the level and the distribution of income, and on the position of natural resources in the economy. Interest in the future of fertility is thus widely shared. By separating generalizable from unique influences in the past, the demographic historian can offer a set of conditional predictions about the future course of fertility.

The variables we have usually used to sort out past fertility patterns are not likely to be of much help in analyzing or predicting future American fertility patterns. The share of population in agriculture, the share in cities, levels of education, rates of infant mortality, rates of immigration, racial shares—none of these traditional variables is likely to shift dramatically in the future. Nor do these variables vary so widely across the national population as they used to. There is the danger that demographic history will seem to offer no predictive power for the United States. That danger can be avoided if an effort is made to measure and apply the general variables that do underlie much of the seeming disunity in American fertility history and will continue to do so.

Conditional predictions can be offered on the basis of a fairly simple model that explains much of the past variations in American fertility. Such a model is sketched here and elsewhere. (See Lindert, forthcoming, for a fuller presentation of the model.) It expands upon suggestions made in different writings by Easterlin (1968, 1969, 1973). When expanded, this line of hypothesis helps to explain cross-sectional fertility patterns and some of the time-series paradoxes surrounding the relationship of the postwar baby boom to other periods. The model stresses past events as an influence on current fertility. The facts do not allow this single model to account for all the American fertility patterns that attract interest. Ad hoc explanations featuring unique influences must still be employed. Yet the tests that follow show that the model fits some past patterns that seemed to resist a unified explanation. The model also predicts that any future economic instability will yield unstable birth rates around low average levels.

INCOME, COSTS, AND TASTES

Since the Civil War or earlier, American fertility has been regulated in the sense that the natural limits to fecundity have played little role in determining the birth rate. A unifying model of fertility must therefore be a model of choice by couples or by married individuals. Economists have traditionally classified the determinants of household or individual choices into three categories: income, prices, and tastes. Applying this taxonomy to fertility decision-making requires considerable care. Couples (or married individuals) do not choose numbers and kinds of children. They must choose instead fertility regulation strategies over periods of time shorter than the whole of their fecund years. Given the children they may already have or have lost, and other information, they choose one gamble or another. This point means that the definition of the relevant price and taste variables must include the prices of, and tastes for, the mode of fertility regulation itself as well as for the childbearing and child-rearing outcomes.

Of the three traditional choice variables, the *income* variable is the one most easily reworked for analyzing fertility decisions. All that is required is a careful treatment of the fact that fertility outcomes themselves affect family income.[1] With this precaution, income remains a familiar fertility influence that should be positive if other things are indeed held equal.

The economic cost of a child obviously far outweighs the economic cost of even the most expensive kind of birth control. Yet the familiar concept of child cost requires some reworking if it is to fit the relative price, or relative cost, concept usually employed in theories of household choice. It seems plausible that changes in the *relative cost* of a child should affect fertility—but *what kind* of child, and cost *relative to what*? Any variation in the real inputs of time and commodities into a child is not a change in price or cost, but a change in the type of child, analogous to a change in the quality of housing a family purchases. The relative cost concept must refer to the relative cost of a fixed bundle of child inputs. To measure the *relative* cost of the fixed child inputs, the absolute index of their cost must be compared with an index of the cost of the time and commodities the family would have put to other uses without the extra child.

Hypothetical as the comparison of these two bundles of time and commodity inputs into life activities may seem, the contents of the two bundles can actually be revealed, roughly, from cross-sectional studies of households' use of time and consumption expenditures. Finding out what inputs go into a child of given birth position and parental characteristics requires detailed regression estimates plus a few key but plausible assumptions. Finding out what amounts of time and various commodities couples would have applied to other activities without an extra child next requires data on how families' total home time and consumption are changed by an extra child. By combining this information about the net effects of a child on family members' home time and total family purchases with the previous estimates of what the extra child actually received, yields estimates of the time and commodity inputs that would have been devoted to other things (extra vacations, new furniture, a career for the wife, and so on) without the extra child. The task of measuring such bundles of inputs in detail is tedious and complicated, as has been performed elsewhere (Lindert, forthcoming, chap. 4, Appendixes A–F). Combining such measures with price

---

[1] See Lindert, forthcoming, for a fuller fitting of the appropriate income, or lifetime wealth, concept to a household-choice model.

and wage series, one gets an index of the relative cost of a first, or of a third, child in low-income urban families, covering the last half-century. This index will be applied in explaining American fertility swings later in this chapter.

For most investigations of fertility patterns, however, it is not necessary to enter into involved calculations of the detailed costs of children and the apparent alternatives to them. All that is usually required is a listing of the time and commodity categories on which a child tends to make a family spend more, or less, of its resources. It appears that all one needs to know to identify what makes the relative cost of a child change is how an extra child affects the family's total consumption of food, luxuries, land and time, and its payment of taxes. An extra child invariably raises family food consumption and reduces spending on luxuries. Urban location or any other force raising the price of food relative to that of luxuries would thus tend to raise the relative cost of a child somewhat. The relative cost of a child also will drop whenever the tax system gives new subsidies to child-rearing; this happened during World War II, when the income tax exemption for dependents suddenly became relevant for the majority of American families. We further know that farm children caused their families to consume more land directly, both by giving the family the extra hands for working more land and by raising the total amount of owned land their parents would want to leave as a bequest. The cost of acquiring land is thus another variable relevant to the relative cost of children in an agricultural setting.

The relationship of family time to the relative cost of children is somewhat more subtle and has been changing over time. An extra child is time-intensive if he makes his parents and older siblings shift a greater economic value of time away from paid work to home activities than the child contributes to the household while a member of it. The extra child is time-supplying if he supplies more time in chores and paid work than he forces others to withdraw from paid work. The relative cost of a time-intensive child would be raised, and that of a time-supplying child would be lowered, by a rise in real wage rates (the cost of time relative to commodities).

The effect of the rise in real wage rates on relative child costs has differed across sectors and over time. It appears that an extra farm child was time-supplying in the nineteenth century, but is now neither time-supplying nor time-intensive. Two long-run developments seem to have caused this change in the relationship of a farm child to the family's supply of home time and time spent in commodity production. The first is the progressive settlement of the land, with unimproved acreage taking a smaller and smaller share of farmland. Much of the farmer's time was occupied with land clearing and preparation, and any child above 6 could contribute valuable labor time in practically any season. It was also relatively easy for a frontier child to leave early and form a new household, thus keeping labor scarce on his parents' farm. The economic value of child labor relative to the average value of farmland must have declined considerably as an area became settled. Second, the secular rise in rural school attendance made children contribute less labor to the family.

These two factors, land settlement and education, meant that by the mid-twentieth century farm children had an effect on the family's labor supply very different from their impact in earlier centuries. Across the nineteenth century, when farm children were still labor-supplying, the secular rise in wages therefore tended to *decrease* the relative cost of a particular way of raising a farm child. By the middle of the twentieth century, the labor supplied by a farm child had dwindled to something like the reduction in the mother's farm work and paid work caused by the child, so that movements in farm wage rates no longer had any strong effect on the relative cost of a farm child.[2]

Outside of agriculture the labor-supply implications of an extra child also have been changing over time. In the late nineteenth century child labor was still widespread enough, especially wherever textiles were produced, to make children labor-supplying on balance. That is, an extra child could have been counted on to work for pay while living with his parents more than he reduced the mother's paid work outside of the home when he was an infant. Thus the upward drift in wage rates in the late nineteenth century tended to reduce the relative cost of raising a nonfarm child (though probably not as strongly as it reduced the relative cost of a farm child). By the middle of the twentieth century nonfarm children had become relatively time-intensive. Each child contributed less time in chores and paid work than he took away from the average mother's earnings outside the home. Thus from sometime between World War I and World War II on, the rise in real wage rates raised the relative cost of a nonfarm child.

Throughout the modern period, it appears, migration from the farm

---

[2] Connections between farm land settlement and the relative cost of children have been noted in somewhat different ways by other authors. See Easterlin (1971, especially p. 401), Yasuba (1961, chap. 5), Forster and Tucker (1972, chap. 2), Leet (1975), and the chapter by R. M. McInnis, this volume.

to the nonfarm sector would have raised the relative cost of a child, both by raising its net time demands and by raising the price of food relative to luxuries. This means that the share of the labor force employed in agriculture, besides being an influence on tastes, is an influence on the relative cost of children. It is also a steadier influence than is the wage rate, which, as just noted, tended to lower the relative cost of a child in some contexts and raise it in others. We shall return to the roles of agriculture's share and wage rates in child costs and fertility when examining American fertility patterns.

The third traditional variable in a theory of choice is likely to be the most important in the case of fertility. As used by the theory of consumer choice, the *tastes* variable is a catchall meaning everything not explained by income and relative prices. To get valuable insights into the determinants of fertility, one must make some committal hypothesis about the forces that lie behind tastes. It is impossible to fit all the influences on tastes into any simple unified pattern. There is, however, one variable that seems to exert a consistent pressure on tastes regarding birth control and childbearing. That variable is the set of *prior inputs* into members of the families in which each generation of young adults grew up. Without ever consciously reflecting on the economic magnitude of the time, energy, and commodities received by each family member when he or she was growing up, a young adult has inculcated these inputs into family members as standards for emulation. Young couples tend to set standards for their own enjoyments that are related to the activities pursued by their own parents. They tend also to feel that each child they have should receive something resembling the inputs they can remember receiving as children. This is not to say that the history of family inputs and activities exactly repeats itself. Each young couple faces different income prospects, different relative prices, and different social pressures from that experienced by their parents, and these other forces will usually prevent exact duplication of family time use and consumption patterns from generation to generation. Yet the inertial force of the prior family inputs, it is hypothesized, remains strong.

Past inputs per family member affect the desire to have or avoid extra children by interacting with the young couple's income constraint and with the prices they face. Though unaware of the total dollar magnitudes involved, young couples and those who advise them develop a sense of how easy or difficult it is for them to afford to raise individual children in a manner influenced by their family history. The initial years of rearing their first child or two sharpen their appreciation for the relationship of their means to their standards. Should their income prospects be much brighter than those their parents faced, they will tend to find that an extra child can be raised the way they want without a severe burden on family funds and energies. Should their income prospects not look so bright as those of the households in which they grew up, extra children will seem more burdensome.

A related hypothesis about prior family inputs has already been applied to the postwar baby boom and subsequent baby bust by Easterlin (1968, 1973). When modified and expanded, the same kind of hypothesis also helps explain why fertility should usually have a negative cross-sectional relationship to couples' income and education in modern settings.[3] One of the major socioeconomic shifts of the last two centuries has been a rise in the share of income earned by human skill rather than by property or muscle. This increasing dependence of income on investments in personal development implies a relationship between tastes and income that constrains couples raised with greater inputs to limit family size more severely on the average. There seem to be diminishing economic returns to inputs into the development of individual humans. In part this may stem from a higher luxury consumption component to the extra inputs spent on high-input children, and in part it may stem from natural limits on the amount of economic returns one person can produce from his extra years of preparation. As a result, persons raised in families in which twice as much was spent on each family member of given age than in some other families will tend *not* to enjoy incomes twice as large on the average. Having tastes geared to input standards that are twice as high, yet not having twice as much income, they tend to feel greater pressure to limit family size to keep up inputs per person. This influence is subtle and vague enough that it need imply a negative cross-sectional relationship between status and

---

[3] The argument advanced in this paragraph is not the only way in which the theory being sketched predicts a generally negative cross-sectional relationship between fertility and such variables as income, education, and occupational status. It also predicts this negative profile on the grounds that higher-status families will face higher wage rates, making their time relatively costly. This should make any set of inputs into a child look relatively more costly to such higher-status couples in the postwar era, when children, as argued earlier, are time-intensive.

The additional argument that higher-status couples have better access to birth control techniques has merit to the extent that they tend to live in more urban settings. This argument is less helpful than it at first appears, however, since apparent access to birth control knowledge and devices varies across classes largely because some are more motivated to search for these means than are others. To ask why that is true is to return to the task of explaining differences in desired fertility. For a more detailed treatment of these issues, see Lindert, forthcoming, Chap. 3.

fertility only generally, a relationship that can be outweighed by other cross-sectional differences in individual modern settings.[4]

This simple hypothesis about inertia in tastes, plus recognition of the importance of other influences on tastes, income, and the relative cost of children, makes a theory of the desirability of birth outcomes. Combining these elements of a theory of birth outcomes with information about the supply and inherent social acceptability of different methods of birth control yields a testable theory of birth probabilities. The rest of this chapter will test this theory against data from the United States in order to determine the roles of the variables singled out here and of other, more traditional variables in explaining fertility patterns.

THE DATA

Only aggregate data can test the ability of the aforementioned hypotheses to account for the intriguing fertility patterns observed for the United States. In part this is because some of the more challenging tasks of explanation relate to the behavior of aggregate time-series. The use of aggregate data is also dictated by the nature of the prior-family-inputs variable that has been placed at the center of a model of taste formation. To measure these prior family inputs at the level of individual young adults requires, if not direct data on the time and commodities they received, at least data on income per family member in their parents' household over the years since their earlier childhood memories. Interviews cannot generate reliable data on the incomes of the parents of young adult interviewees except for the current period. Little faith can be had in the answers to, say, 1970 interview questions asking "How much did your father earn in 1960?" Approximations can be had by finding out the father's occupational history and the respondent's schooling, but these are certainly imperfect substitutes.

What is hard even to approximate at the individual level can be tracked somewhat more accurately at the state level for the United States since the Civil War. Since 1870 the decennial census has recorded the state or country of birth of the persons residing in each state. These

---

[4] Note that the failure of those raised on twice as much to have twice as much income is hypothesized for cases in which incomes come from privately acquired skills and not from birthrights. In societies where privileged families can extract income from the rest of society by right of birth, upper-class couples need not feel the same constraint. The hypothesis thus carries the implication that any lower fertility among the upper classes in a caste-ridden society would have to be collectively enforced, through customs directly limiting fertility or through customs designed to raise class consumption standards so high that couples cannot retain good standing with excessive numbers of children.

place-of-birth data give a fair indication of where the young adults in each state were raised, even though the data are not broken down by age groups. If we know the levels of real income per capita in the various places of birth, these can be combined with the shares coming from each place of birth to produce a rough measure of the earlier income per capita enjoyed by the current generation of young adults as they grew up. The prior-family-inputs variable introduced in the foregoing hypotheses can then be represented by such measures of past income per capita in places of birth, plus current levels of income per person at work, which represent not only income prospects but also the more recent influences on the material standards felt by young couples.

Estimates of state personal incomes per capita are available for the United States for 1840, 1880, 1900, 1919–1921, and annually from 1929.[5] For the fraction of each state's population born abroad, the background income per capita has been estimated on the basis of economic historians' guesses as to the ratios of foreign countries' gross national product (GNP) per capita to United States GNP per capita. These and the data on places of birth will be put to use in estimating background incomes per capita for dates 20 years before each of several censuses.[6] This procedure yields estimates of a background income, or prior income, variable that represents part of the material standards felt by different

[5] For estimates of state income per capita in 1840, see Easterlin (1960, Table A-1); for 1880, 1900, and 1919–1921, see Easterlin (1957, Table Y-1); for 1929–1955, see Schwartz and Graham (1956, Table 2); and for years since 1955, see various issues of the U.S. Department of Commerce, Office of Business Economics, *Survey of Current Business.*

[6] The choice of 20 years as the lead time for the prior income experience variable is, of course, arbitrary, and other lengths of time between past experience and current fertility could have been chosen. It was felt that the combination of a long lead like 20 years plus the implicit taste component of current income per worker would succeed in encompassing the full range of relevant family income experience. With additional time and research funding, one could derive the background incomes per capita for only 10 years earlier (than each census for which fertility is being observed); for the period from the 1930s on, even annual background incomes could be worked up. These might be employed in a large pooled sample covering the states for census years to determine more finely the relative importance of the most recent, vis-à-vis more distant, past income experience in affecting desired fertility.

Aside from refining the choice of time leads for the income experience variable, it would also be desirable to have measures more specific to the recent income experience of *young adults* than the measures used here. For the present it must be assumed that current personal income per worker for all age groups (adjusted for taxes and the cost of living, but *not* for hours worked) is a fair reflection of both the recent experience and the income prospects of young adults.

cohorts of young couples whose fertility is measured in the censuses of 1900 and 1920–1970.[7]

Using state aggregates has another advantage besides allowing us to trace past income experience through place-of-birth data. State aggregates have been presented consistently in each decennial census, with reasonably comparable definitions of demographic and socioeconomic

---

[7] The procedure for calculating this background income per capita, along with the estimates for each state in each census, is described in Appendix G of *Fertility and Scarcity in America* (Lindert, forthcoming). To clarify the procedure, it might help to repeat the example given there. The background (1920) income per capita for the average adult resident of Minnesota in 1940 was derived as follows:

(1) Place of birth	(2) Share of 1940 Minnesotans born there	(3) 1920 personal income per capita there (in 1960 $)	(4) = (2) × (3)
Other countries	.106	$ 465	$49
New England	.0029	1288	1
Middle Atlantic	.0087	1372	12
East North Central	.0747	1159	87
South Atlantic	.0020	601	1
East South Central	.0021	540	1
West South Central	.0026	771	2
Mountain	.0042	869	4
Pacific	.0026	1350	4
Minnesota and all other	.7942	902 (Minn.)	716
Total	1.0000		876 = Background income per capita

As illustrated here, the procedure uses regional rather than state data to economize on calculations. The income level from the state of residence itself is applied not only to those born within the state but also to those born within its geographic division (the West North Central division, in the case of Minnesota) and to miscellaneous births (U.S. overseas territories, birthplace not reported, and so on).

It was not possible to present estimates for background incomes involving Mountain and Pacific states and the District of Columbia before 1920, owing to inadequate data. For this reason these states could not be used as observations before 1940, and it had to be assumed that persons migrating from them to Eastern states by the time of the 1930 and earlier censuses grew up with resources resembling those recorded for the states of their later residence.

variables for different censuses. With samples of states it is thus possible to investigate historic changes in the importance of each of several fertility influences. Survey data based on observations from individual families, by contrast, are seldom so comparable over long periods of time. Since it is likely that the parameters of fertility behavior change over time, the opportunity to identify these structural changes is an important advantage of the use of census aggregates.

The use of aggregates also has its dangers. In particular, there is the danger of attributing the behavior of one group within a state to another group. This danger is due in part to the necessity of investigating the fertility and marriage patterns of all groups added together. It has not proved possible to develop complete state-by-state data sets on the fertility and other attributes of nonwhites versus whites, or Catholics versus others, or foreign-born residents versus natives, or farm families versus others. Some of the key variables, especially the income estimates, are not broken down by such groupings at the state level. Only the demographic variables have some of these breakdowns for states. In what follows it is necessary to proceed with considerable caution in making any inferences about *whose* fertility and marriages are being explained by movements in state incomes and other all-state variables.[8]

With this warning observed, we can derive considerable insight into fertility patterns from the available data. With some investment in time, it has proved possible to draw up a sample of state data covering seven censuses: 1900 and 1920–1970. For the censuses of 1900, 1920, and 1930 there is a set of data for each of 37 states east of the Rocky Mountains (not including the District of Columbia). For 1940–1970 all 48 contiguous states plus the District of Columbia are represented.

[8] An additional problem that could arise with aggregate data has proved to cause little difficulty in the present inquiry. Whenever testing a model of individual behavior from grouped data, one must worry about the fact that the cells—in this case, the states—are of different size. The differences in their sizes threaten to invalidate the assumption of homoscedasticity on which least-squares regression analysis leans. For a uniform variance among individual behavioral units (households), larger states will tend to have lower variance than smaller states. A means of restoring homoscedasticity to the state residuals is to multiply all variables for a state by the square root of the number of units (here the number of females 15–49) and run a regression on such weighted variables without a constant term. This weighted regression technique produced results very similar to the unweighted regression estimates for the postwar period (the only sample for which both techniques were tried). There being little difference, only one of the weighted regressions has been reported here, on the grounds that the unweighted regressions are easier to interpret.

From this overall data base it proves possible to vary the type of statistical regression in three ways. First, the dependent variable can be either a fertility measure or a measure of shares of young women who are married, since the additional information on shares married was an inexpensive by-product of gathering the data needed for fertility analysis. The fertility measure used is, of necessity, simply the ratio of living children 0–4 to females 15–49 after adjustment for estimated under-renumeration. This child–woman ratio is not as desirable for some purposes as an age-specific fertility rate or a total fertility rate, but these are not available. Nevertheless, child–woman ratios have been shown to be reasonable proxies for fertility rates,[9] especially when, as happens later in this chapter, the age distribution of females is included in the list of independent variables. The main difficulty with the child–woman ratio is that it mixes the direct effects of other variables on fertility, the effects of these same variables on infant mortality, and the effect of infant mortality on fertility. In what follows it must be assumed that the overall influences of other variables on fertility are proportional to their influences on the child–woman ratio.

The second variation in type of test made possible by the available census data is alternation between cross sections of states within a single census and pooled samples of states over several censuses. The use of the pooled samples—one for the three postwar censuses and one for all seven censuses—has the advantage of enlarging the sample to permit sharper significance tests where independent variables are somewhat correlated. The use of pooled samples is often suspected of mis-estimating significance statistics because errors in measurement or specification that are specific to certain time periods or states might give too much show of significance to variables associated with those periods or states. This problem is dealt with here in two ways. One is to use dummy variables specific to regions or to certain census years as competing independent variables in the pooled regressions. Any error specific to these regions or censuses should be absorbed by the dummy variables.

Another way of dealing with possible biases in significance tests for the pooled samples is to employ the third variation in type of regression allowed by the data. Having data for consecutive censuses, it is possible to run regressions in which the variables are decadal rates of change

[9] For a discussion of the conditions under which the child–woman ratio is a reasonable proxy for fertility rates, see Bogue and Palmore (1964), Grabill and Cho (1965), and Tuchfeld et al. (1974).

rather than levels. This redefinition of the variables makes each observation consist of differences between magnitudes observed for a given state and the corresponding magnitudes for the same state 10 years earlier. Any errors that are constant for the same state for consecutive censuses will be netted out, providing another means of checking the robustness of the conclusions reached from straightforward cross-sectional regressions using levels rather than rates of change.

CROSS-SECTIONAL INFLUENCES ON FERTILITY AND MARRIAGE: AN OVERVIEW

Using the data and the types of regressions just described, it is possible to follow over time the changes in the roles of different variables in explaining how fertility and marriage vary across the country. Tables 1–4 present selected regressions relating child–woman ratios, shares of females ever married or single, and their rates of change between censuses to a host of explanatory variables. (See appendix for definitions of variables used in Tables 1–4.) These regression results will be examined in this section to identify structural changes in the determinants of cross-sectional fertility and marriage patterns. The remaining sections will use the same information plus the results of other studies to reinterpret several larger patterns in the course of American fertility.

The most consistent influence on fertility differences among states over this century appears to have been the *prior income experience* of young couples. This conclusion comes from the behavior of the present and past income variables—current income per person in the labor force (YWORKER) and income per capita in places of origin 20 years earlier (YCAPORIG)—and their rates of change between censuses. The level of current income is of inconsistent sign and seldom significant, but the past income variable always affects fertility negatively and usually passes the standard tests of statistical significance. This behavior of the income variables is consistent with the hypothesis about taste formation previously introduced. The failure of current income per person in the labor force to show a consistently positive sign can be interpreted as an indication that current income often represents recent influences on couples' material standards (tastes) as much as it represents their current resources. The more consistently negative influence of past income experience (YCAPORIG) can be interpreted as a confirmation of the importance of income history as a determinant of the material standards that make couples limit family size.

TABLE 1
Child-Woman Ratios: Regressions Using State Data, Various Censuses, 1900-1970 (Dependent Variable is CW)

Regression no.:	(1) postwar[a]		(1a) postwar[a]		(2) postwar[a]		(3) all 7 censuses		(4) all 7 censuses	
Indep. variable	coeff.	std.err.	coeff.	std.err.	coeff.	std.err.	coeff.	std.err.	coeff.	std.err.
Constant term	.870***	(.237)	1.208	(.244)	.419	(.222)	.887***	(.143)	.860***	(.139)
WED1529	.002*	(.001)	--	--	--	--	--	--	.007***	(.0008)
WED3044	-.001	(.001)	--	--	--	--	--	--	-.001	(.0008)
PRIMAGE	-.007	(.079)	.289*	(.138)	-.031	(.064)	.194*	(.082)	.228**	(.076)
SEXWH	--	--	--	--	.184*	(.090)	.358***	(.082)	--	--
SEXNW	--	--	--	--	-.097	(.160)	.013	(.038)	--	--
SEXGAP	--	--	.160*	(.078)	--	--	--	--	--	--
YCAPORIG	-.179***	(.027)	-.151***	(.033)	-.131***	(.026)	-.193***	(.017)	-.159***	(.016)
YWORKER	.074*	(.033)	.009	(.045)	.084**	(.029)	.086***	(.014)	.026	(.014)
RELCOST	--	--	--	--	--	--	--	--	--	--
NONWHITE	.013	(.026)	-.041	(.027)	.022	(.026)	.036	(.032)	.008	(.028)
FORBORN	-.0016	(.0014)	-.0005	(.001)	-.0012	(.0011)	-.0015*	(.0006)	-.0030***	(.0007)
AGRIC	.0003	(.0004)	.0001	(.0005)	-.0000	(.0004)	.0012**	(.0004)	.0015***	(.0004)
SCHDY	--	--	.0045	(.0023)[a]	--	--	--	--	--	--
SCHOOLF	.0117*	(.0045)	--	--	.0116**	(.0038)	--	--	--	--
CATHOLIC	--	--	--	--	.064	(.055)	--	--	--	--
CATH5050	.150*	(.063)	--	--	.138**	(.042)	--	--	--	--
CATH5060	.152**	(.047)	--	--	.065	(.040)	--	--	--	--
CATH5070	.073	(.047)	--	--	--	--	--	--	--	--
PILLETC(1970)	-.015***	(.019)	.007	(.015)	-.086***	(.019)	.063***	(.013)	.079***	(.010)
IKE(1960)	.063***	(.012)	.091***	(.010)	-.065***	(.011)	.144***	(.011)	.129***	(.011)
SOUTH	-.033**	(.011)	-.039***	(.010)	-.028**	(.009)	-.020	(.011)	-.041***	(.010)
NENG	--	--	--	--	--	--	.020	(.011)	.009	(.009)
WNCMN	--	--	--	--	--	--	.012	(.010)	.005	(.009)
CW2	--	--	--	--	.318***	(.057)	--	--	--	--
R²adj. / std.err. of estim.	.877	/ .027	.854	/ .029	.904	/ .024	.712	/ .051	.765	/ .046
no. of observ. / deg. of freedom	135	/ 119	147	/ 135	135	/ 118	307	/ 293	307	/ 293

* p < .05   ** p < .01   *** p < .001

[a] Censuses of 1950, 1960, 1970, excluding Alaska and Hawaii, and excluding the District of Columbia Mountain States, and Pacific States for 1950.

TABLE 1
Continued

Regression no.:	(5)		(6)		(7)		(8)		(9)	
Sample:	1900 census		1900 census		1900 census		1900 census		1900 census	
Indep. variable	coeff.	std.err.	coeff.	std.err.	coeff.	std.err.	coeff.	std.err.	coeff.	std.err.
Constant term	.870***	(.237)	1.208	(.244)	.419	(.222)	.887***	(.143)	.860***	(.139)
WED1529	--	--	-.0068	(.0038)	--	--	-.0072	(.0035)	--	--
WED3044	--	--	.0183*	(.0067)	--	--	.014*	(.006)	--	--
PRIMAGE	--	--	--	--	--	--	.089	(.589)	.993	(.497)
SEXWH	--	--	--	--	--	--	--	--	--	--
SEXNW	--	--	--	--	--	--	--	--	--	--
SEXGAP	.116	(.076)	--	--	--	--	--	--	-.008	(.035)
YCAPORIG	-.111	(.060)	-.091	(.082)	-.186***	(.050)	-.147*	(.068)	-.130*	(.061)
YWORKER	.161*	(.074)	.082	(.083)	--	--	.071	(.077)	--	--
UNIMPROV/LANDCOST[b]	.239**	(.081)	-.082	(.055)	--	--	--	--	--	--
NONWHITE	-.010	(.146)	-.149	(.187)	.116	(.274)	-.258	(.168)	-.354*	(.150)
FORBORN	--	--	--	--	--	--	--	--	--	--
AGRIC	.0034***	(.0006)	.0009	(.0013)	--	--	.0003	(.0009)	.0015*	(.0006)
ILLIT	.0055*	(.0027)	.0087*	(.0038)	--	--	.0089	(.0045)	.0068	(.0043)
SCHOOLF	--	--	-.018	(.163)	--	--	-.182	(.189)	-.098	(.153)
CATHOLIC	--	--	--	--	--	--	--	--	--	--
CATH5050	--	--	--	--	--	--	--	--	--	--
CATH5060	--	--	--	--	--	--	--	--	--	--
CATH5070	--	--	--	--	--	--	--	--	--	--
PILLETC(1970)	--	--	--	--	--	--	--	--	--	--
IKE(1960)	--	--	--	--	--	--	--	--	--	--
SOUTH	--	--	--	--	--	--	--	--	--	--
NENG	--	--	--	--	--	--	--	--	--	--
WNCMN	--	--	--	--	--	--	--	--	--	--
CW2	--	--	--	--	--	--	--	--	--	--
R^2adj. / std.err. of estim.	.881 /	.040	.865 /	.043	.597 /	.074	.732 /	.038	.693 /	.060
no. of observ. / deg. of freedom	37 37 /	29	37 /	27	37 /	34	37 /	27	37 /	29

* $p < .05$　** $p < .01$　*** $p < .001$

[a] AGRIC's coefficient was significant at the 6% level, YCAPROIG's at the 9% level, and ILLIT's at the 11% level.

[b] UNIMPROV for (5), LANDCOST for (6).

Continued

Regression no.:	(10) 1930 census		(11) 1930 census		(12) 1940 census		(13) 1940 census		(14) 1950 census	
Indep. variable	coeff.	std.err.	coeff.	std.err.	coeff.	std.err.	coeff.	std.err.	coeff.	std.err.
Constant term	.873	(.653)	1.168**	(.392)	2.186***	(.410)	1.276	(.427)	1.473***	(.402)
WED1529	.0024	(.0021)	--	--	--	--	.0034	(.0020)	--	--
WED3044	.0002	(.0066)	--	--	--	--	.0011	(.0037)	--	--
PRIMAGE	.157	(.103)	.117	(.100)	.524	(.572)	.832	(.545)	.913	(.491)
SEXWH	--	--	--	--	--	--	--	--	--	--
SEXNW	--	--	--	--	--	--	--	--	--	--
SEXGAP	--	--	.179	(.143)	.407***	(.113)	--	--	.196	(.159)
YCAPORIG	-.113[a]	(.064)	-.133*	(.058)	-.222***	(.059)	-.233***	(.060)	-.195***	(.044)
YWORKER	.002	(.070)	--	--	-.078	(.061)	-.012	(.063)	-.030	(.060)
RELCOST	--	--	--	--	--	--	--	--	--	--
NONWHITE	-.419**	(.141)	-.349*	(.132)	-.138*	(.065)	-.237**	(.068)	-.165*	(.062)
FORBORN	--	--	--	--	--	--	--	--	--	--
AGRIC	.0021[a]	(.0010)	.0018***	(.0005)	-.0005	(.0007)	.0005	(.0007)	.0004	(.0008)
ILLIT	.0081[a]	(0049)	.0078	(.0048)	--	--	--	--	--	--
SCHOOLF	--	--	--	--	.0037	(.0020)	.0006	(.0022)	.0120*	(.0054)
CATHOLIC	-.057	(.126)	-.114	(.105)	.010	(.057)	.141[b]	(.070)	.077	(.062)
CATH5050	--	--	--	--	--	--	--	--	--	--
CATH5060	--	--	--	--	--	--	--	--	--	--
CATH5070	--	--	--	--	--	--	--	--	--	--
FILLETC(1970)	--	--	--	--	--	--	--	--	--	--
IKE(1960)	--	--	--	--	--	--	--	--	--	--
SOUTH	--	--	--	--	--	--	--	--	--	--
NENG	--	--	--	--	--	--	--	--	--	--
WNCMN	--	--	--	--	--	--	--	--	--	--
CW2	--	--	--	--	--	--	--	--	--	--
$R^2_{adj.}$ / std.err. of estim.	.767	/ .034	.773	/ .033	.826	/ .029	.827	/ .209	.734	/ .030
no. of observ. / deg.of freedom	37	/ 27	37	/ 29	49	/ 40	49	/ 39	49	/ 40

$* \ p < .05 \quad ** \ p < .01 \quad *** \ p < .001$

[a] Significant at 7% level.
[b] Significant at 6% level.

TABLE 1
Continued

248

Regression no.:	(15)		(16)		(17)		(18)		(19)	
Sample:	1950 census		1960 census		1960 census		1960 census		1960 census	
Indep. variable	coeff.	std.err.	coeff.	std.err.	coeff.	std.err.	coeff.	std.err.	coeff.	std.err.
Constant term	.124	(.401)	.853	(.833)	.252	(.770)	.033	(.713)	-.001	(.005)
WED1529	-.0038	(.0024)	--	--	-.0018	(.0024)	--	--	-.0001	(.0021)
WED3044	.014***	(.004)	--	--	.0041**	(.0014)	--	--	.0023a	(.0012)
PRIMAGE	1.408***	(.317)	.295	(.210)	1.407	(.380)	.134	(.169)	.869	(.332)
SEXWH	--	--	--	--	--	--	--	--	--	--
SEXNW	--	--	--	--	--	--	--	--	--	--
SEXGAP	--	--	.225	(.208)	--	--	.042	(.172)	--	--
YCAPORIG	-.125***	(.042)	-.143**	(.051)	-.085	(.054)	-.046	(.050)	-.019	(.048)
YWORKER	-.088	(.052)	.043	(.106)	-.209	(.103)	.045	(.083)	-.021	(.083)
RELCOST	--	--	.503	(1.168)	.217	(1.060)	.879	(.949)	.900	(.899)
NONWHITE	-.060	(.056)	-.040	(.058)	-.060	(.054)	.044	(.049)	.037	(.049)
FORBORN	--	--	.0011	(.0027)	.001	(.003)	-.0008	(.0025)	-.0002	(.0025)
AGRIC	.0013*	(.0006)	.0008	(.0009)	.0014	(.0009)	.0014a	(.008)	.0017*	(.0007)
ILLIT	--	--	--	--	--	--	--	--	--	--
SCHOOLF	.011*	(.005)	.014	(.008)	.011	(.008)	.015*	(.006)	.011	(.006)
CATHOLIC	.179**	(.060)	--	--	--	--	--	--	--	--
CATH5050	--	--	--	--	--	--	--	--	--	--
CATH5060	--	--	--	--	--	--	.188**	(.062)	.189**	(.064)
CATH5070	--	--	--	--	--	--	--	--	--	--
PILLETC(1970)	--	--	--	--	--	--	--	--	--	--
IKE(1960)	--	--	--	--	--	--	--	--	--	--
SOUTH	--	--	--	--	--	--	--	--	--	--
NENG	--	--	--	--	--	--	--	--	--	--
WNCMN	--	--	--	--	--	--	--	--	--	--
CW2	--	--	--	--	--	--	.484***	(.125)	.399**	(.119)
R^2/std.err. adj./of estim.	.817 /	.025	.446 /	.036	.554 /	.028	.672 /	.028	.714 /	.026
no. of/deg.of obser./freedom	49 / 39		49 / 39		49 / 38		49 / 37		49 / 36	

* $p < .05$ ** $p < .01$ *** $p .001$

[a] significant at the 7% level.

[b] significant at 6% level.

Continued

Regression no.:	(20)		(21)		(22)	
Sample:	1970 census		1970 census		1970 census	
Indep. variable	coeff.	std.err.	coeff.	std.err.	coeff.	std.err.
Constant term	.182	(.514)	.738	(.744)	.232	(.006)
WED1529	--	--	-.0028	(.0023)	-.0001	(.0020)
WED3044	--	--	.0081	(.0049)	.0029	(.0043)
PRIMAGE	.344	(.254)	.238	(.325)	.237	(.267)
SEXWH	--	--	--	--	--	--
SEXNW	--	--	--	--	--	--
SEXGAP	-.182^b	(.091)	--	--	--	--
YCAPORIG	-.030	(.048)	-.120*	(.052)	-.075	(.047)
YWORKER	.006	(.055)	-.028	(.072)	.012	(.058)
RELCOST	.079	(.573)	.275	(.730)	.511	(.620)
NONWHITE	-.012	(.038)	.025	(.055)	.052	(.049)
FORBORN	.0008	(.0017)	.0008	(.0023)	.0008	(.0018)
AGRIC	.00005	(.00006)	.0003	(.0007)	-.001	(.0006)
ILLIT	--	--	--	--	--	--
SCHOOLF	.0003	(.0080)	.003	(.011)	.0029	(.0089)
CATHOLIC	--	--	--	--	--	--
CATH5050	--	--	--	--	--	--
CATH5060	--	--	--	--	--	--
CATH5070	.088*	(.035)	--	--	.121*	(.047)
PILLETC(1970)	--	--	--	--	--	--
IKE(1960)	--	--	--	--	--	--
SOUTH	--	--	--	--	--	--
NENG	--	--	--	--	--	--
WNCMN	--	--	--	--	--	--
CW2	.411***	(.080)	--	--	.330**	(.097)
R^2 adj. / std.err. ofestim.	.569 /	.018	.260 /	.023	.523 /	.019
no. of /deg. of obser. / freedom	49 / 37		49 / 38		49 / 36	

* $p < .05$ ** $p < .01$ *** $p < .001$
[a] significant at 7% level.
[b] significant at 6% level.

TABLE 2
Shares of Women Who Are Ever-Married or Single: Regressions Using State Data, Various Censuses, 1900-1980

Regression no.:	(23) postwar[a] WED1529		(24) postwar[a] LNSPINST		(25) all 7 censuses WED1529		(26) all 7 censuses LNSPINST		(27) 1900 census WED1529	
Sample: Dep. variable:										
Indep. variable	coeff.	std.err.	coeff.	std.err.	coeff.	std.err.	coeff.	std.err.	coeff.	std.err.
Constant term	79.72**	(24.29)	-4.33	(2.87)	6.40	(10.81)	-0.60	(0.83)	21.99	(21.09)
PRIMAGE	--	--	--	--	--	--	--	--	--	--
SEXWH	29.83***	(10.20)	-1.09	(1.21)	38.75***	(6.38)	-2.58***	(0.49)	--	--
SEXNW	--	--	--	--	--	--	--	--	--	--
SEXGAP	--	--	--	--	--	--	--	--	15.51*	(4.79)
YCAPORIG	-7.39**	(2.81)	0.53	(0.33)	-4.70***	(1.35)	0.15	(0.10)	3.45	(3.47)
YWORKER	3.14	(3.51)	-0.18	(0.42)	9.90***	(1.08)	-0.34***	(0.08)	--	--
UNIMPROV	--	--	--	--	--	--	--	--	16.83**	(5.60)
NONWHITE	-12.75***	(2.60)	1.22***	(0.31)	1.20	(2.48)	0.53**	(0.19)	13.20	(10.44)
FORBORN	-0.53***	(0.13)	0.02	(0.02)	-0.70***	(0.05)	0.022***	(0.004)	-0.36***	(0.09)
AGRIC	-0.11*	(0.05)	0.00	(0.01)	-0.00	(0.32)	-0.003	(0.002)	0.14***	(0.04)
ILLIT	--	--	--	--	--	--	--	--	-0.12	(0.19)
SCHOOLF	1.00*	(0.47)	-0.07	(0.06)	--	--	--	--	--	--
CATHOLIC	--	--	--	--	--	--	--	--	-0.53	(10.49)
CATH5050	-22.21**	(6.60)	1.58*	(0.78)	--	--	--	--	--	--
CATH5060	-6.16	(5.13)	1.30*	(0.61)	--	--	--	--	--	--
CATH5070	-15.20**	(4.93)	1.43*	(0.58)	--	--	--	--	--	--
PILLETC(1970)	-3.74	(1.91)	-0.42	(0.22)	-2.15*	(1.01)	-0.45***	(0.08)	--	--
IKE(1960)	-1.40	(1.27)	-0.25	(0.15)	2.53**	(0.80)	-0.39***	(0.06)	--	--
SOUTH	2.15	(1.12)	0.01	(0.13)	3.84***	(0.90)	-0.23***	(0.06)	--	--
NENG	--	--	--	--	0.87	(0.84)	0.09	(0.07)	--	--
WNCMN	--	--	--	--	1.11	(0.78)	-0.12*	(0.06)	--	--
R^2 / std.err. adj. / of estim.	.692 /	2.893	.407 /	0.342	.756 /	3.978	.607 /	.304	.886 /	2.40
no. of / deg. of obser. / freedom	135 / 121		135 / 121		307 / 295		307 / 295		37 / 28	

* p < .05   ** p < .01   *** p < .001

a Censuses of 1950, 1960, 1970, and excluding the District of Columbia and Mountain and Pacific states for 1950.

TABLE 2
Continued

Regression no.:	(28)		(29)		(30)		(31)		(32)	
Sample	1900 census		1920 census		1920 census		1930 census		1930 census	
Dep. variable	LNSPINST		WED1529		LNSPINST		WED1529		LNSPINST	
Indep. variable	coeff.	std.err.	coeff.	std.err.	coeff.	std.err.	coeff.	std.err.	coeff.	std.err.
Constant term	0.95	(1.28)	48.35	(39.93)	-0.10	(2.56)	173.13**	(51.07)	-8.02**	(2.76)
PRIMAGE	--	--	--	--	--	--	--	--	--	--
SEXWH	--	--	--	--	--	--	--	--	--	--
SEXNW	--	--	--	--	--	--	--	--	--	--
SEXGAP	-0.68*	(0.29)	4.86	(2.74)	-0.29	(0.18)	28.48*	(13.33)	-1.95*	(0.72)
YCAPORIG	-0.46*	(0.21)	0.83	(5.61)	0.20	(0.36)	6.66	(5.96)	-0.29	(0.32)
YWORKER	--	--	0.08	(6.05)	-0.40	(0.39)	-19.87**	(6.10)	0.86*	(0.33)
UNIMPROV	-1.51***	(0.34)	--	--	--	--	--	--	--	--
NONWHITE	-1.40*	(0.64)	5.46	(13.88)	-1.01	(0.89)	14.38	(12.71)	-0.35	(0.69)
FORBORN	0.010	(0.005)	-0.33*	(0.14)	-0.003	(0.009)	-0.54***	(0.15)	0.003	(0.009)
AGRIC	-0.016***	(0.003)	-0.03	(0.05)	-0.010**	(0.033)	-0.34**	(0.09)	0.009a	(0.005)
ILLIT	0.030*	(0.012)	0.23	(0.36)	0.015	(0.023)	-0.25	(0.45)	0.008	(0.024)
SCHOOLF	--	--	--	--	--	--	--	--	--	--
CATHOLIC	0.27	(0.64)	-26.24	(15.82)	1.00	(1.01)	-10.38	(11.61)	1.061	(0.627)
CATH5050	--	--	--	--	--	--	--	--	--	--
CATH5060	--	--	--	--	--	--	--	--	--	--
CATH5070	--	--	--	--	--	--	--	--	--	--
PILLETC(1970)	--	--	--	--	--	--	--	--	--	--
IKE(1960)	--	--	--	--	--	--	--	--	--	--
SOUTH	--	--	--	--	--	--	--	--	--	--
$R^2_{adj.}$ / std.err. of estim.	.883 /	.146	.791 /	3.094	.636 /	.198	.803 /	3.14	.684 /	.170
no. of obser. / deg. of freedom	37 / 28		37 / 28		37 / 28		37 / 28		37 / 28	

* $p < .05$ ** $p < .01$ *** $p < .001$
aSignificant at the 7% level.

251

TABLE 2
Continued

Regression no.:	(33)		(34)		(35)		(36)		(37)	
Sample:	1940 census		1940 census		1950 census		1950 census		1960 census	
Dep. variable	WED1529		LNSPINST		WED1529		LNSPINST		WED1529	
Indep. variable	coeff.	std.err.	coeff.	std.err.	coeff.	std.err.	coeff.	std.err.	coeff.	std.err.
Constant term	131.67**	(40.94)	-5.77*	(2.18)	81.66*	(34.79)	-4.32	(2.84)	--	--
PRIMAGE	--	--	--	--	--	--	--	--	--	--
SEXWH	--	--	--	--	--	--	--	--	--	--
SEXNW	--	--	--	--	--	--	--	--	--	--
SEXGAP	60.75***	(12.52)	-3.43***	(0.67)	24.65*	(11.07)	-1.97*	(0.90)	--	--
YCAPORIG	4.53	(6.72)	-0.11	(0.36)	-14.56***	(3.99)	1.15***	(0.33)	-12.75**	(4.33)
YWORKER	-14.28*	(6.81)	0.54	(0.36)	8.25	(5.39)	-0.64	(0.44)	20.41**	(7.27)
RELCOST	--	--	--	--	--	--	--	--	-45.37	(32.44)
NONWHITE	12.74*	(6.28)	-0.11	(0.33)	-5.09	(4.97)	0.86*	(0.41)	-4.58	(4.22)
FORBORN	-0.56**	(0.18)	0.002	(0.009)	-0.56**	(0.17)	0.011	(0.014)	--	--
AGRIC	-0.20*	(0.09)	0.005	(0.005)	-0.14*	(0.07)	0.011[b]	(0.006)	-0.15*	(0.06)
ILLIT	--	--	--	--	--	--	--	--	--	--
SCHOOLF	0.81**	(0.24)	-0.027*	(0.013)	1.35***	(0.48)	-.12**	(0.04)	0.80	(0.55)
CATHOLIC	-19.12*	(8.46)	1.46**	(0.45)	-13.21[a]	(6.70)	1.15*	(0.55)	-17.71***	(4.71)
CATH5050	--	--	--	--	--	--	--	--	--	--
CATH5060	--	--	--	--	--	--	--	--	--	--
CATH5070	--	--	--	--	--	--	--	--	--	--
PILLETC(1970)	--	--	--	--	--	--	--	--	--	--
IKE(1960)	--	--	--	--	--	--	--	--	--	--
CW2	--	--	--	--	--	--	--	--	17.28	(10.63)
R^2 adj. / std.err. of estim.	.774 /	3.380	.669 /	.180	.786 /	2.70	.656 /	.220	.705 /	2.463
no. of obser. / deg. of freedom	49 /	40	49 /	40	49 /	40	49 /	40	49 /	38

$* \ p < .05$ $** \ p < .01$ $*** \ p < .001$

[a] Significant at the 6% level.
[b] Significant at the 7% level.

TABLE 2
Continued

Regression no.:	(38)		(39)	
Sample:	1960 census		1970 census	
Dep. variable	LNSPINST		WED1529	
Indep. variable	coeff.	std.err.	coeff.	std.err.
Constant term	-5.32	(11.24)	35.61	(71.85)
PRIMAGE	--	--	-30.82	(35.54)
SEXWH	--	--	--	--
SEXNW	--	--	--	--
SEXGAP	-1.28	(2.72)	25.35[a]	(12.79)
YCAPORIG	1.30[a]	(0.65)	1.53	(6.77)
YWORKER	-0.70	(1.44)	2.61	(7.23)
RELCOST	-2.06	(16.24)	-99.41	(79.93)
NONWHITE	1.01	(0.83)	-13.03*	(5.42)
FORBORN	--	--	--	--
AGRIC	0.01	(0.01)	-0.14	(0.08)
ILLIT	--	--	--	--
SCHOOLF	-0.10	(0.11)	-0.68	(1.09)
CATHOLIC	--	--	--	--
CATH5050	--	--	--	--
CATH5060	1.12	(0.94)	--	--
CATH5070	--	--	-26.70	(4.48)
PILLETC(1970)	--	--	--	--
IKE(1960)	--	--	--	--
CW2	--	--	28.63	(10.85)
$R^2_{adj.}$ / std.err. of estim.	.103 /	.491	.699 /	2.49
no. of obser. / deg.of freedom	49 / 40		49 / 38	

* $p < .05$ ** $p < .01$ *** $p < .001$

[a] Significant at 6% level.

TABLE 3

Decadal Changes in Child-Woman Ratios: Regressions Using State Data, Various Censuses, 1930ᵃ–1970 (Dependent Variable is DCW)

Regression no.: Sample: Indep. variable	(40) postwar # coeff.	std.err.	(41) postwar # coeff.	std.err.	(42) 1940 census coeff.	std.err.	(43) 1950 census coeff.	std.err.	(44) 1950 census coeff.	std.err.
Constant term	.059***	(.009)	.001***	(.001)	-.005	(.010)	.049**	(.015)	.095***	(.019)
DWED1529	--	--	.001	(.001)	.005**	(.002)	.008***	(.001)	--	--
DPRIMAGE	-.010	(.042)	.056	(.053)	.025	(.078)	.495*	(.209)	.878*	(.354)
DSEXWH	.257**	(.084)	--	--	--	--	--	--	.034ᵇ	(.142)ᵇ
DSEXNW	.060	(.129)	--	--	--	--	--	--	--	--
DYCAPORI	-.065***	(.018)	-.063***	(.018)	-.086**	(.026)	.022	(.031)	.010	(.042)
DYWORK	.015	(.019)	.021	(.018)	.096	(.059)	-.034	(.020)	.007	(.029)
DRELCOST	-.333**	(.114)	-.243	(.147)	--	--	--	--	--	--
DNONWHIT	.195*	(.083)	.197*	(.086)	-.182	(.653)	.007	(.151)	.198	(.207)
DFORBORN	-.004	(.003)	--	--	--	--	--	--	--	--
DAGRIC	.002	(.001)	--	--	.008***	(.002)	-.0024	(.0014)	-.002	(.002)
DSCHOOLF	.023***	(.004)	--	--	--	--	.0015*	(.0006)	.001	(.001)
CATHOLIC	--	--	--	--	-.056	(.45)	--	--	--	--
CATH5050	.062	(.050)	.153**	(.049)	--	--	.001	(.034)	.077	(.042)
CATH5060	-.001	(.042)	.082*	(.041)	--	--	--	--	--	--
CATH5070	-.085*	(.038)	-.038	(.041)	--	--	--	--	--	--
PILLETC(1970)	-.174***	(.011)	-.164***	(.011)	--	--	--	--	--	--
R²adj. / std.err. of estim.	.965 /	.022	.952 /	.026	.538 /	.028	.647 /	.016	.356 /	.022
no. of obser. / deg.of freedom	135 /	120	135 /	124	49 /	41	49 /	40	49 /	40

* p < .05   ** p < .01   *** p < .001

Census of 1950, 1960, 1970, excluding Alaska and Hawaii, and excluding the District of Columbia and Mountain and Pacific states for 1950.

a For the 1930 census, all models with DCW as the dependent variable failed to yield any predictive power (i.e., R²adj. was negative).

b Independent variable is DSEXGAP.

TABLE 3
Continued

| Regression no.: | (45) | | (46) | | (47) | | (48) | | (49) | |
| Sample: | 1960 census | | 1960 census | | 1970 census | | 1970 census | | 1970 census | |
Indep. variable	coeff.	std.err.	coeff.	std.err.	coeff.	std.err.	coeff.	std.err.	coeff.	std.err.
Constant term	.074***	(.014)	.070***	(.014)	-.131***	(.017)	-.141***	(.014)	-.127***	(.017)
DWED1529	--	--	.003*	(.001)	--	--	.0056***	(.014)	--	--
DPRIMAGE	.223	(.127)	.448*	(.184)	.206[a]	(.110)	.794***	(.170)	.247*	(.119)
DSEXWH	--	--	--	--	--	--	--	--	--	--
DSEXGAP	.243*	(.114)	--	--	.259	(.149)	--	--	--	--
DYCAPORI	-.053	(.035)	-.030	(.037)	-.097**	(.030)	-.023	(.030)	-.121***	(.023)
DYWORK	-.003	(.053)	.008	(.053)	.172**	(.049)	.141	(.043)	.185***	(.045)
DRELCOST	--	--	--	--	--	--	--	--	--	--
DNONWHIT	.269*	(.127)	.272*	(.127)	.035	(.128)	.091	(.113)	.009	(.130)
DFORBORN	--	--	--	--	--	--	--	--	--	--
DAGRIC	.0029	(.0015)	.0022	(.0015)	.0020	(.0019)	.0049**	(.0015)	--	--
DSCHOOLF	.021**	(.007)	.014	(.008)	.0108	(.0065)	.0076	(.0058)	--	--
CATHOLIC	--	--	--	--	--	--	--	--	--	--
CATH5050	--	--	--b	--	--	--	--	--	--	--
CATH5060	--b	--	--	--	--	--	--	--	--	--
CATH5070	--	--	--	--	-.059	(.036)	-.023	(.032)	-.044	(.039)
PILLETC(1970)	--	--	--	--	--	--	--	--	--	--
$R^2_{adj.}$ / std.err. of estim.	.475	/ .023	.472	/ .023	.612	/ .021	.703	/ .019	.523	/ .025
no. of obser. / deg.of freedom	49 / 41		49 / 41		49 / 40		49 / 40		49 / 43	

*p < .05   **p < .01   ***p < .001

[a]significant at the 7% level.

[b]A regression identical to this one except for the inclusion of CATH5060 yielded a lower $R^2_{adj.}$ and an insignificantly positive value for CATH5060.

255

TABLE 3
Continued

| Regression no.: | (50) | | (51) | |
| Sample: | 1970 census | | weighted postwar[a] | |
Indep. variable	coeff.	std.err.	coeff.	std.err.
Constant term	-.124***	(.016)	--	--
DWED1529	.0047**	(.0016)	--	--
DFR1MAGE	.703***	(.186)	.389***	(.095)
DSEXWH	--	--	.118	(.066)
DSEXNW	--	--	.094	(.170)
DYCAPORI	-.090***	(.023)	-.061***	(.017)
DYWORK	.134**	(.045)	.025	(.018)
DRELCOST	--	--	-.311**	(.110)
DNONWHIT	.126	(.126)	.099	(.096)
DFORBORN	--	--	-.0045*	(.0020)
DAGRIC	--	--	.0012	(.0008)
DSCHOOLF	--	--	.0018[b]	(.0009)
SCHOOLF50,60	--	--	.0080***	(.0007)
SCHOOLF70	--	--	-.0223***	(.0058)
CATH5050	--	--	.039	(.041)
CATH5060	--	--	.036	(.040)
CATH5070	-.024	(.037)	.0005	(.0356)
PILLETC(1970	--	--	.151*	(.073)
$R^2_{adj.}$ / std.err. of estim.	.591 /	.022	.978[a] /	17.17[a]
no. of / deg.of obser. / freedom	49 / 41		147 / 131	

* $p < .05$ ** $p < .01$ *** $p < .001$

[a]The state coverage of the weighted postwar sample is the same as for the unweighted postwar sample above. For the weighted sample, each variable, including the dependent variable, was multiplied by the square root of the number of females 15-49. This procedure assures that if the underlying individual observations are homoskedastic, the state aggregates used will also be homoskedastic, provided also that the constant term is omitted from the regression. The omission of a constant term, however, means that the R^2 statistic does not have its usual meaning.

TABLE 4
Decadal Changes in Shares of Women Ever-Married or Single: Regressions Using State Data, Various Censuses, 1930-1970

Regression no.:	(52)		(53)		(54)		(55)	
Sample:	postwar[a]		1950 census		1960 census		1970 census	
Dep. variable	DWED1529		DWED1529		DWED1529		DWED1529	
Indep. variable	coeff.	std.err.	coeff.	std.err.	coeff.	std.err.	coeff.	std.err.
Constant term	0.32	(1.26)	5.14	(1.35)	-3.52**	(1.24)	0.38	(1.54)
DPRIMAGE	--	--	--	--	-83.71***	(8.80)	-103.68***	(9.72)
DSEXWH	31.25**	(11.34)	--	--	--	--	--	--
DSEXNW	28.92	(21.68)	--	--	--	--	--	--
DSEXGAP	--	--	23.68**	(7.58)	50.15***	(7.95)	27.19[c]	(13.55)
DYCAPORI	-1.13	(2.41)	0.77	(3.09)	-6.81**	(2.45)	-11.32***	(2.75)
DYWORK	0.69	(2.57)	3.46	(1.81)	-3.17	(3.63)	7.14	(4.41)
DRELCOST	-75.87***	(15.42)	--	--	--	--	--	--
DNONWHIT	-5.61	(11.35)	21.82	(13.97)	9.54	(8.92)	-14.81	(11.51)
DFORBORN	-0.96**	(0.34)	-1.02***	(0.23)	-1.09***	(0.24)	-0.96*	(0.44)
DAGRIC	-0.00	(0.12)	-0.06	(0.13)	-0.12	(0.12)	-0.36*	(0.17)
DILIT	--	--	--	--	--	--	--	--
DSCHOOLF	1.07	(0.56)	0.35**	(0.10)	2.51***	(0.50)	0.89	(0.59)
CATHOLIC	--	--	--	--	--	--	--	--
CATH5050	0.20	(6.88)	1.64	(3.54)	--	--	--	--
CATH5060	9.90	(5.64)	--	--	--[b]	--	--	--
CATH5070	-11.19*	(5.10)	--	--	--	--	-11.60**	(3.99)
PILLETC(1970)	-2.48	(1.39)	--	--	--	--	--	--
$R^2_{adj.}$/std.err. of estim.	.786 /	3.00	.542 /	1.61	.849 /	1.56	.731 /	1.88
no. of/deg. of obser./freedom	135 /	121	49 /	40	49 /	40	49 /	39

* $p < .05$ ** $p < .01$ *** $p < .001$

[a]Censuses of 1950, 1960, and 1970, excluding Alaska and Hawaii, and excluding the District of Columbia and Mountain and Pacific states for 1950.

[b]A regression identical to this one except for the inclusion of CATH5060 yielded a lower $R^2_{adj.}$ and an insignificantly negative value for CATH5060.

[c]Significant at the 6% level.

257

This interpretation in favor of the hypothesis of taste formation through income and family input experience is consistent with the fact that the past income experience variable is statistically significant in some censuses and not in others. The YCAPORIG variable is significant in the censuses of 1920–1950 and in the larger pooled samples, but not in the fertility cross-sections of 1900, 1960, and 1970 (see Regressions 5, 6, 18–20, 22). (Hereafter references to the regressions in Tables 1–4 will be abbreviated: "R.3" for "see Regression 3," and so on.) The failure of significance in these cases can be explained in a way that fits the view that past income experience is an important influence on controlled fertility in all settings. It so happened that in 1900 current income was almost perfectly correlated with the past income variable across states, and in 1960 and 1970 neither the past income variable nor current income varied nearly as greatly across states as these had varied earlier in this century. Therefore in 1900 multicollinearity prevented confirmation of the statistical significance of past income experience, and the lack of significance for 1960 and 1970 regressions stemmed from the fact that past and current incomes did not happen to vary enough to show their influence in these single-census, cross-sections. For the censuses of 1920–1950, by contrast, the American economy had been subjected to enough shocks to cause past incomes to vary considerably across states in ways not mirrored by current incomes, thus yielding a better test of the potential importance of prior income experience.

An alternative interpretation of the consistent influence of past income experience on fertility might be advanced. The performance of the YCAPORIG variable might have reflected nothing more than the influence of past fertility on current fertility. This suspicion is fostered by the fact that YCAPORIG is a measure of prior incomes per capita and not per worker or per adult, and is thus negatively correlated with past fertility. It might be that its apparent explanatory power is in no way related to the hypothesis previously advanced. Perhaps its negative signs only pick up the simple point that whatever affects past fertility for a state affects current fertility similarly. This possibility was tested in several regressions (R.2, 18–20, 22, and others not reported) which included the value of the state's child–woman ratio 20 years earlier as an additional explanatory variable. Not surprisingly, this variable is highly significant, representing as it does all the state-specific forces not captured in other variables. Yet when it is used in a postwar sample large enough to sort out the significance of highly correlated variables (R.2), the coefficient for past income experience still turns out to be highly significant and not much reduced in magnitude. Apparently the hypothesis about past income experience as a consistent determinant of couples' tastes toward childbearing is sustained.[10]

The other variable introduced by the hypothesis is the *relative cost* of a child. Its impact also shows up in the results, though its significance, like the manner in which it is measured, varies for different census samples. The direct measures of the rate of change in relative child costs (outside of agriculture) for the postwar era display a negative influence on both fertility and nuptiality, as theory had suggested (R.40–41, 51, 52). Within single censuses, the relative cost variable, which is a variation on the wage rate, is not statistically significant (and of the "wrong" sign) because of its high correlation with the current and past income variables used in the same regressions (R.16–22, 37–39). Across the postwar era, the rate of change in relative child cost is a clearly significant influence on the rate of change in fertility. Its significance stems essentially from the fact that the high fertility of the late 1940s accompanied a drop in relative child cost caused by the new relevance of the income tax exemption per child, while in later years no such drop occurred. I shall return to this point in reexamining the postwar fertility wave.

The relative cost of a child must be measured differently for the era before World War I. In that less urbanized and industrialized setting the two main forces making children look more expensive relative to the things with which they competed were the migration out of agriculture and, within agriculture, the scarcity of land. The prewar influence of these two forces on relative child cost is incorporated into (but not necessarily equal to) the 1900 regression coefficients for the share of the male work force employed in agriculture (AGRIC) and two proxies for the relative availability of farm land (UNIMPROV and LANDCOST). These variables explain much of the variation of fertility and marriage among states in the 1900 census (R.5, 6, 27, 28), with one of the proxies for land availability (UNIMPROV) performing better than the other (LANDCOST). The clear tendency of the availability of unimproved land in West North Central and West South Central states to encourage marriage and fertility seems to confirm the argument of several authors that land availability is an important fertility determinant within largely agricultural societies. The interpretation taken here is that the

---

[10] The issue of how the interplay of past and current incomes relates to nuptiality has been investigated by the regressions in Tables 2 and 4. The regressions from the large pooled samples and the single-census regressions from the postwar era show that marriage is encouraged by higher current incomes relative to past income experience, as one would have guessed. But this relationship does not hold for most earlier censuses.

importance of land availability, like that of the share of the population in agriculture, reflects a response of fertility and marriage to differences in relative child costs.[11]

In contrast to the relatively steady influence of present and past income on fertility and marriage, the impact of *agriculture and urbanization* has shown some striking changes over this century. Both of these forces must be represented by the single variable AGRIC in the present regressions, since state data on the shares in cities are too highly correlated with the shares outside of agriculture for analysis of their separate roles. The cross-sectional impact of the agricultural variable on marriages has swung from positive to negative and back to insignificance between 1900 and 1970. In the 1900 census, females tended to marry considerably earlier in more agricultural states, other things equal (R.27, 28). In the 1920 census, the share of women 30–44 who were ever married was again significantly higher in more agricultural settings, other things equal (R.30), but this was no longer true for the younger (15–29) age group, suggesting that some sort of influence on the timing of marriage had tipped in favor of urban as opposed to farm marriage around World War I (R.29). By the time of the 1930 census, marriage seemed to be strongly discouraged by agricultural settings especially for the younger age group (R.31, 32). The same was true for the next three decades, though the antinuptial impact of agriculture (or the positive impact of urbanization?) was smaller for 1940–1960 than for the 1930 census. By 1970 the distribution of a state's population between agriculture and other sectors no longer seemed relevant to the share of females married (R.39).

---

[11] This conclusion is supported by the fact that AGRIC and UNIMPROV showed considerable explanatory power in regressions that included other independent variables for which they might have served as misleading proxies. The relevance of available land (UNIMPROV) is not to be explained away as merely reflecting the fact that the newer farm areas to the west had higher ratios of males to females and a predominance of females in the prime childbearing age range (20–34). The importance of available unimproved land held up in a regression also including the net excess of males over females (SEXGAP vs. UNIMPROV in R.5), and there was in fact no correlation between the availability of new farm land and the share of females 15–49 in the prime 20–34 age group in 1900.

Nor is the share in agriculture or the availability of farmland an implicit proxy for the interplay between present and past incomes, since these variables were also given their due in the same regressions showing the importance of AGRIC and UNIMPROV for 1900. The suspicion that settlement on the frontier is another proxy for a jump in income prospects relative to past income experience is also countered by the fact that frontier states in 1900 failed to show any extraordinarily high ratio of current to past (place of birth) incomes in 1900. Hence the importance of AGRIC and UNIMPROV must bespeak either the relevance of relative child costs or an unidentified influence on tastes.

The agricultural variable has a less pronounced and more erratic impact on fertility when the shares of females married are held constant. A more agricultural state, other things equal, had a level of fertility (for constant married share) that was no different in most cases, but significantly greater in a minority of cases. The cases of positive relationship between agriculture and fertility for constant marriage were the censuses of 1930, 1950, and 1960 (R.10, 15, 19). The overall effect of agriculture on fertility, now combining its effect on marriage with its effect on fertility within and outside of marriage, appears to have declined across this century (R.5, 9, 11, 12, 14, 18, 20), from a strong positive stimulus in 1900 to irrelevance in 1970.

It is not clear why the role of agriculture–urbanization should have shown these movements. The mere fact that the population has migrated away from agriculture, for example, does not explain why the overall fertility impact of a given difference in the share in agriculture should have dropped. The patterns of effects on marriage do fit the swings in the relative economic fortunes of agriculture (downward from 1910 to 1940 and upward thereafter), but the long-run decline in agriculture's *unit* fertility relevance does not. Faced with this pattern and with the convergence in rural–urban differences in child–woman ratios from 1940 to 1960, one could construct an ad hoc hypothesis that across World War II some social force made farm and urban tastes converge, but the issue must remain unresolved here.

Swings may also have occurred in the fertility and nuptiality effects of *Roman Catholicism*. We have state data, such as they are, on membership in the Roman Catholic church for years near each census from 1890 through 1940. At the risk of further distortion, one could also apply the last state-by-state membership figures, those for 1936, to states' 1950 population for an examination of the relevance of Catholicism in the postwar period. This information has been employed in various regressions in Tables 1–4. Taken at face value, the regressions on marriage patterns imply that Catholics between World War I and the 1950s had a greater tendency to postpone or completely avoid marriage than did others (R.29–36), this tendency being statistically significant for the censuses of 1940 and 1950. In the 1960 and 1970 censuses, as in 1900, the shaky measures of Catholic shares of population imply that marriage patterns were not statistically significant between Catholics and non-Catholics.[12]

When the shares married are held constant, the effect of higher

[12] The statement about the absence of religious differences in marriage patterns in 1960 and 1970 is based on the fact that the impact of the Catholicism variable in these censuses seemed to be the same whether or not the shares married were held constant. This

concentrations of Roman Catholics on fertility seems to have swung from negative for 1900–1930 to significantly positive for 1940–1970 (R.6, 8, 10, 13, 15, 19, 22). These estimates, like recent fertility surveys, also suggest a marked dip in the marital fertility differential between Catholics and non-Catholics across the 1960s (R.19, 22, 40, 41, 47–51). When the effects on marriage and the effects on fertility for constant married shares are combined, it appears that the overall fertility effect of Roman Catholicism, other things equal, swung from negative in the 1920s to a statistically significant peak fertility stimulus in the late 1950s (i.e., in the 1960 census) and dropped off again across the 1960s (R.9, 11, 12, 14, 18, 20).

The observed pattern of fertility and nuptiality differentials by religion happen to fit expectations one might have had from swings in Catholic and Protestant policy and attitudes toward birth control. It was in 1930 that Pius XI's encyclical *Casti Connubii* firmly labeled any couples who attempt to frustrate the natural power of the sex act to generate life as "branded with guilt of grave sin." No such new toughness was apparent in official Protestant pronouncements. It is for the 1930s (1940 census) that the regression estimates begin to reveal greater fertility among Catholics than non-Catholics, holding marriage and other variables constant. It is also in the censuses of 1940 and 1950 that Catholicism appears to become a statistically significant factor postponing marriage. Both the fertility and the nuptiality effects associated with a large share of Catholics in the state appear to support the hypothesis that after *Casti Connubii* Catholics increasingly felt constrained not to limit births by effective means within marriage. The reduction in the fertility differential between Catholics and non-Catholics in the 1960s can be linked to a shift in lay Catholic attitudes. Around 1964 many American Catholics, probably encouraged by the publicized ecuminism and reform at the Second Vatican Council and by a series of lay American books defending modern contraception, shifted to the pill and other modern practices. This shift in attitude was not reversed by Pope Paul VI's condemnation of the pill in 1968.[13]

---

contradicts the regressions reporting a significant effect of Catholicism toward postponement of marriage in 1960 and 1970 (R.37, 39). These regressions happen to have no variable for sex ratios or immigration, which are correlated negatively and positively respectively with Catholicism in the state-by-state cross section. These variables may have caused the influence attributed to Catholicism in the regressions. At the same time, the postwar estimates of shares Catholic are particularly shaky, based as they are on state membership in 1936.

[13] For an annual series on the use of the pill and intrauterine devices by interviewed Catholics, see Ryder (1972). On the shift in attitudes, see Noonan (1967, pp. 580–581, 595–597, 602–609).

This view of the shifts in the impact of Catholicism should be treated with caution, however. As noted, the postwar estimates of the state shares of Catholics are not to be leaned on. And there is always the danger that Catholicism may be displaying influences that belong to omitted variables associated with heavily Catholic states.

The effect of *educational attainment* on fertility changed in a manner somewhat resembling the swing in the apparent fertility effect of Catholicism, whereas the effects of schooling and Catholicism on marriage moved quite differently. Education is represented inversely in the censuses up through 1930 by the share of persons over 21 who are illiterate, and directly for 1940 and beyond by the median years of schooling of females 25 and over. In 1900 education seems to have been a factor promoting earlier marriage but lowering fertility (see ILLIT in R.5, 6, 27, 28). Its negative effect on fertility remains essentially unchanged through 1930, though it appears to have no effect on marriage patterns in the censuses of 1920 and 1930 (R.8–11, 29–32). In the 1940 census, schooling shows no influence on the fertility patterns of the late 1930s when marriage is held constant (R.13). Yet it has again become a factor encouraging marriage (R.33, 34), as in 1900, so that its overall effect on fertility is positive and almost statistically significant (R.12).

In the postwar era, the relationship of schooling to fertility and marriage jumps and falls sharply. In the 1950 census schooling achieves its peak positive influence on both fertility and marriage (R.14, 15, 35, 36, 43, 44, 53). Where the census data had shown a reduction in the fertility differentials between low-education and high-education groups, in the baby boom, the regressions now add the observation that the effect of schooling on fertility became strongly positive for the late 1940s, other variables held constant. The same positive effects on marriage and fertility continue through the 1960 census, though their statistical significance and magnitude generally appear to have been lower than in the 1950 census (R.16, 18, 19, 37, 38, 45, 46, 51, 53). With the 1970 census, all such effects on fertility and marriage disappear (R.20, 21, 22, 39, 47, 48, 51, 55). The task of interpreting these swings in the impact of differences in schooling is undertaken in the next section.

The effect of *race* on fertility is left unclear by the regression results. The regressions of Tables 1 through 4 seem in general to argue that having a higher share of nonwhites may lower a state's aggregate fertility ratio, given the aggregate levels of income, schooling, and so forth. This antinatal effect is statistically significant about half the time. It occurs even in the censuses before World War II, despite some possible tendency for nonwhites to marry earlier then than their levels of income, and so on, would have predicted for a white population.

There is no obvious explanation for this tendency toward extra birth restriction, other things equal. The racial variable may well be playing the role of Southern residence (SOUTH), whose significantly negative influence removes any significance from the racial variable whenever both appear in the same regression (R.1–4). Accepting this interpretation, however, leaves the role of Southern residence itself unexplained.

The consistency of the likely impact of race, at any rate, suggests that over a long period the levels of fertility one would predict for nonwhites would generally follow the same trends as for whites. Indeed one of the striking features of nonwhite fertility is that it did follow a trend very much like that of white fertility, declining from 1880 to the 1930s, then rising with the baby boom and falling again since. The similarity in the shape of the trends for different races suggests that their fertility rates may be responding to influences shared by all races. One set of roughly common influences, of course, is the growth path of incomes, education, and life expectancies. Perhaps the history of blacks' relative deprivation changed slowly enough so that forces felt by both blacks and whites governed trends in their fertility rates more visibly than did changes that discriminated against or for blacks. To make this point convincingly for the years before World War II, however, we would need better data on income and other variables by race than are now available.

THE POSTWAR BABY BOOM AND BUST

With these insights into changes in the determinants of fertility differences over time, one can better interpret some of the developments in the history of American population growth that have attracted attention and puzzlement.

The surge and crash of birth rates in the postwar era can be better understood in terms of interactions between past income experience, current incomes, relative child costs, and schooling. An explanation for most of or all the boom and bust swings seems implicit in the cross-sectional patterns already revealed by the regressions that examined one census at a time. But to make this explanation as clear as possible, it is best to look at pooled regressions covering more than one census and ask: "What combination of other explanatory variables would be able to remove any significance from the *Zeitgeist* dummy variables identifying each recent decade's experience as a special case?" If no plausible combination of other variables can do that, then one would have to conclude either that variables have been mis-specified or that the explanation for the fertility swings lies in factors the models used here have failed to capture.

The pooled samples, like the single-census samples, show that the past income, current income, and relative cost variables indeed have a role to play in accounting for the rise and fall of fertility in the postwar era (R.1–4, 40, 41, 51). The relationship of current to past income appears to play a part like that assigned to it by Easterlin's hypothesis of relative economic status. In the late 1940s and 1950s fertility was promoted in part by the very high ratio of current to prewar incomes. By the 1960s, the relevance of the prewar experience for the decision making of young couples was rapidly waning, and though the growth rate of the 1960s was somewhat higher than that for the 1950s, income prospects in the late 1960s were not so greatly improved over the experience of the previous two decades as was the case for the baby boom cohorts of young couples. It thus appears that fertility was being adjusted to the ratio of current means over the material standards per family member that were formed by both recent and more distant past income experience. This is the same sort of conclusion reached by Easterlin on the basis of different measures. His measures of relative income status compare the recent incomes (and the unemployment history) of young adults with those of adults a generation older (e.g., 1973, Figures 2, 3) for the nation as a whole.

What we know about the movement of relative child costs also helps to explain the postwar fertility swings. The relative cost of an extra child was cut when World War II swept the majority of American families into the ranks of income-tax payers. This made the income-tax exemption per child suddenly relevant, cutting the relative cost of a third child in nonfarm families by 16% between 1940 and 1945, a cut that was partly offset by a 3% cost increase due to wage increases over the same years and a further 8% cost increase in the later 1940s.[14] Taken by itself, the 16% wartime cut in the cost index due to the tax-exemption effect raised the child–woman ratio significantly. The coefficient on the relative-cost term in R.41 in Table 3 implies that this 16% cost reduction raised the child–woman ratio by .0533, or about 17% of the 1940

---

[14] For the calculations of relative child cost, see Appendix F of *Fertility and Scarcity in America* (Lindert, forthcoming).

It is certainly reasonable to wonder whether or not different cohorts of young couples could have been responding to movements in a measure of relative child cost they had never even heard of. On this issue, see the section on "Bedside Calculators" in Chapter 4 of the same book, which makes the argument that such movements could indeed have affected their behavior through their perceptions of the extent to which extra children seemed to increase couples' burdens or joys.

child–woman ratio for the entire United States. For the 1940s as a whole, the net cost reduction of about 5% implies a fertility stimulus of a little over 5% of the 1940 level (again according to R.41, which gives the highest coefficient to child costs). These cost effects account for only a small part, though a statistically significant part, of the observed baby boom, which saw fertility rise by about a third in the 1940s and rise further in the 1950s. Correspondingly, the slight postwar upward drift in relative child costs caused by the rise in real wages cut fertility only slightly, and not enough to prevent the rise in the 1950s or to account for the sharp drop in fertility after the early 1960s.

Yet when income history and relative costs have been entered directly into pooled regressions spanning the postwar period, with or without help from Catholicism variables specific to individual decades, there still seems to be something significant and special—that is, something unexplained—about the fertility of the last two decades. Fertility was still higher in the late 1950s (1960 census) and lower in the late 1960s (1970 census) than the direct effects of the variables just mentioned would have predicted.

Another influence can be added to cut down the special unexplained differences between the decades. The extra force to be added is suggested by the behavior of the schooling variables in the regressions. It will be recalled that the cross-sectional impact of the schooling variable within individual censuses varied noticeably from decade to decade. Schooling had slight influence, if any, on fertility in both the 1940 and 1970 censuses, yet it seemed to raise fertility greatly within the censuses of 1950 and 1960.

Why has the impact of differences in levels of schooling been so different for different periods? More specifically, why should it have become strongly positive during the 1940s and then insignificant during the 1960s? One possibility, of course, is that its influence is a mirage caused by omitting some other variables that happen to be strongly correlated with schooling levels across states in the baby boom years but not at other times. A simpler and more promising explanation is that the increased control over births at lower completed parities, an outcome strongly associated with schooling in the past, actually raises the sensitivity of fertility to economic and other changes affecting the desirability of extra births.[15]

There are two reasons for expecting such a pattern. First, a given percentage change in, say, incomes is likely to affect more strongly the

---

[15] I am indebted to my colleague Larry L. Bumpass for suggesting that I test this hypothesis in connection with the fluctuations in American fertility since the Depression.

demand for something that is a large commitment than the demand for something that takes little resources. Manufacturers of spices and other infrequent-purchase products have often noted a low price elasticity of demand for products on which households spend little money or thought. It may well be that income elasticity of demand is also less strongly affected where the object of expenditure is a smaller share of total family resources. The marginal children in families that will be large with or without them will take a lower percentage of family resources than marginal additions to small families. Perhaps groups with lower parities, such as those with more schooling, find a greater effect on the desirability of one more child in response to a given percentage change in incomes.

Second, for any given change in the desirability of extra children, it seems likely that the responsiveness of birth probabilities will be greater for those groups who have invested more energy in gaining access to effective birth control options. These more informed and contracepting groups will tend to be those nearer their margins of desired family size. The smaller the likely completed parity, the greater the share of couples in the relevant group who are near their margins of wanted versus unwanted births for any given state of income, costs, contraceptive technology, and so forth. More schooled, or higher-input, couples will tend to be those who have fewer children on the average. Should conditions in the economy take a turn for the worse, they will cut their birth probabilities more effectively (as long as they had not already been preventing births altogether). Should conditions for raising a family seem to brighten, they will raise their birth probabilities considerably, while those groups who would tend to have had more anyway would tend to stick with a relatively ineffective method of contraception (rhythm, withdrawal) and end up wanting a greater share of a relatively constant number of births.[16] The same movements in income and costs can generate greater responses among those with greater control over their fertility.

This interpretation of the results suggests the following explanation of the relationship of education to the baby boom and bust. The more educated had achieved a considerably lower fertility than those with

---

[16] This argument might seem to draw support from the fact that the baby boom brought a greater response of births at lower than at higher birth orders (Kirk, 1960, p. 251). But the present hypothesis relates to differences in the responsiveness of different *completed* parities, not different current birth orders. There is little tendency for the share of "marginal" (lastborn) children in any birth order to change from the second to the seventh order, so that the Kirk data on the responsiveness of different birth orders cannot serve as a proxy for the responsiveness of different completed parities.

less education by 1940. Having greater control over fertility, they were able to raise their birth probabilities more sharply and certainly when the economy revived with World War II. They continued with levels of fertility that were historically not much lower than those of the less educated groups, for as long as the climate seemed bright for large families. In the 1960s, when the climate began to become less favorable, they were more prompt in once again cutting down on birth probabilities.

If this interpretation is accepted, it carries the important implication that modernizing countries, led by the more educated and higher-input couples, acquire fertility patterns characterized by greater responsiveness to economic fluctuations and other changes, as well as by lower average fertility over the long run. Should conditions fluctuate, low-fertility groups and countries will show instability in their fertility patterns. Should conditions change slowly, this instability will not appear despite their keener sensitivity.

Although it is plausible that more-schooled and contracepting couples may be adjusting their fertility more sensitively to changing economic conditions, the present aggregate tests do *not* provide firm confirmation of the importance of this tendency for explaining recent experience. Regressions were run on the pooled postwar sample using interaction terms relating schooling to the rate of growth in incomes (SCHDY in R.1a, SCHOOLF50,60 and SCHOOLF70 in R.51). The theory just advanced predicts that such variables should pick up the pronatal effect of extra schooling when incomes are rising rapidly and the antinatal effect of extra schooling when they are not. The results do show the significance of the hypothesized effect on regressions reported here (R.1a, 51), but in other (unreported) regressions the special interaction variable lost its significance when forced to compete with Catholicism proxies. The special argument about contraceptive sensitivity to changing economic conditions is thus consistent with the data, but one is left with the suspicion that other explanations could also fit the observed twists in the relationship of schooling to fertility.

It must also be noted that none of the regressions, even those with the special interaction terms, convincingly removed all that was special about individual postwar decades. In the pooled regressions on levels of the child–woman ratio, the *Zeitgeist* dummies for the 1960 and 1970 censuses accounted for only a small share of the shifts observed for the United States as a whole, (R.1–4), yet in the rate-of-change regressions (R.40, 41) the dummy for the 1970 census accounted for all the observed decline in the child–woman ratio. It thus appears that income, education, and the other socioeconomic variables used here account for some of, but not all of, the special instability of postwar fertility.

THE NOT-SO-PUZZLING 1920s

To judge from the regressions, it appears that the same kinds of models that help to bring order to postwar fertility history fit the census of 1930 quite well. This seems to contradict the view of Coale and of Sweezy that the experience of the 1920s does not fit the "economic" hypotheses used for explaining the baby boom. The puzzle they posed, again, was that the prosperity following World War II was accompanied by a surge in births but the prosperity following World War I brought a further decline in births.

The conundrum of the 1920s disappears when the economic history of that decade is examined. The prosperity of the 1920s could not compare to the boom of the 1940s. Output per man-hour rose 19.8% per decade between 1913 and 1929 or 28.2% in the decade of the 1920s (1919–1929). It rose 32.9% across the 1940s and at the rate of 36.0% per decade across the 1940s and 1950s combined (U.S. Bureau of Economic Analysis, 1973). The contrast in postwar eras is sharpened by the fact that unemployment, which is not reflected in the figures on output per man-hour, was at least as high in the 1920s as in 1913 (Coen, 1973), whereas unemployment dropped from over 14.5% to less than 6.0% in the 1940s.

What we know of the movement of the distribution of income in the 1920s also served to account for the absence of a baby boom in that decade. The 1920s saw a widening of inequalities in wealth and income. The shift toward inequality was sufficiently pronounced, in fact, that the gains in real income were taken up almost entirely by the top 7% of nonfarm families.[17] Wage rates remained nearly fixed, and farm families suffered such large capital losses in the 1920–1921 crash in land values that their small current income gains over the rest of the decade failed to bring an overall gain in purchasing power. In other words, for families that would account for nearly all of the nation's births, income was rising less rapidly than in previous decades. It is hardly surprising that fertility failed to surge in the 1920s the way it did in the ascent from depression to boom in the 1940s.

---

[17] Based on a reworking of the Simon Kuznets figures of upper-income groups' shares of total income by Charles F. Holt in Holt (1972).

THE STEADY DECLINE: 1860–1935

One historical development that helped to make the baby boom so unexpected was the steadiness of the previous long fertility decline. From the early nineteenth century to the middle of the Depression, the rate of decline in fertility fluctuated less than it has since. This is not to say that the decline was entirely uniform. As already noted, the fertility of native-born New Englanders was no lower in the 1920s than around the Civil War, and Southern white fertility fell less rapidly than the white national rate between 1870 and 1900. The national child–woman ratio had a slight sawtooth pattern, falling faster in the censuses of 1870, 1890, 1910, and 1930 than in 1880, 1900, or 1920. Each of these variations deserves to be studied by itself.

The theory advanced here cannot be tested against all the features of the long fertility decline, because of insufficient data. It is not difficult, however, to reconcile the present framework with the steadiness of the decline. All the major influences on fertility identified by the models for twentieth century censuses moved more steadily before 1935 than since. Incomes fluctuated in response to local harvest failures, World War I, and short recessions marked by bank panics. But each of these fluctuations was too brief to affect fertility behavior greatly. The rise of schooling and the decline of agriculture also proceeded too evenly to cause major swings in fertility. The relative stability of the downward trend may also be explained in part by the interaction hypothesized earlier between the degree of control over fertility and the sensitivity of fertility response to changing conditions. In the later nineteenth century, fertility was still controlled by a few crude means—postponement of marriage, abstinence, withdrawal, rhythm. As economic prospects varied, young adults had less ability than their descendants to vary their own birth probabilities. This greater imperfection of birth control may have dampened their responsiveness to economic fluctuations.

Used with care, the family of models tried out in Tables 1–4 could explain part of the variation in regional rates of fertility decline before 1935. One variation it *cannot* at present explain, because the necessary economic data are lacking, is the failure of the fertility of native-born New Englanders to decline from the 1860s to the 1920s. We lack series on the incomes, income history, agricultural employment share, and schooling of persons within a region classified by nativity. Another variation may prove more tractable. It has been noted that the fertility of Southern whites failed to drop much between 1870 and 1900. The same fact seems less anomalous if this period is broken at 1880. In the wake of the Civil War the Southern states experienced an abnormally low ratio of young males to young females. Southern whites also suffered from a loss of income from slaves and nonhuman capital, plus crop failures. All these factors could easily have lowered fertility for the 1870 census. (The lower child–woman ratio for that census may also be due in part, but probably not entirely, to a bias in the serious undercount in Southern states in the 1870 census.) It is thus not surprising that Southern white fertility dropped little if at all from the 1870 census to that of 1880. From 1880 on there is less of a drift of Southern white fertility to be explained, so that relative steadiness in the ratio of Southern white fertility holds during the era (after 1880) when there is no further pronounced movement in the ratios of Southern to national income, schooling, share in agriculture, and so forth.

CONCLUSION

It seems possible to use a single framework to tie together seemingly inconsistent patterns of American fertility. A framework featuring the interplay of past income experience, present income, relative costs, and the prior efficacy of fertility control seems capable of interpreting the baby boom and bust, the previous long decline in fertility, and cross-sectional fertility patterns. It provides these interpretations in a way that should strike historians as sensible: It makes the case for a general model by taking care to identify unique historical forces and changes in structure over time.

The same framework offers some conditional forecasts regarding American fertility. First, its reasons for predicting a negative relationship between fertility and modernization variables imply that, over the long run, fertility should indeed remain low, and at rates below those of the baby boom. It also points out the possibility, however, that instability in the economy will produce instability in fertility. As argued previously, the more fertility becomes controlled in general, the more it moves from having a high random component for individual couples to having less randomness and more systematic response to the economic and other factors that govern the desirability of extra children. This hypothesis says, in effect, that if birth rates should jump in response to economic conditions in the future, we have good reason to hold back on cries of "Standing room only!" in the expectation that if the economic conditions producing the jump are temporary, so is the jump in fertility itself. Conversely, the record lows in fertility in the mid-1970s, which also seem affected by unfavorable short-run economic conditions, may be somewhat below the long-run average level of fertility to be expected.

When aligned with the present kind of model, the history of American fertility over the last 100 years also suggests a relationship between the rate of economic growth and the trend in fertility. Past fertility patterns have shown that the negative influence of income experience on desired family size outweighs the positive influence of family income prospects. This suggests that as long as future American income growth resembles past growth in its degree of emphasis on investments in education, the faster the long-run rate of growth the greater the downward pressure on fertility will be, even though higher income growth can raise fertility in the short run. This forecast, however, is an extension of the present results beyond the sample on which they are based. Incomes are near record highs and fertility rates have never been lower. It is not implausible to argue that fertility cannot drop further because it is now as low as the natural desire of a majority of young adults to be parents will permit. Having not tested this hypothesis, the present tests cannot reject it. They do lead, however, to a presumption that the long-run trend in American fertility will at least not be upward.

APPENDIX: DEFINITIONS OF VARIABLES USED IN REGRESSIONS IN TABLES 1–4

DEPENDENT VARIABLES

CW = child–woman ratio; the ratio of children 0–4 to women 15–49, all races. The census data were adjusted for underenumeration, using the underenumeration estimates of Coale and Zelnik (1963) for whites and those of Coale and Rives (1973) for all non-whites.

DCW = decadal change in the child–woman ratio; CW for the state in a given census minus CW for the previous census.

$WED1529$ = the share of women 15–29 who are ever married. (WED1529 was computed by taking the simple average of the shares married in each 5-year age interval.)

$LNSPINST$ = the natural logarithm of the share of never marrieds (spinsters) among women 30–44 (= $1 - .01WED3044$). (This variable was put into natural log form to conform to a clear nonlinearity in the relationship of the share married in the 30–44 age group to the independent variables.)

$DWED1529$ = decadal change in the share of women 15–29 ever married.

INDEPENDENT VARIABLES

Demographic Variables

$WED1529$ = the share of women 15–29 who are ever married (as in preceding section).

$WED3044$ = the share of women 30–44 who are ever married. (WED3044 was computed by taking the simple average of the shares married in each 5-year age interval.)

PRIMAGE = the share of women 15–49 who are 20–34 (prime childbearing age), after adjusting the underlying figures for whites and nonwhites for estimated census underenumeration.

SEXWH = a measure of the excess of white males 15–49 over white females 15–49; the natural log of the ratio of white males 15–49 to white females 15–49 (both adjusted for estimated underenumeration) times the share of females 15–49 who are white (i.e., times 1 − NONWHITE).

SEXNW = a measure of the excess of nonwhite males 15–49 over nonwhite females 15–49; the natural log of the ratio of nonwhite males 15–49 to nonwhite females 15–49 (both adjusted for estimated underenumeration), times the share of females 15–49 who are nonwhite.

SEXGAP = the average imbalance of males 15–49 over females 15–49, all races together; equal to SEXWH + SEXNW.

DWED1529 = decadal change in the share of women 15–29 ever married.

DPRIMAGE = decadal change in the share of women 15–49 who are 20–34.

DSEXWH = decadal change in SEXWH, a measure of the excess of white males 15–49 over white females 15–49.

DSEXNW = decadal change in SEXNW, a measure of the excess of nonwhite males 15–49 over nonwhite females 15–49.

DSEXGAP = decadal change in SEXGAP, the average imbalance of males 15–49 over females 15–49.

Prior Income, Current Income, and Relative Child Costs

YCAPORIG = prior income per capita; the natural log of personal income per capita, adjusted for income taxes and the cost of living, in "places of origin" 20 years earlier. For further details on its calculation, see Lindert (forthcoming, Appendix G).

YWORKER = current income per person in the labor force; the natural log of personal income, adjusted for income taxes and the cost of living, per person in the labor force, 1940–1970, and per person gainfully employed, 1900–1930.

RELCOST = an index of the relative cost of a nonfarm third child, 1960 and 1970 observations only; equal to .069 × share outside of agriculture (see AGRIC) × the natural log of the ratio of the state's average earnings per man-hour in manufacturing to the same earnings average for the United States.

DYCAPORI = decadal rate of growth in prior income per capita; the decadal rate of growth in the antilog of YCAPORIG.

DYWORK = decadal rate of growth in current income per person in the labor force; the decadal rate of growth in the antilog of YWORKER.

DRELCOST = decadal rate of change in the relative cost of a nonfarm third child for the entire United States. The same value was applied to each state for a given decade. (DRELCOST was calculated from a time-series index of the relative cost of a third child, derived in Lindert (forthcoming, Appendix F).

UNIMPROV = an index of the availability of unimproved land in 1900, and a proxy for the relative cheapness of an extra farm child in 1900. (UNIMPROV was calculated as follows: The share of the highest acreage in the state ever in farms in the twentieth century that was not improved acreage in 1900 was divided by the same share for the contiguous United States. This new ratio minus one was then weighted (multiplied) by the share of the state's working males who were employed in agriculture.)

LANDCOST = an index of the average labor cost of farm land in 1900, and a proxy for the relative cost of an extra farm child in 1900. (LANDCOST was calculated as follows: The ratio of the state's average value of farm real estate per acre to the annual average daily farm wage without board was divided by the same ratio for the contiguous United States. This new ratio minus one was then weighted (multiplied) by the share of the state's working males who were employed in agriculture.)

Socioeconomic and Religious Variables

NOTE: In expressing percentages, use, e.g., 12.0, not .12.

NONWHITE = share of nonwhites in females 15–49, after adjusting for estimated underenumeration.

FORBORN = percentage of the state's population born in other countries.

AGRIC = percentage of working males employed in agriculture.

ILLIT = percentage of all persons 21 and over who are illiterate (1900–1930 only).

SCHOOLF = median years of schooling completed by females 25 and over.

SCHOOLF50,60 = SCHOOLF times one for each observation of the 1950 and 1960 censuses; zero for other censuses.

SCHOOLF70 = SCHOOLF times one for each observation of the 1970 census; zero for other censuses.

CATHOLIC = for 1900–1940 only, the ratio of membership in the Roman Catholic church 4 years earlier to the population of the state at the time of the census.

CATH5050 = for 1950 only, the ratio of membership in the Roman Catholic church in 1936, the last year for state religious membership, to the state's 1950 population.

CATH5060 = the value of CATH5050, applied to each 1960 observation instead of to each 1950 observation.

CATH5070 = the value of CATH5050, applied to each 1970 observation instead of to each 1950 observation.

DNONWHIT = the decadal change in the share of nonwhites in females 15–49.

DFORBORN = the decadal change in the percentage of the state's population born in other countries.

DAGRIC = the decadal change in the percentage of the state's working males who are employed in agriculture.

DSCHOOLF = the decadal change in the median years of schooling completed by females 25 and over.

SCHDY = interaction term relating schooling of females to the rate of growth in income; SCHOOLF × (YWORKER − YCAPORIG).

Other Variables

PILLETC(1970) = 1 if the observation is from the 1970 census, 0 otherwise.

IKE(1960) = 1 if the observation is from the 1960 census, 0 otherwise.

SOUTH = regional dummy for the South; equal to 1 if the state is in the South Atlantic, East South Central, or West South Central divisions, except for Maryland, Delaware, and the District of Columbia; and 0 for other states (including Maryland, Delaware, and the District of Columbia).

NENG = regional dummy for New England.

WNCMN = regional dummy for the West North Central plus Mountain states.

CW2 = the child–woman ratio for the same state 20 years earlier.

REFERENCES

Bogue, Donald J., & Palmore, James A. (1964). "Some Empirical and Analytical Relations among Demographic Fertility Measures with Regression Models for Fertility Estimation," *Demography*, Vol. 1, pp. 316–338.

Coale, Ansley J. (1960). Introduction to Ansley J. Coale, ed., *Demographic and Economic Change in Developed Countries*. Princeton, N.J.: Princeton University Press.

Coale, Ansley J., & Rives, Norfleet W., Jr. (1973). "A Statistical Reconstruction of the Black Population of the United States: 1880–1970: Estimates of True Numbers by Age and Sex, Birth Rates, and Total Fertility," *Population Index*, Vol. 39 (January), pp. 3–36.

Coale, Ansley J., & Zelnik, Melvin (1963). *New Estimates of Fertility and Population in the United States*. Princeton, N.J.: Princeton University Press.

Coen, Robert M. (1973). "Labor Force and Unemployment in the 1920's and 1930's: A Re-examination Based on Postwar Experience," *Review of Economics and Statistics*, Vol. 55 No. 1, (February), pp. 46–55.

Easterlin, Richard A. (1957). "State Income Estimates," in Simon Kuznets, Dorothy Swaine Thomas, *et al.*, *Population Redistribution and Economic Growth*. Vol. 1. Philadelphia: American Philosophical Society.

Easterlin, Richard A. (1960). "Interregional Differences in per Capita Income, Population, and Total Income." In National Bureau of Economic Research, *Trends in the American Economy in the Nineteenth Century*. Studies in Income and Wealth, No. 24. Princeton, N.J.: Princeton University Press.

Easterlin, Richard A. (1968). *Population, Labor Force, and Long Swings in Economic Growth: The American Experience*. New York: Columbia University Press.

Easterlin, Richard A. (1969). "Towards a Socio-economic Theory of Fertility," in S. S. Behrman, L. Corsa, & R. Freedman, *Fertility and Family Planning: A World View*. Ann Arbor: University of Michigan Press.

Easterlin, Richard A. (1971). "Does Human Fertility Adjust to the Environment?" *American Economic Review*, Vol. 61 (May), pp. 399–407.

Easterlin, Richard A. (1972/1973). "The Economics and Sociology of Fertility: A Synthesis." Unpublished manuscript.

Easterlin, Richard A. (1973). "Relative Economic Status and the American Fertility Swing," in Eleanor B. Sheldon, ed., *Economics and Family Behavior*. Philadelphia: Lippincott.

Engerman, Stanley (1974). "Changes in Black Fertility, 1880–1940." Working paper prepared for the MSSB Conference on Family History, July 1974, Williamstown, Massachusetts.

Forster, Colin, & Tucker, G. L. S. (1972). *Economic Opportunity and White American Fertility Ratios, 1800–1860*. New Haven, Conn.: Yale University Press.

Grabill, Wilson; Kiser, C. V.; & Whelpton, P. K. (1958). *The Fertility of American Women*. New York: Wiley.

Grabill, Wilson, & Cho, Lee Jay (1965). "Methodology for the Measurement of Current Fertility from Population Data on Young Children," *Demography*, Vol. 2, pp. 50–73.

Himes, Norman E. (1936). *The Medical History of Contraception*. New York: Gamut Press.

Holt, Charles F. (1972). "Size Distribution of Income and the Prosperity of the Twenties." Unpublished manuscript.

Kirk, Dudley (1960). "The Influence of Business Cycles on Marriage and Birth Rates," in Ansley J. Coale, ed., *Demographic and Economic Change in Developed Countries*. Princeton, N.J.: Princeton University Press.

Kiser, Clyde V. (1960). "Differential Fertility in the United States," in National Bureau of
    Economic Research, *Demographic and Economic Change in Developed Countries.*
    Princeton, N.J.: Princeton University Press.
Kuznets, Simon (1953). *Shares of Upper Income Groups in Income and Savings.* New York:
    National Bureau of Economic Research.
Leet, Don R. (1975). "Human Fertility and Agricultural Opportunities in Ohio Counties:
    From Frontier to Maturity, 1810–1860," in Richard K. Vedder & David C. Klinga-
    man, eds., *Essays in Nineteenth Century Economic History.* Athens: Ohio University
    Press.
Lindert, Peter H. (forthcoming). *Fertility and Scarcity in America* (Princeton, N.J.: Prince-
    ton University Press).
Noonan, John T. (1967). *Contraception: A History of Its Treatment by the Catholic Theolo-
    gians and Canonists.* New York: Mentor.
Ryder, Norman B. (1972). "Time Series of Pill and IUD Use: United States, 1961–1970,"
    Studies in Family Planning, Vol. 3 (October), pp. 233–240.
Schwartz, Charles F., & Graham, Robert E. (1956). *Personal Income by States since 1929.*
    Washington, D.C.: U.S. Government Printing Office.
Spengler, Joseph J. (1930). *The Fecundity of Native and Foreign-Born Women in New
    England.* Brookings Pamphlet Series, Vol. 2, No. 1. Washington, D.C.: Brookings.
Sweezy, Alan. (1971). "The Economic Explanation of Fertility Changes in the United
    States," *Population Studies,* Vol. 25 (July), pp. 255–268.
Tuchfeld, Barry S., *et al.* (1974). "The Bogue–Palmore Technique for Estimating Direct
    Fertility Measures from Indirect Indicators as Applied to Tennessee Counties, 1960
    and 1970," *Demography,* Vol. 2 (May), pp. 195–206.
U.S. Bureau of Economic Analysis (1973). *Long Term Economic Growth, 1860–1970.* Series
    A168. Washington, D.C.: U.S. Government Printing Office.
Yasuba, Yasukichi. (1961). *Birth Rates of the White Population in the United States, 1800–
    1860: An Economic Study.* Baltimore, Md.: Johns Hopkins.

Who Chose the Cities?
Migrants to Moscow and
St. Petersburg Cities in
the Late Nineteenth Century*

BARBARA A. ANDERSON

Brown University

Who chose the cities? This is a question of interest in any developing country. The problems of overcrowding and masses of migrants unaccustomed to urban life are familiar. Most explanations offered, usually by development economists, suggest a model of men in the aggregate deciding whether to migrate and choosing their destinations in order to maximize their expected income or raise their standard of living (Todaro, 1969; Jorgenson, 1961). Thus to any given destination, especially to one of the most advanced, industrial destinations in a society, the normal economic model would predict that migration rates would be higher, the poorer and more backward the place of origin. Also, from any given origin, one might expect that the persons who were most disadvantaged at that origin would be most likely to migrate.

There has been some evidence to the contrary, most notably research that shows selectivity of migrants according to those with the greatest skills. The recent literature on the brain drain and the mobility of professionals is along these lines (Long, 1973; Grubel and Scott, 1969; Thomas, 1964). Aside from the evidence on selectivity of individuals within a given origin according to the possession of modern characteris-

*The research for this chapter was supported in part by a National Institutes of Health Traineeship in Demography at Princeton University and by NSF GS-3173X2 at the Institute for Advanced Study. The preparation was supported by Rockefeller Foundation Grant #70051 at the Economic Growth Center, Yale University.

277

tics, there is also reason to hypothesize that migration rates to modern, advanced destinations would be positively related to the level of development of the origin. The social psychological literature on attitude changes during modernization indicates that with modernization, there is an increased willingness to take risks, to engage in wage work, and to associate with strangers (Inkeles and Smith, 1974; Simmel, 1960; Levy, 1972:56–59; Lewis, 1955:42–44). All of these new attitudes should be intimately related to whether a person would be willing to migrate from his place of birth and, if he is, which destination would appear attractive.

This chapter hypothesizes that migration to modern, advanced destinations would be positively selective of persons with advanced skills, but also that migration rates should be positively related to the level of modernization of the origin. For instance, it is expected that an illiterate person in an area with a high literacy rate will be more willing to move and have more information about other places than an illiterate in an area with a lower literacy rate.

Modernization has been conceptualized in many different ways. Generally definitions have focused on either cultural or industrial aspects of social change. Stressing the cultural aspect, Cyril E. Black has defined modernization as "the process by which historically evolved institutions are adapted to the rapidly changing functions that reflect the unprecedented increase in man's knowledge, permitting control over his environment, which accompanied the scientific revolution . . . [Black, 1966:7]." More concisely, it is ". . . a process by which the traditional institutions are adapted to modern functions . . . [Black, 1966:46]." This definition stresses the importance of knowledge in a period of rapid change.

Others have emphasized industrial aspects of social change, with the level of modernization of a society defined as the ratio of inanimate to animate power used in that society (Levy, 1966:11). Animate sources are men and animals, and inanimate sources are primarily machines.

E. A. Wrigley has suggested considering the two aspects simultaneously as cultural and industrial factors (Wrigley, 1969). The cultural aspect includes an increase in literacy, an increase in the proportion living in urban places and the adoption of fertility control in marriage. The industrial aspect includes an increase in per capita gross national product and the utilization of modern production methods. Both cultural and industrial changes usually occur together, although not in any set order. England was quite industrialized before it experienced a substantial increase in literacy, while the opposite was true of France (Wrigley, 1969; Bendix, 1967:29).

Hypotheses based on consideration of the social psychological and sociological literature on modernization are tested for migrants to Moscow and St. Petersburg at the end of the nineteenth century who were born in 45 provinces of European Russia.[1] Concisely, the hypotheses are:

Migration rates to culturally modern destinations are higher the greater the level of cultural modernization of the origin, both in terms of absolute rates and in terms of rates of migration to the modern destinations relative to migration rates to less culturally modern destinations.

Migration rates to industrially modern destinations are higher the greater the level of industrial modernization of the origin, both in terms of absolute rates and in terms of migration rates to modern destinations relative to migration rates to less industrially modern destinations.

Migration rates to industrially or culturally modern destinations will be higher, the less important agriculture is at the origin as the sole source of support.

Population pressure at an origin is not a major positive cause of migration to culturally or industrially modern destinations.

The level of modernization of the origin affects migration rates to modern destinations positively apart from the tendency of persons possessing modern characteristics to migrate with a higher probability than persons without modern characteristics.

EUROPEAN RUSSIA IN THE NINETEENTH CENTURY AS A MODERNIZING SOCIETY

In terms of both cultural and industrial changes, European Russia at the end of the nineteenth century was a rapidly developing, modernizing society. Literacy rates were increasing as was the proportion of the population engaged in industry. Figure 1 shows the percentage of military recruits who were literate for a number of dates (Rashin, 1956: 305–306). Values are shown separately for areas with high and those

[1] Five of the 50 provinces of European Russia were excluded from the set of origins studied in this chapter. They were the three Baltic provinces, Estland, Lifland, and Kurland, and Moscow and St. Petersburg provinces. The three Baltic provinces were excluded because there is a great deal of evidence that they constituted a separate social system and thus were not in the same "universe" as the other European Russian provinces. Moscow and St. Petersburg provinces were excluded from the origins, because it was not possible to distinguish those who were born in the capital cities from those who were born elsewhere in the province. For denominators all 50 provinces were used. Hereafter, "Moscow" and "St. Petersburg" will refer to the cities rather than the provinces.

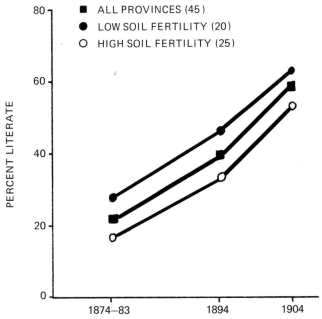

Figure 1.   Percentage of military recruits literate, 1874–1904.

with low soil fertility. Essentially, in the areas of high soil fertility, agriculture was much more important than in the areas of low soil fertility. At every date, the literacy rate of recruits was higher in the low soil fertility area than in the high soil fertility area.[2] Figure 2 shows the proportion of the population engaged in industry at various dates. This also increased rapidly throughout the nineteenth century. Again, industrial work was more common in the areas of low soil fertility than in the high soil fertility areas. Like currently developing countries, primarily imported rather than indigenously developed technology was used, which resulted in a more rapid reaction to technological change than occurred during Western European industrialization.

   Sidney Goldstein (1973) has noted that the best single indicator of cultural modernization is probably literacy. In this study, the percent-

   [2] De Tegoborskii's soil fertility variable is generally based on the length of the growing season and the amount of precipitation. The inherent fertility of the soil was a better agricultural variable than the proportion of the population engaged in agriculture, since the latter variable had a very small variance. The level of soil fertility was highly correlated with the extent to which workers in agriculture had an auxiliary occupation. Such an auxiliary occupation was usually cottage industry. The lower the soil fertility, the more likely a person in agriculture was to have an auxiliary occupation. Low soil fertility was levels 1–3; high soil fertility was levels 4–5.

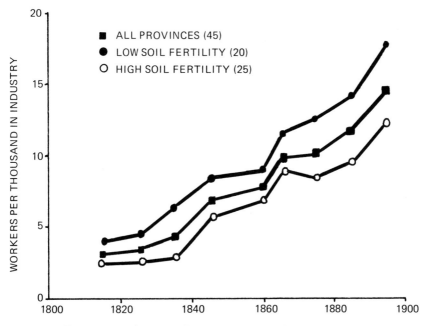

Figure 2. Workers in industry per 1000 population, 1815–1900.

age of military recruits, 1874–1883, who were literate is used as the indicator of the level of cultural modernization of a province (Rashin, 1956:305–306).[3]

J. N. Sinha (1974) has noted that a good occupational indicator of the level of industrial modernization of a society is the proportion of the population engaged in secondary industry. For data referring to 1897, the number of males engaged in secondary industry per 1000 males in the population of a province is used as the indicator of the level of industrial modernization of the province (Russia, 1905a; Russia, 1905b). For 1869, the number of workers per 1000 population in 1860 is used (Rashin 1940:3a, Rashin 1956:44–45).[4]

---

[3] Literacy of military recruits, 1874–1883, is used since it is the first data for which the literacy rate of a subpopulation of each province is available. The first date for which the literacy rate of the entire population is available is 1897, which is later than one would like to use, since most of the migration data was also gathered in 1897. The correlation between the literacy of military recruits, 1874–1883, and the literacy of all males by province in 1897 is +.810. Also the literacy of recruits is likely to be more closely related to the literacy of persons who grew up in a province than is the literacy rate of the entire population, which is more likely to be seriously affected by migration.

[4] 1897 was the first date for which the proportion of the population in secondary industry was available by province. Wokers in industry per thousand population 1860 is

TABLE 1
Workers and Servants Resident in Moscow, St. Petersburg and Odessa Cities in 1897

	Moscow		St. Petersburg		Odessa	
	Male	*Female*	*Male*	*Female*	*Male*	*Female*
Population	591,852	446,739	692,667	572,253	216,792	187,023
Number of workers and servants	299,438	134,446	291,584	141,586	65,019	28,139
Percentage of population who were workers or servants	50.6%	30.1%	42.1%	24.1%	30.0%	15.0%
Percentage distribution of workers and servants						
Workers in secondary industry	59.5%	32.2%	50.4%	24.2%	40.6%	13.7%
Workers in transportation, communication or commerce	21.0	6.2	21.5	3.1	19.7	5.8
Household servants	10.0	53.6	12.3	61.5	12.1	71.3
Unskilled and day-laborers	5.3	3.3	9.0	7.4	21.5	7.8
Other	4.2	3.7	5.8	3.8	6.1	1.4
Total	*100.0%*	*100.0%*	*100.0%*	*100.0%*	*100.0%*	*100.0%*

Moscow and St. Petersburg were the most modern places, both culturally and industrially, in European Russia. Tables 1 and 2 compare Moscow and St. Petersburg with Odessa, which in 1897 was the third largest city in European Russia (Rashin, 1956:247–250; Russia, 1905a; Russia, 1905b). Almost any urban place would have had a higher literacy rate and a higher proportion of the population engaged in industry than any rural place, but the contrast between Moscow and St. Petersburg and Odessa is striking. Even of those engaged in wage work, Moscow and St. Petersburg had a higher proportion of each sex engaged in relatively modern secondary industry and a smaller proportion of females in servant positions than did Odessa. As shown in Table 2, Moscow and St. Petersburg had far more literate populations of each

used for the analysis of migration data in 1869, since 1897 seemed too late a date to use. The 1860 industrial variable is not entirely satisfactory. Values by province were only available for the 25 provinces with the largest absolute number of workers in industry. The average rate across the other provinces was used for the provinces with a smaller absolute number of workers in industry.

TABLE 2
Percent Literate in St. Petersburg , Moscow
and Odessa Circa 1870

	Year	Male	Female
St. Petersburg	1869	62%	46%
Moscow City	1871	50%	34%
Odessa	1873	36%	22%

sex than did Odessa. Between the two cities however, St. Petersburg was more highly developed culturally, while Moscow was more advanced industrially. This is indicated by the higher literacy rate in St. Petersburg and by the higher proportion in secondary industry in Moscow.

Another factor which may be important in ascertaining the modernization status of an area in a society where most persons are engaged in agriculture is the extent to which persons in agriculture have no other source of support, such as cottage industry. In this study, the classification by Michael de Tegoborskii of the provinces of European Russia into five levels of soil fertility is used. The evidence is that the higher the level of soil fertility in a province, the less persons in that province engaged in any activity other than normal agriculture. (de-Tegoborskii, 1972:30). Such an areal classification is more sensible in Russia than it might be in other countries, since in Russia, unlike France, there were not sharp changes in climate or soil across small distances. Rather changes across space were quite gradual (Parker, 1969:27).

A common hypothesis in the economic development literature is that persons migrate to a city because of population pressure at the origin (Myrdal, 1968:470–471; Carroll, 1970:12, Todaro, 1969). I do not believe population pressure would be important for migration to a modern, advanced destination. Rather, it is expected that if migration were largely motivated by population pressure at the origin, relatively scarcely inhabited frontier destinations would be chosen rather than advanced cities. In this study, the indicator for population pressure is the natural rate of increase of population 1881–1885. For the 1869 data, natural r 1861–1865 is used (Rashin, 1956:217–218).[5]

---

[5] The natural rate of increase is the number per thousand population by which the population increases each year due to fertility and mortality. It is the crude birth rate minus the crude death rate. The growth rate was not used, since it is affected by

TABLE 3
Means, Standard Deviations and Descriptions of Explanatory Variables

Name	Mean	s.d.	Description
Soilfert	3.333	1.414	A five-level soil fertility variable 1 = lowest, 5 = highest
Litrec	21.822	10.633	The percentage of military recruits who were literate 1874-1883
Work60	7.424	10.302	The number of workers per thousand population in 1860
Worksec97	16.116	14.115	The number of male workers in secondary industry per thousand males in 1897
Nat r 61	14.689	4.446	The natural rate of increase per thousand population 1861-1865
Nat r 81	14.044	3.919	The natural rate of increase per thousand population 1881-1885
LndistSP	3.817	.461	The natural logarithm of the distance to St. Petersburg City, measured in arbitrary units
LndistMSP	3.348	.553	The natural logarithm of the distance to Moscow or St. Petersburg City, whichever is closer, measured in arbitrary units
%CloserSP	-.381	.449	The percentage St. Petersburg City is closer than Moscow City

The means and standard deviations of all the explanatory variables appear in Table 3, and the correlations among the explanatory variables are in Table 4. Places with a high literacy rate and high proportion of the population in secondary industry tended to be near Moscow and St. Petersburg. Thus it is necessary to take distance into account in order to ascertain whether literacy and industry have independent effects on migration rates or whether they only seem to have effects due to their geographic distribution. The natural logarithm of distance is generally used as the distance variable, since it increases less rapidly than distance. Thus the difference between 500 and 550 miles is not considered to be as great as the difference between 50 and 100 miles. For migration to Moscow and St. Petersburg as one destination, the natural logarithm of the distance to the closer of the two cities is used, while for the study of the distribution of migrants between Moscow and St. Petersburg, the percentage which the origin was closer to St. Petersburg than Moscow is the distance variable used. This is discussed in greater detail later.

---

migration. The density of the population was also not used, since its interpretation is strongly affected by the use to which the land is put. Although the economic literature is generally unclear about what population pressure means, the natural rate of increase seemed the most reasonable candidate.

TABLE 4
Correlations among Explanatory Variables

	Soilfert	Litrec	Work60	Worksec97	Nat r 61	Nat r 81	LndistSP	LndistMSP	%CloserSP
Soilfert	1.000	-.610***	-.305*	-.264	.320*	.370*	.652***	.404**	-.372*
Litrec		1.000	.270	.671***	-.409***	-.571***	-.489***	-.659***	-.215
Work60			1.000	.787***	-.170	-.180	-.035	-.301	-.358*
Worksec97				1.000	-.250	-.368*	-.157	-.512***	-.470***
Nat r 61					1.000	.653***	.345**	.390*	.004
Nat r 81						1.000	.546***	.609***	.043
LndistSP							1.000	.792***	-.391*
LndistMSP								1.000	.309*
%CloserSP									1.000

*p < .05.
**p < .01.
***p < .001.

SELECTIVITY OF MIGRANTS

Data from the 1869 St. Petersburg City Census (Russia, 1872:118) permit the testing of the hypothesis that ecological characteristics of origins affect migration rates apart from the characteristics of individual migrants as compared to nonmigrants. They also allow examination of some aspects of the selectivity of migrants according to possession of advanced skills.

The relevant data were in a table which presented, for peasants only, the number of migrants in St. Petersburg City cross-classified by province of origin, sex, whether over or under 7 years of age, and for those over 7 years of age whether literate or not.

Table 5 shows the correlations between explanatory variables and the migration rates in columns 1–2 and the standardized multiple regression coefficients for migration rates to St. Petersburg of peasants over age 7 in columns 5–6.[6] The strong positive effect of literacy at the origin and the strong negative effect of distance on migration rates for females is striking in the regressions. This supports the hypothesis that migration rates to advanced destinations are positively related to the level of cultural modernization of the origin. The common population pressure hypothesis is rejected as expected. The industrial modernization hypothesis is also countered, against expectations.

The classification of migrants by literacy allows the calculation of the ratio (literate migrants from Province A/all migrants from Province A) for each sex. This shows quite a different pattern, as presented in the correlations in columns 3–4 in Table 5. There is no significant correlation between this ratio and literacy for men, and it is significantly negative for women.[7] If high migration rates from highly literate provinces were simply the result of a greater tendency for literates than illiterates to migrate, independent of the ecological characteristics of the origin, a strong positive correlation would have resulted. Since the correlation was insignificant or negative, it is clear that migrants were

---

[6] Migration rates to St. Petersburg City 1869 for the population at least 7 years of age were of the form:

$$1000 m_{ip}/(.5\ P_i)$$

where m_{ip} = the number of persons of the given sex at least age 7 who migrated from Province i and in 1869 lived in St. Petersburg City

P_i = the total population of Province i in 1863

[7] The problem with this interpretation of literacy is that it is not known how many of the migrants were literate before migration to St. Petersburg and how many acquired literacy in the city.

TABLE 5

Relationships for Overall Migration and Selectivity of Migrants by Literacy for St. Petersburg City 1869 (on 45 Provinces)

	Correlations				Standardized multiple regressions	
	Male migra- tion rate (1)	Female migra- tion rate (2)	Male literate proportion (3)	Female literate proportion (4)	Male migra- tion rate (5)	Female migra- tion rate (6)
Soilfert	-.511***	-.699***	.149	.204	.129	-.098
Litrec	.807***	.691***	-.089	-.375***	.810***	.414***
Work60	-.067	-.094	.063	-.050	-.316***	-.263**
Nat r 61	-.493***	-.505***	.039	.143	-.202*	-.205*
Lndist SP	-.531***	-.746***	.409***	.384**	-.161	-.418***
Multiple R^2					.794	.792
p					<.001	<.001

*p < .05.
**p < .01.
***p < .001.

not a random sample of residents at the origin and that, for females, the less literate the origin, the more selective migration was of literate persons. For both sexes, there is a significant positive correlation with the natural logarithm of distance, which is the opposite of what was found in correlations for overall migration rates. This positive relationship with distance suggests long distances were a lesser obstacle to literate than to illiterate persons. Perhaps the less modern the place of origin generally, the more important it was that an individual have a characteristic, such as literacy, which would make migration to a city attractive to him. All these findings support the interpretation of characteristics of origins as factors which generally affect persons, apart from their individual characteristics.

The distribution of origins of migrants to St. Petersburg did not change greatly between 1869 and 1897. The correlation between the male migration rate to St. Petersburg in 1869 and that rate for 1897 is .939 (Anderson, 1974). Thus in the remainder of this chapter, based on the findings for 1869, the characteristics of an origin are interpreted as factors forming an environment affecting persons in that area.

MIGRATION TO MOSCOW OR ST. PETERSBURG, 1897

Migration to Moscow or St. Petersburg can be viewed in two ways. First one can consider the rate of migration out of one's province of birth to either city. For this, for each sex, the proper rate for migration from Province A is the number of persons born in Province A who in 1897 lived in either Moscow or St. Petersburg per 1000 persons born in Province A who in 1897 lived anywhere in the Russian Empire, including the two major cities and Province A. The second approach is to visualize migration as a two-stage process. First a person may decide whether to migrate. If he decides to migrate, he then chooses his destination. In this case, the relative distribution of migrants between Moscow and St. Petersburg on one hand and all other destinations on the other is the proper consideration. We restrict our attention to other destinations in European Russia because there is evidence that migration within European Russia differed considerably from migration to other destinations in the Russian Empire, such as Siberia (Anderson, 1974). In this two-stage model of migration, the proper rate is the conditional probability that a person chooses Moscow or St. Petersburg as a destination, given that he migrates out of his province of birth to some other province in European Russia. Thus the conditional rate for each sex for migration from Province A is the number of persons born in province A who in 1897 lived in Moscow or St. Petersburg per 1000 persons born in Province A who in 1897 lived somewhere in European Russia other than their province of birth.

The calculation of both types of rates comes from the same data set (Russia, 1905b).[8] The source is a table in the 1897 Imperial Russian Census which presents for each sex a cross-classification of province of birth by province of residence in 1897. Moscow and St. Petersburg are included separately as places of residence in 1897.

The hypotheses for both types of rate are similar. It is expected that choice of Moscow or St. Petersburg will be positively related to the level of cultural and industrial modernization of the origin, and it may be negatively related to the soil fertility of the origin, due to possibly

BLE 6
rrelations for Migration Rates in European Russia 1897

	Male M-SP (1)	Female M-SP (2)	Male M-SP/ER (3)	Female M-SP/ER (4)	Male M/M-SP (5)	Female M/M-SP (6)
ilfert	-.538***	-.639***	-.727***	-.751***	.504***	.536***
trec	.847***	.799***	.812***	.780***	-.096	-.089
rksec97	.471**	.411**	.400**	.382**	.308*	.315*
t r 81	-.510***	-.528***	-.538***	-.549***	-.007	.119
distMSP	-.758***	-.801***	-.776***	-.769***		
loserSP					-.679***	-.799***
le M-SP	1.000	.924***	.915***	.851***	-.053	-.095
male M-SP		1.000	.960***	.954***	-.137	-.193
le M-SP/ER			1.000	.983***	-.239	-.288
male M-SP/ER				1.000	-.283	-.337*
le M/M-SP					1.000	.890***
male M/M-SP						1.000

*p < .05.
*p < .01.
*p < .001.

[8] The problem with a lifetime migration rate is that one does not know where a person was between birth and the time of the assessment of place of residence. Also such a rate does not account for international emigration or mortality. International emigration was slight before 1900, so this aspect is a minor problem. Differential mortality according to migration status should not introduce serious biases.

TABLE 7
Multiple Regressions for Migration Rates in European Russia 1897 [a]

	Male M-SP (1)	Female M-SP (2)	Male M-SP/ER (3)	Female M-SP/ER (4)	Male M/M-SP (5)	Female M/M-SP (6)
Standardized						
Soilfert	.019	-.184	-.314	-.386	.224	.157
	(.214)	(2.237)	(4.326)	(5.081)	(1.333)	(1.152)
Litrec	.803	.546	.506	.388	-.378	-.291
	(6.298)	(4.556)	(4.789)	(3.507)	(1.937)	(1.845)
Worksec97	-.240	-.254	-.244	-.220	.314	.227
	(2.541)	(2.851)	(3.116)	(2.675)	(2.050)	(1.832)
Nat r 81	.115	.097	.072	.033	-.168	.008
	(1.297)	(1.166)	(.982)	(.428)	(1.352)	(.084)
LndistMSP	-.430	-.556	-.485	-.490		
	(4.440)	(6.058)	(5.997)	(5.782)		
%CloserSP					-.521	-.697
					(3.502)	(5.792)
R^2	.824	.844	.879	.867	.601	.739
p	<.001	<.001	<.001	<.001	<.001	<.001
n	45	45	45	45	45	45
Unstandardized						
Constant	46.934	57.074	706.136	790.746	403.669	272.576
Soilfert	.443	-2.243	-43.942	-53.568	34.426	23.327
Litrec	2.504	.885	9.423	7.161	-7.717	-5.765
Worksec97	-.565	-.310	-3.428	-3.054	4.831	3.387
Nat r 81	.973	.427	3.645	1.648	-9.278	.436
LndistMSP	-25.768	-17.310	-173.650	-173.756	-252.073	-327.085
Mean	21.3	12.0	179.9	160.7	393.5	409.7
S.D.	33.2	17.2	198.0	196.2	217.0	210.7

[a] t-values are in parentheses. Underlined values have *p* < .05 for a two-tailed test.

conservative influences of being in a setting where agriculture is important to the exclusion of most other forms of economic activity (Geertz, 1963). Natural *r* is not expected to be strongly positively related to either migration rate.

The correlations between the migration rates by residence in 1897 and the explanatory variables appear in Table 6 in columns 1–4. All correlations are as hypothesized. Migration rates to Moscow and St. Petersburg whether absolute or conditional are significantly positively related to literacy and activity of the population in secondary industry at the origin and negatively with soil fertility, natural r and distance from the cities. However, the geographic distribution of these characteristics, as reflected in Table 4, makes it especially necessary to examine their joint affect when ln distance is included in multiple regressions. These appear in Table 7 in columns 1–4. The multiple R^2 values are very high, indicating that most of the variability in the migration rates can be accounted for by the explanatory variables chosen. In examining the individual coefficients, the hypothesis that cultural modernization of the origin positively affects migration to advanced destinations is strongly supported, as it was for migration to St. Petersburg in 1869. The expectation about the effect of natural r is also fulfilled, since rather than being strongly positive, its coefficients are insignificant and quite close to zero. The soil fertility of the origin differentiates among origins significantly with the expected sign for the distribution of migrants between the two major cities and the rest of European Russia, but is not significant for males when total migration rates out of a province are considered. This suggests the importance of agriculture at an origin may affect choice of migration destination more than overall willingness to migrate. The hypothesis about industrial modernization is rejected in the multiple regressions. This will be examined further in the distribution of migrants between Moscow and St. Petersburg.

DISTRIBUTION OF MIGRANTS BETWEEN MOSCOW AND ST. PETERSBURG

Moscow and St. Petersburg to this point have been considered together, as one destination. This is due to their relative similarity when compared to other destinations in European Russia. However some migrants chose one city, while others chose the other. It was expected that one major factor determining which city was chosen would be simply which was closer to the province of birth. To examine this, a different kind of distance variable is used. It is the percentage which St. Petersburg is closer than Moscow. This is the distance to St. Petersburg divided by the average of the distance to Moscow and the distance to St. Petersburg.

Although there were many similarities, as shown in Tables 1 and 2, there were important differences between the cities. Moscow was mainly an industrial center, while St. Petersburg (the capital) was mainly a cultural center. If conditions at one's origin make one seek destinations which are relatively similar to that origin, then migrants from relatively industrially modern origins should have tended to choose Moscow, while migrants from relatively culturally modern origins should have chosen St. Petersburg.

The migration variable used to study this has the same form as the variable for the distribution of migrants between the two major cities and the rest of European Russia. For Province A, for each sex, it is the number of persons born in Province A who in 1897 lived in Moscow per 1000 persons born in Province A who in 1897 lived in either Moscow or St. Petersburg. In other words, it is the conditional probability that a migrant chose Moscow as a destination, given he migrated to either Moscow or St. Petersburg.

The correlations appear in columns 5 and 6 of Table 6. Although the correlations with other migration rates are generally negative, except in one case, they are not statistically significant, supporting the idea that neither city was intrinsically more "modern" than the other. The correlations with workers in secondary industry per 1000 are significant and, as expected, positive. The correlations with literacy are negative but quite close to zero. The correlations with soil fertility are positive. The high soil fertility provinces were generally closer to Moscow than to St. Petersburg. The correlations with natural r are insignificant and are of opposite signs for the two sexes, indicating that population pressure was not a differentiating cause of migration to these two cities. As expected, which city was closer seems to have been an important factor, as indicated by the strong negative coefficients for the percentage St. Petersburg was closer than Moscow.

The multiple regressions appear in columns 5 and 6 of Table 7. The multiple R^2 values are reasonably high. As expected, the coefficient for workers in secondary industry is positive and significant for males. Thus, although industrial modernization of the origin did not relate in the expected way to migration rates to advanced destinations generally, it may serve to differentiate between advanced destinations of different types. Males from industrially advanced origins do seem to have chosen the industrially advanced destination. The coefficients for literacy are negative, as expected, but are not significant at the .05 level. Natural r remains insignificant, as expected. In the multiple regressions, the coefficients for soil fertility remain positive but become insignificant. The coefficients for the distance variable remain negative and significant for both sexes.[9] Although which city was closer did affect the

[9] A number of other forms of explanatory variables were used in order to investigate the sensitivity of the results to the exact form of the independent variables. For the agricultural variable, the proportion of males whose primary occupation was agriculture

choice of destination, other characteristics of the two cities as related to characteristics of provinces of birth were important, especially for males.

CONCLUSIONS

First consider the results for the hypotheses as stated at the beginning of the chapter:

Migration rates to culturally modern destinations are higher the greater the level of cultural modernization of the origin both in terms of absolute rates and in terms of migration to the modern destinations relative to migration rates or the less modern destinations.—Confirmed both absolutely and relatively for migration to Moscow and St. Petersburg as opposed to the rest of European Russia.

Migration rates to industrially modern destinations are higher the greater the level of industrial modernization of the origin, both in terms of absolute migration rates and migration rates to modern destinations elative to migration rates to less industrially modern destinations.— Confirmed only for the distribution of males between Moscow and St. Petersburg Cities. Refuted in all other cases.

Migration rates to industrially or culturally modern destinations will be higher, the less important agriculture is at the origin as a sole source of support.—Confirmed for the distribution of migrants between the two cities and rest of European Russia and for females to the two cities. Not supported otherwise.

Population pressure at an origin is not a major positive cause of migration to industrially or culturally modern destinations.—Confirmed in all cases.

The level of modernization of the origin affects migration rates to modern destinations positively apart from the tendency of persons possessing modern characteristics to migrate with a higher probability than persons without modern characteristics.—Supported for St. Petersburg 1869, especially for females.

---

was tried in place of the soil fertility variable, as was the proportion of males whose primary occupation was in agriculture who had an auxiliary occupation. The growth rate of the population and the density of the population were also tried in place of the rate of natural increase as a population pressure variable. Other forms of the distance variable were also used. Distance (rather than the logarithm) and also the reciprocal of the square of distance were tried instead of the natural logarithm of distance. Also for the allocation of migrants between the two cities, the arbitrary number of units of distance which the origin was closer to St. Petersburg City was also tried. None of these modifications made any substantial difference in the results.

The strong relationship between the literacy of origins and migration rates to Moscow and St. Petersburg counters the concept of migrants as country bumpkins. Although the migrants may appear naive compared to urban natives, they tend to come from the relatively more culturally advanced places among all possible origins. The insignificance of natural r as a cause for migration also counters the concept of destitute migrants streaming to the city due to intolerable crowding at their origin. The significance of industrial modernization of the origin in differentiating between Moscow and St. Petersburg as destinations for males gives some support to the contention that there are separate cultural and industrial factors in modernization. Only further research can determine to what extent these patterns are general and to what extent they may have been peculiar to nineteenth century European Russia.

REFERENCES

Anderson, Barbara A. (1974). *Internal migration in a modernizing society: The case of late nineteenth century European Russia*. Ph.D. dissertation, Princeton University.

Bendix, Reinhard (1967). "Preconditions of Development: A Comparison of Japan and Germany," in R. P. Dore (ed.), *Aspects of Social Change in Modern Japan*. Princeton: Princeton University Press.

Black, Cyril E. (1966). *The Dynamics of Modernization*. New York: Harper & Row.

Carroll, John J. (1970). "The Family in a Time of Change," in John J. Carroll (ed.), *Philippine Institutions*, p. 12 Manila: Solidaridad Publishing House.

de Tegoborskii, Michael L. (1972). *Commentaries on the Productive Forces of Russia, Volume I*. New York: Johnson Reprint, Reprinted from 1855 publication (London: Longman).

Geertz, Clifford (1963). *Agricultural Involution: The Process of Ecological Change in Indonesia*. Berkeley: University of California Press.

Goldstein, Sidney (1973). "The Effect of Broken Marriage on Fertility Levels in Thailand." Paper at annual meeting of The Population Association of America, New Orleans, unpublished.

Grubel, H. G. and A. D. Scott (1969). "The International Flow of Human Capital," in M. Blaug (ed.), *Economics of Education 2*. Middlesex, England: Penguin.

Inkeles, Alex and David Smith (1974). *Becoming Modern*. Cambridge: Harvard University Press.

Jorgenson, D. W. (1961). "The Development of the Dual Economy." *Economic Journal 71*: 309–334.

Levy, Jr., Marion J. (1966). *Modernization and the Structure of Societies*. Princeton: Princeton University Press.

Levy, Jr., and Marion, J. (1972). *Modernization: Latecomers and Survivors*. New York: Basic Books.

Lewis, W. Arthur (1955). *The Theory of Economic Growth*. Homewood: Irwin.

Long, Larry H. (1973). "Migration Differentials by Education and Occupation: Trends and Variations." *Demography 10*:243–258.

Myrdal, Gunnar (1968). *Asian Drama: An Inquiry into the Poverty of Nations.* New York: Pantheon.

Parker, W. H. (1969). *An Historical Geography of Russia.* Chicago: Aldine.

Rashin, A. G. (1940). *Formirovanie Promishlennogo Proletariata v Rossii.* Moscow: Sotzekliz.

Rashin, A. G. (1956). *Naseleniia Rossii na 100 Let.* Moscow: Gosstatizdat.

Russia, Tzentral'nyi Statisticheskii Komitet (1872). *Sanktpeterburg po Perepis Dekabry 1869 Goda.* St. Petersburg: A. B. Tipo-Lit.

Russia, Tzentral'nyi Statisticheskii Komitet (1905a). *Raspredlenie Rabochix i Prislygi po Gryppam Zanyiti i po Mesty Rozdeniia po Osnovanyi Dannykh Pervoi Vseobschei Perepisi Naseleniia Rossiskoi Imperii 28, Yanvaria 1897 Goda.* St. Petersburg: Tipo-Lit.

Russia, Tzentral'nyi Statisticheskii Komitet (1905b). *Obschi Svod po Imperii Rezul'tatov Razvabotki Dannykh Pervoi Vseobschei Perepisi Naseleniia, Proizvedennoi 28 Yanvaria 1897 Goda.* St. Petersburg: Tipo lit.

Simmel, Georg (1960). "The Metropolis and Mental Life," in C. Wright Mills (ed.), *Images of Man.* New York: Braziller.

Sinha, J. N. (1974). "Population Growth and Structural Changes in the Labor Force." Paper at annual meeting of the Population Association of America, New York, unpublished.

Thomas, Brinley (1969). "Brain Drain Again," in M. Blaug (ed.), *Economics of Education 2.* Middlesex, England: Penguin Books: 241–249.

Todaro, Michael P. (1969). "A Model of Labor Migration and Unemployment in Less Developed Countries." *American Economic Review LIX:* 138–148.

Wrigley, E. A. (1969). *Population and History.* New York: McGraw-Hill.

A Repertory of Stable Populations

M. DEMONET
School of Advanced Studies in the Social Sciences

J. DUPÂQUIER
Laboratory of Historical Demography

H. LE BRAS
National Institute of Demographic Studies

In the course of 1974, we assembled a repertory of stable populations (to be published by the French National Institute for Demographic Studies). The repertory consists of a collection of imaginary populations simulated on a computer by combining three series of hypotheses relative to nuptiality, fertility, and mortality. Each combination generated a well-defined population structure, which was then the object of a detailed description. The purpose is to allow scholars to make relevant comparisons with real populations and to recognize any similarities that may exist.

The repertory has been designed as a tool for demographic historians, or more generally for those who have only incomplete or faulty data. It does not claim, however, to be a universal key to the study of populations, and certainly not in a period of "demographic explosion." It is based on Lotka's stable population theory, and on the development of demographic analysis (see Keyfitz, 1968). The latter made it possible to define basic parameters of population change and to provide their mathematical expressions. If the distribution by age and sex of a population and its fertility and mortality schedules are known, we can predict, to the digit, its course for a period, however long, in the future, and the age distribution it will reach, provided the two following conditions are fulfilled:

1. There is no change whatsoever in either fertility or mortality.
2. The population is closed (there is no migration).

Things are not so simple in practice, because all societies regulate their fertility by the social phenomenon of marriage. Although illegitimate fertility is not always negligible (6 or 7% of all births in France), the combination of a nuptiality table and a set of age-specific marital fertility rates is much more useful than overall fertility rates to describe the process of reproduction of a population. This led to the inclusion of three parameters in our computations: nuptiality, marital fertility, and mortality. Each of their combinations results in a stable population model.

In theory, it would have been necessary to take illegitimate fertility into account; this, however, would have resulted in an excessive increase in the number of combinations, and would not have changed results appreciably. Moreover, the frequency of illegitimate births is very low in traditional populations (1–3%). The user who would be reluctant to neglect them will have no problem in modifying the nuptiality table of the observed population so that the new table combined with an age distribution and a marital fertility schedule will produce a total number of births equal to the sum of legitimate births and illegitimate births.

The construction of stable population models, which is greatly facilitated by electronic computation, is not new in demography and does not offer major difficulties. The models presented here are different from others, not only by the choice of hypotheses, but by the computed characteristics. We have not restricted ourselves to elementary indices (birth, death, marriage, and net reproduction rates, and age distribution). We have tried to present all the data that a historical demographer would have observed if he were studying these populations with conventional methods: distributions of deaths by age, proportion of widows, average age at marriage, ratio of births to marriages, percentage of mothers alive at the marriage of their sons and daughters, and, most of all, distribution of families by the age of the mother and the number of live children aged less than 14 years.

This choice, which might surprise the students of present-day populations, corresponds roughly to what can be computed from conventional sources in historical demography. The documents that constitute the basis of analysis in historical demography were not assembled because of their scientific interest. Baptism, marriage, and burial registers were a response to the Catholic church's need to control the administration of sacraments; taxation rolls, hearth counts, and most nominal

lists reflected fiscal or military concerns: a better distribution of taxa-
tions, draft, and subsistence; land maps and cadastres recording the
structure of land ownership; marriage contracts and inventories after
death regulating the transmission of patrimonies. It is only through a
kind of data smuggling that historians have been able to make use of
these sources in their demographic studies.

However ingenious the methods used to extract a maximum of information from these sources, they cannot be expected to tell us everything about the functioning of historical populations. For example,
nobody has ever succeeded in constructing an acceptable life table for
the seventeenth century, nor a nuptiality table, nor a good age pyramid.
We do not even know the crude birth and death rates for the France of
Louis XIV. There was a spectacular breakthrough in the area of fertility,
thanks to the method of family reconstitution developed by Louis Henry
(see Gautier, 1958); but the complexity and slowness of the procedure
greatly limits the potential of the method so that we have good information on about 20 parishes for the seventeenth century and about 100 for
the eighteenth.

Meanwhile, we have at our disposal a great mass of statistical data
assembled by contemporary administrations or scholars. Much more
could be collected at the cost of a moderate effort. Unfortunately, these
are dirty data, rough-hewn materials that would not yield the indices
that we really want. Some are the results of more or less accurate tallies
of parish registers: e.g., yearly or monthly fluctuations in the numbers
of baptisms, marriages, or burials; collections of ages at death or at
marriage; proportions of parents alive at the marriage of their children;
frequencies of remarriages. Others originate in surveys of population
structure: distributions by sex and marital status, ratio of widows to
married women, tabulations of families by the number of dependent
children, and so on.

Analysis of these anonymous data is made difficult by their inclusion
of random or systematic errors. Some of these can be easily identified
and corrected (for instance the tendency to age heaping); others can be
recognized but are difficult to correct (for instance the underregistration
of infant deaths). Some of the results are partial, and it becomes essential to know whether they can be held representative of the whole.
Thus, it is certain that the proportions never married, computed from
the proportion of women who died after their fiftieth birthday, have
been underestimated in village monographs because single people are
more likely to migrate out than are married people.

Even if these secondary data were clean, or could be cleaned, they
would not allow us to infer the basic parameters: They are only by-

products of the great, complex demographic mixer. For example, the ratio of the number of baptisms to the number of marriages is not just a reflection of the level of marital fertility. It is influenced by mortality, which depresses it by breaking unions prematurely, and by the age distribution of the population, which may introduce a lag between the size of marrying cohorts and that of the older groups that provide the baptisms.

And indeed, the interaction between population structure and change complicates the problem. A rise of fertility like the one that occurred in France after 1945 will first cause an increase in the crude birth rate; but, until the new generation reaches reproductive ages, the rate must go down even if fertility is constant, because the size of the population increases without a parallel growth of the number of women of childbearing ages. Similarly, the crude death rate depends more on the proportion of old people than on the expectation of life itself. This is well known, and it would be pointless to add further examples.

We have attempted to make use of these secondary data through the construction of models, because we were convinced that some of these data were specific, i.e., that they could be the result of only one, two, or three combinations of the basic parameters (nuptiality, fertility, and mortality), at least in the case of stable populations. If we knew the ratio of baptisms to marriages on the one hand, and the distribution of families by number of dependent children on the other hand, might it not be possible to find a stable population with similar characteristics in the repertory, and in the process to infer some conclusions about fertility, nuptiality, and mortality?

Of course, some secondary data have no specific character; this is the case with seasonal fluctuations. Other data are poor indicators: for example, the unadjusted distribution of families by size. But we hope to find some sensitive and effective measuring devices in the demographic weaponry of historical documents. Ideally they will react differentially to variations in fertility, nuptiality, or mortality. But this can only be assessed by testing. We have thus discovered that the ratio of births to marriages gave a better—i.e., more specific—measure of legitimate fertility than did the birth rate. Our repertory therefore finds another justification in providing a test of demographic indices. We hope to be able to go further in the near future, and to investigate what relationship links secondary and primary data, basic parameters, and observable results.

This approach seems more reliable than that which would attempt to construct models directly from secondary data. It is very difficult to provide a system of equations that will link secondary data without passing through the basic parameters. The resulting model would be a hybrid, somewhat like a clock with missing gears, which would function only by manual prodding.

The main problem consisted in the choice of hypotheses. In principle, one could have combined all known nuptiality tables with all fertility schedules and life tables. Such a publication would have filled thousands of pages and missed the mark. The fact is that almost all the available tables are provided by developed countries of today, with fairly similar characteristics. High-mortality and early-marriage regimes would hardly have been represented; nor would have historical populations. The adopted solution was quite different: Take extreme cases and fill in intermediary situations by interpolation.

As far as fertility was concerned, we had first resolved to use age-specific marital fertility schedules. The latest German data (both from the German Democratic Republic and from the German Federal Republic) had provided the minimal variant; the example of the Hutterites and the French Canadians in the early eighteenth century gave the maximal variant and three intermediary situations were defined by interpolation. But experience demonstrated that this method led to misleading conclusions about the distribution of families as a function of the age of the mother. This is so because the timing of family formation varies greatly between a system of natural fertility and one based on birth control. It became necessary to complicate the model, and this led H. Le Bras to the exploration of new avenues of research; this will be the subject of separate publications.

Mortality hypotheses raised another type of problem. There are few usable tables for historical populations: Almost all of them had a lower expectation of life than present-day populations. Moreover, the relationship between the mortality of children and that of adults seems to have been different from period to period and population to population. We decided to use a system of model life tables, specifically that of Lederman (1969). His network No. 1 has an enormous advantage over the United Nations tables, or over those of Coale and Demeny: It has two entries, the probability of dying for children under 5, and that for adults between 45 and 65.

The following extreme values were chosen for the probabilities of dying under 5:

1. At one extreme, 20 per 1000, corresponding to the average of the country most advanced in the prevention of mortality. This record can hardly be improved further; our results would not be modified if it were.

2. At the other extreme, 650 per 1000; this implies an infant mortality rate on the order of 380 per 1000 for boys and 350 per 1000 for girls.

The intervening levels are based first on a geometric progression: 50 per 1000, 100 per 1000, 200 per 1000; then on an arithmetic progression: 350 per 1000, and 500 per 1000 to avoid excessive jump and provide intermediate reference points. The following values were retained for adult mortality between 45 and 65 years: 120, 150, 200, 300, 450, and 600 per 1000.

The last available child mortality rate for the French population is 22 per 1000, close to the minimum; at the other extreme, there were two reference points: 418 per 1000 according to Halley's table, 465 per 1000 according to Wargentin's. The decision to continue up to 600 aimed at covering the entire conceivable historical experience.

With these two sets of hypotheses, it appeared unnecessary to look for all possible combinations, since there is no complete independence between infant and adult mortality. The 12 following combinations were considered:

	$_5q_0$	$_{20}q_{45}$
1	0.020	0.120
2	0.050	0.120
3	0.050	0.150
4	0.100	0.150
5	0.100	0.200
6	0.200	0.200
7	0.200	0.300
8	0.350	0.300
9	0.350	0.450
10	0.500	0.450
11	0.500	0.600
12	0.650	0.600

It will be observed that the last combination represents an extreme case, and that the survival of the population can only be ensured by nuptiality and marital fertility close to the maximum. The life tables corresponding to these 12 combinations have been computed by H. Le Bras for single years of age.

Nuptiality is one of the weak points in our model—and in all demographic models. The analysis of nuptiality offers specific difficulties, because it is an "open" phenomenon confronting two groups—marriageable men and marriageable women—with numbers by age, and chances of meeting a partner that may significantly differ.

Since our study is restricted to stable populations characterized by regular age distributions, it seemed that the phenomenon could be described by female nuptiality tables and cross-tabulations of ages at marriage from which male nuptiality would be computed at a later stage. The cross-tabulations of ages at marriage were computed by H. Le Bras with lags and frequency distributions that varied by age of the spouse. The female nuptiality tables were computed by M. Demonet from A. J. Coale's model patterns (see Coale, 1971).

The extreme values were close to those observed for Ireland in 1936 (youngest age at first marriage, 17.5 years; proportions never marrying, 25%; very slow pace, 1) and for India in 1960 (youngest age at first marriage, 14.3; proportions never marrying, 1%; very rapid pace, .33). The three intermediate variants were computed by linear interpolation between these values. Here are the average ages at first marriage in the five variants:

1	29.02
2	26.33
3	23.60
4	20.87
5	18.18

Remarriages introduce an additional difficulty. They have never been systematically studied. In addition to age at widowhood, mortality, and the number of dependent children, one would have to take into account the frequency of, and the interval before, a remarriage. The latter factors are a function of the marriage market and of regional customs. Similarly, we had to neglect divorces, de facto separations, and polygamy; these areas do not lend themselves to absolute generalizations. A rough approximation had to do, so we assigned the same probabilities of marriage to the widows as to single girls, and twice the probabilities of single boys to the widowers.

Unfortunately, such a rule cannot be applied to most stable populations with a high nuptiality. After considering the differences in ages at marriage by sex, and excess male mortality, it was obvious that the number of male candidates for marriage was too small for that of females derived from the selected nuptiality table. In fact, the problem is solved in most populations with very high female nuptiality (in the Middle East, North Africa, or South Asia) either by the interdiction of widow remarriage (India), by polygyny, or by the custom of repudiation (the latter interpreted as sequential polygyny).

Since we could not diversify our models so that they would fit any cultural situation, we kept only those combinations that were compatible with the nuptiality rules defined. Let us mention in passing that the introduction of divorce (frequently followed by remarriage) would in-

TABLE 963
HYPOTHESES : LIFE TABLE   9
             FERTILITY TABLE   6
             NUPTIALITY TABLE 3

1) CORRESPONDING STABLE POPULATION

AGES	MEN				WOMEN				TOTAL
	SINGLE	MARRIED	WID.	TOTAL	SINGLE	MARRIED	WID.	TOTAL	
0	1754	0	0	1754	1708	0	0	1708	3462
1	1521	0	0	1521	1501	0	0	1501	3023
2	1397	0	0	1397	1378	0	0	1378	2775
3- 7	6308	0	0	6308	6186	0	0	6186	12495
8-12	5681	0	0	5681	5553	0	0	5553	11235
13-17	5195	11	0	5207	5035	25	0	5061	10268
18-22	4079	633	7	4720	3510	1033	14	4559	9279
23-27	2289	1860	46	4196	1497	2465	90	4054	8250
28-32	1072	2500	92	3665	713	2683	187	3583	7248

304

33-37	586	2498	144	3229	468	2403	283	3156	6386
38-42	413	2191	215	2820	367	2012	388	2768	5589
43-47	331	1801	290	2424	311	1608	497	2417	4841
48-52	273	1417	351	2042	268	1233	591	2093	4135
53-57	222	1058	389	1670	226	891	654	1773	3443
58-62	173	732	398	1304	184	588	671	1445	2749
63-67	126	452	374	953	141	339	625	1106	2060
68-72	83	235	310	629	98	159	510	768	1397
73-77	46	94	211	352	58	56	344	459	811
78-82	21	26	110	158	28	13	182	224	383
83 AND OVER	8	5	49	62	12	1	85	100	162
TOTAL	31588	15518	2994	50101	29251	15518	5128	49899	100000

2) DISTRIBUTION OF DEATHS BY AGE

AGES	MEN	WOMEN	TOTAL
0	16370	13792	30163
1	5201	5018	10219
2	2217	2310	4528
3-7	3146	3370	6517
8-12	1124	1233	2357
13-17	1041	1246	2288
18-22	1506	1623	3130
23-27	2007	1694	3701
28-32	1817	1598	3416
33-37	1480	1488	2969

3) GENERAL FERTILITY RATE

RATE
0.0000
0.0570
0.2441
0.3095
0.2843

4) INDICES

CRUDE BIRTH RATE	:	0.0418
CRUDE DEATH RATE	:	0.0295
INFANT MORTALITY RATE	:	0.2130
NUPTIALITY RATE	:	-0.0078
GROSS REPRODUCTION RATE	:	2.8687
NET REPRODUCTION RATE	:	1.4728
MEAN AGE AT FIRST MARRIAGE - BOYS	:	26.6614
- GIRLS	:	24.0379
PROPORTION OF REMARRIAGES (1)	:	0.0518
PROPORTION OF WIDOWS (2)	:	0.2484

38-42	1617	1389	3006	0.1928
43-47	1667	1300	2967	0.0741
48-52	1748	1322	3070	0.0162
53-57	1859	1491	3351	
58-62	1948	1706	3655	
63-67	1957	1901	3858	
68-72	1863	1974	3838	
73-77	1515	1739	3255	
78-82	958	1218	2176	
83 AND OVER	613	914	1528	
TOTAL	51664	48336	100000	

PROPORTION OF DEFINITIVE CELIBACIES

    - BOYS : 0.1329

    - GIRLS : 0.1278

RATIO OF THE NUMBER OF BIRTHS

    TO THAT OF MARRIAGES : 5.3555

PROPORTION OF MOTHERS SURVIVING

    -AT SON'MARRIAGE : 62.0793

    -AT DAUGHTER'MARRIAGE : 67.5513

(1) AS A RATIO OF THE TOTAL NUMBER OF MARRIAGES

(2) AS A RATIO OF EVER-MARRIED WOMEN

307

5) DISTRIBUTION OF FAMILIES BY SIZE AND AGE OF THE WOMAN

AGE OF WOMAN	PROPORTION OF FAMILIES WITH FOLLOWING NUMBER OF LIVE CHILDREN							DISTRIBUTION OF CHILDREN
	0	1	2	3	4	5 OR MORE	TOTAL	
UNDER 23 YRS	5043	671	129	14	0	0	5859	502
23-27	7465	3506	1918	767	229	60	13948	6306
28-32	4446	3393	3236	2350	1333	898	15659	15955
33-37	2241	2077	2671	2710	2204	2754	14659	23603
38-42	1736	1438	2077	2397	2204	3242	13096	23697
43-47	2185	1669	2093	2078	1636	1822	11485	17067
48-52	3533	2016	1879	1325	729	469	9954	8938
53-57	5275	1624	932	406	142	52	8434	3226
58-62	6077	554	183	47	9	1	6873	838
TOTAL	38005	16951	15122	12098	8489	9302	100000	100000

PROPORTION 0 TO 14   37.2134
PROPORTION 15 TO 64   58.8767
PROPORTION 65 AND OVER 3.9099

troduce no important bias in the tables, except as far as the nuptiality indices are concerned.

Finally, because this repertory is meant as a working instrument, and not as a toy for demographers, we have also eliminated all nonrealistic combinations (resulting in net reproduction rates of less than .7 or of more than 3). This brought the number of tables from a theoretical total of 420 to 226.

We present a sample table to illustrate the range of information that is provided.

We hope that this repertory will be of use not only to population historians, but also to those who work with incomplete data, and perhaps as a teaching device. We intend to use it to analyze the demographic meaning of what we called secondary data, including crude birth and death rates.

REFERENCES

Coale, Ansley J. (1971). "Age Patterns of Marriage," *Population Studies,* Vol. 25, No. 2 (July), pp. 193–214.

Gautier, Etienne and Louis Henry (1958). *La Population de Crulai.* Paris: Presses Universitaires de France.

Keyfitz, Nathan (1968). *Introduction to the Mathematics of Population.* Reading, Massachusetts: Addison-Wesley.

Lederman, Sully (1969). *Nouvelles Tables-Types de Mortalite.* Cahier No. 53, Institut National d'Etudes Demographiques. Paris: Presses Universitaires de France.

Can Anything Be Said about Demographic Trends When Only Aggregate Vital Statistics Are Available?*

MASSIMO LIVI BACCI

University of Florence

1. THE PROBLEM

In this chapter I shall reconsider a problem that intrigued the first demographers. Can anything be said about demographic trends when only vital statistics are available? Is it possible to estimate the level of fertility, mortality, or nuptiality when births, deaths, and marriages are known, but a reliable estimate of the size of the population is missing? Demographers of the old times—Petty and Graunt, Halley and Sussmilch, and many others—based many of their findings on the assumption of the existence of fixed, or relatively fixed, ratios of births, deaths, and marriages to the population. Whenever the ratio could be estimated, generally by analogy, and the number of vital events was known, then the level of the population could be easily calculated. The

---

* This chapter presents some of the results obtained during my visit at the Office of Population Research, Princeton University, in the first half of 1974. I wish to express my gratitude to many friends and colleagues at the Office of Population Research and in particular to its director, Ansley Coale, for encouraging me in pursuing my research.

The hypothesis and methodologies presented here are still in the experimental stage. They need extensive testing, both on historical material and through simulation models. This by no means justifies errors in the logic of the procedures or the interpretation of the results. However, when an attempt at breaking new ground is made, the first priority should be that of stimulating the debate even at the price of attracting criticism.

advance in the collection of statistics, particularly census statistics, soon showed that the conditions of stability and analogy on which many findings were based were not fulfilled. Ratios and rates could be computed by referring vital events to census statistics and the interest of demographers turned to other matters.

In many instances, however, the demographer may not be in the ideal situation for carrying on his analysis. The combination of census and vital statistics, very common in the developed countries during the twentieth century, is as rare in developing nations as in premodern populations. In the first case, census statistics are often available, but vital statistics are lacking or unreliable. The reverse is true for premodern populations of Europe: vital data were frequently collected by the parish priests, but censuses were rare and incomplete.

During the last two decades, demographers have struggled to develop methodologies for inferring demographic trends from census statistics. Models based on stable or quasi-stable techniques of analysis, combined with a skillful use of census data, have enabled demographers to estimate levels and trends of fertility and mortality with a good degree of precision. Thanks to these models, much more is now known about the demography of the developing countries than the use of traditional techniques would have permitted. The application of these techniques to historical demography has been advocated in several instances and would probably increase our knowledge of the past (van de Walle, 1972).

On the other hand, often little use is made of the very rich historical material accumulated by the continuous and meticulous work of the parish priests. For many areas and cities of Europe continuous series of births, deaths, and marriages exist from the sixteenth century. In some cases data have been published; in others, they still await a patient but not impossible work of collection. Always, demographers have paid little attention to them whenever population statistics were missing. My aim is to show that these series can provide precious indications as to the levels and trends of nuptiality, mortality, and fertility. What are needed are long, annual series of vital events. Although this task might be easier when a population is closed, it is not essential to make the assumption of its stability.

2. AN INDICATOR OF THE TIMING OF MARRIAGE

2.1

The years 1772 and 1773 were years of severe mortality in Sweden (Sundbärg, 1907). The number of deaths rose from an average of 55,000 in 1767–1771 to 76,000 in 1772 and 105,000 in 1773, falling then to slightly less than 50,000 in the following 5 years. The adverse conditions affected also the level of births that, from an average of 68,000 in 1767–1771, fell to 59,000 in 1772 and 51,000 in 1772, rising again to the normal level of 69,000 in 1773–1777. Common sense suggests that the small size of the 1772–1773 cohorts must have depressed the number of marriages in the two cohorts, under the hypothesis of relatively stable mortality. Since the age distribution of marriages is also highly concentrated around the modal age at marriage, it is likely that the low number of births in the years 1772–1773 had produced a lower than normal number of marriages toward the end of the century. Inspection of the series of marriages shows that this is the case: The number of marriages falls from 19,000 in 1794–1799 to 17,000 in 1799–1801, and rises again to 19,500 in 1802–1806.

Are the two fluctuations—in births and 27 years later in marriages—related one to the other? Inspection of long series of births and marriages for various countries reveals a number of instances in which peaks or hollows in the number of births due to exceptional reasons (bad or good harvests, the end or the beginning of an epidemic or of a war, etc.) are reflected in peaks and hollows in the number of marriages after a number of years reasonably close to the expected modal age at marriage of the cohort. But, on the other hand, fluctuations of marriages are also caused by factors other than the numerical dimensions of the birth cohorts coming of age, so that any coincidence in the nature of the fluctuations of births and of marriages may be spurious.

2.2

The hypothesis to be tested is that a shortage in one or more birth cohorts will cause, with a lag close to the modal age at marriage of females, a shortage in the number of marriages, and, conversely, a peak in births will generate a peak in marriages. More generally, fluctuations of births will be reproduced, with a certain lag of time, in the fluctuations of marriages. Two main considerations have to be kept in mind:

1. That each marriage cohort (marriages concluded in any given year) is formed by the marriages of several birth cohorts (i.e., birth cohorts born 15 to 40 or 50 years before). Therefore fluctuations of births will be reproduced in the fluctuations of marriages, but the latter will be dampened. The dampening effect will diminish, the more concentrated around the modal age at marriage the nuptiality schedule of each cohort is (there would be no dampening effect should everybody get married at the modal age). The reverse is also true, and the dampening effect increases the more spread out is the nuptiality schedule.

2. Fluctuations in marriages have various sources. Any crisis (an epidemic, depression, war, etc.) may produce a short-term or even a medium-term fluctuation in marriages. Fluctuations in marriages may be also imputable to changes in the "timing" of nuptiality in the various cohorts (mean age at marriage goes up or down). All these fluctuations are not produced by the fluctuations of birth cohorts and therefore introduce a spurious element. It is desirable, therefore, to eliminate the short-term fluctuations through a smoothing procedure.

In order to test the hypothesis formulated at the beginning of this section, the simplest way would be to correlate births to marriages, the latter with varying lags (for instance, between 18 and 30 years), and assume as the estimated modal age at marriage the lag yielding the highest correlation. However, this procedure does not take into account the *dampening* effects of the age distribution at marriage and does not eliminate the spurious fluctuations of marriages not imputable to the fluctuation of birth cohorts.

The suggested procedure calls, in the first place, for the elimination of the dampening effect. This can be done through a conversion of births into "hypothetical" marriages. Marriages in a given year can be expressed by the following formula:

$$M_t = \sum_{x=a}^{b} B_{t-x} \cdot P_x^t \cdot N_x^t$$

Marriages in t, (M_t), equal the sum of the products of each birth cohort times its probability of surviving to the year t, (P_x^t), combined with the probability of getting married in the year t, (N_x^t). The birth cohorts taken into consideration are from t-a to t-b, where a is the number of years corresponding to the minimum age at marriage and b is the number of years corresponding to the maximum age at which there is still a significant number of marriages (for our purpose, 40 years will be sufficient). In other words, with this procedure we do convert birth cohorts into hypothetical marriages, assuming a standard mortality and nuptiality. The series of hypothetical marriages fluctuates only because of the changes in the size of the birth cohorts, and the consequences of changes in the marriage or mortality pattern are eliminated.

In practice all this amounts to a weighted moving average of births, with weights proportional to the values $P_x \cdot N_x$. Since the minimum age at marriage is 15 and the maximum at least 40, the weighted average will involve at least 25 terms. A good number of years of the series is therefore sacrificed at the head and at the tail of the series. In practice, it will be sufficient to follow an abbreviated procedure, with a weighted average of about 10 terms, with weights proportional to the $P_x \cdot N_x$ of the ages around the modal age at marriage.[1]

Second, the series of actual marriages (to be correlated with the series of hypothetical marriages) is also smoothed with a 5-year moving average, in an attempt to minimize the influence of short-term fluctuations not imputable to the fluctuations of the birth cohorts.

Third, the percentage of change of hypothetical and actual marriages of each year over the preceding year is computed.

Fourth, a correlogram between the two series of changes in percentages is computed. The interval between "converted births" and "actual marriages" yielding the highest correlation coefficient will be taken as an estimate of the modal age at marriage.

Table 1 gives an example of the procedure employed based on Swedish data; columns 4 and 7 give the annual rates of growth of the weighted average of births (hypothetical marriages) and of the smoothed series of actual marriages; the first of the two series has been correlated with successive 10-year series of the second: 1872–1881, 1873–1882 . . . 1882–1891. The correlogram yields the highest value (.779) when births are combined with the actual marriages of 1879–1888, corresponding to a lag of 27 years.

Table 2 reports the results of a more systematic application of the method to the statistics of Tuscany. For the eight groups of birth cohorts considered, the highest values of the correlogram are reached at an assumed modal age varying between 21 and 24 years, with an average slightly higher than 22 years. The results are consistent with the expectations and with the modal age of brides at first marriage of about 23 years between 1861 and the end of the century. Similar estimates for Sweden give values of 26.2 for the 1750–1799 cohorts and of 28.0 for 1800–1859. For Norway, the estimated modal age is 25.0 for 1770–1799, 27.2 in 1800–1849, and 24.7 for 1850–1880. For both Sweden and Norway the variability of the estimates for shorter (10-year) periods is much higher than for Tuscany. The results, however, suggest that the Scandinavian populations had a higher age at marriage than the Tuscan, and

---

[1] In our calculations, the values $P_x \cdot N_x$ have been obtained in the following way: The P_x values have been derived from Coale and Demeny's (1966) model life tables, model West, $e = 35$ years. The N_x values are taken from Coale (1971, p. 200), assuming that 10% is the proportion remaining single. If we assume that the minimum age at marriage is 16, then the modal age falls at age 24. If we take the weights (in other words, the values of $P_x \cdot N_x$) corresponding to the 9 years centered on the modal age (in this case the ages from 20 to 28), we take almost 2/3 (62.3%) of the total of the weights (sum of the $P_x \cdot N_x$ from age 16 to age 56). The calculations in Table 1 consider 40 years (40 weights); the results reported in Table 2 and section 2.2 are based on weighted averages with 9 terms (9 weights).

TABLE 1
Scheme for the Computation of the Correlogram: Hypothetical Marriages Obtained by Multiplying Birth Cohorts by Appropriate First Marriage Frequencies and Survival Rates, and Actual Marriages, Sweden

Birth cohorts	Hypothetical marriages deriving from weighted average of the birth cohorts	Change of hypothetical marriages over preceding year (%)	Year	Actual[a] marriages	Percentage change of actual marriage over preceding year
1821-1860	24,750	.5	1872	27,164	3.9
1822-1861	24,883	.8	1873	28,236	2.7
1823-1862	25,077	1.2	1874	28,992	.8
1824-1863	25,385	2.8	1875	29,238	-1.3
1825-1864	26,104	2.8	1876	28,853	-1.6
1826-1865	26,833	2.0	1877	28,352	-1.0
1827-1866	27,361	1.7	1878	28,064	-1.7
1828-1867	27,828	2.1	1879	27,596	-1.0
1829-1868	28,422	1.8	1880	27,332	.4
1830-1869	28,927	.8	1881	27,447	1.2
1831-1870	29,171	.4	1882	27,784	1.5
1832-1871	29,288		1883	28,204	1.2
			1884	28,556	.5
			1885	28,693	- .9
			1886	28,448	-1.3
			1887	28,086	-1.5
			1888	27,670	-1.5
			1889	27,266	-1.6
			1890	26,840	- .6
			1891	26,671	

[a]First marriages; series smoothed with a 5-term moving average.

this is, again, in line with what we know about the marriage patterns of the two populations during the nineteenth century.

2.3

The procedure outlined in the preceding section does not claim to give precise estimates of the age pattern of nuptiality. But it is, perhaps, the only way to learn something about the age at marriage whenever any other source of information is mute. The correlation between fluctuations of births and marriages may help the demographer understand whether, in past times, the age pattern at marriage was early or late; when, during long historical periods, there has been a significant change in the marriage pattern in the same population, or appreciable differences between populations.

Although the rationale of the methodology is clear, the methodology

TABLE 2
Correlogram, Hypothetical Marriages and Actual Marriages, Tuscany, 19th Century

	Assumed modal age at marriage												Estimated modal age
	19	20	21	22	23	24	25	26	27	28	29	30	
1810–1815/1819–1824	-.013	.462	.717	.860	.226	.440	-.069	-.409	-.657	-.686	-.511	-.491	22
1820–1825/1829–1834	.558	.673	.698	.504	.340	-.033	-.424	-.671	-.689	-.569	-.321	.236	21
1830–1835/1836–1841	-.784	-.253	.422	.874	.682	.651	--	--	--	--	--	.307	22
1846–1850/1851–1856	-.377	.525	-.113	.514	.740	.688	.453	.331	-.757	-.466	-.728	-.490	23
1850–1855/1859–1864	-.572	-.314	.098	.595	.753	.706	.511	-.136	-.586	-.831	-.814	-.780	23
1860–1865/1870–1874	.620	.568	.774	.654	.474	.093	.330	-.189	-.347	-.515	-.376	-.521	21
1870–1875/1880–1884	.015	.231	-.115	-.019	-.093	.549	.101	-.103	-.412	-.646	-.479	-.377	24
1880–1885/1887–1892	.287	.414	.516	.572	.411	--	--	--	--	--	--	--	22

317

could, perhaps, undergo refinements. In the first place, it is necessary to understand what type of fluctuations have to be correlated. I have already said that these are not those of short duration (1 or 2 years, for instance), generally associated with exogenous events. What we want to measure and correlate are the medium-term deviations from the marriage trends, or, better, deviations from the trends that are imputable mainly, if not exclusively, to the changing size of cohorts reaching the age of marriage. More ought to be known as to the nature of the fluctuations in order to devise adequate techniques.

Second, there are the complex problems of the interpretation of the correlogram and of the significance of the correlation coefficients. It is also likely that cross-spectral techniques might be more powerful and suitable tools for our purposes.

Third, the interpretation of the estimated modal age is far from being crystal clear. Main among the many problems: Is it the modal age at marriage of females, or of males, or of an average of the two sexes? The hypothesis is that a shortage in a few birth cohorts (or a peak) will generate, a number of years later, a shortage of females in ages suitable for marriage and therefore a shortage of marriages. But the interconnections between the supply of males and of females in the marriage market is a very complicated one. It is true, however, that the age pattern of marriage is more concentrated among females than among males, and it is likely that fluctuations in birth cohorts are more closely reflected in the fluctuations of marriages at an interval corresponding to the modal age at marriage of females rather than the modal age of males.

We recognize, therefore, that the subject needs more investigation; what is particularly needed is more empirical evidence and the application of alternative techniques in the effort of measuring a relationship that certainly exists but is obscured by many factors.

3.   AN INDICATOR OF THE PROPORTION REMAINING SINGLE

3.1

Some further indications as to the nuptiality pattern can be gained with a different procedure. Let us make the hypothesis that mortality is zero and that everybody gets married. Then, persons born in the year t (belonging to the cohort t) will all be married during the period $t + a/t + b$, where a and b are the minimum and maximum age at marriage. In practice, the large majority of the cohort's members will get married around the modal age. If the modal age at marriage for females is, for instance, 24 years, the largest part of the female cohort will get married

20 to 29 years after birth. The standard schedule of first marriage frequencies conceived by Coale (1971, p. 200) on the basis of the Swedish experience shows that about two out of three of the cohort's first marriages take place in the 10 years centered around the modal age. The Swedish distribution is, however, very dispersed, and this proportion is much higher in other European populations.

If we consider a 10-year cohort, born in $t/(t + 9)$, we may safely assume that the majority of the cohort's members (again under the assumption of a modal age at marriage close to 24 or 25 years) will get married 25 years later, or during the period $(t + 25)/(t + 34)$. During these years, the oldest cohort, born in t, will be 25–34 years old and—assuming the standard schedule recalled earlier—about 49% of its members will get married between these two ages. The following cohorts (born in $t + 1, \ldots, t + 9$) will be younger (24–33, . . . , 16–25). The proportion of marriages taking place in each cohort 25 to 34 years after the year t is reported in Table 3.

In total, 57.6% of the members of the 10 cohorts (assumed to be equal in size) will get married during the decade $(t + 25)/(t + 34)$. If we assume a stationary state, we can also say that 57.6% of all marriages of the decade $(t + 25)/(t + 34)$ derive from the cohorts born $t/(t + 9)$ or, on the average, 25 years before. Coale's standard schedule is based on the Swedish experience with a particularly widespread age distribution of marriages; in other European populations, the proportion would rise to 2/3 to 3/4 of all marriages of the cohort.

We may now affirm that, given 10 annual cohorts of female births and assuming that no one dies and everybody reaches marriage, a majority of the cohorts' members will get married 25 to 34 years after the birth of the oldest cohort and that, during this period, the majority of the total

TABLE 3
Proportion of the First Marriage Frequencies During Different
Spans of Life: Females, Coale's Standard Schedule[a]

Age	Percentage of all marriages of the cohort	Age	Percentage of all marriages of the cohort
16–25	45.8	21–30	65.0
17–26	53.0	22–31	62.9
18–27	58.8	23–32	59.1
19–28	63.0	24–33	54.3
20–29	65.1	25–34	48.8

[a]From A. J. Coale, Age Pattern of Marriage, *Population Studies*, 25(2), 200, 1971.

number of marriages concluded will have a bride belonging to these cohorts. We may also infer that there must be a high correlation between the total number of marriages of the cohorts born in $t/(t + 9)$ and the total number of marriages concluded in $(t + 25)/(t + 34)$, and that we may indeed be justified in considering the latter as an indicator of the former.

We may now compute the difference

$$B_{t/(t+9)} - M_{(t+25)/(t+34)} = \Delta_{t/(t+9)}$$

where $\Delta_{t/(t+9)}$ represents, or is a close indicator of, those among the members of the cohort $B_{t/(t+9)}$ who do not reach marriage because (1) they die (or migrate) before marriage, or (2) they remain single. We may also say that

$$\Delta_{t/(t+9)} = \Delta^{\lambda}_{t/(t+9)} + \Delta^{\mu}_{t/(t+9)}$$

where Δ^{λ} represents those dying before the age at marriage and Δ^{μ} those remaining single. In a cohort (if the age distribution of marriages does not undergo extraordinary changes) Δ^{λ} is a constant fraction of all deaths when mortality is constant. In a population with a stable level of fertility, the proportion of total deaths occurring before age 20 or 25 is approximately constant for levels of mortality below an expectation of life at birth of 40 years.[2] Now, members of the cohort $B_{t/(t+9)}$ dying before the age at marriage (assume here that all marriages happen at the mean age) die mostly during the first 5 years of life. For instance, in a life table with an expectation of life of 30 years, about 50% of deaths occur before age 25, but almost 80% of these die before their fifth birthday. Therefore, the large majority of those born in $t/(t + 9)$ and who do not reach marriage because they die before, will die in $t/(t + 14)$. The total deaths in this period will include all deaths before the fifteenth birthday of the generation born in t, and all deaths before the fifth birthday for the generation born in $t/(t + 9)$. On the other hand, these deaths account for a considerable proportion of the total deaths of the period $t/(t + 14)$ (in stationary situations, they will account for 1/2 when $e_0 = 22.5$; 2/5 when $e_0 = 30.0$; 1/3 when $e_0 = 35$; 1/4 when $e_0 = 42.5$).

Now, if Δ^{λ} represents those who do not reach marriage because they die before, they will constitute an approximately constant proportion of

[2] The percentage of total deaths under age 25 (females, West model, stable population with a GRR of 2) is 46.3 with $e_0 = 20$; 47.1(25); 47.2(30); 46.8(35); 45.6(40); 44.2(45); and 42.0(50).

$D_{t/(t+14)}$ when fertility remains steady and mortality is high and below an expectation of life of 40. We will therefore compute:

$$\frac{\Delta_{t/(t+9)}}{D_{t/(t+9)}} = \frac{\Delta^\lambda_{t/(t+9)}}{D_{t/(t+9)}} + \frac{\Delta^\mu_{t/(t+9)}}{D_{t/(t+9)}}$$

We will call this ratio "S". Variations over time of S will be, therefore, mainly imputable to changes in the "unknown" quantity Δ^λ, or the proportion of the cohort's members not reaching marriage because they remain single.

3.2

The reader will probably contend that the series of assumptions are piled one on top of the other and that our hypothesis is based on the high correlation existing between events in a cohort or number of cohorts and events taking place in a given period of time. We have, in fact, made four assumptions:

1. That the number of marriages taking place in a 10-year cohort is closely represented by all marriages taking place in a 10-year period, on the average 25 years later;
2. that the difference between the size of the cohorts and the number of marriages 25 years later closely represent the members of the cohort who do not reach marriage;
3. that the cohort's members who do not reach marriage because they die are closely represented by those dying before age 15;
4. that the proportion dying before marriage is a constant fraction of all deaths occurring in $t/(t + 14)$.

Hypothesis 1 is affected by changes in the nuptiality schedule (the lower the dispersion about the mean, the truer the hypothesis); the validity of hypothesis 2 is linked to the validity of hypothesis 1 and, of course, to the existence of migration; hypothesis 3 is affected by the dispersion of the marriage schedule and by the changes in the marriage schedule; hypothesis 4 is true in a cohort only when mortality is stationary and, in a population, when fertility is constant and expectation of life at birth below 40 years. Furthermore, the entire set of relations is disturbed by the short-term fluctuations affecting births, marriages, and deaths.

The correspondence between marriages in the cohort and marriages in the population 25 years later and between deaths in the cohort before marriage and deaths in the population $t/(t + 14)$ can, however, be improved with some further refinement.

The first refinement consists in taking a weighted average of the marriages occurring in $(t + 25)/(t + 34)$. The weights will be proportional to the presumed incidence, on the marriages of each year, of the marriages of the members of the cohorts born in $t/(t + 9)$. However, when the number of marriages is close to stationarity, and given the low variability of the weights (see Table 3), weighted and unweighted marriages in the $(t + 25)/(t + 34)$ period give rather close values.

The second refinement regards the number of deaths in $t/(t + 14)$. Only a relatively low proportion of the deaths in each of these years proceeds from the cohorts born in $t/(t + 9)$ (for the deaths in t, cohort t; in $(t + 1)$, cohorts $t/(t + 1)$; in $t + 9$, cohorts $t/(t + 9)$, aged respectively 1–10, 2–11, . . . , 5–14). The number of deaths in $t/(t + 14)$ is, therefore, a weighted average of the annual deaths, with weights proportional to the estimated incidence, in each year, of the deaths originating from the cohorts $t/(t + 9)$ over the total number of deaths.[3]

3.3

There are two ways to prove the empirical value of this procedure. The first is through a model simulating the functional relationships among births, marriages, and deaths at given levels of fertility, nuptiality, and mortality. The model could also simulate changing trends and fluctuations.

[3] With the West model life tables, females, $e_0 = 35$, we obtain the following weights:

Years	Age of the cohorts $t/(t + 9)$	Percentage of total deaths occurring to cohorts $t/(t + 9)$
t	0	21.4
$t + 1$	0–1	27.2
$t + 2$	0–2	29.9
$t + 3$	0–3	31.5
$t + 4$	0–4	32.9
$t + 5$	0–5	33.5
$t + 6$	0–6	34.0
$t + 7$	0–7	34.6
$t + 8$	0–8	35.1
$t + 9$	0–9	35.7
$t + 10$	1–10	14.7
$t + 11$	2–11	9.3
$t + 12$	3–12	7.1
$t + 13$	4–13	5.8
$t + 14$	5–14	4.9

Given the low proportions at years $t + 10$ to $t + 14$, it may be sufficient to consider only the years t to $t + 9$.

A second and simpler model consists in applying this procedure to concrete populations of the past, for which long series of vital statistics are available, together with valid estimates of the proportion remaining single. I have followed this second way; the examination of the results will teach us something about the limits of applicability.

In Table 4 are reported the results for Sweden, cohorts 1751 to 1880. The two series (S and the proportion remaining single at age 40–45 derived from Sundbärg's estimates) show a remarkable coincidence. The proportion remaining single goes down from the initial level to a minimum for the 1791–1800 cohorts, then increases gradually, reaching a maximum with the last cohort considered. Very similar, although with the expected fluctuations, is the trend of S that shows an initial decrease (minimum in 1801–1810) and then an almost continuous increase until the last cohort considered. The correlation between the two series is .879. We may, however, observe that the increase of S for the cohorts born after the mid-nineteenth century could be due to emigration: The higher emigration is the higher is the difference between births and marriages of a given cohort and—in a regime of approximately constant mortality—the higher is S. Mortality, however, was not constant and was already slowly declining since the first decades of the nineteenth century, and a decline of mortality produces—other factors being constant—a decrease of S.

In the case of Tuscany (cohorts of 1810–1819 to 1890–1899) S does not show any visible trend, and the same is true for the proportion remaining single at age 50–54:

	1810–1819	1820–1829	1830–1839	1840–1849	1850–1859	1860–1869	1870–1879	1880–1889	1890–1899
S^a	.311	.411	.302	.343	.296	.330	.339	.301	.294
% single[b]	10.7	11.4	11.0	—	9.7	9.5	9.6	10.0	10.2

[a]The value of S is sensibly lower than for Sweden. This is due to the fact that we have considered only female births, whereas deaths are for both sexes.
[b]The values of the proportion of single females at age 50–54 are taken from the censuses of 1861, 1871, 1881, 1901, 1911, 1921, 1931, and 1936.

Again, S shows large fluctuations, with a peak in 1820–1829, but a definite trend is not visible. In other words, S and the proportion remaining single give the impression of a relative stability of the marriage pattern.

Italian statistics offer also the possibility of a cross-section test of the method using regional vital statistics. In Table 5 we show the values of S (cohorts of 1862–1871) and the corresponding proportion remaining single. It is a period of still-high fertility and mortality; the test, how-

TABLE 4
Proportions Remaining Single at Age 40-45 and Indicator S', Sweden Female Population, Cohorts 1751-1760 to 1871-1880[a]

Cohorts	Female births (1)	Weighted Marriages $t+25/t+34$ (2)	Weighted Deaths $t,t+14$ (3)	Births minus marriages $(1)-(2)$ (4)	S' $(4):(3)$ (5)	Proportion remaining single 40-45 (6)
1751-1760	32.413	15.256	26,165	17,157	.656	14.8
1761-1770	33.053	16.357	28,256	16,696	.591	14.6
1771-1780	32.903	16.301	29,286	16,602	.567	14.7
1781-1790	33.662	18.325	29,518	15,337	.520	13.5
1791-1800	37.104	20.229	29,002	16,875	.582	12.7
1801-1810	36.152	19.664	34,136	16,488	.483	14.4
1811-1820	40.275	20.065	31,255	20,210	.647	16.4
1821-1830	46.519	23.687	32,107	22,832	.711	17.8
1831-1840	46.279	27.040	33,402	19,239	.576	19.2
1841-1850	50.182	25.674	33,848	24,508	.724	20.4
1851-1860	58.276	28.032	38,813	30,244	.779	21.8
1861-1870	62.516	27.078	40,118	35,438	.883	23.0
1871-1880	65.260	29.610	39,705	35,650	.898	23.2

[a]From G. Sundbarg, *Bevolkerungsstatistik Schwedens 1750-1900*, Stockholm, 1907.

[b]The proportion single in the cohort 1751-1760 is an average of the percent single at age 40-45 for 1795 and 1800, etc.

TABLE 5
Proportion Remaining Single at Age 50-54 (Females, 1911 Census) and S, Cohorts
1862-1871, Italian Regions

Regions	S	Proportion remaining single
Piemonte	.684	14.2
Liguria	.707	15.6
Lombardia	.647	12.5
Emilia	.643	10.0
Toscana	.678	9.5
Marche	.603	9.2
Umbria	.580	8.3
Abruzzi	.553	5.6
Campania	.592	10.8
Puglia	.590	8.1
Basilicata	.634	7.4
Calabria	.581	9.9
Sicilia	.610	9.4
Sardegna	.590	9.9
Italy	*.627*	*10.9*

ever, is disturbed by emigration, rapidly increasing at the end of the century, particularly in the south.

The correlation between the two series is .758 (57% of the variance), not very high, but significant, given the disturbing effects of emigration.

Finally, Table 6 reports the results of the calculations for S for the United Kingdom—nine 10-year cohorts for England and Wales, three for Scotland, and two for Ireland. The correlation between S and the proportion remaining single is extremely close: .918 for England and Wales and, when Ireland and Scotland are included, the time and cross-section correlation increases to .952, explaining 91% of the variance. Here, again, the bias introduced by emigration cannot be measured, although partially offset by the decreasing mortality in the second half of the nineteenth century.

The empirical relationships examined in this section work in a satisfactory way. More extensive tests, with time-series and cross-section applications, would be very useful. In many instances, in the examples given, the second half of the nineteenth century is not suitable for testing our hypothesis because of the fall of mortality and the rise of mobility. The two tendencies have opposite effects on S, but they certainly do not completely offset each other. Furthermore, we are not in a position to estimate the proportion remaining single from S. The conclusion is that S may be used in order to infer the long-run tendencies of the proportion remaining single in a population, or in order to

TABLE 6
Proportion Remaining Single at Age 45-54 and Indicator S, British Isles, Circa XIX
Century[a]

Cohorts	Female births	Female deaths t,t + 14	Marriages t + 25/t + 34	Births minus marriages	S	Proportion remaining single age 45-54	
			England and Wales[b]				
1780-1789	237.0	190.8	84.0	153.0	.401	11.5[c]	(1851)
1790-1799	262.1	195.3	97.3	164.8	.422	12.2	(1851)
1800-1809	283.5	195.2	111.6	171.9	.440	11.9	(1861)
1810-1819	321.0	208.7	116.5[d]	204.5	.490	12.1	(1871)
—	—	—	—	—	—	—	—
1839-1848	259.0	186.9	186.5	72.5	.388	12.9	(1891)
1849-1858	306.5	208.7	197.0	109.5	.525	13.6	(1901)
1859-1868	357.6	232.3	211.3	146.3	.630	15.8	(1911)
1869-1878	411.5	248.7	250.2	161.3	.649	16.4	(1921)
1879-1888	436.5	259.3	170.6	165.9	.640	16.4	(1931)
			Scotland				
1855-1864	51.1	33.8	25.6	25.5	.754	20.8	(1911)
1865-1874	58.5	37.3	29.4	29.1	.780	20.7	(1921)
1875-1884	61.4	37.4	32.0	29.4	.786	21.5	(1931)
			Ireland				
1864-1873	70.9	46.5	22.0	48.9	1.952	24.0	(1911)
1874-1883	64.4	46.7	22.6	41.8	.895	26.9	(1926)

[a]From B. R. Mitchell, Abstract of British Historical Statistics, Cambridge, 1962.

[b]For England and Wales, the modern series of vital statistics start in 1838
(Annual Report of the Registrar General). Data source for 1780 to 1840 is the
Parish Register Abstract. Calculation for the 1780-1819 period have been based
on the statistics from the first source.

[c]Age group 55-64.

[d]1835-1840.

separate, within a population, areas with significantly different nuptiality patterns.

4.   AN ESTIMATE OF MORTALITY BEFORE MARRIAGE

4.1

Let us now assume that we know something about the marriage
pattern. The most likely situation is one in which, by analogy or with
the help of scanty statistical or historical information, we know that the
typical pattern is one of early or late marriage and that the proportion

remaining single is low or high. Let us also suppose that this information is confirmed by the systematic cross-analysis of fluctuations of births and marriages and by the levels and trends of the indicator of the proportion remaining single, S. In this situation, can anything be said about the pattern of mortality?

Recalling the formula reported in 2.2 we can say that

$$M_t = \sum_{x=a}^{b} B_{t-x} \cdot P_x^t \cdot N_x^t$$

The number of marriages in a given year equals the sum of the products of the various birth cohorts times the appropriate marriage and survival rates. Let us advance the usual hypothesis that all members of each cohort will avoid death but will marry. The sum of the marriage frequencies (N) in any given cohort will be 1; similarly, the survival rate to the various ages will be equal to 1. In this case,

$$\overline{M}_t = \sum_{x=a}^{b} B_{t-x} \cdot \overline{N}_x^t$$

Let us apply this formula to the various birth cohorts likely to produce marriages in the year t (we will also make the hypothesis of a stable marriage pattern in the various cohorts), choosing an appropriate nuptiality schedule likely to fit the experience of the population. The ratio $M_t/\overline{M}_t$, between the actual marriages and the hypothetical marriages (nobody remains single and nobody dies) is affected by the incidence of the following three factors:

1. the level of mortality between birth and marriage—the lower the mortality, the lower the ratio;
2. the age pattern of nuptiality. A late pattern implies—with constant mortality—a lower proportion of survivors to the age of marriage. Given, however, the low mortality risks in the young adult ages and the relatively low variability of the age pattern of marriage, the importance of this factor is relatively weak;
3. the proportion remaining single; the higher this proportion, the lower the ratio.

It is possible to compute model tables expressing the ratio of first marriages to births as a function of the level of mortality (model life tables already exist); of the mean age at marriage;[4] of the proportion remaining single.

---

[4] Actually, the proportion surviving to the age at marriage is a weighted average of the l_x between the minimum and the maximum age at marriage with weights proportional to

4.2

Table 7 reports the calculations of the ratio of actual to hypothetical marriages for Tuscany in the nineteenth century. The standard distribution of first marriage frequencies (O being the lowest age at marriage, see Coale, 1971) is reported in column 4 and multiplied by the appropriate birth cohorts (column 2). The number of hypothetical marriages (column 6) is then matched with the appropriate number of actual marriages (column 8) and the ratio computed (column 9). The value of the ratio is close to .5, which, given the prevailing marriage pattern, corresponds to an expectation of life at birth of about 35 years. The procedure for the estimate of the expectation of life will become clear through the inspection of Table 8, where we have reported the ratios of actual to hypothetical marriages for cohorts having a typical nuptiality age-pattern (mean age at marriage 23.5 years), different mortality levels (e_0 from 20 to 50 years, West model life tables) and different values of the proportion remaining single (from 0 to 30%).

The ratio of actual to hypothetical marriages for Tuscany was, during the nineteenth century, close to .5, the proportion remaining single about 10%, and the mean age at marriage between 23 and 24 years. The corresponding estimate of e_0 is about 35 years, an estimate consistent with the late nineteenth century experience.[5]

4.3

It is interesting to note that, given a fixed age pattern of nuptiality, the same ratio of actual to hypothetical marriages may be determined by different combinations of levels of mortality and proportion remaining single.

Let us assume that $M/\overline{M}$ for a given population yields a value of .350. This ratio (mean age at marriage, 23.5) may be the result of an e_0 of 20 and a proportion remaining single of zero, or of an e_0 of 30 years and a proportion remaining single of 30% (and of the appropriate intermediate values). If we know nothing about the marriage pattern (0 and 30% represent the lower and upper limit of the known European demographic history) then our calculations are not of great help, since the

---

the marriage frequencies. This weighted average of l_x would coincide with the value of e at the mean age at marriage only in the absence of mortality in the ages at which marriage is contracted. Owing to the characteristics of the l_x curve, the proportion of the cohort's members surviving to the age at marriage corresponds to a value of l_x between 1 and 2 years older than the mean age at marriage.

[5] The expectation of life at birth for the Italian population (1881–1882, national life table) was 35 years.

TABLE 7

Proportions of Birth Cohorts Surviving to Marriage Tuscany, XIX Century

Years	Female live births	Standard schedule of first marriage frequencies (per 1000 women) (3)	(4)	Hypothetical marriages Cohorts from which they derive (5)	Number (6)	Corresponding Actual marriages[a] Year (7)	Number (8)	Proportion of births surviving to marriage[b] (8) : (6) (9)
1810-1814	114,791	35-39	1.09	1795-1834	(27,961)[c]	1845-1849	14,041	.502
1815-1819	110,569	30-34	2.74	1800-1839	(29,028)[c]	1850-1854	13,372	.461
1820-1824	143,790	25-29	5.50	1805-1844	(29,260)[c]	1855-1859	16,615	.568
1825-1829	153,138	20-24	12.67	1810-1849	29,295	1860-1864	16,438	.561
1830-1834	149,994	15-19	28.51	1815-1854	30,136	1865-1869	13,274	.440
1835-1839	146,130	10-14	57.85	1820-1859	31,388	1870-1874	14,465	.461
1840-1844	143,686	5-9	72.22	1825-1864	32,658	1875-1879	15,704	.480
1845-1849	155,240	0-4	19.42	1830-1869	34,613	1880-1884	16,539	.478
1850-1854	163,589			1835-1874	36,546	1885-1889	18,282	.500
1855-1859	166,734			1849-1879	37,499	1890-1894	17,578	.469
1860-1864	182,914			1845-1884	37,646	1895-1899	16,836	.447
1865-1869	194,192			1850-1889	37,531	1900-1904	18,035	.481
1870-1874	190,843			1855-1894	38,096	1905-1909	20,668	.543
1875-1879	189,155			1860-1899	38,278	1910-1914	20,574	.537
1880-1884	183,146							
1885-1889	196,655						Mean, 1845-1879 = .496	
1890-1894	192,410						Mean, 1880-1914 = .493	
1895-1899	185,683							

[a] Assuming a modal age at marriage of 22-23 years, see Table 2 last column.

[b] The computation of this ratio with first marriages only would yield values approximately 5% lower (in 1883-1886, 4.6% of brides were widows).

[c] Assuming a constant number of births for 1795-1809, equal to 114,000.

TABLE 8

Proportion of Births Surviving and Getting Married for Different Levels of Mortality Combined with Different Levels of the Proportion Remaining Single, Mean Age at Marriage = 23.5 years

e_0	Proportion remaining single (%)															
	0	2	4	6	8	10	12	14	16	18	20	22	24	26	28	30
20.0	.345	.338	.331	.324	.317	.311	.304	.297	.290	.283	.276	.269	.262	.255	.248	.242
22.5	.384	.376	.369	.361	.353	.346	.338	.330	.323	.315	.307	.300	.292	.284	.276	.269
25.0	.423	.415	.406	.398	.389	.381	.372	.364	.355	.347	.338	.330	.321	.313	.305	.296
27.5	.461	.452	.443	.433	.424	.415	.406	.396	.387	.378	.369	.360	.350	.341	.331	.323
30.0	.496	.486	.476	.466	.456	.446	.436	.427	.417	.407	.397	.387	.377	.367	.357	.347
32.5	.531	.520	.510	.499	.488	.478	.467	.457	.446	.435	.425	.414	.404	.393	.382	.372
35.0	.565	.554	.542	.531	.520	.509	.497	.486	.475	.463	.452	.441	.429	.418	.407	.396
37.5	.598	.586	.574	.562	.550	.538	.526	.514	.502	.490	.478	.466	.454	.443	.431	.419
40.0	.629	.616	.604	.591	.579	.566	.553	.541	.528	.516	.503	.491	.478	.465	.453	.440
42.5	.661	.648	.635	.621	.608	.595	.582	.568	.555	.542	.529	.516	.502	.489	.476	.463
45.0	.690	.676	.662	.649	.635	.621	.607	.593	.580	.566	.552	.538	.524	.511	.531	.483
47.5	.719	.705	.690	.676	.661	.647	.633	.618	.604	.590	.515	.561	.546	.532	.518	.503
50.0	.748	.733	.718	.703	.688	.673	.658	.643	.628	.613	.598	.583	.568	.554	.539	.524

two expectations of life at the lower and upper limits—20 and 30 years—are very much distant and represent widely differing situations. But if we have even a very unprecise estimate of the proportion remaining single (e.g., low, between 0 and 10%; medium, between 10 and 20%; and high, over 20%), then our estimate of mortality becomes more precise. If the proportion is low, e_0 will be between 20 and 22.5; if it is medium, e_0 will be between 22.5 and 26; if it is high, e_0 will be between 26 and 30. The limits of the estimates are relatively narrow, and therefore the procedure may turn out to be very useful.

When the ratio $M/\overline{M}$ rises, the error's margins increase. If the ratio is .500, and the proportion remaining single low, e_0 may vary between 30 and 34; if the same proportion is medium, e_0 will be between 34 and 39; if high, e_0 will be between 39 and 47. However, the experience of the populations of the past centuries suggests that expectations of life at birth above 40 years (and even less) were extremely rare, if not impossible, at least for large populations and relatively long historical periods. On the other hand, the indicator S seems to be able to explain a large part of the variance of the proportion remaining single and seems therefore suitable for closer estimates then the low, medium, and high assumed here.

Finally, it is also interesting to note that the age at marriage has little effect on the ratio $M/\overline{M}$ at least within the limits of the European marriage pattern. Table 9 reports the values of the ratio for different values of the mean age at marriage and given values of e_0 and of the proportion remaining single. The effect of a variation in the mean age at marriage is much lower than the effect of a corresponding variation of the proportion remaining single or of the level of mortality.

Summing up, and concluding, we may note the following four points:

1. The level of the ratio of actual to hypothetical marriages in a cohort

TABLE 9
Ratio of Actual to Hypothetical Marriages (M/$\overline{M}$) for Different Combinations of e_0 and Mean Age at Marriage

e_0	Mean age at marriage					
	23.5	24.5	25.5	26.5	27.5	28.5
20	.311	.304	.297	.291	.284	.278
30	.446	.440	.434	.428	.421	.415
40	.566	.561	.555	.549	.544	.538
50	.673	.669	.664	.660	.655	.651

is due to the levels of mortality, of the proportion remaining single, and of the age at marriage.

2. When mortality is high—for example, e_0 below 40—as it is almost universally in the history of the pre-nineteenth century population, the level of the ratio is much more affected by the level of mortality than by the marriage pattern. Even large variations of the latter have a relatively mild effect on the ratio.

3. Variations in the proportion remaining single account for larger variations of the ratio $M/\overline{M}$ than variations in the age at marriage.

4. This method estimates mortality before the age at marriage.

5. ESTIMATING THE NUMBER OF CHILDREN PER MARRIAGE

5.1

It is possible to study fertility in the absence of census statistics and without resorting to family reconstitution. When births are recorded by duration of marriage, marriage–duration fertility rates can be computed for any given year. The sum of these rates gives a period measure of family size, or the mean number of children per marriage. In symbols, if i is the duration of marriage and x the years of observation, n_i^x the legitimate births in the year x from marriages concluded i years before, and M_{x+i} the marriages concluded in the year $x-i$, the duration specific rates are

$$f_i = n_i^x/M_i$$

Obviously, terminations of unions because of divorce, migration, or mortality are ignored. The average number of children per marriage is

$$F = \sum_{i=0}^{\omega} n_i^x/M_i = \sum_{i=0}^{\omega} f_i$$

where ω is the longest duration of marriage for which there is a significant level of fertility.

Obviously, this method can only be employed when rather sophisticated statistics on births by duration of marriage are available. It is well known, however, that the distribution of the duration-specific fertility rates tends to change very slowly, generally with a progressive concentration of childbearing in the low durations of marriage.[6] It is therefore

---

[6] The proportions of the final family size achieved between durations 0 and 5, 5 and 10, and over 10, were, for Fiesole, 1630–1680 ($F = 6$), 38.6, 28.1, and 33.3%. The same values for Italy, 1927 ($F = 3.6$), were 46.9, 24.9, and 28.2%; for Italy, 1965 ($F = 2.5$), 58.2, 23.9, and 17.9%.

possible to assume a standard distribution of f_i and, having at hand a continuous series of legitimate births and marriages, to compute,

$$\overline{N}_x = \sum_{i=0}^{\omega} \bar{f}_i \cdot M_i$$

or the standard number of legitimate births that would occur in the year x if the marriages performed in the year x and in the preceding years had experienced a fertility level equal to $\bar{f}_i$. On the other hand,

$$N_x/\overline{N}_x \cdot \overline{F} = F_x$$

or the product of the ratio of actual to standard births times the standard family size ($\overline{F}$, or the mean number of children per marriage resulting from the $\bar{f}_i$ schedule), gives an estimate of the family size in the year x.[7]

5.2

The simple procedure explained earlier may give useful indications as to the fertility trends even when estimates of the population are available. Table 10 reports the mean number of children per marriage (F) for Tuscany from 1820–1824 to 1895–1899 and the birth rate for the same period. F has been computed with the help of a standard distribution of births by duration of marriage based on the experience of a Tuscan village (Fiesole, marriages of 1630–1680, $\overline{F} = 6.0$) with pre-decline levels of fertility.[8] The mean number of children per marriage declines almost continuously from 1820–1824 to the end of the century. F is above 5.5 during the 1820–1829 decade, and falls below this level in 1830–1834, below 5.0 in 1850–1854, below 4.5 in 1880–1884, reaching 4.2 in 1895–1899. The decline is almost uninterrupted but for two slight comebacks in 1865–1869 (4.77 against 4.69 in 1860–1864) and 1885–1889 (4.50 against 4.44). On the whole, from 1820–1824 to 1895–1899, F declines by 1.4 points, or 25% below its initial level.

Of a very different nature is the trend of the birth rate, although the overall decline is about the same (-26.9%). The birth rate is about 43 per 1000 in 1820–1829; falls thereafter, remaining around 34–36 from 1835–1860 onward; rises to almost 40 in 1865–1869; and declines continuously until the end of the century. Summing up the birth rate shows three well-identified movements: a decline until 1840–1844, a

---

[7] Gini (1934) applied this method for the first time 40 years ago. See also a critical discussion of Gini's procedure in Mortara (1933).

[8] In general, when the size of birth cohorts is relatively stable, the choice of the standard distribution does not greatly matter. Similar results are often obtained with relatively different fertility schedules.

TABLE 10
Number of Children per Marriage and Birth Rate in Tuscany, 1820-1899

| Period | Absolute values | | Index numbers (1820-1824 = 100) | |
	Children per marriage[a]	Birth rate	Children per marriage	Birth rate
1820-1824	5.64	43.2	100.0	100.0
1825-1829	5.52	42.6	97.9	98.6
1830-1834	5.33	39.3	94.5	91.0
1835-1839	5.12	36.2	90.8	83.8
1840-1844	5.06	34.3	89.7	79.4
1845-1849	5.06	35.4	89.7	81.9
1850-1854	4.90	35.8	86.9	82.9
1855-1859	4.74	36.0	84.0	83.3
1860-1864	4.69	38.7	83.2	89.6
1865-1869	4.77	39.6	84.6	91.7
1870-1874	4.67	37.5	82.8	86.8
1875-1879	4.62	36.7	81.9	85.0
1880-1884	4.44	34.7	78.7	80.3
1885-1889	4.50	35.5	79.8	82.2
1890-1894	4.45	33.7	78.9	78.0
1895-1899	4.23	31.6	75.0	73.1

[a]From 1820 to 1862 live births minus illegitimate live and still births.

rise until 1865–1869, and a subsequent decrease until the end of the century. On the other hand, the decline of F is practically continuous throughout the period.

Changes of F may derive from at least four factors:

1. changes in the frequency of termination of marriages before the end of the fertile period (because of death, divorce, or migration);
2. changes in the age at marriage;
3. changes in the timing of births, not affecting the final family size;
4. an actual change in the attitude of the couple.

Factor 4 is the one we want to isolate. In other words, we want to know whether the modification of F is the consequence of an increasing (seldom decreasing) deliberate control of fertility by the couple. Factor 3, on the other hand, is of lesser influence, because changes in timing may be responsible for short-lived fluctuations but certainly not for long-term, gradual changes of F. The action of factor 1 can be neutralized by estimating how many marriages contracted in the years x, $x - 1$, $x - 2$, and so on survive to the year x and may, therefore, be exposed to the risk of giving birth to a child in the year x. If a life table is available, it is possible to estimate the number of surviving unions 1, 2,

. . . , 30 years after marriage by combining male and female survivorship between the time of marriage and duration 1, 2, . . . , 30. The higher the mortality level is, the higher the new estimate of F incorporating the effects of mortality will be. Since mortality decreased in Tuscany during the nineteenth century or—at best—remained constant, it cannot be responsible for the decline of F. On the other hand, the results of the cross-analysis of birth and marriage fluctuations (see Table 2) are consistent with a relatively stable age at marriage during the century.

The conclusion is that the decrease of F during the first part of the century cannot be attributed either to mortality rate (which decreased, therefore producing—with unchanged fertility rates—an increase of F) or to changes in the age at marriage, which remained constant.

5.3

The Tuscan example shows that the interpretation of F can be facilitated by indications as to the level of mortality and the age pattern of nuptiality. When only long series of aggregate vital statistics are available, then the indications on nuptiality and morality reached with the techniques outlined in this chapter may be particularly useful.

Here, again, there is ample need for further research and empirical testing. It would be useful to develop a series of model fertility schedules by duration of marriage, according to the overall level of fertility (F) and the age at marriage. This would very much help in selecting the appropriate f_i schedule for the estimate of F.

Secondly, the computation of model tables of terminations of marriages, according to the level of mortality and the nuptiality pattern (late or early marriage, etc.) could be an useful instrument for estimating the net effect of mortality on the level of F.

6. CONCLUSION

I started from the assumption that aggregate historical series of vital statistics can yield more information on demographic trends than demographers usually believe possible.

First, I have shown that the peculiarities of the series themselves—peaks and hollows and short- or medium-term deviations from the trend—can be exploited in order to estimate the modal interval between birth and marriage.

Second, the interrelations between births (by cohort) and marriages (by calendar year), in a regime of approximate stability, can yield useful indications as to the proportion of the cohort remaining single.

Third, the estimate of the proportion of a cohort not reaching marriage, associated with indications as to the age at marriage and the proportion remaining single, can be used for estimating the level of mortality before marriage.

Fourth, the application of a standard schedule of duration-specific fertility rates to the series of marriages permits the calculation of the (hypothetical) number of births, given a certain regime of fertility; the comparison with the actual number of births yields an estimate of the mean number of children per marriage. This measure can be refined and interpreted when the level of mortality and the age pattern of nuptiality are known.

Throughout the chapter, I have insisted that the ideas and methodologies explained here need (1) further refinement (and I have indicated the nature of such refinement), (2) further empirical testing, and (3) testing through simulation.

REFERENCES

Coale, A. J. and Paul Demeny (1966). *Regional Model Life Tables and Stable Populations*. Princeton: Princeton University Press.

Coale, A. J. (1971). "Age Patterns of Marriage," *Population Studies*, Vol. 25 (July), pp. 193–214.

Gini, C. (1934). "Di un procedimento per la determinazione del numero medio dei figli legittimi per matrimonio," *Atti del Congresso Internazionale per gli Studi sulla Popolazione*, Vol. 10, Rome, pp. 41–68.

Mortara, G. (1933). "Sui metodi di studio della fecondità dei matrimoni," *Giornale degli Economisti*, Vol. 48 (December), pp. 890–897.

Sundbärg, G. (1907). *Bevölkerungsstatistik Schwedends 1750–1900*. Stockholm: P. A. Norstedt and Söner.

van de Walle, E. (1972). "De l'emploi des modèles en démographie historique," *Annales de Démographie Historique 1972*. Actes du Colloque de Florence, 1–3 October 1971, pp. 153–177.

Methods and Models for Analyzing Historical Series of Births, Deaths, and Marriages*

RONALD DEMOS LEE

University of Michigan

1. INTRODUCTION AND SUMMARY

Long time-series of baptisms, burials, and marriages are widely available for preindustrial Europe, occasionally at the national level, but most typically for parishes or groups of parishes. From the point of view of temporal demographic analysis, this body of data is largely unexploited, in part because of the methodological problems its analysis presents: The data concern numbers of events, whereas the interesting hypotheses concern rates.[1] How can we relate the hypotheses and evidence when we know neither the base population size and age structure nor the age distributions of the events? How can we study behavioral phenomena when these cannot be distinguished from purely demographic interactions? These difficulties have discouraged analysis of a whole range of problems and have led to casual and

* This chapter was prepared for the conference, "Behavioral Models in Historical Demography," held in Philadelphia 24–26 October 1974, sponsored by the Mathematical Social Sciences Board and funded by the National Science Foundation. This research was supported by grant HD08586-01 from NICHD. The author gratefully acknowledges the research assistance of Michael Kipling, and typing and preparation of diagrams by Carolyn Copley.

[1] Reconstitution methods provide a wealth of information but are nonetheless mute concerning temporal change except over the longer run.

sometimes entirely fallacious inference from the raw demographic series.[2]

Nonetheless there are many interesting and important hypotheses relating to variations over time in demographic series, and to evaluate these hypotheses we must resort to the only data at hand: the long series of baptisms, burials, and marriages.

This chapter develops a basic model for the analysis of series of baptisms and burials.[3] In most applications this model is a stochastic linear approximation to the discrete renewal equation. Various hypotheses are introduced as specifications of the relations between fluctuations in fertility and mortality. In this way implications of the hypotheses for the time-series behavior of births and deaths may be studied. Spectral analysis is then used to compare the observed behavior with the behavior implied by each of the hypotheses considered.[4] Throughout, the methods and models are illustrated with data from Colyton and Hartland.[5]

Because much of the material in this chapter is quite technical, I will first give a detailed nontechnical summary of the principal issues and results. This summary is organized around quotations from the historical demography literature, which, I hope, will help illustrate the practical implications of the analysis.

The analysis begins, in Part 2 of this chapter, by measuring the amount of variation in the baptism, burial, and marriage series that did in fact occur. I concentrate on the short-run fluctuations, because these (as I later show) were substantially independent of age and marital structure, and accurately reflect the changes in marital fertility, nuptiality, and mortality.

> Every study so far made shows that the number of marriages shows more violent fluctuations than those for births or deaths [Eversley, 1965, p. 44].

Our findings for the two parishes studied fit this generalization (although they would not if purely random fluctuation were excluded). For both Colyton and Hartland, the calculated coefficients of short-run

---

[2] An important example is the often stated, nonetheless false, notion that fluctuations in baptism series are explained by parallel fluctuations in marriage series. See van de Walle (1968, p. 488) and Lee (1975 and in press).

[3] This chapter may be regarded as a companion piece to Lee (1975 and in press), in which a model relating series of births and marriages is developed.

[4] There is growing interest in using spectral methods to analyze historical demographic data; for example, see Gluckman, Herlihy, and Pori (1973), Deprez, Hum, and Spencer (1974), and my own work.

[5] Professor E. A. Wrigley generously sent me the aggregate series for these parishes.

variation[6] were as follows: births, .17; deaths, .34; marriages, .38 (see Table 2).

One of my goals in this chapter is to explain such annual variation. But can it, even in principle, be explained?

> The most striking feature of Hartland's population . . . is the rarity of any changes in the number of baptisms and burials which could not be the product of chance given the small number of events which took place each year [Wrigley, 1969, p. 71].

As Wrigley's statement suggests, there is much purely random variation in the series for small parishes. This variation would occur even if true vital rates were constant. It is pure randomness, and intrinsically unexplainable. Its existence sets an upper bound to the proportion of variance that can be explained, and to the correlation coefficients that can ideally be obtained.

In Part 2 I will evaluate the proportion of variation in parish register series that is of this purely random form. The proportion depends on the size of the population, and on the amount of systematic variance that occurs, which in turn is different for births, deaths, and marriages. The calculated proportion ranged from a low of 22% for deaths in Colyton to a high of 61% for marriages in Hartland (see Table 1 and Figure 1). These results suggest that the parish population may be too small for a satisfactory analysis of annual variation. With larger base populations, the random component of variation declines sharply.

> The bare record of numbers of baptisms, burials and marriages is enough to suggest that great changes in fertility and mortality had taken place, but it is not sufficient to show what these changes were [Wrigley, 1969, p. 82].

Actually, considerable information about changes in fertility and mortality can be gained from deeper analysis of aggregate baptism and burial series, as is shown in Part 4. Using the basic demographic model, plus some additional assumptions, it is possible to estimate the population size and age structure, life expectancy, and gross reproduction rates at annual or 5-year intervals. Results are illustrated in Figure 2. If the method proves to be more generally applicable, it should considerably enrich our knowledge of trends and fluctuations in historical populations.

> On the population graphs of baptisms, marriages and sometimes of deaths, an alternation of full generations and depleted generations produces "bumps and

---

[6] The coefficient of variation is the standard deviation divided by the mean; thus in a "typical" year, births would be 17% above or below their long-run mean.

hollows" which succeed one another every thirty years or thereabouts [Goubert, 1965, p. 472].

It is well known that birth and marriage series often move in waves of approximately 30 years' duration, presumably due to the succession of generations. Though the suggested reason is intuitively appealing (although not unquestioned; see Carlsson, 1970), a satisfactory theoretical analysis leading to testable hypotheses has yet to be made. In Part 5 I shall outline such an analysis and compare its implications to estimates from Colyton's baptism series (Figures 3 and 4). The correspondence is acceptable but not striking.

Other population-generating mechanisms, leading to quite different dynamic implications, have also been suggested.

> The situation of the laborer being then again tolerably comfortable, the restraints to population are in some degree loosened, and the same retrograde and progressive movements with respect to happiness are repeated [Malthus, 1798/1970, p. 77].

Malthus argued that population size tended toward an equilibrium corresponding to subsistence level wages, and that the lags between birth and labor force entry would cause long oscillations of population and wages about their equilibrium levels. This would produce a pattern of birth series behavior that might be quite different from the 30-year wave. In Part 6 I shall integrate the Malthusian mechanism with the basic demographic model and study the implied dynamic behavior. As it happens, for plausible parameter values the 30-year cycle is unaffected, and the Malthusian oscillations that might arise are so long as to be undetectable (see Figure 5).

Let us now turn to the main concern of this chapter, which is modeling, estimating, and testing the relations between series of births and deaths.

> The fluctuations in the death rate . . . appear often to have been the effective cause of the fluctuations in the birth rate [Habakkuk, 1965, p. 272].

In Part 7 I shall estimate the relations of series of births to deaths for Colyton and Akershus, Norway. We find for Akershus a very strong negative association of the two, but for Colyton we find a weak negative relation (see Figure 6). In both cases decreases in births lag slightly behind increases in deaths.

The literature of historical demography contains many hypotheses about the relationships between fertility and mortality and between births and deaths. These relationships will be investigated, theoretically and empirically, in subsequent parts of this chapter.

A portion of the relationship between series of births and deaths is due to purely demographic factors; these are explored in Part 8. For example, both series are affected by the size and age structure of the base population, and therefore should exhibit some similarities in behavior. Furthermore, when births increase sharply, about one-fifth of the increase will succumb to infant mortality in the first year of life, and will consequently cause an increase in total deaths. There are many other effects, more subtle and indirect, which are incorporated in the analysis of this part.

It is impossible to assess the quantitative importance of these links without going through a difficult and complex analysis. Having done so (see Figure 7), we are able to conclude that if fertility and mortality vary independently so that only demographic interactions are present, then,

1. For fluctuations of periods less than 20 years, the interrelation of the series explains only an insignificant portion of their variance (5 to 10%).

2. The small association that exists is *positive*, with deaths lagging slightly behind births.

3. The 30-year cycle that occurs in birth series should *not* occur in death series.

Though demographic interactions thus appear to generate only meager effects, biological (i.e., nonvoluntary) connections between fertility and mortality may cause large effects, as suggested by Hotelling and Hotelling for one of the links:

> Such an influence is found in the recurrence of epidemics which lead to profound depressions in births seven to nine months later [Hotelling & Hotelling, 1931, p. 149].

In Part 9 I shall examine these links, which include lactation interruption, fecundity impairment, and fetal mortality.[7] After building specifications of these effects into the demographic model, I conclude that

---

[7] In each case it is also possible that malnutrition plays a role, as R. E. Frisch has suggested. Thus malnutrition of the mother would prolong the effect of lactation on fecundity, and it might operate independently to cause infecundity and fetal mortality. See Frisch (1974).

1. Lactation interruption could have no significant effect on time-series behavior of births and deaths.

2. Though there is less certainty about appropriate parameter values, it nonetheless appears that the mortality–fetal mortality link would likewise produce only weak association of births and deaths over time.

3. Morbidity as a common cause of both infecundity and mortality might well explain the observed association of births and deaths.

In Part 10, I shall take up social and voluntary links.

> In the period after years of high mortality, people could afford to marry earlier. . . . Hence earlier marriages and more births [Habakkuk, 1965, pp. 272–273].

Habakkuk here expresses the conventional view. But after incorporating this mechanism and the replacement fertility mechanism in the basic model, I have come to the following conclusion:

1. The mortality–nuptiality–fertility mechanism, under the most favorable possible assumptions, cannot explain the covariance of births and deaths for fluctuations of less than 20-year periods, and in any case suggests a *positive* association, not a negative one.

With respect to other possible links, I conclude,

2. The efforts of couples to replace dead children with new births (if such efforts were made) could not lead to a significant covariation of births and deaths over time.

3. If the conditions leading to high mortality also led to voluntary restriction of fertility, the results would be indistinguishable from fecundity impairment, and would likewise account for the observed associations.

So far, only the interrelations of demographic series and the inferences that may be drawn from them have been considered. In Part 11, I shall briefly consider meteorological and economic sources of disturbance to the demographic system. The results are generally weak, but in the expected direction. High grain prices are associated with higher mortality and lower marital fertility and nuptiality (net of the effects of rainfall and temperature change); cold winters and springs caused high mortality (net of the effect of price changes). (See Figures 8 and 9.) However, the weakness of the results, taken together with findings on pure randomness in parish series, suggests that larger populations must be used for this kind of analysis.

2. RANDOM AND SYSTEMATIC VARIATION IN PARISH POPULATIONS

Plots against time of the yearly totals of baptisms, burials, and marriages occurring in a parish reveal considerable annual variation. It is natural to assume that these variations in recorded events reflect variations in the underlying vital rates, and to search for social, economic, and meteorological explanations. However, it is prudent first to consider the null hypothesis that these variations arise by pure chance when a small population is subject to constant vital rates; after all, vital rates are only probabilities at the individual level, and with parish-size populations at risk, a good deal of annual variation in numbers of vital events would in any case occur.

The formal mathematics of this source of demographic variability has been worked out in sophisticated detail by a number of authors (Chiang, 1968; Henry, 1972b; Pollard, 1973; Schweder, 1971; Sheps & Menken, 1973; Sykes, 1969; and others). Unfortunately I have not been able to find results in the form required. So I have had to develop approximate results under the simplifying assumptions that the population at risk is homogeneous, and that events are the outcome of Bernoulli trials. (Spencer, 1975, is working along similar lines.)

Suppose that in a roughly stationary parish population of $n = 1000$ people life expectancy at birth is 30 years, so that on the average the crude death rate is .033 and there are 33 deaths per year. Abstracting from age structure, each individual each year has a probability of $q = .033$ of dying, and $p = .967$ of surviving. Then the variance of the number of deaths actually occurring in a year is given by $npq = (1000) (.033) (.967) = 32$.[8]

Now consider births. Here we must acknowledge that only a fraction of the population is at risk. Following the work of Gautier and Henry (1958, p. 115) and others, we may take the average fertility of women at risk to be about .4 births per year (in the context of preindustrial Europe). However this makes no allowance for pregnancy and postpartum amenorrhea; a minimal adjustment would raise the average fertility of women at risk to .5. Since in a stationary population births equal deaths, there must on the average be 33 births per year, and about 33/.5 or 66 women at risk. The variance of annual births will therefore be npq

---

[8] Since both the age structure of the population and its size will actually be varying randomly over time, the observed variance should be somewhat larger. We can finesse this problem by looking only at the short-run component of variation in empirical applications.

= (66)(.5)(.5) = 16.5. This ignores an additional component of fertility variation due to negative autocorrelation imparted by postpartum amenorrhea; this might be expected to generate a periodicity of about 1/.4, or 2.5 years. (See, e.g., the diagram on p. 55 in Henry, 1972b.)

It is more difficult to define the population at risk to marriage, although interesting theoretical work has been done recently by Henry (1972b) and by Coale and McNeil (1971). Since marriage in Europe was late, suppose that the average wait until marriage, after in some sense becoming at risk, was about 5 years, and that the annual probability of marriage for those at risk was therefore 1/5, or .2. Given a typical marriage rate of .008, then eight marriages per year would require 8/.2 or 40 "potential couples" at risk. The variance of marriages would then be $npq = (40)(.2)(.8) = 6.4$. This is close to 8, the variance if the entire population were at risk.

These figures take on more meaning when compared to the observed annual variance of parish register series. As noted earlier, we can avoid the complicating factors of population size and age distribution by restricting our attention to shorter-run fluctuations. We do this with the help of spectral analysis, a technique that I shall now explain briefly.

Suppose we have calculated in the usual way the variance of a series of births. Casual inspection of the time-series may suggest that some of the calculated variance is due to longer-run fluctuations, such as the characteristic long waves of perhaps 30-years period which often appear in birth series; and some due to shorter-run fluctuations, such as the 2- or 3-year ups and downs which sometimes give birth series a sawtooth appearance. The *spectrum* of a series gives the contribution of variation at each *wavelength, periodicity,* or *frequency* to the total variance of the series. Variance at long wavelengths or low frequencies corresponds closely, but not exactly, to long-run variation, while that at short wave lengths or high frequencies corresponds closely to short-run variation. The decomposition is additive, so the integral of the spectrum gives the total variance.[9] For an exposition of spectral analysis, see Granger and Hatanaka (1964) or Jenkins and Watts (1968).

While spectral analysis is useful for the investigation of cyclic behavior (the existence of a cycle is revealed by a peak in the spectrum at the appropriate cycle length or period), its usefulness is by no means restricted to analysis of series with cyclic behavior. In this part, for example, we shall use the technique solely to distinguish approximately between long-run and short-run variation in the demographic series.

We have calculated the spectra of baptisms, burials, and marriages for

[9] Or, 2π times the total variance, depending on the convention followed. This holds for 2 true spectrum, but not necessarily for the estimated spectrum.

two English parishes: Hartland, which had a tranquil demographic history, and Colyton, which had a violent one (for descriptions of these parishes and their demographic histories, see Wrigley 1966, 1968, 1969). The estimated spectra are shown for Hartland in Figure 1. Consider the spectrum of baptisms. It is very high for low frequency, long period fluctuations (at the left of the diagram), and is much lower for shorter periods (to the right). The spectrum suggests a tendency for births to move in short cycles of 2 and 3 years, a point which does not concern us here.[10]

On Figure 1, the 95% confidence interval for the true spectrum is indicated by a vertical bar, which may be visually added or subtracted from the log-scale plot of the estimated spectrum (see Jenkins & Watts, 1968, p. 255).

On the same diagram, the contribution of purely random variance is also shown. This source of variation is assumed to be *white noise*, independent from one year to the next. The spectrum of white noise is constant, so the random contribution to the spectrum is drawn as a horizontal line of appropriate height. It is clear that the random variation makes up a substantial portion of the total, particularly for marriages. The component of variation that is not random, and which we may therefore seek to explain, is different for the three series, and also varies by frequency.

The average portion of variance that is intrinsically unexplainable is shown in Table 1 for both parishes. We see that it ranges from a low of 22% for deaths in Colyton to a high of 61% for marriages in Hartland.[11]

The similarity of the figures for the two parishes is surprising; I had anticipated that for Colyton, pure randomness would have been relatively much less important, in light of its disturbed history. But, in fact, Colyton demographic history was no more variable *in the short run* than was Hartland's, as is shown by Table 2, which gives coefficients of variation.

Apparently the difference between the two parishes held only for secular changes in the demographic rates, or possibly lay only in the relative degree of closure of the two parishes.[12]

---

[10] Such cycles could well be generated by biological features of the reproductive cycle in response to stochastic disturbance.

[11] For Colyton I have omitted burials in the crisis year 1646, since this year alone doubled the variance (burials were about 10 times their average number).

[12] For Crulai, 1680–1800, coefficients of variation are very similar to those for Hartland and Colyton; for Sweden, 1748–1880, the coefficients are much less. This is not surprising since Sweden's national population was larger and more geographically dispersed than that of a parish.

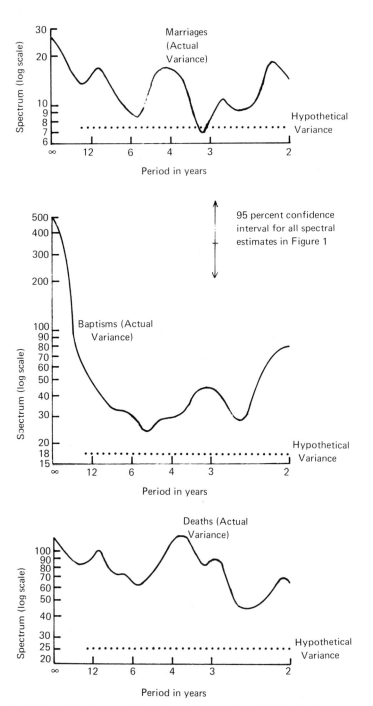

Figure 1. Estimated variance and purely random variance for Hartland, 1558–1838.

TABLE 1
Purely Random Variance as Proportion of Total
Variance (Excluding Low Frequencies)[a]

	Colyton (1545-1838)	Hartland (1558-1838)
Baptisms	.42	.43
Burials	.22	.32
Marriages	.55	.61

[a]Calculated as theoretical variance (assuming constant rates) divided by average spectral estimate for periods of 13 years and less.

TABLE 2
Coefficients of Short-Run Variation[a]

	Colyton (1545-1838)	Hartland (1558-1838)
Baptisms	.17	.18
Burials	.34	.34
Marriages	.38	.37

[a]Square root of average spectral estimate, divided by mean, for periods of 13 years and less. Colyton burial total for 1646 excluded.

3. THE BASIC DEMOGRAPHIC MODEL

Having discussed the purely random element in demographic time-series, we now focus our attention more systematically on the demographic processes generating the series.

Let B_t and D_t refer to births and deaths in year t. Let $m_{a,t}$ be the fertility rate for all persons (of both sexes) age a at exact time t, during the following year. The mortality rate $q_{a,t}$ is similarly defined (with $q_{-1,t}$ equal to the mortality rate for B_t). The cohort survival rate for age group a, $p_{a,t}$, is given by

$$p_{a,t} = \prod_{i=-1}^{a-1} (1 - q_{i,t-a+i})$$

The series B_t and D_t are generated (by definition) as follows:

$$B_t = \Sigma m_{a,t}\, p_{a,t}\, B_{t-a} \tag{3.1}$$

$$D_t = \Sigma q_{a,t}\, p_{a,t}\, B_{t-a} \tag{3.2}$$

Now suppose that variations in $m_{a,t}$ and $q_{a,t}$ follow a fixed age-pattern, so that $m_{a,t} = f_t m_a$ and $q_{a,t} = q_a + \eta_t \delta_a$.[13] If m_a is normalized to add to unity, then f_t measures the gross reproduction rate; η_t is an index of the force of mortality.

The equations can now be rewritten:

$$B_t = f_t \Sigma m_a p_{a,t} B_{t-a} \tag{3.3}$$

$$D_t = \eta_t \Sigma \delta_a p_a B_{t-a} + \Sigma q_a p_{a,t} B_{t-a} \tag{3.4}$$

(We could, of course, also express $p_{a,t}$ in terms of η_{t-i}.)

This basic model will be drawn on in subsequent sections.

4. ESTIMATING VITAL RATES AND AGE STRUCTURES FROM PARISH DATA SERIES

In some cases it is possible to estimate time-series of population size and age structure, and fertility and mortality, from series of births and deaths.[14] Suppose that we know the size and age distribution of the generating population for some initial period $t = 0$.[15] In a closed population this is equivalent to knowledge of $p_{a,0} B_{0-a}$ for all ages. If we also know D_0 and B_0, then we may calculate η_1 from equation 3.4. This in turn allows us to find $p_{a,1} = 1 - q_a - \eta_1 \delta_a$ for each a, and then to calculate $p_{a,1} B_{1-a}$ for all ages. Continuing in this way, we can estimate η_t, $q_{a,t}$, $p_{a,t}$, and the population age structure over the entire length of the series B and D. This in turn enables us to estimate f_t, the gross reproduction rate, using equation 3.3. Figure 2 shows estimates of Colyton's population size, gross reproduction rates, and period life expectancy for 5-year intervals, 1545 to 1834. These estimates agree well with Wrigley's (1966, 1968) reconstitution estimates when averaged over appropriate intervals. Not all applications are so successful, which is not surprising since the method requires stringent assumptions about closure and completeness of registration.[16]

[13] The δ_a are measured as differences between mortality rates by age in adjacent model life tables, and then normalized so that $\Sigma p_a\, \delta_a = 1$; m_a is an appropriate model fertility schedule.

[14] The material in this section is discussed in detail in Lee (1974a).

[15] Alternatively, one could start from a known population size and distribution and work backward in time.

[16] In collaboration with David Levine, I am currently experimenting with methods for dealing with underregistration and migration.

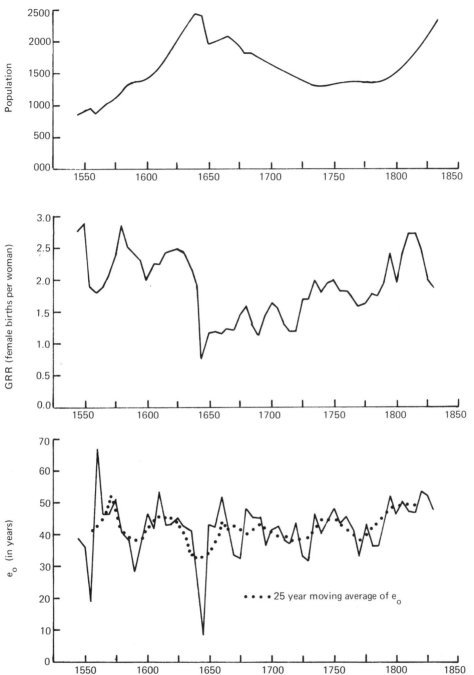

Figure 2. Estimated population, gross reproduction rate (GRR), and life expectancy (e_0) for Colyton, 1545–1834. Reprinted, with permission, from *Population Studies*, Vol. 28, No. 3 (November 1974), p. 501.

5. THE 30-YEAR WAVE IN BAPTISM SERIES

The preceding section concerned the chronology of changing vital rates in historical time. From here on, I shall analyze the variance–covariance structure of demographic events, or the probabilities that certain combinations of events would occur, independently of historical time.[17] It is simplest to begin by analyzing the internal structure of the series of births.

Let us begin by assuming that the gross reproduction rate $f_t = f(1 + \epsilon_t)$ is a stationary random variable with mean f and variance $f^2\sigma_\epsilon^2$, and an arbitrary autocovariance structure. (Presumably, variations in f_t, represented by ϵ_t, reflect social, economic, and meteorological influences.)

Let us also assume for now that mortality is constant. Define ϕ_a, the average net maternity function, by $\phi_a = fm_a p_a$. Suppose the average net reproduction rate (NRR), equal to the sum over a of ϕ_a, is roughly unity, so that the population is roughly constant over time.[18] Then the birth process is generated by

$$B_t = (1 + \epsilon_t)\Sigma\phi_a B_{t-a} \qquad (5.1)$$

If B denotes the average number of births, and we let b_t represent proportional variations in births [so that $b_t = (B_t - B)/B$], then equation 5.1 is approximated by

$$b_t \doteq \epsilon_t + \Sigma\phi_a b_{t-a} \qquad (5.2)$$

or

$$\Sigma c_i b_{t-i} = \epsilon_t \qquad (5.3)$$

where $c_0 = 1$ and $c_j = -\phi_j$ for $j > 0$.

This represents the birth process as an autoregressive process with a disturbance term equal to proportional variations in the gross reproduction rate (or absolute variations in the NRR).[19]

In Part 2 we used spectral analysis to separate short-run from long-run variation, at least approximately. Here we will use it to analyze the cyclic behavior of a series. On the one hand we can use spectral analysis to derive the cyclic behavior implied by our model of the birth series.

---

[17] The analysis in this section is in many respects similar to an analysis in Coale (1972), which was carried out for a different purpose.

[18] This assumption is unnecessary, as is shown in Lee (1974c).

[19] See Lee (1974b). This representation is also approximately correct when mortality and nuptiality are stochastic, as is shown in Lee (1975).

On the other hand, we can use it to study cyclic tendencies in actual series of births.

The spectrum, $g_b(\lambda)$, decomposes the variance of b by frequency, λ. If b has no cyclic tendencies, then its spectrum will have no peaks. If b tends to fluctuate with a period of 15 years, the spectrum will be relatively great at the appropriate frequency ($\lambda = 1/15$ cycles per year). Equation 5.3 implies that the spectrum of births will be related to the spectrum of fertility variation, $g_\epsilon(\lambda)$, as follows (see Granger & Hatanaka, 1964):

$$g_b(\lambda) = |A(\lambda)|^2 \, g_\epsilon(\lambda) \qquad (5.4)$$

where

$$|A(\lambda)|^2 = 1/|(2\pi)^{-1} \, \Sigma c_j e^{-ij\lambda}|^2 \qquad (5.5)$$

$A(\lambda)^2$ is called a *squared gain* function, and it can be calculated from equation 5.5 for any given net maternity schedule. Such a function based on Crulai's net maternity schedule is shown in Figure 3. If fertility variation ϵ has no autocorrelation, so that its spectrum is constant, then $|A(\lambda)|^2$ is also the shape of the birth spectrum $g_b(\lambda)$. The

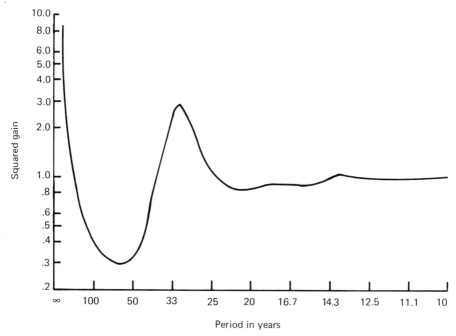

Figure 3. Squared gain for births over fertility, based on Crulai vital rates. The squared gain is shown only for periods over 10 years. For shorter periods, it is very close to unity.

strong peak in this function at a period of 32 years indicates a tendency for the age structure of reproduction to generate cycles of this length out of nonperiodic fertility variation. (For a deterministic theory of these cycles, see Bernardelli, 1941, or Keyfitz, 1972.)

More realistically, we should take account of the inertia (autocorrelation) of fertility variation. This is partly due to nuptiality variation, and partly to the structure of variations in price and climate. If we assume that $\epsilon_t = .5\epsilon_{t-1} + \theta_t$, where θ_t is serially independent, then the spectrum of both births and fertility will be higher at lower frequencies. The implied spectrum is drawn in Figure 4.

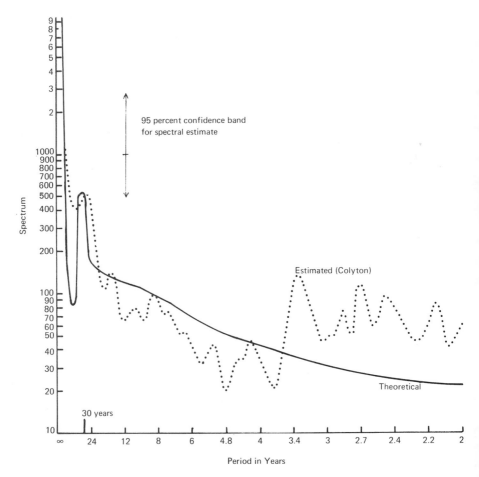

Figure 4. Birth spectra: estimated for Colyton, 1545–1837, and theoretical, with autocorrelated fertility variation. It is assumed that $\epsilon_t = .5\epsilon_{t-1} + \theta_t$, where θ_t is white noise.

Figure 4 also shows the estimated spectrum of baptisms for Colyton, 1545–1837. There is indeed a peak in the spectrum at 28 years, which corresponds fairly well with the theory.[20] However, the confidence bands indicate that this peak is probably spurious. There are also numerous cyclic tendencies of less importance that are presumably forced on the series by environmental variation—climate and harvest.

6. MALTHUSIAN OSCILLATIONS

So far I have considered only the purely demographic explanation of population fluctuations. But if preindustrial populations were subject to autoregulatory mechanisms tending to bring them to equilibrium with their economic environments, then the possibility of Malthusian oscillations about equilibrium exists. These would arise from the age–time lags in reproduction and labor force entry, and reflect undershootings and overshootings of equilibrium (Lee, 1970, 1974c; Malthus, 1798/1970, pp. 77–78; Wrigley, 1969, p. 70; Yule, 1906).

If we assume that regulation took the form of fertility control by way of nuptiality or marital fertility, and that variations in mortality were largely exogenous (as is argued by Chambers, 1972; Lee, forthcoming; Ohlin, 1955) then we may easily incorporate control in our basic model, and study its dynamics (this is done in detail in Lee, 1974c).

Let w represent a real wage index, or some other welfare measure. Fertility depends in part on w: $f_t = g(w_t) + u_t$, where u_t represents other exogenous determinants, and $dg/dw > 0$. Value w_t depends on the number of workers, L_t, so, $w_t = w(L_t) + v_t$ and $dw/dL < 0$. Eliminating w, we can write $f_t = h(L_t) + \epsilon_t$ with $dh/dL < 0$. Specifically, assume $f_t = \alpha L_t^{-\beta} + \epsilon_t$ for appropriate α, β (for estimates of these parameters, see Lee, 1973, forthcoming).

If everybody aged 15 to 65 works, then $L_t = \Sigma_{15}^{64} p_a B_{t-a}$. Referring to equation 3.3, the renewal equation becomes

$$B_t = [\alpha(\Sigma_{15}^{64} p_a B_{t-a})^{-\beta} + \epsilon_t] \Sigma_{15}^{44} \phi_a B_{t-a} \qquad (6.1)$$

As in the last section we may simplify this expression, and find that

$$b_t \doteq \epsilon_t = \Sigma_{15}^{64} (\phi_a - \beta k_a) b_{t-a} \qquad (6.2)$$

where $k_a = p_a/(e_{15} - e_{64})$, with e_x denoting life expectancy at age x.

Once again the calculated squared-gain function allows us to examine the dynamic behavior of b. Figure 5 shows the results for several values

---

[20] The peak in the empirical spectrum is less clearly distinguished than that in the theoretical spectrum; this is perhaps partly because the empirical spectral estimate is actually an average over a band of frequencies.

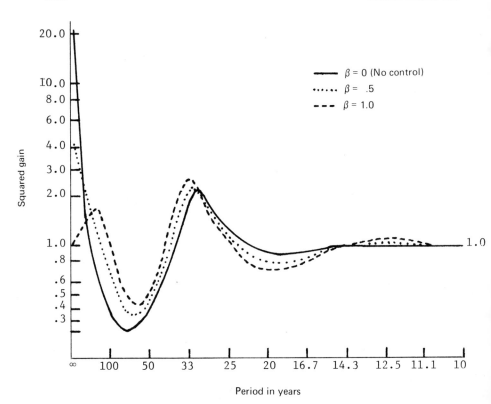

Figure 5. Squared gain for births in a Malthusian system. Calculated from age distributions of vital rates in Coale and Demeny (1966), with $e_0 = 30$ and $\bar{m} = 31$. The squared gain is shown only for periods over 10 years; for shorter periods it remains close to unity.

of β. Values of β between 0 and .5 seem most plausible, based on *a priori* considerations and some empirical research. For these values we see that the generational cycle is virtually unaffected, and that the behavior of the birth series would look different only in the long run. This is not really helpful, since too much is variable in the long run. For example Colyton *does* show a very long "cycle" of 150 to 200 years length as the controlled model predicts (with $\beta = 1$); however, the cause is exogenous secular variation in mortality. Of course in any case the model is really applicable only to closed populations, and not to parishes.[21]

---

[21] Recent U.S. demographic behavior conforms to this model with a high control elasticity of $\beta = 7.5$. See Lee (1970, 1974c).

7. THE RELATION OF BIRTHS TO DEATHS:
EMPIRICAL ESTIMATES

The preceding two sections developed models to account for the internal structure of a single series. Let us now consider more complicated models that concern the relations between two series, or internal structures when there is more than one source of disturbance. Elsewhere I have dealt in detail with the joint analysis of series of births and marriages (Lee, 1975). In this and the following section, I will analyze the more complicated relation between births and deaths using a similar approach. For this purpose we use cross-spectral analysis—a bivariate or multivariate extension of the spectral techniques introduced earlier (see Granger & Hatanaka, 1964, or Jenkins & Watts, 1968).

The spectrum measures the variance of a series by period or frequency. The cross-spectrum measures the association (covariance) of two or more series also by period or frequency. It is closely analogous to a regression; it is as if one performed a separate regression for variations at each periodicity. The R^2 of a regression gives the proportion of the variance of the dependent variable that is explained by the association; the corresponding cross-spectral concept is the *coherence squared*, denoted $\gamma^2(\lambda)$, which gives the proportion of the variance at period or frequency λ that is explained by the association. The regression coefficient measures the sensitivity of the dependent variable to changes in the independent variable; the corresponding cross-spectral function is the "gain." We have already encountered the squared gain in Part 5. To simplify our analysis here, the estimated gain in what follows will be ignored. Finally a regression equation may involve a lagged relation; in cross-spectral analysis, the lags are not specified in advance. Rather the optimal lag is calculated for each period. This lag is indicated by the *phase shift* or *phase angle* denoted $\phi(\lambda)$. It is measured in radians.[22] A phase angle of 0 or 2π indicates a positive relation of the variables with zero lag. A phase angle of π indicates a negative relation of the series, again with zero lag: When one variable is at a peak, the other is at a trough. Phase angles that are neither 0 nor 2π are difficult to interpret, because a lag of a year, for example, goes with a different phase angle at each period.

Figure 6 shows estimated cross-spectral functions for births and deaths in Colyton and in Akershus, Norway. The Akershus estimates are included just to show what strong results look like. By contrast the

---

[22] There are 2π radians to a full cycle, or π radians to a half-cycle. Phase angles of 0 and 2π are indistinguishable.

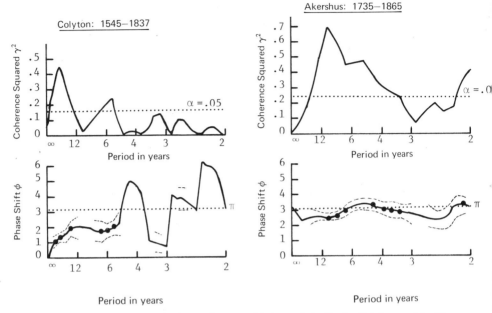

Figure 6. The estimated relation between births and deaths in Colyton and in Akershus. Estimates of γ^2 are significantly different from zero at the 5% level when they lie above the dotted line. Corresponding phase estimates are more reliable and are marked by heavy dots; 95% confidence intervals for phase estimates are indicated by dashed lines, for all frequencies with estimated coherence squared of at least .1.

Colyton estimates are indecisive. For Norway there can be no doubt about the high significance of a negative relation between births and deaths, since most coherence-squared estimates are significantly greater than zero at well above the .05 significance level, and the phase shift fluctuates about π. For Colyton the coherence squared is not consistently significant, and the phase diagram is less clear.[23] The variance of the phase estimate depends on the coherence. If we restrict our attention to the Colyton phase estimates corresponding to significant coherence estimates (shown as heavy dots in Figure 6) the agreement with Akershus is closer.

How are we to interpret these results? The literature of historical demography abounds with discussions of the relations between fluctuations in series of births and deaths (e.g., Habakkuk, 1965, pp. 272–273). This is particularly true of the demography of crises, when mortal-

---

[23] There are global tests of the null hypothesis that the two series are independent, but I have not applied them.

ity rose sharply as births first dropped and then rebounded. A large number of mechanisms linking birth and death series have been mentioned. These may be classified according to demographic effects (predictable solely on the basis of the population renewal equation), biological effects (lactation interruption, fetal mortality, fecundity impairment), and effects arising from individual decision or social institutions (replacement fertility, opportunity for marriage, or voluntary control). In subsequent sections I shall model these and derive the implied cross-spectral functions.

8. DEMOGRAPHIC INTERACTIONS OF BIRTHS AND DEATHS

In this section demographic effects only are considered. Equations 3.1 and 3.2 provide the starting point. The goal is to express births and deaths as approximate linear functions of past and current variations in fertility and mortality rates. After this is done, it is possible to derive the cross-spectral description of the relations between the series. The mathematical procedure is outlined in Appendix 1, so we need only look at the results here. It is shown in the Appendix that

$$\Sigma c_i b_{t-i} \doteq \epsilon_t + \Sigma y_i \eta_{t-i} \tag{8.1}$$

$$\Sigma c_i d_{t-i} \doteq \Sigma w_a \epsilon_{t-a} + \Sigma (r_i + s_i) \eta_{t-i} \tag{8.2}$$

where b, c, ϵ, and η are defined as before, $d_t = (D_t - D)/D$ is a proportional deviation of deaths, and w, y, r, and s are appropriate sets of coefficients. In Equation 8.1, ϵ is the effect of current fertility on current births, and $\Sigma y_i \eta_{t-i}$ reflects the depleting effect of past mortality on the reproductive-aged population. In Equation 8.2, $\Sigma w_a \epsilon_{t-a}$ reflects the effect of current births (via infant mortality) and past births (via $w_a = q_a p_a$) on current deaths. $\Sigma r_i \eta_{t-i}$ reflects the effect of past mortality on past births and hence indirectly on current deaths, and $\Sigma s_i \eta_{t-i}$ reflects the direct effect of past mortality on the population at risk to current mortality.

This completes the expression of the birth and death processes as approximately linear mixed autoregressive and moving average processes in fertility and mortality. We can now derive the cross-spectral functions, as explained in Lee (1975). These are shown in Figure 7, along with functions resulting from hypotheses to be discussed in the next two sections.

The coherence squared for the "demographic" case is extremely small except for very low frequencies or long fluctuations. This means that the coherences estimated for Norway and Colyton are not due to common

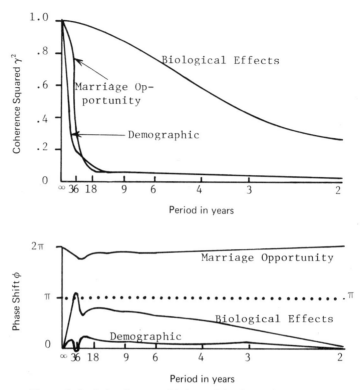

Figure 7. Theoretical relation between births and deaths under three hypotheses. The demographic effect is incorporated in all three theoretical cross-spectra.

age-structure effects, or the birth–infant mortality link; rather, they must reflect covariation of fertility and mortality.

The phase diagram suggests a positive relation of births and deaths, with births leading by about .6 years.[24] This is inconsistent with the Akershus and Colyton phase shifts.

9. BIOLOGICAL LINKS OF BIRTHS AND DEATHS

The ground is cleared for specification of hypotheses concerning the relation of ϵ_t (fertility variation) to η_t (mortality variation). We begin by considering biological effects due to lactation interruption, fecundity impairment, and fetal wastage.[25] The lactation-interruption effect arises

[24] For example, at 9 years, the lead is about $(.4/6.28) \cdot (9)$ or about .6 years.
[25] Ansley Coale has pointed out to me that all the links discussed in this section are strengthened by considerations of the effects of malnourishment on lactation-induced amenorrhea, on fetal mortality, and on fecundity impairment. See Frisch (1974).

because lactation prolongs amenorrhea. An infant death, by interrupting lactation, may shorten the interval to the subsequent birth, thereby raising fertility. The importance of this effect for cross-sectional birth interval differentials has been repeatedly demonstrated by reconstitution studies, following Gautier and Henry's classic study of Crulai (1958). These studies typically show the birth interval to be about 20 months following an infant death, and about 30 months otherwise.

From the distribution of birth intervals (e.g., Charbonneau, 1970, p. 148), we find that ordinarily the probability that a woman will give birth in the calendar year following a previous birth is roughly .3 to .4, which agrees approximately with the inverse of the average interval, or 12/30 = .4. The inverse of the interval shortened by lactation interruption is 12/20, or .6. Let us suppose, then, that an infant death will raise the mother's birth probability by about .2 in the following calendar year. Out of a typical increment of deaths, about one out of four will be infant deaths, each leading to .2 additional births in the following year. Let $\epsilon_{1,t}$ be the component of fertility variation due to lactation interruption. Then we have

$$\epsilon_{1,t} = .05\eta_{t-1} \tag{9.1}$$

Now consider fetal mortality: How might it covary with general mortality and what lags should we expect? Fetal mortality is very heavily concentrated in the first 2 months after conception,[26] but it is not clear whether this portion of fetal mortality is particularly sensitive to disease or malnutrition of the mother.[27] Studies of women during and following periods of near-starvation in Holland and Leningrad during World War II show that although birth weights decreased and stillbirths increased, the effect on fetal mortality was of little quantitative importance (Antonov, 1947; Robson, 1972; Smith, 1947). On the other hand, the Hotellings' (1931) interesting study of English birth fluctuations, 1838 to 1914, argues that much of the variance can be explained by epidemics of cholera, dysentery, smallpox, or influenza, which increased fetal mortality and thereby reduced births 7–9 months later. Likewise Leridon (1973b) finds a strong negative effect of influenza on births 9 months later.

With little to go on, I have based the specification on the following assumptions:

---

[26] According to figures cited by Leridon (1973a, p. 55), about 65% of deaths occur in the first 8 weeks.

[27] Bourgeois-Pichat has argued that early high mortality is primarily due to chromosomal irregularities, and that the portion that is environmentally determined is fairly constant over the gestation period (as cited in United Nations, 1973, p. 75).

1. On the average, about 10% of conceptions experience fetal mortality that is environmental.
2. This component of fetal mortality is proportional to general mortality.
3. This environmental fetal mortality occurs on the average 3 months after conception.

These assumptions lead to the specification,

$$\epsilon_{2,t} = -.05\eta_t - .05\eta_{t-1} \tag{9.2}$$

where $\epsilon_{2,t}$ is fertility variation due to fetal mortality.

The third source of covariation of fertility and mortality is fecundity impairment: We may regard both death and inability to conceive as extreme consequences of an unobserved variable, ill health. Striking evidence of the effect of undernourishment on fecundity comes from the study of women in Holland, cited previously. There, 50% of the reproductive-age women ceased menstruating, and about half of the remainder experienced menstrual irregularity. Births declined to about 30% of their expected level (Smith, 1947). If we assume, as seems reasonable, that fecundity impairment covaries simultaneously with mortality, then fertility will covary with a lag of 9 months. If both mortality and fecundity impairment have the same elasticity with respect to ill health, then we may specify that

$$\epsilon_{3,t} = -.25\eta_t - .75\eta_{t-1} \tag{9.3}$$

where $\epsilon_{3,t}$ is the appropriate source of fertility variation.[28]

In addition to the components of variation in fertility that are related to mortality, there is an important component due either to other factors (economic, meteorological, political, and the like) or to pure demographic randomness. This component we will call ϵ'_t. Adding all these sources of variation, we find

$$\epsilon_t = \epsilon'_t - .3\eta_t - .75\eta_{t-1} \tag{9.4}$$

It is clear that the fecundity-impairment effect dominates the others in this calculation, and unless we assumed a much lower elasticity for the relation between fecundity and mortality, this would remain the case with altered assumptions.

Following methods described in Lee (1975), we can calculate the cross-spectral functions for the old system (equations 8.1 and 8.2) plus the new equation (9.4). The results are shown in Figure 7.

[28] It would be more accurate to distinguish a systematic and random component of mortality.

The fecundity impairment link yields a high coherence at low frequencies, which diminishes at higher frequencies. The phase diagram suggests that births and deaths are negatively related, with low births lagging high deaths by about 1 year.[29] This specification evidently fits the estimated cross-spectrum much better than the independent fertility and mortality specification.

However, the phase diagrams for Akershus (see Figure 6) and Sweden (not shown here) indicate a *zero-lag* negative relationship. It is difficult to see how this could be reconciled with the model in this section unless (1) fetal mortality was more important than I assumed, and occurred in a late month of pregnancy, (2) fecundity impairment responded to adverse conditions several months before mortality did, or (3) Scandinavian variations in mortality and fecundity occurred primarily in January, February, and March.[30]

10. VOLUNTARY AND INSTITUTIONAL LINKS OF BIRTHS AND DEATHS

Now let us consider possible effects of replacement fertility and of mortality-linked marriage. I know of no evidence that couples in preindustrial Europe attempted to replace child deaths through higher subsequent fertility. In any case, such replacement fertility would be difficult to distinguish from the lactation-interruption effect. However if we do take the hypothesis seriously, we might suppose that about one-third of the incremental deaths were of young children, and that of these, about one-half were replaced over a period of 5 years.[31] This would suggest

$$\epsilon_{4,t} = .033 \sum_{i=1}^{5} \eta_{t-i} \qquad (10.1)$$

The implied effect would be so weak that it could not be determined from time-series studies.

Now consider marriage. Habakkuk expressed a widely held view when he wrote,

> In the period after years of high mortality, people could afford to marry earlier;
> . . . hence earlier marriages and more births [1965, pp. 272–273].

[29] For example, at 9 years, $[(3.14 - 2.3)/6.28] \cdot (9)$ is about 1.2 years.

[30] In fact Leridon (1973b) found the strongest relation between mortality in January and February and births 9 months later—still in the same calendar year. The data were for France, 1946 to 1963.

[31] These numbers are loosely drawn from Rutstein (1971).

The long-run consequences of a rigid mortality–marriage link have been modeled and analyzed by Ohlin (1961). Here I shall make the strongest possible time-series interpretation of the operation of this mechanism. Suppose that marriages occur when, and only when, the death of an adult male occurs.[32] Assuming marriage occurs in the same year as the death, this can be shown to imply that $m_t = d_t$, where m_t is the proportional deviation of marriages [i.e., $m_t = (M_t - M)/M$]. This suggests that the more tractable $m_t = \eta_t$ is approximately true. Let f_x be the distribution of births to a married couple by duration of marriage x, normalized so that $\Sigma f_x = 1$ (see Connor, 1926). Then, drawing on results in Lee (1975) we have

$$\epsilon_t = \epsilon'_t + \Sigma f_x m_{t-x} \qquad (10.2)$$

or

$$\epsilon_t = \epsilon'_t + \sum_{x=0}^{25} f_x \eta_{t-x}$$

Once again we can calculate the implied cross-spectrum of births and deaths, this time including the assumed relation of nuptiality to mortality as expressed in Equation 10.2.

The result, shown in Figure 7, is nearly indistinguishable from the simple demographic case. The coherence is now higher at some low frequencies, and births lag deaths by a minute amount. We can conclude that the link between mortality and marriage opportunity cannot possibly account for the relation of births to deaths for fluctuations of less than 20-year periods, in these or any other series.

Another possible link, not yet mentioned, is that the same adverse conditions that led to high mortality also led married couples voluntarily to restrict their fertility, or to experience a decline in libido. If conceptions were negatively related to the mortality of the same period, this would suggest

$$\epsilon_{6,t} = \epsilon'_t - .25k\eta_t - .75k\eta_{t-1} \qquad (10.3)$$

However, comparison of this equation with equation 9.4 shows that they are virtually indistinguishable.

---

[32] If this were true, estimated coherences for marriages and deaths should approach unity. In fact, for Hartland, Colyton, and Crulai, the estimated coherence squared is not significant. For the much larger populations of Sweden and Norway, there is a very strong coherence, but the phase shift indicates a *negative* relation between deaths and marriages, not a positive one.

We conclude that for fluctuations of less than 20 years, association of births and deaths can only have reflected fecundity impairment or voluntary control of marital fertility.

The analyses in the preceding three sections also enable us to calculate the theoretical spectra of births and deaths under each hypothesis. The spectrum of births (not shown here) suggests a strong 30-year generational cycle, and generally looks very similar to Figure 3. However, the spectrum of deaths shows no evidence of a 30-year cycle; apparently the age structure of mortality filters out variation in births at this frequency.[33] We can conclude that any 30-year cycle in a death series is "forced" by a corresponding cycle in mortality, and is not generated demographically as are the birth and marriage cycles.

11.   PRICES, CLIMATE, AND VITAL RATES

I have discussed the internal structure of the demographic series and their relations to one another. I now briefly discuss the exogenous sources of variation in the demographic system. Since short-run fluctuations in the series have been shown to be unaffected by age structure (or duration structure of marriages), we may take them as proxies for variations in marital fertility, nuptiality, and mortality. In this section I shall discuss estimated cross-spectra of the demographic series with various economic and meteorological series (for a discussion of the role of meteorological variables, see Utterström, 1955).

We have used the following independent variables: Exeter grain prices (Mitchell & Deane, 1962); severity-of-Western-European-winter index (Easton, 1928); German tree-ring series (LeRoy Ladurie, 1971); British rainfall series (Glasspoole, 1928); British monthly temperature series (Manley, 1953) (aggregated to the four seasons). There is space here only for selected results.

Figure 8 shows the estimated coherence squared and phase shift for Hartland baptisms and burials, and Colyton marriages, against Exeter wheat prices. We see that marital fertility in Hartland was negatively related to prices, with a lag of about 1 year.[34] The relation is strongest for fluctuations of periods of 4–13 years, and in this range accounts for 20 to 25% of the variance.

[33] Elsewhere (Lee, 1975), I have shown that marriages will exhibit a strong 30-year cycle, leading births by a few years.

[34] These estimated lags should not be taken too seriously. A high price for one year, measured at Michelmas, sometimes goes with an even higher price 6 months later in the following year, although the Michelmas price for the second year may be normal. Thus an estimated lag of a year behind prices could be consistent with no *true* lag at all.

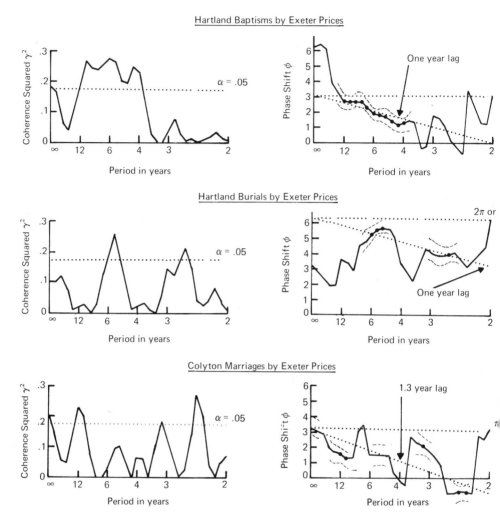

Figure 8. Exeter wheat prices and vital events in Hartland and Colyton. Estimates of γ^2 are significantly different from zero at the 5% level when they lie above the dotted line. Corresponding phase estimates are more reliable and are marked by heavy dots; 95% confidence intervals for phase estimates are indicated by dashed lines, for all frequencies with estimated coherence squared of at least .1.

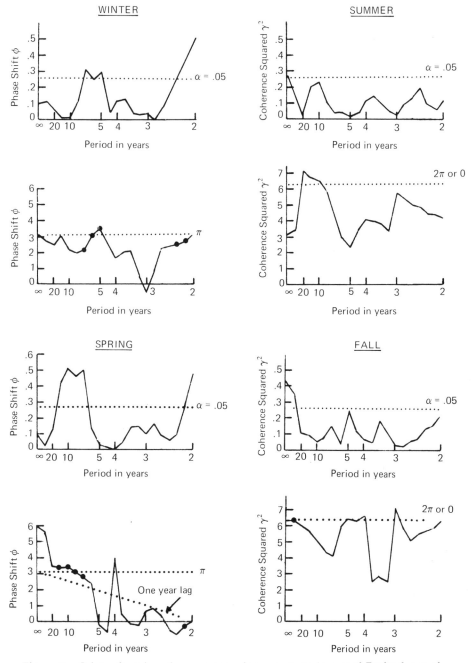

Figure 9. Colyton burials and mean seasonal temperatures in central England, net of Exeter wheat prices, 1698–1820. Estimates of γ² are significantly different from zero at the 5% level when they lie above the dotted line. Corresponding phase estimates are more reliable and are marked by heavy dots.

The cross-spectrum for Hartland deaths and Exeter prices shows a weak tendency for high mortality to follow high prices after a lag of about a year or less. The peak coherence squared, at a period of 5½ years, is 25%.

The cross-spectrum for Colyton marriages and Exeter prices shows a weak negative association, with low nuptiality lagging high prices by about a year.[35]

Meteorological variation may either affect vital rates directly, or by way of an effect on grain prices; for this reason it would be better to estimate multivariate cross-spectra. However the quality of the meteorological data before the eighteenth century precluded this. I did try using Easton's severity-of-Western-European-winter index, which was available over the whole period, but there were no significant associations. I also tried a German tree-ring series (reproduced in LeRoy Ladurie, 1971), which correlated moderately with a British rainfall series when they overlapped (1727–1927), but again there were no significant associations.

For the eighteenth century, better temperature and rainfall series were available. I estimated multivariate cross-spectra of Colyton burials against five variables: Exeter prices, and mean temperature in winter, spring, summer, and fall (calculated from Manley, 1953). The results (except for price) are shown in Figure 9. Apparently cold winters and springs caused high mortality; the effect of summer and fall temperatures is less clear.

I made similar estimates substituting rainfall for prices. The partial association of rainfall with mortality was marginally significant, and suggested that higher mortality went with *drier* weather.

As this chapter began with a listing of its conclusions, there is no need to reiterate them now. However, in view of the tentative or negative nature of many of the empirical results, it is worth emphasizing once more that the analysis of larger populations yields much more satisfactory results.

APPENDIX 1: MATHEMATICAL DERIVATION OF THE DEMOGRAPHIC INTERACTIONS

The first-order Taylor approximations to equations 3.1 and 3.2 are as follows:

$$B_t \doteq B + \Sigma\phi_a(B_{t-a} - B) + \Sigma Bp_a(m_{a,t} - m_a) + \Sigma m_a B(p_{a,t} - p_a) \qquad (A.1)$$

$$D_t \doteq D + \Sigma q_a p_a(B_{t-a} - B) + \Sigma Bq_a(p_{a,t} - p_a) + \Sigma Bp_a(q_{a,t} - q_a) \qquad (A.2)$$

[35] The other three cross-spectra (Exeter prices with Hartland marriages and Colyton baptisms and burials) showed weaker association.

where B, D, ϕ_a, q_a, p_a, and m_a all represent long-run mean values. Recalling that $m_{a,t} = fm_a(1 + \epsilon_t)$, and $q_{a,t} = q_a + \eta_t \delta_a$, these approximations may be rewritten as,

$$b_t = \Sigma \phi_a b_{t-a} + \epsilon_t + \Sigma m_a(p_{a,t} - p_a) \tag{A.3}$$

$$d_t = \Sigma q_a p_a b_{t-a} + \Sigma q_a(p_{a,t} - p_a) + \eta_t \tag{A.4}$$

where b_t and d_t represent proportional deviations of births and deaths from their long-run means—e.g., $b_t = (B_t - B)/B$.

We have made some progress, but the analysis is incomplete, since $(p_{a,t} - p_a)$ of course depends on an accumulation of past η's, and we must take explicit account of this. By definition,

$$p_{a,t} = \prod_{i=-1}^{a-1} (1 - q_{a-i,t-i}).$$

After substituting for $q_{i,t}$, taking a first-order Taylor approximation, and simplifying, we find that

$$p_{a,t} - p_a \doteq \sum_{i=-1}^{a-1} p_a[-\delta_{a-i}/(1 - q_{a-i})]\eta_{t-i} \tag{A.5}$$

Define $x_i = -\delta_i/(1 - q_i)$, $y_j = \Sigma_{i=15}^{50} \phi_i x_{i-j}$, and $c_i = -\phi_i$ except $c_0 = 1$. Then the birth equation can be expressed as

$$\Sigma c_i b_{t-i} = \epsilon_t + \sum_{i=0}^{50} y_i \eta_{t-i} \tag{A.6}$$

For the death equation, let $w_a = q_a p_a$; this corresponds roughly to the life table distribution of deaths to a cohort of births. Let $h_a = \Sigma_{i=0}^{a-1} w_i x_{a-i}$ except $h_0 = 1 + w_0 x_0$. Then,

$$d_t = \sum_{a=0}^{85} w_a b_{t-a} + \sum_{i=0}^{85} h_i \eta_{t-i} \tag{A.7}$$

To complete the derivation, we must eliminate b from this equation. Multiplying both sides by c_i, $i = 0, \ldots, 45$, and summing appropriately, gives:

$$\sum_{i=0}^{45} c_i d_{t-i} = \sum_{a=0}^{85} w_a \epsilon_{t-a} + \sum_{i=0}^{85} z_i \eta_{t-i} \tag{A.8}$$

where $z_a = (\Sigma w_j y_{a-j} + \Sigma c_j g_{a-j}) = (r_a + s_a)$.

APPENDIX 2: SPECTRAL PROCEDURES USED IN THIS CHAPTER

Spectral analysis is properly applied to so-called *covariance stationary* processes, that is, ones having no time trend in mean or variance–covariance. Some demographic series conform to this requirement (Hartland, Crulai), but others do not (Colyton, Sweden). When vital rates fluctuate about a constant level, then births and deaths will tend to grow geometrically. In this case dividing them by an estimated geometric trend transforms them to stationarity. This method was used for Sweden. In other cases, the vital rates undergo secular swings, and dividing by a long moving average is more satisfactory (see Granger & Hughes, 1971; and Gluckman *et al.*, 1973). The Colyton series was transformed by dividing by a 61-year moving average that was progressively shortened at each end of the series to avoid losing observations. When identical transformations of this sort are applied to several series, there is no mathematical effect on their cross-spectrum, but it increases the efficiency of the estimates. On the other hand, moving averages introduce spurious peaks in the simple spectra, and a correction should be made. Thus division by a 61-year moving average induces a strong cycle of 42 years in the data.

Spectral analysis requires rather long series (say at least 75 observations), and the ratio of number of observations to number of lags used should be higher than 3, preferably on the order of 5 to 10. When this ratio is low, a strong bias occurs in the results, and confidence bands become very wide. It is then easy to convince oneself that insignificant results are meaningful.

There is not space here to discuss additional details of the procedure. Suffice it to say that the cross-spectral estimates in this chapter were made by a multivariate program using a Parzen window. In addition to the detrending described earlier the series were "prewhitened" by the operation $y_t = x_t - kx_{t-x}$ for various values of k between .125 and .85. The estimated spectra were then recolored to remove the effects of detrending and prewhitening.

REFERENCES

Antonov, A. N. (1947). "Children Born During the Siege of Leningrad in 1942," *Journal of Pediatrics*, Vol. 30, p. 250.

Bernardelli, Harro (1941). "Population Waves," *Journal of the Burma Research Society*, Vol. 31, No. 1 (April), pp. 1–18.

Carlsson, Gosta (1970). "Nineteenth Century Fertility Oscillations," *Population Studies*, Vol. 24, No. 3 (November), pp. 413–422.

Chambers, J. D. (1972). *Population, Economy and Society in Preindustrial England*. Oxford: Oxford University Press.

Charbonneau, Hubert (1970). *Tourouvre-au-Perche Aux XVIIe et XVIIIe Siècles*. Paris: Presses Universitaires de France.

Chiang, C. L. (1968). *Introduction to Stochastic Processes in Biostatistics*. New York: Wiley.

Coale, Ansley (1972). *The Growth and Structure of Human Populations: A Mathematical Investigation*. Princeton, N.J.: Princeton University Press.

Coale, A. J. and Demeny, Paul (1966). *Regional Model Life Tables and Stable Populations*, Princeton: Princeton University Press.

Coale, A. J., & McNeil, D. R. (1971). "The Distribution of Age of the Frequency of First Marriage in a Female Cohort." Office of Population Research, TR9, Series 2 (December). Unpublished manuscript.

Connor, L. R. (1926). "Fertility of Marriage and Population Growth," *Journal of the Royal Statistical Society*, Vol. 89, Pt. 3 (May), pp. 553–566.

Deprez, P., Hum, D., & Spencer, B. (1974). "Spectral Analysis and the Study of Seasonal Fluctuations in Historical Demography." Department of Economics, University of Manitoba. Unpublished manuscript.

Easton, E. (1928). *Les Hivers dans L'Europe Occidentale*. Leyde.

Eversley, D. E. C. (1965). "Population, Economy and Society," in D. V. Glass & D. E. C. Eversley, eds., *Population in History*. London: Edward Arnold.

Frisch, Rose E. (1974). "Demographic Implications of the Biological Determinants of Female Fecundity." Center for Population Studies, Harvard University, Research Paper 6, July 1974. Unpublished manuscript.

Gautier, Etienne, & Henry, Louis (1958). *La Population de Crulai*. Paris: Presses Universitaires de France.

Glasspoole, J. (1928). "Two Centuries of Rainfall," *Meteorological Magazine,* Vol. 63, No. 745 (February), pp. 1–7.

Gluckman, Perry; Herlihy, David; & Pori, Mary (1973). "A Spectral Analysis of Deaths in Florence." Center for Advanced Study in the Behavioral Sciences, Stanford University. Unpublished manuscript.

Goubert, Pierre (1965). "Recent Theories and Research in French Population Between 1500 and 1700," in D. V. Glass & D. E. C. Eversley, eds., *Population in History.* London: Edward Arnold.

Granger, C. W. J., & Hatanaka, M. (1964). *Spectral Analysis of Economic Time Series.* Princeton, N.J.: Princeton University Press.

Granger, C. W. J., & Hughes, A. O. (1971). "A New Look at Some Old Data: the Beveridge Wheat Price Series," *Journal of the Royal Statistical Society,* Ser. A, Vol. 134, Pt. 3, pp. 413–428.

Habakkuk, H. J. (1965). "English Population in the Eighteenth Century," in D. V. Glass & D. E. C. Eversley, eds., *Population in History.* London: Edward Arnold.

Henry, Louis (1972a). "Nuptiality," *Theoretical Population Biology,* Vol. 3, No. 2 (June), pp. 135–153.

Henry, Louis (1972b). *On the Measurement of Human Fertility.* New York: American Elsevier.

Hotelling, Harold, & Hotelling, Floy (1931). "Causes of Birth Rate Fluctuations," *Journal of the American Statistical Association,* Vol. 26, pp. 135–149.

Jenkins, Gwilym, & Watts, Donald (1968). *Spectral Analysis and Its Applications.* San Francisco: Holden-Day.

Keyfitz, Nathan (1972). "Population Waves," in T. N. E. Greville, ed., *Population Dynamics.* New York: Academic Press.

Lee, Ronald D. (1970). "Econometric Studies of Topics in Demographic History." Ph.D. dissertation, Harvard University.

Lee, Ronald D. (1973). "Population in Preindustrial England: An Econometric Analysis," *Quarterly Journal of Economics,* Vol. 87, No. 4 (November), pp. 581–607.

Lee, Ronald D. (1974a). "Estimating Series of Vital Rates and Age Structures from Baptisms and Burials: A New Technique, with Applications to Preindustrial England," *Population Studies,* Vol. 28, No. 3 (November), pp. 495–512.

Lee, Ronald D. (1974b). "Forecasting Births in Post-Transition Populations: Stochastic Renewal with Serially Correlated Fertility," *Journal of the American Statistical Association,* Vol. 69, No. 347 (September), pp. 607–617.

Lee, Ronald D. (1974c). "The Formal Dynamics of Controlled Populations and the Echo, the Boom and the Bust," *Demography,* Vol. 11, No. 4 (November), pp. 563–585.

Lee, Ronald D. (1975). "Natural Fertility, Population Cycles, and the Spectral Analysis of Series of Births and Marriages," *Journal of the American Statistical Association,* Vol. 70, No. 350. pp. 295–304.

Lee, Ronald D. (forthcoming). "Models of Preindustrial Population Dynamics, with Applications to England," in Charles Tilly, ed., *Historical Studies of Changing Fertility.* Princeton, N.J.: Princeton University Press.

Leridon, Henry (1973a). *Aspects Biometriques de La Fecondite Humaine.* Paris: Presses Universitaires de France.

Leridon, Henry (1973b). *Natalité, Saisons et Conjoncture Economique.* Paris: Presses Universitaires de France.

LeRoy Ladurie, Emmanuel (1971). *Times of Feast, Times of Famine: A History of Climate Since the Year 1000.* New York: Doubleday.

Malthus, Thomas Robert (1798/1970). *An Essay on the Principle of Population, (1798),* ed. Anthony Flew. Baltimore, Md.: Penguin.

Manley, G. (1953). "The Mean Temperature of Central England, 1698–1952," *Quarterly Journal of the Royal Meteorological Society*, Vol. 79, pp. 242–262.

Mitchell, B. R., & Deane, Phyllis (1962). *Abstract of British Historical Statistics*. London: Cambridge University Press.

Ohlin, Goran (1955). "The Positive and the Preventive Check." Ph.D. dissertation, Harvard University.

Ohlin, Goran (1961). "Mortality, Marriage, and Growth in Pre-industrial Populations," *Population Studies*, Vol. 14, No. 3 (March), pp. 190–197.

Pollard, J. H. (1973). *Mathematical Models for the Growth of Human Populations*. Cambridge: Cambridge University Press.

Robson, John R. K. (1972). *Malnutrition, Its Causation and Control*. New York: Gordon and Breach.

Rutstein, Shea O. (1971). "The Influence of Child Mortality on Fertility in Taiwan: A Study Based on Sample Surveys Conducted in 1967 and 1969." Ph.D. dissertation, Department of Economics, University of Michigan.

Schweder, Tore (1971). "The Precision of Population Projections Studied by Multiple Projection Methods," *Demography*, Vol. 8, No. 4 (November), pp. 441–450.

Sheps, Mindel, & Menken, Jane (1973). *Mathematical Models of Conception and Birth*. Chicago: University of Chicago Press.

Smith, C. A. (1947). "The Effect of War-Time Starvation in Holland Upon Pregnancy and Its Products," *American Journal of Obstetrics and Gynecology*, Vol. 53, p. 599.

Spencer, Barbara (1975). "Size of Population and Variability of Demographic Data (17th–18th centuries)." Department of Economics, University of Manitoba. Unpublished manuscript.

Sykes, Z. M. (1969). "Some Stochastic Versions of the Matrix Model for Population Dynamics," *Journal of the American Statistical Association*, Vol. 64, No. 325, pp. 111–131.

United Nations, Department of Economic and Social Affairs. *The Determinants and Consequences of Population Trends: New Summary of Findings on Interaction of Demographic, Economic and Social Factors*. Vol. 1. New York: United Nations.

Utterström, G. (1955). "Climatic Fluctuations and Population Problems in Early Modern History," *Scandinavian Economic Historical Review*. Vol. 3, No. 1, pp. 3–47.

van de Walle, Etienne (1968). "Marriage and Marital Fertility," *Daedalus*, Vol. 97, (Spring), pp. 486–501.

Wrigley, E. A. (1966). "Family Limitation in Pre-Industrial England," *Economic History Review*, Vol. 19, pp. 82–109.

Wrigley, E. A. (1968). "Mortality in Preindustrial England: The Example of Colyton Devon, Over Three Centuries," *Daedalus*, Vol. 97 (Spring) pp. 546–580.

Wrigley, E. A. (1969). *Population and History*. New York: McGraw-Hill.

Yule, G. Udney (1906). "Changes in the Marriage and Birth Rates in England and Wales During the Past Half Century," *Journal of the Royal Statistical Society*, Vol. 69, Pt. 1 (March), pp. 18–132.

Index